AF545170

Values and Policies in Controversy

AN INTRODUCTION TO ARGUMENTATION AND DEBATE

Values and Policies in Controversy

AN INTRODUCTION TO ARGUMENTATION AND DEBATE

Russell T. Church
UNIVERSITY OF TENNESSEE

Charles Wilbanks
UNIVERSITY OF SOUTH CAROLINA

Gorsuch Scarisbrick, Publishers
SCOTTSDALE, ARIZONA

Gorsuch Scarisbrick, Publishers
8233 Via Paseo Del Norte, Suite E-400
Scottsdale, AZ 85258

10 9 8 7 6 5 4 3 2 1

ISBN 0-89787-326-2

Printed in the United States of America.

Contents

Preface

Values and Policies in Controversy presents a systematic and comprehensive treatment of argumentation and debate. This book provides the student with a foundation in the major concepts of argumentation and debate theory. In addition, it will provide a solid practical base for both the student who wishes to pursue debate in competition and the student who desires to improve proficiency in public debate.

We view educational debate as primarily co-curricular. That is, the *activity* provides definite pedagogical benefits that go beyond and build upon the knowledge of the theoretical bases presented in the text itself. The usefulness of such skills as poise, organizational proficiency, research skills, and analysis is enduring. Long after the course is over, the student will continue to utilize these benefits.

Values and Policies in Controversy is intended to enhance that learning opportunity, and offers as comprehensive a view of argumentation and debate as space would allow. We believe that the book uniquely contributes to the student and the instructor of the basic argumentation and debate course through its presentation of the topics.

The underlying importance of human values to all types of argument—the role of *values* in controversy—is discussed here. Noting the growth of non-policy debating on the intercollegiate level, we have reclassified propositions. The traditional fact–value–policy taxonomy has been replaced with a much more sensible and instructive classification system, within which we identify seven distinctive categories: trait inferences, relational inferences, historical inferences, predictive inferences, value comparison claims, policy evaluation claims, and policy advocacy claims.

This reclassification of the propositions offers the reader an opportunity to understand specific burdens with more clarity than previous classifications, and makes it possible for the arguments used to support the claims to be evaluated with more facility.

Within the discussion of non-policy debate, we offer descriptions of case formats in propositions of inference and value as well as policy propositions. Such a discussion is rare in contemporary argumentation and debate texts.

Also included is a treatment of negative strategies for all types of propositions; this, too, is seldom available in today's texts.

We have included a comprehensive treatment of ethics and credibility. Believing that the ethical and credible advocate is usually more successful than a debater who lacks these qualities, we are convinced that such a discussion is essential. Based upon that same conviction, style and delivery have been afforded a prominent place in *Values and Policies in Controversy.* Finally, the text offers a practical guide to debater adaptation to judges of various paradigm orientations.

As is almost always true of projects of this magnitude, its successful completion could not have been accomplished without the contributions and support of many people. We want to thank Dr. William Strickland for his comments on early drafts of portions of the work, and for the same contribution we are indebted to Dr. Karl Krayer. For more substantial reviews we thank Drs. James Brooks and Warren Decker.

Dr. Thomas Cooke, Chair of the Department of Theatre and Speech at the University of South Carolina, could scarcely have been more cooperative in allowing us to use the facilities and supplies of the department in this effort. We appreciate the indulgence and support of the department faculty and staff.

We also wish to acknowledge the American Forensic Association, Raymond Bud Zeuschner, and Penn State Press for allowing us to utilize protected material. To all of those who encouraged and otherwise supported this project we are grateful.

ONE

Introduction

During the 1984 national elections public opinion was formed, in part, due to the open debate that took place between the opposing parties. Sometimes that debate became heated. Walter Mondale was charged with being a "doomsayer" and George Bush was labeled "vulgar." Geraldine Ferraro was called "dishonest" and a "token." Regardless of the truth or falsity of these labels, such debate was at times awkward and disconcerting. However, despite the unease that such exchange engenders, few Americans would suggest that public argument and political debate be stifled. For example, as public opinion was being formed in 1973 concerning the Watergate affair, Americans were asked whether a great nation such as ours should air its problems in such an open and even embarrassing manner. Americans responded as they always have—affirmatively. We know that public debate has always been essential to democratic government. As with the Watergate affair and the 1984 election, open debate may not always be pleasant, but if a free people are to make informed decisions they must be allowed to generate and participate in such debate.

Debate and Democracy

A democracy may be described in many different ways, but all definitions will include one common characteristic: citizen participation. The great educator John Dewey once wrote that "democracy as a way of life may be expressed as the necessity for participation of every human being in the formation of the values that regulate the living of men together."[1] Dewey's words imply two imperatives for citizens living in a free society. One imperative is participation, the other is cooperation. In a society as large and complex as ours, made up of very diverse human beings, disagreement is inevitable. On the one hand, we generally agree that the majority should always prevail. On the other hand, in order for democracy to work the minority must be heard and must be given fair consideration. Through the participation of everyone and the cooperation of the majority, democracy is strengthened.

Debate is a vehicle that allows citizens to participate in their government. In closed societies debate is discouraged and even punished. In democracies such as ours, it is cherished and encouraged. Debate has had a long and proud tradition in the political development of our country. It is recognized not as an ideal, but as an absolutely essential means by which conflicting values are treated in the marketplace of ideas. The majority may rule but the majority does not monopolize the flow of ideas that leads to the development of our societal values. In a sense the majority must earn its status by supporting the give and take, the thrust and parry, that may allow the minorities to become majorities or may build the groundwork for the majority itself to become stronger.

Debate exposes conflicting ideas to the scrutiny of the public. Debate allows for objective, informed, and dynamic decision-making. It encourages objectivity because both sides are allowed and encouraged to defend their views vigorously; the best case for each side is made. Debate is informative because objective presentation leads to rational choices on great issues of common concern. Finally, debate is dynamic because competing views are adjusted to meet the demands of the opponent's arguments and to satisfy a questioning public.

Certainly, a vigorous and flourishing democracy demands the exercise of reasoned intercourse of ideas. Even in our personal day-to-day decision-making debate plays an important role. We often carefully weigh the advantages and disadvantages of the various options that confront us. Is a Ford a better choice than a Toyota or a Buick? Should we go to an Italian restaurant or one that serves Chinese food? Should I take English 310 or Biology 201

Chapter Outline

this semester? Such decisions are usually made after careful introspection and self-debate. If one applies this introspection to societal decision-making, the importance of debate to a democratic nation is more apparent. It is difficult to imagine how a democracy would function without public debate on questions such as: "Should we raise taxes to reduce the budget deficit?" or "Should we send military aid to El Salvador?" or "Should the state university raise tuition for the coming semester?" Debate involves minor issues and issues of the utmost gravity. Democracy simply could not flourish without it.

Educational Debate

Public debate takes place every day in our society. It involves almost everyone who claims a role in our society. Even though some people in our society never make a public pronouncement of their opinions, even though many people never make a speech, or engage in discussions on public policy, virtually everyone is a *receiver* of opinions, or has heard speeches, or has listened to discussions on public policy. As a receiver, a person becomes a participant in the debate. This is the nature of public debate—the public forum. Whether or not we actually contribute to the messaages being advanced in public discussions, we participate just by being present and by functioning within our society.

Educational debate is different from public debate in that the participation is more certain. It is structured and it is more directly guided. Definite rules and expectations that guide the function of an educational debate are usually unknown to the participant in a public debate. Despite the differences between public and educational debate, training in the latter offers the student an excellent opportunity not only to gain skills in the peculiarities of educational debate, but to gain competence in public debate as well.

The benefits gained through studying educational debate are lasting ones. Even though the topic you will be debating, the format and the vocabulary you will learn, and the decision rules that you will follow may not be used in public debate, the skills you will learn in this course will continue to be useful long after the semester is over. As you become proficient as a classroom debater, you will acquire the necessary skills for public debate. If you use a saw, nails, glue, a plane, and paint to construct a bookcase, it is relatively unimportant whether you will ever again use those same tools. The bookcase continues to be useful. In the same way, the skills you will acquire in this course, including analytical ability, poise, organizational skills, research prowess, eloquence, and cooperation will continue to be valuable to you in the "real world."

Debate and Discussion

Educational debate should not be confused with discussion. They may both have decision-making as a goal, and both may lead to decisions, but there is a difference. Debate focuses on a *proposition,* whereas a discussion centers on a *question.* A proposition is a declarative statement; a question, of course, is not. If a decision were to be made on U.S. foreign policy in El Salvador, a discussion might center on the question, "What should be the nature of U.S. foreign policy in El Salvador?" A debate on the same topic would focus on a declarative statement or proposition, such as, "The U.S. should withdraw all military personnel from El Salvador." In a discussion there are many positions, some of which may not be clearly defined. In a debate there are only two possible positions—one supports the proposition and one does not. In public argument there is often the same distinction. When Congressional committees hold hearings, they solicit opinions from many sources and they hear many approaches to the topics being discussed. Although at times they may be contentious, committee hearings are not generally debates. When a particular bill is being considerd by Congress, however, the passage of that piece of legislation becomes the focus. There are effectively only two positions—for or against the bill. Arguments on the floor of Congress on these occasions, then, are debates.

The advantage of a discussion is that it accomodates many different positions on a given topic, but this characteristic can also be a disadvantage. Discussions often fail to resolve the question. Debate, on the other hand, is more efficient. Only two major positions are considered and there is always a decision. The proposition is either adopted or it is rejected. In our Congressional example, the bill passes or it does not. Thus, a debate is more efficient as a tool of decision-making because it is more certain of resolution.

There is another difference in the two processes. In a discussion, the answer to the question must be achieved through agreement of the parties involved. In order for a discussion to work, a compromised solution is sought—a solution that is at least acceptable to the participants. Often, of course, such an agreement is never reached and the question remains unresolved. This is the major disadvantage to the discussion approach. In debate, on the other hand, an individual or collective arbitrator decides which position prevails, again making the debate more certain of resolution.

Formats

As we mentioned earlier, an educational debate is usually more structured than a public debate. The precise structure of an educational debate is called a *format.* A format indicates the order of speeches and the time limits of each speaker. A number of formats are available in educational debate. The two most widely used are the traditional cross-examination and the Lincoln–Douglas formats.

The role of each side in an educational debate can be understood fully only in the context of the format that the debaters follow. The traditional cross-examination format is organized as follows:

CONSTRUCTIVE SPEECHES

First affirmative constructive speech
Cross-examination by negative speaker
First negative constructive speech
Cross-examination by affirmative speaker
Second affirmative constructive speech
Cross-examination by negative speaker
Second negative constructive speech
Cross-examination by affirmative speaker

REBUTTAL SPEECHES

First negative rebuttal speech
First affirmative rebuttal speech
Second negative rebuttal speech
Second affirmative rebuttal speech

Although the times allocated to each speech and cross-examination periods may vary, the constructive speeches will usually be 8 or 10 minutes in length and the rebuttals will usually be 4 or 5 minutes in length.

This format affords the affirmative both advantages and disadvantages. For example, the affirmative both begins and ends the debate. Thus, it is the affirmative's responsibility in the first speech to indicate a sufficient rationale to justify the consideration of the proposition, and later to deal with all the important issues remaining in the debate.

As the above organization indicates, a debate is divided into two major sections—constructives and rebuttals. In the constructive speeches both the affirmative and the negative teams must present all the issues to be considered. In intercollegiate debate new issues should not be introduced after constructives are concluded. For the affirmative, this limitation means that all the rationales that will be used to justify the adoption of the resolution should be introduced in the constructive speeches. The specific responsibilities and strategies of affirmative and negative teams will be treated in Chapters Nine and Ten.

Another format that is used often in educational debate is the Lincoln–Douglas organization. As you may have guessed, the name of the format is based upon the historic series of debates between Abraham Lincoln and Stephen Douglas. It is distinctive from the traditional cross-examination format in that it involves only two speakers, one representing each side. As such the debate is usually more brief than the traditional format, and the order of the speeches is different. Although the times may vary, the Lincoln–Douglas format usually follows this structure:

LINCOLN–DOUGLAS FORMAT	
Affirmative constructive	6 minutes
Cross-examination by the negative speaker	
Negative constructive	7 minutes
Cross-examination by the affirmative speaker	
Affirmative rebuttal	4 minutes
Negative rebuttal	6 minutes
Affirmative rebuttal	3 minutes

Under this format the general speaker responsibilities are very similar, although of course the responsibilities of each side are not divided between two speakers.

Debate and Argumentation

The difference between debate and argumentation might appear at first to be vague. The essential difference between the two is much like the difference between an automobile and the concept of travel: Debate (the car) is the vehicle, argumentation (travel) is the process. There are other ways to travel than by automobile; there are other ways to argue than by debate. We can forward arguments in a discussion or simply in an interpersonal exchange. While there may be differing formats and particular decision rules, the nature of argument and the process of argumentation remain largely the same regardless of the vehicle.

Values, Practicality, and Argumentation

A detailed treatment of the process of argumentation appears in Chapter Two; here we will treat the fundamental issues involved in argumentation and decision-making. Debate allows for the cooperative development of the values and attitudes that regulate our society. All public policy decisions are based, at least in part, on the *prevailing values* of society. Our attitudes toward specific issues are not formed in a vacuum, but rather require each of us to consider a variety of attitudes and issues. Importantly, considerations of value seem to be crucial in the decision-making process. When we make decisions about possible courses of action, most of us resolve the question, "Is it right?" before we consider such questions as "Will it work?" or "Is it necessary?" If, for example, we are given an opportunity to purchase tickets to a big football game, the first question likely to be considered might be similar to "Is it right that I attend the game instead of studying?" or "Is the football game more important than visiting my family?" Those kinds of questions are likely to be addressed before the more practical questions of cost, time commitment, or transportation problems. W. D. Ross writes eloquently of the primacy of value considerations in decision-making:

> When a plain man fulfills a promise because he thinks he ought to do so, it seems clear that he does so with no thoughts of its total consequences, still less with any opinion that these likely will be the best possible. He thinks, in fact, more of the past than of the future. What makes him think it right to act in a certain way is the fact that he has promised to do so—that and usually nothing more. That his act will produce the best possible consequences is not his reason for calling it right.[2]

When we approach the process of argumentation and decision-making, therefore, questions of value are likely to dominate our study.

The importance of value considerations admitted, it can also be accurately stated that the resolution of those considerations almost always leads to discussions, debate, or contemplation on more practical issues. Argumentation is a rather complex process involving issues with both value and practical implications.

Components of Argumentation

Attitudes and values are developed through interaction with other people and through varied experiences. We observe our environment, we make judgments about what we observe, and then we generate predictions about things we have yet to observe. For instance, suppose we ate a Bronco Burger on Wednesday and found that it was delicious. Suppose we ate a Bronco Burger again on Friday and again found that it was delicious. If someone suggested that we eat Bronco Burgers on Sunday, our prediction would likely be that they would be delicious. On the other hand, without ever having experienced Bronco Burgers or something similar, we could not make a comfortable prediction. Experience underlies any judgment. What we know to be true or what we assume to be true is the first step in forming opinions and arguments.

Stephen Toulmin has developed a model of argument that labels the components of the process. Toulmin's model will be discussed in detail in the following chapter. In this chapter we will offer a brief presentation of its components.

The first component is *data*. Data are observations. They are known or are assumed to be true. Suppose two people were arguing about the university football team. Data would include such things as the team's record, the names of the players and the statistics of their performances, their schedule, the name of their coach, and even public statements made by the players or by the coach. If we know what the team's record is, the players' identities and their abilities and their schedule and their coach, we can make various judgments about the team. For instance, if the team has a record of no wins and six losses, we might safely conclude that the team is not very good. That judgment is made based upon the evaluation of the data. If we not only look at the record, but also look at the team's schedule we might find that the football team has played five of the top ten teams in the country. That knowledge might alter our judgment about their strength. We cannot evaluate the data, however, without standards.

Standards tell us on what basis we can evaluate the data. They indicate the importance of the data. Is a team's record an important measure of worth? How important is the ranking of the opposition? Toulmin identifies these standards or criteria as *warrants*. If we believe that the most accurate measure of a team's strength is their record, then at no wins and six losses we must conclude that the team is not strong. The warrant (the most accurate measure of strength is the win–loss record) connects the data (the team has no wins and six losses) to the conclusion (the team is not strong). Thus the value question (that of our choice of criteria or standards) underlies the conclusion, which Toulmin calls the *claim*.

Figure 1–1 dissects a more complex argument. Sam and Pete turned in term papers that were identical in length, topic organization, and conclusion. Given that data, what can one claim? The claim depends upon the warrant we choose to employ. If we infer that the two very similar papers must have

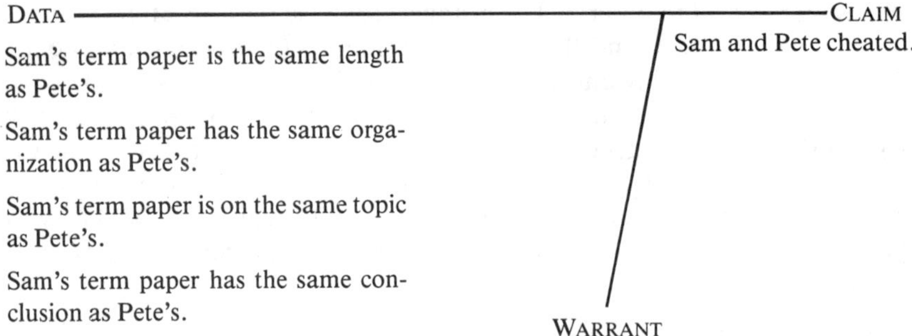

Two papers that are of the same length, on the same topic, organized identically, and have the same conclusion were probably prepared jointly.

It is dishonest to prepare papers jointly.

FIGURE 1–1

been prepared together, and that if two papers are jointly prepared it would be dishonest, then we must conclude or claim that Sam and Pete cheated. The warrant, then, allows for the evaluation of the data. A claim cannot be made without the criteria for evaluation.

When we make the claim that Sam and Pete cheated, the implications of our conclusion go further. Assuming that the inference is correct, then what do we do about it? What course of action might follow the judgment that the students were dishonest? In Figure 1–2 an additional claim is made. In the first example, the claim did not suggest any course of action, but simply implied that the two students had cheated. In the latter example, the claim proposes a specific course of action—expulsion. That claim could not be reached, however, without first evaluating the data and making an inference based on that evaluation. If two arguers focus on the latter claim, whether formally or not, they must consider the judgment that Sam and Pete cheated.

The complexity of argument is illustrated in those two examples. When we argue, we do not simply make a conclusion. That conclusion or claim is based upon data, and mediated through warrants, which are standards by which we evaluate the data. Moreover, argument is a dynamic process. The claims we make today lead to other perhaps more complex claims tomorrow. Just as the claim that Sam and Pete cheated led to the claim that the two students should be expelled, other claims might well follow. Because the process of argument is both complex and dynamic, this text will discuss argument containing claims of action as well as claims that do not prescribe action.

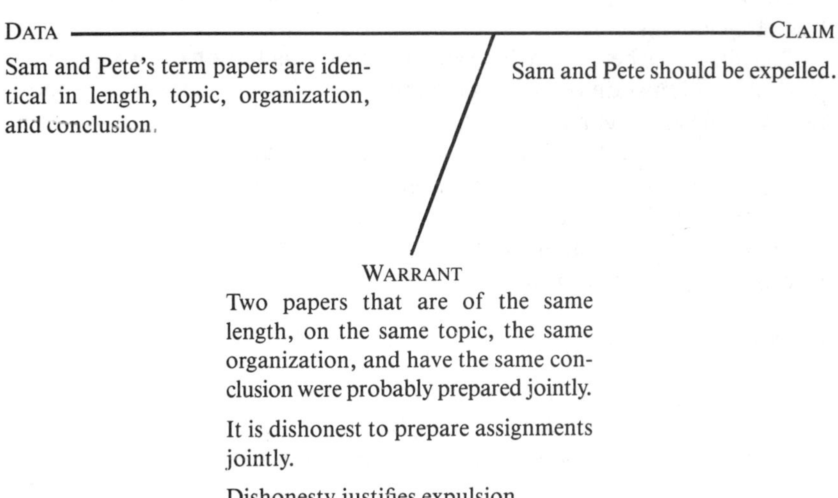

FIGURE 1–2

In the next three chapters we will treat in more detail the nature of argument, propositions of argument, and the nature of reasoning. Beginning with Chapter Six we will introduce you to debating. The discovery of issues, organization and evidence, research, refutation, cross-examination, credibility, and the construction of affirmative and negative cases are included in the coming chapters.

Summary

As long as we live in an open and free society, our citizens must be trained in argument and debate. Debate provides a vehicle through which citizens participate in their governments. Through debate, we educate ourselves and others so that rational decisions may be made; we forcefully advocate our positions on crucial issues so that competing interests may be heard, and in so doing we energize our society. While debate encourages the clash of disagreement, it also encourages problem-solving through that very clash of ideas. Misunderstanding can be avoided only by allowing both sides of any issue to be fully aired.

Democracies have forgotten the importance of argument and debate only at their peril. A democracy cannot long survive without the participation and the cooperation of its citizens. Indeed, debate and argument are bound to democracy as surely as the pages are bound to make a book.

The differences between public debate and educational debate are structure and level of participation. Educational debate requires from all participants more active participation. The structure of educational debate is called format. Two widely used formats are traditional cross-examination and Lincoln–Douglas.

The difference between debate and discussion centers on the focus of each process. A discussion centers on a question, a debate focuses on a proposition. Debate and argumentation differ in the same way an automobile differs from the concept of travel. Debate is the vehicle of an argument.

Stephen Toulmin has offered an excellent model of argument that includes three basic components: data, warrant, and claim. Values and practicality underly most arguments and can be understood by viewing argument through the Toulmin model.

Notes

1. John Dewey, "Democracy and Educational Administration," *School and Society,* Vol. 45 April 3, 1937, p. 457.
2. W. D. Ross, *The Right and the Good* (Oxford: Clarendon Press, 1973), p. 17.

Questions and Exercises

1. What are the two imperatives of a free society and how are they related to argument and debate?
2. Debate allows for objective, informative, and dynamic decision-making. Explain what is meant by that statement.
3. What skills may be acquired by participating in educational debate?
4. What is the difference between public debate and educational debate?
5. What is the difference between debate and discussion?
6. Describe the two formats of educational debate discussed in Chapter One. Describe the general obligations of each side within each format.
7. Explain the distinction between debate and argumentation.
8. According to Stephen Toulmin, what are the fundamental components of argument?
9. Scan the newspaper for three days and log each instance in which there is a public debate reported. Note the proposition being debated, the participants in the debate, and its outcome.
10. Select a particular decade in our nation's history (1840s, 1910s, 1950s, 1970s, and so on) and through library research find a debate of national importance that took place during those years. Identify the proposition being debated, the participants in the debate, its importance and its outcome.

Suggested Readings

Tomlinson, James. "The Philosophy and Development of CEDA." *CEDA Yearbook, 1983*. California State University, Northridge: Don Brownlee, 1983, pp. 1–5.

Louden, Allan and Austin, Curtis. "CEDA vs. NDT: A Dysfunctional Myth." *CEDA Yearbook, 1983*. California State University, Northridge: Don Brownlee, 1983, pp. 6–12.

TWO

The Nature of Argument

In Chapter One, you learned the difference between debate and argument. Debate is a vehicle by which an argument can be forwarded. In this chapter we will investigate in more detail the nature of an argument—a definition, its structure, and its components.

A Definition

An argument is a reason or a "line" of reasons that is meant to support a belief or opinion. Several necessary components are indicated by this definition: (1) There is an audience that might disagree with the belief or opinion; (2) the argument is to some degree designed; (3) the argument is aimed at those who disagree; and (4) the sources of the audience's disagreement can be predicted. It can be said, then, that argument is aimed at *persuasion*. Argument is aimed at moving the listeners from support of their positions to support of the position of the arguer.

Simply put, argument consists of the reasons for the opinions and attitudes that we hold and wish to forward. That is not to say, however, that all "reasons" constitute arguments. As the conditions enumerated above indicate, controversy is at the heart of argument. For example, if we were to claim that in order to freeze water we need to expose the water to a temperature of 32 degrees Farenheit or colder because the freezing point of water is 32 degrees, an argument would not be forwarded. The claim is demonstrable, the reason for the claim is not controversial. On the other hand, if one were to claim that Candidate X should be elected to Congress because he or she is honest and patriotic, the validity of the reasons cited cannot be determined with much certainty. Arguments consist of reasons for our beliefs that reflect some degree of uncertainty or controversy.

If the audience already holds the same view as the speaker, then the speaker is not engaged in argument. If during the summer of 1984, a speaker were addressing a meeting of Students for Mondale suggesting that the audience support Walter Mondale for president, no real argument would have taken place. In order for argument to occur there needs to be a prediction of attitude change. Attitude change cannot be predicted if the audience already accepts a speaker's conclusion. Figure 2–1 depicts situations that allow a prediction of attitude change and situations that would prevent such predictions.

Fritz Hieder developed the theory depicted in this illustration, and Heider believes that before attitude change can take place a state of psychological imbalance must exist. If a speaker (P1) addresses a message about an object of discussion (X) to an individual (P2), assuming that the individual (P2) holds no negative attitude toward the speaker (P1), the situation would be balanced if both hold the same attitude toward the object of discussion.

Chapter Outline

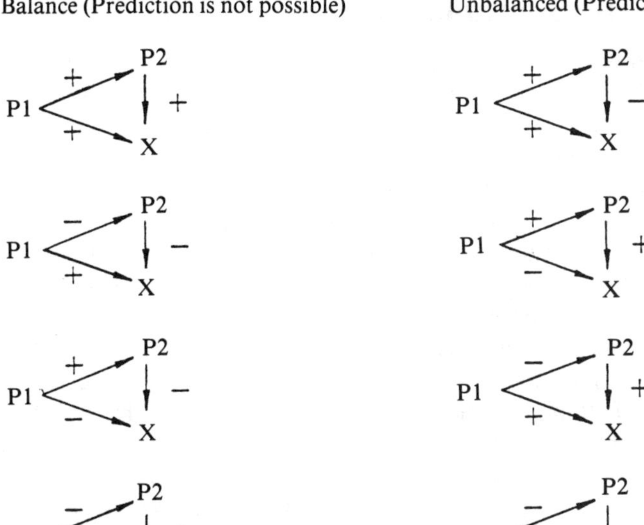

FIGURE 2–1 Predictability of attitude change.

The situation is unbalanced when any of the following are true: (1) When the speakers already hold negative feelings toward each other, but hold the same attitude toward the object of discussion; (2) when the speaker and individual have favorable dispositions toward each other but disagree about the object of discussion; (3) when there is a condition of audience neutrality toward the speaker or the object of persuasion. Under any of those conditions a prediction of attitude change can be made.

The above definition of argument also indicates that argument is *designed.* This means that argument is "aimed" toward an end and that the reasons chosen to support one's claim are selected with that particular end in mind. For example, if you know that the audience disagrees with your opinion and you know why the audience is likely to disagree, then supporting material can be selected to overcome the particular reservations of your audience. A speaker, then, does not simply present "reasons" without design. Even when audience disagreement is assumed and the reasons for disagreement are only estimated, an arguer "designs" the message.

Argument, then, consists of reasons for our opinions determined and designed for an audience that considers the message controversial. In the following section we investigate the relationship between argument and the audience in greater detail.

Conviction and Persuasion

One component of argument that is almost always essential to ultimate success is *information.* That is, it is often necessary to educate the audience before persuading them. It is important to understand, however, that information alone is not argument. For example, if a speaker were to attempt to persuade an audience to support the president's tax reform proposal, a necessary task would be to "instruct" the audience as to the nature of the president's proposal as well as the details of the current tax system. This would be unnecessary only if the audience was already knowledgeable regarding such matters. The president's proposal cannot be supported until the audience understands it. Moreover, an audience is unlikely to support the proposal if its advantages over current policy cannot be demonstrated. The process of "educating" or "informing" the audience leads to conviction. That is, information is often necessary to convince the audience that the speaker's point of view makes sense. In the example above, the audience has to be informed of the strengths of the president's proposal as well as of the flaws of the current tax system before they can be moved to support the speaker's position.

There is a conviction–persuasion duality involved in most argument. Information alone is not argument, but information is certainly important to successful argument. That is, there needs to be a "disposition" toward a point of view before one can fully embrace the point of view. That "disposition" is often achieved by information.

Of course, the distinction between "information" and "argument" is not always clear. The following example illustrates how the same message can be interpreted in different ways:

> The Catholic priest teaching the precepts of the Catholic religion to the children of his parish is doing the work of an educator, but he becomes a propagandist when, with the same object, he addresses the adult members of another religious group.[1]

The audience perceives the message according to their particular characteristics. In the example above, the children of the parish perceive the message as information, but the adult members of the other religious group perceive it as argument. Audiences are different in many respects and that often makes the task of the arguer a difficult one.

Argument and the Universal Audience

Chiam Perelman writes of a "universal audience," one that the speaker assumes already possesses general knowledge of the subject and a similar value orientation to the speaker's. If those assumptions are fair, then the arguer's task is easier and the design of the argument is more certain.

A consideration of the audience has been a concern of rhetorical theorists for centuries. An argument is designed to influence people. The amalgam of those individuals whom a speaker wishes to influence must be considered before a successful argument can be designed. Chiam Perelman underscores the audience's importance:

> In real argumentation, care must be taken to form a concept of the anticipated audience as close as possible to reality. An inadequate picture of the audience, resulting from either ignorance or an unforseen set of circumstances, can have very unfortunate results. Argumentation which an orator considers persuasive may well cause opposition in an audience for which 'reasons for' are actually 'reasons against.' Thus, if one argues for a certain measure that is likely to reduce social tension, such argument will set against the measure all those who would like to see disturbances.[2]

For an arguer to adapt to an audience is not always an easy task, even if it is essential. People who make up audiences possess a variety of emotions, express opposing opinions, rely on assumptions that are not widely held, and offer attention to widely divergent interests. Perelman writes of the difficulty in arguing before diverse audiences:

> It often happens that an orator must persuade a composite audience, embracing people different in character, loyalties and functions. To win over the different elements in his audience, the orator will have to use a multiplicity of arguments. A great orator is one who possesses the art of taking into consideration, in his argumentation, the composite nature of his audience.[3]

It is clear that a means of viewing audiences as more monolithic will facilitate the arguer's task of designing his or her message. Arguments accepted by only a few in the audience will not be as successful, obviously, as arguments that can be accepted "universally." Perelman's view of a universal audience is important, then, to an arguer interested in success. At the heart of the universal audience's unity are *values*. The speaker can appeal to these values through analogy, comparison, maxims, or direct appeal. However the value appeals are implemented, they substantially strengthen an argument.

Even though the aim of persuasion is to change the audience's opinions, attitudes, or behavior in a particular way, this can only be accomplished by appealing to their opinions, attitudes, or behavior in other respects. The noted psychologist and value theorist Milton Rokeach argues that cultures possess values that are universal throughout the culture.[4] For instance, the value of honesty is virtually universally held in our culture and in other cultures as well. The same can be said for the value of patriotism, or propriety, or success. These values transcend particular differences within an audience or between audiences. Because of the universality of such values, an appeal to these values can be made to otherwise disparate audiences, and to many different audiences, with success.

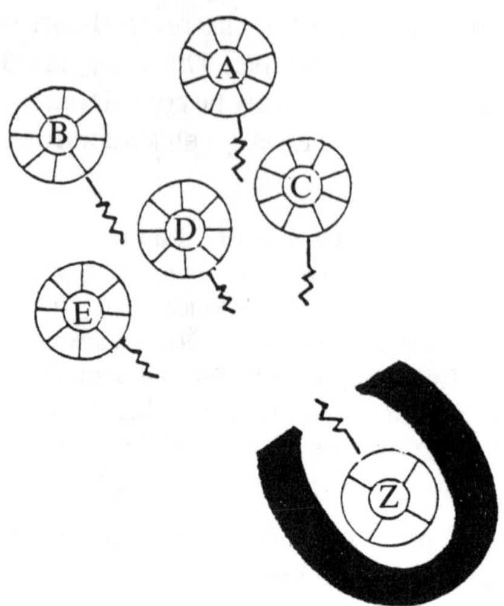

A: Audience Faction I; Value Base I
B: Audience Faction II; Value Base II
C: Audience Faction III; Value Base III
D: Audience Faction IV; Value Base IV
E: Audience Faction V; Value Base V

Z: Universal Audience; Value Base which transcends those of each Faction; Factions are thus joined

FIGURE 2–2 A conceptual model of the universal audience.

As an example, let's look at the United States' "argument" for freedom, The Declaration of Independence. The passage, "We hold these truths to be self-evident, that all men are created equal," clearly appeals to a universal audience. A less universal argument for revolution might have been perceived very differently by the various segments of colonial society. The Declaration allows the various segments to come together as a universal audience reacting to the appeal of a value-ladened argument. No matter what grievance each colonist or group of colonists had against the king, all could accept the call of the Declaration. The Declaration caused different audience factions to join and become a universal audience.

So far we have learned that arguments are reasons for one's opinions which are perceived by the audience as controversial. We have learned that argument cannot take place without a prediction of attitude change, and that attitude change cannot be predicted if an audience already accepts a speaker's conclusion. We have learned that an important component of argument is information, and finally that an arguer has better success designing his or her message for a universal audience.

The Structure of Argument

In the previous section we defined argument and identified its essential components. In this section, you will learn about the *structure* of argument. The Toulmin model, to which you were introduced in the first chapter, will again be used.

The Toulmin Model

In Chapter One you learned the basic components of the Toulmin model, which are data (observations), warrant (standard of evaluation), and the claim (conclusion). The Declaration of Independence is an appropriate illustration of these basic components. Much of the Declaration is devoted to recounting the abuses visited upon the colonies by the king of England. The listing of these abuses constitutes the data:

> The history of the present king of Great Britain is a history of repeated injuries and usurpations, and all having in direct object, the establishment of an absolute tyranny over these states. To prove this, let facts be submitted to a candid world:
>
> He has refused his assent to laws the most wholesome and necessary for the public good.
>
> He has forbidden his governors to pass laws of immediate and pressing importance, unless suspended in their operation until his assent should be obtained; and when so suspended he has utterly neglected to attend to them. . . .
>
> He has plundered our seas, ravaged our coasts, burnt our towns, and destroyed the lives of our people.
>
> He is, at this time, transporting large armies of foreign mercenaries to complete the works of death, desolation, and tyranny. . . .
>
> He has constrained our fellow citizens, taken captive on the high seas, to bear arms against their country, to become the executioners of their friends, and brethren, or to fall themselves by their hands.
>
> He has excited domestic insurrections amongst us, and has endeavored to bring on the inhabitants of our frontiers, the merciless Indian savages, whose known rule of warfare is an undistinguished destruction of all ages, sexes, and conditions.

These many observations make up the data. From the data, the colonists could claim:

> We, therefore, the representatives of the United States of America, in general Congress assembled, appealing to the Supreme Judge of the world for the rectitude of our intentions, do, in the name, and by the authority of the good people of these colonies, solemnly publish and declare that these united colonies, are and of right ought to be, free and independent states. . . .

Before the data can persuasively justify the claim, however, there must be a way to evaluate the data. Just how do these abuses by the king justify a new government? The standard for such evaluation, the warrant, is presented at the beginning of the Declaration:

> We hold these truths to be self-evident, that all men are created equal; that they are endowed by their Creator with certain unalienable rights; that among these

> are life, liberty, and the pursuit of happiness. That, to secure these rights, governments are instituted among men, deriving their just powers from the consent of the governed; that, whenever any form of government becomes destructive of these ends, it is the right of the people to alter or to abolish it, and to institute a new government. . . .

The Declaration of Independence, then, has the necessary components of successful argument. It has a claim that is supported by data, and mediated through a warrant, the standard by which we judge the data.

Toulmin offers three other components of the structure of the argument. These are *support for the warrant,* the *qualifier,* and the *rebuttal.*

The validity of a warrant might not be self-evident and thus might need further support or defense. When further strengthening of the warrant is needed an arguer might utilize support for the warrant. To illustrate the use of this component, we can look again at the Declaration of Independence. In the declaration, the necessary conditions justifying an alteration of the government are supported or underscored by the statement:

> But when a long train of abuses and usurpations, pursuing invariably the same object, evinces a design to reduce them under absolute despotism, it is their right, it is their duty, to throw off such government and to provide new guards for their future security.

The warrant is thus strengthened and further supported.

Often an arguer does not wish to maintain that his or her claim is absolutely certain, or that the claim can be applied universally to all situations. In such circumstances, the speaker might attach a qualifier to the claim. When a qualifier is used, it often takes the form of the term "probably" or the phrase "almost always." In other words, a qualifier indicates that the claim might be excepted under certain unusual circumstances or conditions.

When such excepted conditions or circumstances exist, they can be specified in the form of a rebuttal; that is, a statement specifying exceptions to the claim. Rebuttals usually include phrases like "except in the case of . . . ," or "I recognize that the claim would be true only for. . . ." Rebuttals should not be viewed as a weakening of the claim. A rebuttal allows the arguer to recognize legitimate limitations on the applicability of the claim. By doing so, the speaker may increase his or her credibility since it is not wise to claim more than can be reasonably supported. It is always better to recognize limitations than to stubbornly uphold an untenable position.

Toulmin's analysis also emphasizes two important considerations in argument: probability and assumptions. These considerations are most often central to the warrant portion of an argument, but can also be important in other parts of argument.

Probability

Most topics of public and educational debates involve *probabilities.* In other words, the questions considered in these debates can never be answered with certainty, as some scientific questions might be. Toulmin's model of argumentation is a strong one precisely because it recognizes the role of probability in argument and makes provision for it in the form of qualifiers and rebuttals.

The nature of probability will be discussed in greater detail in Chapter Five. A distinction should be made here, however, between *probability* and *plausibility,* terms that are sometimes confused. A plausible explanation is one that is possible, but not necessarily likely. For example, suppose a couple discovers the disappearance of their automobile upon returning from a date. One plausible explanation could be that someone took the car by mistake, thinking it was their own. That *could* have happened—it is possible. A more likely explanation, however, is that the car was stolen. The latter explanation is probable, the former is not. Both are plausible.

Facts and Assumptions

What is a fact? The answer to that question is not as simple as it might appear. One audience might perceive a message as factual or informative in nature, while another audience would perceive the same message as argumentative. Suppose an astronomy professor, speaking to a physics class at the University of Tennessee, stated that the earth was spherical. In all likelihood, the students would receive the message as factual. If the same astronomy professor were to address a meeting of the Flat Earth Society with the same message, the chances are that the audience would not accept the statement as fact.

The same message or statement, therefore, can be perceived very differently by different audiences. This consideration is an important one. For argument to be successful, one must recognize which statements will be accepted as fact and which statements will require support or further argument. Chapters Six and Seven also discuss facts and assumptions in argument.

Kinds of Arguments

Assuming that the audience has been considered, the type of argument that will be used must be chosen. The arguer may choose from several types of argument, and the choice (the strategy) will ultimately be based upon the analysis of the audience, the subject matter of the argument, and the position taken by the speaker. This section will discuss five types of argument: (1) cause to effect, (2) effect to cause, (3) argument from past association,

(4) argument by comparison, and (5) argument by generalization. Some of these types of arguments will also be discussed in Chapter Five on reasoning.

Cause to Effect

This type of argument begins with an assumption about the cause of an event, or with a description of the cause that is not in dispute. It then moves to explain an effect that *is* in dispute. If one wishes to argue that an increase in military spending is responsible for the large budget deficit, an argument from cause to effect might be useful. It could be argued that (1) military spending accounts for 30% of the budget; (2) military spending has increased more rapidly than any other budget item; (3) military spending is capital intensive, and therefore produces little revenue; and (4) military spending is exponential. These descriptions of military spending would then be cited as the cause of the large budget deficits.

This type of argument is effective only if several conditions are met. First, there must not be intervening forces that interfere with the causal relationship established. In the example above, if taxes were raised at the same rate as military spending had increased, then the increase in such spending would not contribute to the budget deficit. Or, if any other budget item was reduced to the same degree that military spending had increased, then again there would be no effect on the budget deficit.

The second necessary condition is that the cause must be strong enough to result in the inferred effect. Using the same example, if military spending had increased by 5% and that represented 30% of the budget, then it would only account for a very small percentage of the entire budget and budget deficit. In that instance, the cited cause would not seem strong enough to produce the effect.

The final necessary condition is that the effect that is in dispute must not be caused by additional factors. It is possible, for instance, that the budget deficit is largely fueled by increases in military spending *and* increases in other budget items. Suppose that the budget deficit is $150 billion dollars and that the increase in military spending accounted for $30 billion, and the increase in Social Security outlays accounted for $30 billion, and Revenue Sharing accounted for $20 billion. While military spending represents a large percentage of the total, other items account for large percentages as well. If this is true then it is probably unsound to claim that the increase in military spending is responsible for the deficit.

Effect to Cause

As you might have guessed, this type of argument is opposite in structure to the type previously discussed. Effect to cause argument begins with an effect that is not in dispute and then infers a cause.

Suppose the police stop a car in the vicinity of several reported robberies that have taken place just minutes before. In the car is a man wearing gloves. Beside him are several small locksmith tools. In the back seat and in the trunk are television sets, toasters, microwave ovens, silverware, and radios that might have been taken in the reported robberies. The police charge the man with the robberies, arguing that the man's possession of these stolen items indicates that he has stolen them. In such a case the cause (the man has committed the robberies) is inferred from the undisputed signs or effects (the suspicious circumstances surrounding the man).

As with cause to effect, effect to cause argument must meet certain conditions in order to be strong. First, the undisputed effect or effects must not be due to any cause other than the one inferred. In the above example, if the man who was apprehended had actually just purchased the stolen items from another individual in the vicinity, the charge against him would be inappropriate. An arguer must weigh all possible causes and choose the one that demonstrates the most clear relationship between the effects and the cause. If the inferred cause is reasonable, and care has been taken to consider other possible causes, such an argument can be strong indeed.

Secondly, it is necessary in effect to cause argument that the inferred cause is strong enough to result in the undisputed effect. For instance, in the example above, if only one house had been robbed, and the man apprehended had many more appliances than could have been taken from a single residence, the cause would not have been sufficient to result in the effect.

Finally, for such an argument to be persuasive, the effect must indeed be undisputed. If there is controversy as to the exact nature of the effect, the inference to the cause will be rather meaningless and profoundly unpersuasive.

Argument from Past Association

This argument is an easy one to understand and it is also a very powerful one. We have all shared experiences that connect the occurence of two or more events: when there is lightning there is thunder, where there is lightning and thunder there is rain, and where there is smoke there is flame. Such associations, of which there are many, can be used as a basis for argument. For example, a few years ago when the military registration law was being debated, some opponents of the legislation argued that there had never been military registration that did not lead to a draft, and that there had never been a draft that did not lead to a war. These opponents were arguing from past association to establish that the proposed law should not be passed.

The strength of this argument, of course, depends upon the validity of the association. If the alleged association did not actually occur, or if examples of the past association are so few as to weaken the inference, then the argument will not be persuasive.

Argument by Comparison

Argument by comparison is exactly what the name implies. It compares or likens the qualities of a lesser-known object or idea to those of a well-known object or idea. It implies that the two objects or ideas share a common characteristic, thus evoking a familiar image to generate and support a new and perhaps controversial idea.

For example, one might argue that the Soviet Union is stretching its tentacles and drawing helpless nations under its domination like the giant octopus of the sea draws in its prey. This argument does not suggest that the Soviet Union is an octopus, but that an octopus and the Soviet Union have certain characteristics in common. If the implication can be supported, this type of argument can be very dramatic and persuasive. Comparison and analogy are also discussed in Chapter Five.

Argument by Generalization

This kind of argument moves from the observation of several typical examples from a class of objects and generalizes their characteristics to the entire class. If someone were arguing that foreign cars are of poor quality, the argument might be constructed in this way: (a) Toyotas are of poor quality, Datsuns are of poor quality, Volkswagens are of poor quality; (b) since Toyotas, Datsuns, and Volkswagens are typical of all foreign cars, (c) foreign cars are of poor quality.

The possible deficiencies of this type of argument are obvious. First, the examples must actually be a part of the class to which the generalization applies. Second, the examples must indeed be typical of the class from which the examples are drawn. Finally, the examples must be legitimate. In the example above, for instance, the speaker would have to support the initial observations adequately. If the speaker claims that Toyotas are of poor quality, evidence must be shown to support the observation. If the examples are not legitimate, and not accepted by the audience, then the argument will fail to be persuasive.

The Interaction of Claims

As you read in Chapter One, argument is complex and dynamic. That is to say, one argument often depends upon or leads to another. For example, if we want to suggest a solution to a problem, it might be necessary to first persuade our audience that a problem indeed exists. Consider the following arguments.

I

DATA: Senator Jones employs his wife, his brother, his sister, his two daughters, and his cousin on his staff.

WARRANT: Nepotism is improper.

SUPPORT FOR THE WARRANT: Nepotism misuses public funds. Nepotism reduces the possibility of oversight of improper conduct.

CLAIM: Senator Jones operates his office improperly.

II

DATA: Senator Jones mailed campaign material paid for with government funds.

WARRANT: Mailing campaign material with government funds is improper.

SUPPORT FOR THE WARRANT: The law prohibits such action.

CLAIM: Senator Jones operates his office improperly.

III

DATA: Senator Jones accepted a $200,000 campaign contribution from Acme Steel Corporation.

WARRANT: Accepting campaign contributions from corporations is improper.

SUPPORT FOR THE WARRANT: Accepting such contributions is illegal. Accepting such contributions is a conflict of interest.

CLAIM: Senator Jones operates his office improperly.

IV

DATA: Senator Jones is engaged in improper and illegal activities.

WARRANT: Improper and illegal activities justify removal from office.

SUPPORT FOR THE WARRANT: Such activities constitute a violation of public trust.

CLAIM: Senator Jones should be removed from office.

One can readily see that Argument IV above depends upon the first three arguments for its strength. In the same way, Argument II is strengthened in its impact by the presentation of Argument I. Also, Argument III is strengthened by the first two arguments.

Argument from Effect to Effect

In the previous section on types of arguments, the types *effect to cause* and *cause to effect* were discussed. Argument from *effect to effect* is a combination of these two arguments, and it consists of two steps. The first step is an effect-to-cause structure. The second step is a cause-to-effect structure, maintaining that the inferred cause claimed in the first argument structure results in another effect that is in dispute, the acceptance of which is the purpose of the argument.

Suppose an attorney argues that her client should be released on bail. She begins her argument by establishing that her client is a leader in his community. He is the chief of the local volunteer fire department, he is a deacon in his church, he has volunteered to raise money for the orphan's fund, and he coaches a little league baseball team. To complete the effect-to-cause structure, the attorney then reasons that only a person of much integrity, dependability, and sense of civic responsibility would be able to accomplish the service that her client has achieved. The second step, then, is to argue that because of the impeccable reputation and character of her client (based on the above effect to cause argument), there is no reason to deny him bail. The final inference depended on a prior argument structure for its persuasiveness.

In this way, an argument from effect to effect is an interaction of two separate claims. The strength of this type of interaction depends upon the validity and acceptance of the first argument structure, the effect to cause relationship.

Presumption and Burden of Proof

For centuries, based upon British common law, an accused person held for trial has been presumed innocent until proven otherwise—that is, the burden of proving a defendant's guilt rests with the accuser.

In the nineteenth century Richard Whately applied the legal doctrine of burden of proof to non-legal argument. In the brilliant *The Elements of Rhetoric,* Whately included an impressive section on the role of presumption and burden of proof in non-legal argument, and most of the material included there is still useful to today's arguers.

Whately presents two distinct instances of presumption; the first in favor of existing institutions and the second against paradox. To those instances of presumption can be added at least two others: in favor of substantial majority opinion and in favor of substantial majority behavior. When we say that a position has *presumption,* we mean that the burden of proof lies with the advocates of the opposing position. This concept will be explained in more detail in the following examples.

Presumption is very important to the resolution of argument, but its precise function must be clearly understood. *Presumption does not equal probability.* Presumption focuses upon the burdens that each arguer must meet, not on the likelihood of validity. An accused brought to trial is not considered to be "probably innocent;" we know only that the accuser must prove his guilt. If the case against the accused is insufficient, that is enough for a finding of innocent.

In Favor of Existing Institutions

Those who are defending existing institutions or policies have presumption. Conversely, those who are suggesting deficiencies in or changes to existing institutions have the burden of proof. For instance, if advocates argued that the state of South Carolina should mandate the use of seat belts in automobiles, presumption would be against them. Since the state of South Carolina does not now mandate the use of seat belts, the burden of proof would lie with those who suggest change.

Even if those who would call for a change or who suggest deficiencies in existing institutions do not have presumption, they might nevertheless have a strong argument. Presumption of one position does not invalidate the other. Just because we presume South Carolina should not mandate seat belts prior to any argument does not mean that we would not be persuaded by a strong argument suggesting it.

Against Paradox

A paradox is a statement that is seemingly contradictory or opposed to common sense. Examples of paradoxical statements would include: "If we lowered taxes we would raise revenue," "If we raised standards for policemen we would attract more applicants," "If we lowered the price of theatre tickets we would make more money," or "As the economy grows, poverty increases."

Presumption lies with those who oppose paradox. If one chooses to claim a paradox, then the burden of proof lies with the advocate. Again, presumption against paradox does not mean that the paradox is necessarily or probably invalid, it simply places standards for weighing arguments.

In Favor of Substantial Majority Opinion

If one understands the reason why presumption is against paradox, then it is easy to see why presumption lies in favor of substantial majority opinion. Public opinion can, of course, be wrong. If a substantial majority supports a particular position, however, that position is presumed to be valid. The strength of the presumption lies in the strength of the majority. If it can be claimed that only 51% support a particular position, then the presumption in its favor would not be at all strong. On the other hand, if a position is supported by 95% of public opinion, then the presumption would be strong indeed.

Most people utilize presumption in public argument even if they do not recognize it. In a political campaign, for instance, the candidate that is seen as leading the race often increases the lead, for no other reason than the fact that he or she is the leader. Political scientists call this the "bandwagon effect" and it is a substantial asset to any leading candidate.

In Favor of Substantial Majority Behavior

Actions as well as opinions can be measured for the purpose of assigning presumption in argument. Suppose someone was arguing that all motorcyclists should wear helmets. Suppose further that less than 20% of all motorcyclists actually do wear helmets. Presumption would then lie with those who oppose such a notion.

As with public opinion, the size of the majority determines the strength of the presumption. In the above example, the 80% who do not wear helmets constitute a substantial majority. Suppose, however, that only 55% fail to wear helmets. The latter percentage would indeed be a majority, but certainly a less tenable one. The presumption would not be as great. In the presidential election of 1980, President Reagan won with a substantial electoral majority. As a result of that landslide, many of his proposals sailed through Congress with only token opposition. Because of the majority behavior of the electorate in that election, presumption was heavy for the proposals that the president offered. This was an example of the impact of presumption in favor of substantial majority behavior. The importance of the size of majority is clearly illustrated when the Reagan example is contrasted with the close 51% victory Jimmy Carter received just four years earlier. Even with a friendly Congress, Carter's proposals met much more opposition.

Summary

Argument consists of reasons for the opinions and attitudes that we hold and wish to forward. Argument can take place when there is disagreement and when a message or messages are designed for and aimed at those who would disagree. In this chapter you have learned that there is a difference between conviction and persuasion, between information and argument.

This chapter also discussed the concept and the characteristics of the universal audience, which is founded upon the commonality of all possible audiences. That commonality can be discovered by an investigation into the values that people share. In designing an argument for a universal audience, appeals based on values become an important strategy.

The structure of argument consists of six possible components: data, warrant, claim, support for the warrant, qualifier, and rebuttal. This structure suggests a consideration of probability and plausibility. Five distinct types of argument were presented and discussed: cause to effect, effect to cause, argument from past association, argument by comparison, and argument by generalization.

The interaction of *claims* is an important aspect of the complex, dynamic nature of argument. If we understand this interaction, we can present claims in tandem to increase the force of our individual arguments; one argument can actually serve as the basis of another separate claim.

Finally, presumption and burden of proof are fundamental issues in argument. The determination of presumption and burden of proof not only provides assistance in the resolution of arguments, but is also instructive for the arguers. In argument, presumption lies in favor of existing institutions and policies, in favor of substantial majority opinion, in favor of substantial majority behavior, and against paradox.

Notes

1. Chiam Perelman and L. Olbrechts-Tyteca, *The New Rhetoric,* trans., John Wilkinson and Purcell Weaver (South Bend: University of Notre Dame Press, 1969), p. 52.
2. Ibid., p. 20.
3. Ibid., p. 21–22.
4. Milton Rokeach, *The Nature of Human Values,* (New York: The Free Press, 1973), pp. 3, 19, 23–24.
5. Richard Whately, *Elements of Rhetoric,* reprint of 1846 edition (Carbondale: Southern Illinois University Press, 1963), pp. 112–115.

Questions and Exercises

1. Define *argument.*
2. What are the necessary conditions of argument?
3. Attitude change can only be predicted if there is disagreement. Explain that statement.
4. What is the difference between conviction and persuasion?
5. Define the "universal audience." What is at the heart of its unity?
6. Identify and define the six components of argument as presented by Stephen Toulmin.
7. Explain what is meant by an argument from effect to cause.
8. Explain what is meant by arguing from cause to effect.
9. Define argument by past association.
10. What is an argument by generalization?
11. What is the difference between probability and plausibility? Why are these concepts important in argument?
12. Briefly explain how various related claims interact.
13. An argument from effect to effect is an example of an interaction of claims. Explain that interaction.
14. Define "presumption." Define "burden of proof."
15. What are the four instances in which presumption is granted?

16. Select a recent newspaper editorial. Analyze the editorial in the following manner:
    a. Dissect the argument into its components.
    b. Determine the issues involved that indicate a consideration of probability or plausibility.
    c. Does the editorial's argument carry presumption? Why? or why not?
17. Select a speech from a recent issue of *Vital Speeches of the Day.* Identify the arguments found within the speech. For each argument found, identify the "data" which leads to the claim.
18. Using this same speech, explain the interaction of the arguments found. Do the arguments depend upon those that preceed them? If so, how? Does the impact of one or more arguments strengthen the others? If so, how?

Suggested Readings

Ulrich, Walter. "Philosophical Systems as Paradigms for Value Debate." *CEDA Yearbook, 1983*. California State University, Northridge: Don Brownlee, 1983, pp. 22–29.

Podgurski, Dwight T. "Presumption in the Value Proposition Realm." *CEDA Yearbook, 1983*. California State University, Northridge: Don Brownlee, 1983, pp. 34–39.

THREE

The Nature of Propositions

In the first chapter you learned that debates, unlike discussions, are concerned with the verification of specific *statements* or propositions. Propositions are framed positively and never in question form. Simply put, propositions are what the debaters talk about. They are the claims on which the arguments within the debate focus. *A proposition can be defined as a claim that requires, for its verification, the mediation of complex judgments.*

A good way to understand how a proposition functions within a debate is to compare debate to scientific decision-making, and to compare a proposition to a scientist's hypothesis. A hypothesis is not a question and neither is a proposition. A hypothesis is a positive claim that requires verification through various tests. Suppose that a scientist hypothesizes that water, when cooled to a temperature of 32 degrees, becomes a solid or freezes. To determine if the hypothesis is correct, the scientist would conduct an experiment or a series of experiments. She might actually expose a volume of water to a temperature of 32 degrees. If the water freezes we know that the hypothesis is correct. If it does not freeze, the hypothesis was wrong and she must alter the hypothesis or reject it.

A proposition functions in much the same way as a hypothesis. The debate is the experiment that "tests" the validity of the proposition. Debate propositions cannot be verified with as much certainty as the scientific example above, but they function in much the same way.

Functions of Propositions

Without propositions, it would be difficult for debaters to frame their arguments, or even to know which arguments would be relevant. Just as a scientist must first frame a hypothesis in order to design the experiment that tests it, debaters must know the proposition in order to frame the arguments that will collectively form the debate or "test" for the claim. A proposition serves four basic functions in debate: (1) It provides common ground upon which the debate takes place; (2) it provides a research focus; (3) it helps to establish burdens for proof during the debate; and (4) it simplifies complex controversies.

Common Ground

The existence of a proposition makes certain that both sides debate the same topic. The debate would be unmanageable and rather meaningless if the debaters were on completely different tracks. There would be no direct clash of ideas and no way to evaluate the relative merits of the arguments put forward by the debaters. The debate must begin with the two teams and the judge or audience on the same or common ground. In 1980, Iranian militants held American hostages at the U.S. Embassy in Tehran. For more than a year negotiations for their emancipation were fruitless. Upon his eventual release, one of the hostages remarked that neither side seemed to understand the arguments or grievances of the other. The negotiations were begun and promulgated on different ground with vastly different assumptions. The grievances of the American government did not directly respond to the basic complaint that Iran had lodged against the United States. In much the same

Chapter Outline

way, if debaters do not begin on the same plane with common basic assumptions, their arguments cannot be evaluated easily.

Research Focus

As you will soon learn, preparing for a debate demands considerable and careful research. That demand is difficult under the best of circumstances, but it would be virtually impossible if the task were not narrowed by the proposition. Before an attorney can begin preparing for a criminal defense he must first know what specific charge has been filed against his client. That knowledge focuses the attorney's attention to the body of law related to the charge. Knowing the specific charge allows the attorney to focus his research which makes his job more manageable. In the same way, knowing the proposition allows a debater to focus research and make a difficult job less so.

Burdens for Proof

As we will learn in a later chapter, the way in which a proposition is worded and classified will largely determine what burdens each team assumes. Just as the attorney is guided by the wording of an indictment and the specific charge to determine his client's burdens for proof during trial, the proposition indicates what must be proven by whom during the debate. Suppose a person were charged with first degree murder. The state would probably have to prove that the accused premeditated the commission of the crime. But if the accused were charged with second degree murder, the state's burden would be less, perhaps only that the accused was wanton or reckless in the commission of the crime.

Simplification of Controversies

In the first chapter you learned that debate has an advantage over discussion as a decision-making tool in that it is more efficient. As you recall, in a discussion the participants are not guided by a single statement but by a question. The discussion can become quite complex with many different positions being aired with no one solution being fairly considered. The proposition ensures that the debate is focused. It simplifies the complexity in that it allows for detailed investigation into a particular proposal or claim. The controversies surrounding that claim become clearer and can be seen in sharper focus.

Bases for Propositions

A claim or proposition is akin to a hypothesis in science and answers a question similar to a research question posed by a scientist. If an astronomer is researching the planet Saturn he might pose many research questions related to the planet. Such questions would range from, "How large is Saturn?" to "Is there life on Saturn?" The astronomer's responses to those research questions become hypotheses. In debate, we can also identify "research questions" that underlie the proposition. If a debate were to be held on the U.S. economy several questions could be asked about the topic, and answers to such questions might form propositions. We could ask about the nature of the economy, the worth or strength of the economy, what relationship it has to other institutions, or what changes should be made in its management. Each of the questions requires answers that would form very different propositions.

Descriptive Inquiries

There are four kinds of argument inquiries or "research questions" the answers to which can form propositions. First, there are *descriptive inquiries.* These questions include those such as "What is it?" or "What are its components?" or "By what method does it function?" If a debate were to focus on the U.S. economy, for example, a descriptive inquiry would be "What is the state of the economy?" One might answer that question by "hypothesizing" that the economy is weak. To form a proposition from that claim we only have to state it as "*Resolved, that the state of the U.S. economy is weak.*"

Analytical Inquiries

A second type of argument inquiry comprises *analytical inquiries.* These questions ask consideration of relationships. If we know or assume that the U.S. economy is weak, an inquiry might be made into the cause of the weakness, or regarding the effects the weak economy might have. A proposition formed from an answer to an analytical inquiry might be: *Resolved, that the budget deficit undermines continued economic growth.* The focus, in this example, is not on description but on relationships.

Inquiries of Comparison

The third type of argument inquiry includes *inquiries of comparison.* These are questions posed about comparisons. Questions such as "Is the U.S. economy better than that of the Soviet Union?" or "Is a deficit economy better than a stagnant economy?" or "Is economic growth more important than economic fairness?" pose inquiries of comparison. Answers to those questions can form propositions. For instance, a proposition that is based upon an inquiry of comparison would be: *Resolved, that economic fairness is more important than economic growth.*

Prescriptive Inquiries

The fourth type of argument inquiry is *prescriptive inquiries.* These questions deal with proposed solutions or possible solutions to problems and with existing and future policies. An example of a prescriptive inquiry would be, "Will a flat based income tax system guarantee a healthy economy?" Another example would be, "Is a system of immigration quotas desirable?" Propositions that contain answers to these kinds of inquiries often contain the words "should" or "desirable" or "effective." An example would be: *Resolved, that immigration quotas are desirable.*

Just as scientific hypotheses are built upon research questions, argument inquiries can be identified as the basis of propositions. The nature of an inquiry determines the nature of the proposition.

Classification of Propositions

There are several types of propositions. That is, there are many ways in which propositions can be worded, and each variation may produce different burdens upon the debaters and require different standards by which the debate is judged. As the previous section illustrates, the type of proposition is not determined by the subject it treats, but by the nature of the argument inquiry it answers and by specific wording. For example, the following propositions all deal with the United Nations but each would be classified differently:

RESOLVED, that the United Nations is pro-communist.

RESOLVED, that the United Nations encourages communist expansion.

RESOLVED, that U.S. membership in the United Nations is more valuable than U.S. membership in NATO.

RESOLVED, that the United States should withdraw membership from the United Nations.

All of these statements deal with the United Nations, but each is fundamentally different from the others. The difference lies in the type of inquiry each answers.

Three general categories of propositions will be identified in this chapter: (1) propositions of inference, (2) propositions of value, and (3) propositions of policy.

Propositions of Inference

An *inference* is a conclusion gained by reasoning from something known or assumed. For instance, the statement that "President Reagan's cabinet is politically conservative," is an inference. It is a claim or conclusion based on several characteristics of Reagan's cabinet that we know to be true or that we assume to be true. We know who makes up the president's cabinet, we know the public statements they have made, and we know of the policies initiated by their departments. The evaluation of those characteristics is an inference. Knowing who the Secretary of State is, knowing his public statements, and knowing his policies provide a base upon which the inference is made.

Propositions of inference make up a large category, and therefore a further division is needed to clarify the classification. There are four ways in which an inference can be worded: (1) trait inference, that which deals with description of conditions or characteristics; (2) relational inference, that which deals with relationships, (3) historical inference; that which deals with the past; and (4) predictive inference, that which deals with the future.

A *trait inference* makes a claim about the condition or characteristics of something known or assumed. Suppose we are talking about college football. What traits can be assigned to college football? One might conclude that college football is semi-professional, or that it is corrupt, or that it is self-supporting. All are inferences about the condition or characteristics of college football—its traits. Trait inferences in proposition form would include:

RESOLVED, that the United Nations is effective.

RESOLVED, that the Animal Protection Council is poorly administrated.

RESOLVED, that public education is obsolete.

RESOLVED, that the World Court is anti-democratic.

RESOLVED, that the Supreme Court exercises excessive power.

Another kind of inference is one that suggests relationships or effects. These *relational inferences* are claims about the cause of something known or assumed, or the effects exerted by that which is known. Suppose we were debating the nature of Student Health Services on campus. One might conclude that Student Health Services neglects the well-being of students, or that Student Health Services damages the image of the University. It could also be concluded that Student Health Services undermines the rapport between the students and the administration. All of these examples center on the relationship between Student Health Services and another object or group of objects. Other examples of relational inferences include:

RESOLVED, that the method of conducting presidential elections in the United States is detrimental to democracy.

RESOLVED, that commercial television is harmful to children.

RESOLVED, that labor unions cause inflation.

RESOLVED, that Congress exerts excessive influence over the president.

The verification of propositions of relational inference demands a demonstration of a relationship between the key elements in the claim. If we conclude that diet and exercise have grown in importance and popularity and are able to support the claim with ample evidence and solid logic, and we further find that the incidence of heart attacks has decreased over the same period, could we then claim that one caused the other? The answer is no. If nothing else is argued, those two findings are not enough to support the claim that diet and exercise lead to a decrease in heart attacks. In supporting a relational inference, an advocate affirming the proposition must prove that the growing popularity of diet and exercise *caused* or directly *led to* the decrease in the incidence of heart attack. Propositions of relational inference, then, are a bit more complex and perhaps more difficult to support than those that infer traits.

A third type of inference is one of an historical nature, and includes conclusions made about something known or assumed that has existed or has taken place in the past. We can infer many things from the examination of historical facts. An example of an *historical inference* would be the claim that Knute Rockne was a great football coach. We might infer that he was a great coach after discovering that he was the first to utilize the forward pass in college football, that he generated fierce loyalty from his players, and that he won over seventy percent of his games. Examples of propositions of historical inference include:

RESOLVED, that Knute Rockne was a great coach.

RESOLVED, that Lee Harvey Oswald acted alone in assassinating President Kennedy.

RESOLVED, that Abraham Lincoln was an effective president.

RESOLVED, that the atomic bombing of Nagasaki, Japan was unnecessary.

You might notice that the examples above also deal with questions of description and/or relationships, and in that sense each could be classified in either of the first two classifications. Historical inferences, though, pose a peculiar problem for the debater. Without exception, the preparation for debating a proposition of historical inference requires historical research. A debater might have to research relationships, but they would be relationships of the past. A debater might have to research conditions, but they would be historical conditions. That kind of analysis requires special understanding.

The same caution can be issued for debating a final type of inference. Although propositions of *predictive inference* also deal with either conditions or relationships, placing them in a separate class is justified. The conditions or relationships suggested by predictive inferences are in the future, and so the analysis and nature of the research would be different from that of the other categories. A predictive inference speculates on the future based upon present knowledge and assumptions. For instance, since there is much dissatisfaction with the college football championship procedures, and since both the television networks and a majority of fans support a playoff system, one might claim that there will soon be a college football playoff system. Another predictive inference would be that there will be an increased number of ethical violations in the next decade in college football. That inference may be based on several factors now known or assumed. Examples of propositions of predictive inference would be:

RESOLVED, that there will be a space-based anti-ballistic missile system in place by the year 2000.

RESOLVED, that the structure of the Catholic church will be significantly altered within the current decade.

RESOLVED, that a southerner will win the next presidential election.

RESOLVED, that there will be a tax increase during the next fiscal year.

RESOLVED, that the United States will sever all economic and diplomatic relations with South Africa before the next presidential election.

Propositions of Value

The next of our main categories of proposition classifications is *propositions of value.* Values are not always an easy concept to understand. What are values and how do they operate in argument? Those are two of the questions we will discuss before specifically treating propositions of value.

It is easy to confuse "attitudes" with "values" because both are kinds of evaluations. What they evaluate is fundamentally different, however. Attitudes are beliefs that make judgments about specific objects, persons, or situations. Attitudes are also time-bound. That is to say, as time and situations change so might our attitudes. For instance, you might dislike Mr. Snodgrass. Your dislike for Mr. Snodgrass is a disposition that is confined to him alone, and attitudes serve as the basis for that disposition. Your dislike for Mr. Snodgrass might be based on the evaluation that he is selfish or unfriendly. If you make those evaluations about him, your disposition towards the man will most likely be negative. If Mr. Snodgrass saves your life tomorrow, your disposition toward him will likely change because you would no longer hold the same attitudes regarding him. Most likely, you would no longer view him as selfish nor unfriendly.

A value, on the other hand, is not time- or situation-specific. Attitudes are based upon values, so one's values are more enduring. They are enduring beliefs that specify our behavior preferences and help determine the goals for which we strive.[1] Generosity is a value because it is preferable to its opposite—greed. Success is a value, preferable to failure. No matter what happens we are not likely to change those beliefs very easily. We will always believe that generosity is better than greed and that success is better than failure.

To clarify the way in which attitudes are based upon values, let's return to our Mr. Snodgrass example. You might dislike Mr. Snodgrass (disposition) because you perceive him to be selfish (attitude). In this case the attitude leads to the disposition because you *value* generosity. When Snodgrass saves your life you no longer perceive him to be selfish or unfriendly and therefore your attitude toward him might change. In this situation, however, your values would remain unchanged.

As beliefs of preference, values serve as guides or criteria for conduct. We behave as we do largely because we believe that it is the "right" way to behave, or that it will lead to the "right" goal. Humans perceive all values as preferable to their opposites. Otherwise values would not be recognized as values. As such, values cannot be judged in isolation. It would be utterly ridiculous to debate a proposition such as: *Resolved, that generosity is desirable.* Values cannot be debated unless they are compared with other values, or unless some valued thing is compared with another valued thing. We can only judge values within a context of specific behaviors when one value conflicts with another. Therefore, we can conclude that *propositions of value are comparisons.* A debatable value proposition would be: *Resolved, that generosity is preferable to success.* Both generosity and success are values that carry importance relative to specific situations. Propositions of value are either comparisons of one value to another, or of one valued thing to another. Examples of propositions of value would include:

RESOLVED, that individual rights of privacy are more important than national security.

RESOLVED, that commercial television is more beneficial to society than is public television.

RESOLVED, that economic equity is better than economic growth.

RESOLVED, that academic responsibilities are more important to college students than extra-curricular activities.

In the above examples, the value of each element is not being debated, but rather that value relative to another. Milton Rokeach, a respected authority in value theory explains:

> Often a person is confronted with a situation in which he cannot behave in a manner congruent with all of his values. The situation will activate two or more values in conflict with one another. For example, a person may have to choose between behaving compassionately or behaving competently, but not both; between behaving truthfully or patriotically, but not both.[2]

A value claim seeks a resolution of such conflicts. No one would likely question that being truthful is better than lying—that is not debatable. However, when one compares truthfulness to patriotism, another value, then the claim is arguable.

In supporting a proposition of value, then, one cannot focus on just one or the other element, but must compare the values and valued things and produce standards by which they may be compared. The inclusion of a value in a proposition does not necessarily indicate that it is a proposition of value. Only when two values are compared do we have a proposition of value.

Propositions of Policy

Propositions of policy deal with specific courses of action. A policy must specify an action that has distinct and certain limits. Some propositions of policy answer prescriptive inquiries, if the proposition deals with a future course of action. Other policy propositions answer analytical inquiries, if the proposition deals with present or past courses of action.

There are two kinds of policy propositions—those that evaluate and those that advocate. The former are propositions that make evaluative judgments about a course of action without suggesting the adoption of the policy, and these are called propositions of *policy evaluation*. Propositions of policy evaluation almost always suggest relationships or effects, which means that in one respect these propositions can also be considered as propositions of relational inference. Relational inferences gleaned from policies, however, involve issues that might not be found in controversies involving other relational inferences. For this reason we think that it is justified to consider propositions of policy evaluation as a separate class.

Propositions of policy evaluation stop short of actually advocating the implementation of a policy. It is possible to evaluate a course of action positively and not advocate its implementation. I might have nothing but praiseworthy comments to make about political candidate X but vote for his opponent, candidate Y, on election day. No matter how great candidate X might be, candidate Y might be a better candidate. Believing candidate X is a good candidate is different from believing that candidate X is the best candidate or that candidate X should be elected. That is the difference between evaluation and advocacy.

A policy evaluation generally demands a judgment on the justification of a course of action. One can justify a policy on moral grounds, or one can evaluate a policy on practical or legal grounds. For example, to claim the U.S. military intervention into El Salvador is legal is only one level of justification and does not suggest that the policy should be continued. An example of a proposition of policy evaluation would be: *Resolved, that a national flat-rate income tax is desirable.* The proposition clearly deals with a policy —a flat-rate income tax. In analyzing the proposition we might ask, is a flat-rate income tax morally justified? We could find that it is morally justified in that it treats all taxpayers equally. We could ask if it was legally proper. Since the federal government has the power to tax, it would seem to be legal. Finally we might ask if the tax scheme is practical. We might determine that it would be workable, that it would raise revenue and would reduce the deficit. All of the above analysis would strongly support the proposition that a flat tax is desirable. The proposition, however, stops short of advocating the actual implementation of a flat tax.

Indeed, one could agree with all of the analysis above and not support the implementation of a flat tax. Even though a flat rate income tax is morally and legally justified, and even though such a tax would raise revenue and reduce the deficit, one still might not support its implementation. Some other tax plan, or the present one, might enjoy the same justifications. More than one tax plan may be justified as workable or desirable.

Other examples of propositions of policy evaluation are:

RESOLVED, that a tuition increase at the state university is justified.

RESOLVED, that wage and price controls on durable goods are effective.

RESOLVED, that raising the drinking age to 21 is desirable.

RESOLVED, that the 55 MPH speed limit saves lives.

RESOLVED, that the repaving of Percival Road is cost efficient.

The second type of policy proposition is one that goes beyond simply making an evaluation and actually advocates the implementation of a policy. Most propositions of *policy advocacy* include the word "should." Examples of such propositions are:

RESOLVED, that the state university should reduce tuition.

RESOLVED, that advertising aimed at children should be prohibited.

RESOLVED, that victimless crimes should be legalized.

RESOLVED, that wage and price controls should be implemented.

When one claims that a particular policy should be implemented, the claim is a complex one. The claim suggests not only that the policy is workable, but also that it is needed (that it is aimed at solving some actual problem or to accrue some tangible benefits), and that it can actually achieve those goals. Since most propositions of policy advocacy are complex, a specific plan is generally required to indicate how the policy will be implemented.

With that in mind, supporting a proposition of policy advocacy requires an evaluation of its justification, as well as a statement of its necessity, its workability, and its efficacy. In addition, a plan is needed to specify how the policy will be implemented. It is not difficult to see the difference between propositions of policy advocacy and those of policy evaluation. Those of advocacy are much more complex and perhaps more difficult to support.

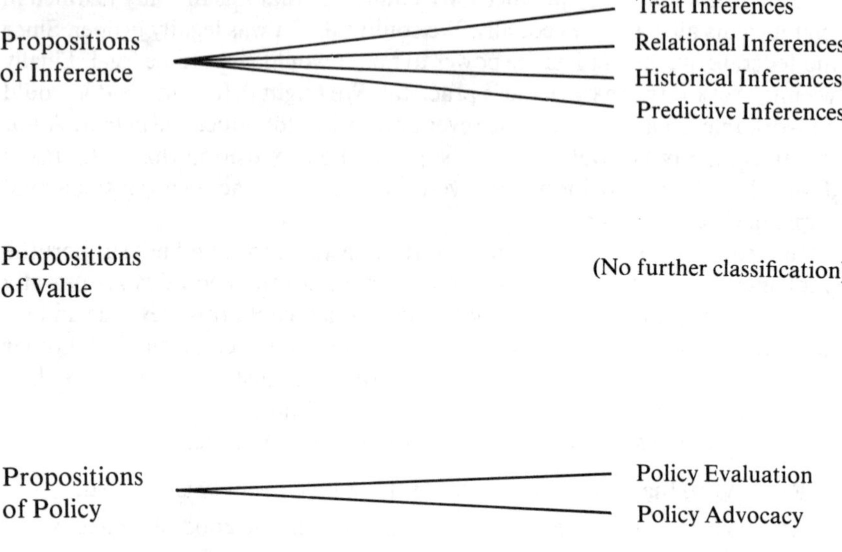

FIGURE 3–1

The Wording of Propositions

The proper wording of a proposition is crucial because it determines the classification, the nature of the debater's analysis, the burdens for proof, and the requirements for research. So far in this chapter you have learned how propositions can be worded in order to correspond to one or the other classifications treated. We will now discuss additional wording guidelines that make it easier for debaters to fulfill their burdens during a debate.

The first guideline is that *propositions should be worded positively.* If the proposition is worded negatively, its advocates will find themselves opposing the suggested traits, relationships, value comparisons, or policies; this is a confusing and ineffective means of debate. For instance, the following proposition is improperly worded: *Resolved, that the United Nations is not obsolete.* To support this proposition, one would have to take a "negative" position—against the United Nations being obsolete. To correct the example, the word "not" could be left out of the proposition, or the inference could be changed. One could change the inference to, "the United Nations is an effective tool for peace in the modern world." Other examples with suggested corrections would include:

Wrong: RESOLVED, that the United States should not resume diplomatic relations with Cuba.

Better: RESOLVED, that the United States should resume diplomatic relations with Cuba.

Better: RESOLVED, that the United States should significantly alter its relationship with Cuba.

Wrong: RESOLVED, that the federal government should not fund abortions.

Better: RESOLVED, that the funding of abortions are outside the legitimate function of government.

Better: RESOLVED, that the federal government is justified in funding abortions.

A second guideline is that *propositions should be simple claims.* A proposition should make a single claim, a single inference, one value comparison, or suggest a single policy. A proposition that violates this guideline would make more than one inference, multiple comparisons, or would advocate two or more policies. Simple claims allow for the clarity needed to make the debater's task more managable. An example of an overly-complex claim and suggested improvements would be:

Wrong: RESOLVED, that commercial television is damaging to children and exploits performers.

Better: RESOLVED, that commercial television is damaging to children.

Better: RESOLVED, that commercial television exploits performers.

Propositions should also be debatable. That is to say, there ought to be approximately equal ground afforded both affirmative and negative positions. The following proposition would not afford equal ground: *Resolved, that proper nutrition is important to one's health.* The evidence and logic supporting the proposition is so strong that a negative team would have difficulty arguing against it. Other examples of undebatable propositions with possible corrections are:

Wrong: RESOLVED, that education is beneficial to society.

Better: RESOLVED, that education is more important to society than a healthy economy.

Better: RESOLVED, that the quality of higher education has been sacrificed for institutional survival.

Wrong: RESOLVED, that the United States should strengthen its economy.

Better: RESOLVED, that the economy of the United States is weak.

Better: RESOLVED, that the United States should implement wage and price controls.

In addition, *propositions should contain terms that are capable of common definition.* This simply means that words which are excessively vague or abstract should not be used in propositions as key terms. If the terms are vague, the debate might degenerate into narrow definitional arguments without any real clash on the inference, comparison, or policy suggested by the proposition. To avoid this, propositions should employ words that are as concrete as possible. In the following proposition common definition of key terms might be difficult: *Resolved, that government regulation is excessive.* The phrase "government regulation" is vague. The proposition does not indicate the level of government with which the inference deals. Does the inference deal with municipal government? What about the federal government? The word regulation is not specific either. What sort of regulation? Regulation of whom or what? The key terms in such a proposition need to be more concrete. Other examples and possible corrections follow.

Wrong: RESOLVED, that sports are beneficial.

Better: RESOLVED, that professional sports are beneficial to society.

Better: RESOLVED, that college football is beneficial to higher education.

Better: RESOLVED, that professional football franchises are beneficial to civic pride.

Wrong: RESOLVED, that government assistance should be changed.

Better: RESOLVED, that the social security system should be made voluntary.

Better: RESOLVED, that the medicare system should be significantly altered.

Better: RESOLVED, that disaster relief should be expanded.

Finally, *propositions should focus on significant issues.* Simply put, propositions should be worth debating. Will the debate be instructive? Will the debate generate discussion of significant social, political, or academic issues? These questions should be answered in the affirmative. The following example is not of lasting concern: *Resolved, that brown cars are preferable to blue cars.* A proposition of that sort would not generate arguments about any issue of much political, social, or academic worth. Other examples of propositions that are of less than sufficient depth are:

Wrong: RESOLVED, that Howdy Doody has made more of an impact on our society than Yogi Bear.

Wrong: RESOLVED, that Snickers bars taste better chilled than not.

Wrong: RESOLVED, that chess is more intellectually stimulating than Backgammon.

Wrong: RESOLVED, that apple pie is more nutritious than pumpkin pie.

Summary

It is clear that the proposition is the basis of debate. Without it, a debater's task of research would be more difficult, as would his or her burden of analysis. In the absence of a proposition debaters would perhaps be confused as to the arguments they should advance, and judges would find no clear standard by which to compare affirmative and negative arguments.

Understanding propositions as hypotheses that answer argument inquiries or "research questions" clarifies research demands and assists debaters in discovering issues. You learned that there are three kinds of propositions: those of inference, of value, and of policy. The relationship between the particular type of proposition and the kind of argument inquiry that is answered is an important one for the debater to understand. By understanding that relationship one simplifies the controversy and promotes a common approach to its resolution.

The wording of the proposition is important. Propositions should be worded positively, should be constructed with a simple claim, should be debatable, should contain terms that are capable of common definition, and should focus on significant issues.

There is no more important consideration in debate than understanding the proposition. Just as scientists would have difficulty in resolving scientific controversies without hypotheses, debaters would have difficulty resolving controversies without propositions.

Notes

1. Milton Rokeach, *Beliefs, Attitudes and Values* (San Francisco: Jossey-Bass, 1976), pp. 159–161.
2. Ibid., p. 161.

Questions and Exercises

1. What are the four functions of propositions?
2. What are analytical inquiries and why are they considered the bases of propositions?
3. Name and briefly explain the four types of argument inquiries.
4. Identify the argument inquiry answered by the following propositions:
   a. RESOLVED, that the state of the U.S. economy is weak.
   b. RESOLVED, that the magnitude of the U.S. budget deficit undermines economic growth.
   c. RESOLVED, that inflation is better than recession.
   d. RESOLVED, that immigration quotas are desirable.

5. You learned that there are several classifications of propositions: trait inference, relational inference, historical inference, predictive inference, value, policy evaluation, and policy advocacy. Classify the following propositions:
   a. RESOLVED, that the United Nations is pro-communist.
   b. RESOLVED, that U.S. policy regarding El Salvador should be significantly changed.
   c. RESOLVED, that vocational education is more important than liberal education.
   d. RESOLVED, that the United States should withdraw from NATO.
   e. RESOLVED, that South Korea is more important to our national security than Taiwan.
   f. RESOLVED, that television advertising aimed at children should be prohibited.
   g. RESOLVED, that personal income taxes undermine the principle of individual liberty.
   h. RESOLVED, that Woodrow Wilson was responsible for the demise of the League of Nations.
   i. RESOLVED, that economic equity is better than prosperity.
   j. RESOLVED, that wage and price controls are effective weapons against inflation.
   k. RESOLVED, that there will be a woman elected president by the year 2000.
   l. RESOLVED, that Abraham Lincoln was an effective president.
   m. RESOLVED, that college basketball exploits student athletes.
   n. RESOLVED, that the Supreme Court exercises excessive power.
   o. RESOLVED, that U.S. foreign policy encourages communist expansion.
6. What are the five guidelines for the wording of propositions?
7. Through library research, find a recently delivered persuasive speech. Identify at least three argument inquiries addressed in the speech. Then frame two propositions that could be formed from those argument inquiries.

Suggested Readings

Ulrich, Walter. "The Nature of the Topic in Value Debate." *CEDA Yearbook, 1984*. California State University, Northridge: Don Brownlee, 1984, pp. 1–6.

Zarefsky, David. "Criteria for Evaluating Non-Policy Argument." *CEDA Yearbook, 1980*. California State University, Northridge: Don Brownlee, 1980, pp. 9–16.

FOUR

Discovering the Issues

In every controversy there are issues that should be raised or special questions that should be asked before the dispute can be resolved. Even in public debates in which propositions may not be explicitly stated, there should be a clear statement and a treatment of those special questions.

The Nature of Issues

Issues may therefore be defined as the vital questions that are inherent to the subject or proposition being argued. For example, suppose the students in your argumentation and debate class are debating this topic: *Resolved, that the college honor code should be significantly strengthened.* An issue that should be raised would center on the present state of the honor code: Is the existing honor code seriously weak? As another example, in the event that the U.S. House of Representatives were debating a bill that would reduce taxes, the participants would need to determine if existing taxes were indeed too high.

This definition of issues implies several important principles. First, *issues exist within the proposition being argued.* The term *issues* does not apply to any and all questions that the advocate chooses to address or that audiences would like to hear argued. Instead, issues are the vital questions that exist within the context and the history of the subject matter. Advocates may choose not to raise the vital questions, but if and when that occurs, the dispute will not be intelligently discussed or effectively resolved. Audiences may also choose not to make a decision based on the answers to these vital questions, but when that happens they risk making an irresponsible and perhaps damaging decision.

Second, *the issues in a debate determine what specific claims must be proven.* In disputing the university honor code, a debater will need to document that there are particular and serious weaknesses within the existing code. Once those claims are established, other issues should be raised that will require other claims to be demonstrated. Thus, issues identify specific burdens as well as points of clash for debaters.

Perhaps the most important question, however, is how you discover issues. The rest of this chapter provides answers to this question in the following sections: analysis of non-policy propositions, issues in propositions of inference, issues in propositions of value, analyzing propositions of policy advocacy, stock issues, a systems approach to stock issues, finding issues in propositions of policy evaluation, and finally, the special issues in educational debate—topicality and extratopicality.

Analyzing Non-Policy Propositions

Although non-policy questions will vary greatly in specific content and do raise very different kinds of questions, discovery of the issues can nonetheless begin with certain common questions. These questions, based on the nature of non-policy propositions, will provide the starting points for the analysis of most non-policy propositions.

The first task is to discover the key term or key terms in the proposition. Both propositions of inference and those of value will feature terms that must be identified in order to determine the precise meaning of the proposi-

Chapter Outline

tion. Pinpointing and understanding these terms is central to an intelligent debate of the topic. For example, in the following proposition, the key term is "detrimental": *Resolved, that unauthorized immigration is detrimental to the United States.* Some propositions may utilize a key phrase instead of a single term. An example would be: *Resolved, that commercial television is more detrimental than beneficial to American society.* In this proposition, the words "more detrimental than beneficial" constitute a key evaluative phrase.

Second, once the key evaluative term or phrase is identified, how should it be defined? This should be a crucial issue within any non-policy debate. The meaning of the key term or phrase will determine whether a particular debate is meaningful and will also limit the arguments that are relevant to a resolution of the debate. The failure to define "detrimental" when debating the immigration topic cited above could result in a debate that would be unfocused or meaningless. In resolving the proposition on commercial television, a failure to define the phrase "more detrimental than beneficial" would prevent any resolution of the arguments. Without a common understanding of the central phrase there would be no way to balance the advantages against the disadvantages of commercial television.

Third, do conditions exist such that the evaluation can be confirmed or denied? Most non-policy propositions pose a question about an evaluation and its applicability to a situation. Once the meaning of the evaluation has been determined, then the application of that evaluation can be tested. For example, in the immigration topic, the key questions is: Does unauthorized immigration in the United States (conditions) deserve the description "detrimental" (evaluation)? In the commercial television topic, the central question is: Can the state of commercial television (conditions) be appropriately described as "more detrimental than beneficial to American society" (evaluation)?

Thus, the three starting points for the analysis of most non-policy propositions can be found in the answers to these three questions:

1. What is the key evaluative term or phrase?
2. How should the key evaluative term or phrase be defined?
3. Do conditions exist such that the evaluation can be affirmed or denied?*

---

*If the wording of the proposition is in the past or future tense, the wording of this question would also change accordingly, as follows:

Past Tense: Did conditions exist such that the evaluation could be affirmed or denied?

Future Tense: Will conditions exist such that the evaluation can be affirmed or denied?

Advocates should answer these questions by establishing a criterion or a set of criteria for the measurement of conditions. Such criteria will specify, by certain standards, at what point the conditions would justify the evaluative description found in the proposition. For example, established criteria for the immigration topic would enable debaters to answer the following inquiry: At what point does unauthorized immigration become detrimental to the United States? In a debate on the commercial television topic, a similar question could be answered: At what point do the detriments of commercial television outweigh its benefits?

The establishment of the criteria, as with any important argument, will be based on analysis, reasoning, knowledge of the particular subject matter, and appropriate authoritative evidence. In an educational debate on a non-policy topic, the affirmative team has the burden of defending the proposition and therefore must provide and must defend a criterion or set of criteria. Without criteria or equivalent arguments defining the key evaluative terms, non-policy propositions would be neither understood nor debated.

The answers to questions such as the three we list above provide the central issues in most non-policy debates. In this sense these questions are similar to the *stock issues* in policy debate, which we will discuss later in this chapter. The stock issues in a policy advocacy debate usually generate an *outline* for the affirmative or negative case. However, this is not the case with the questions we have raised here. Debaters analyzing non-policy propositions will generally discover that the research into the specific topic, the consideration of possible case formats, and the specific characteristics of each kind of non-policy proposition will guide case construction.

In the following sections, the specifics of each kind of non-policy proposition are considered.

Issues in Propositions of Inference

Discovering the specific issues in propositions of inference depends upon analyzing the wording of the particular proposition and focusing on several elements: (1) the structure of the statement, (2) the classification of the claim, and (3) the use of specific qualifiers. Each of these three aspects will be discussed below.

The structure of the statement. The structure of an inference might be classified as either simple or complex. A *simple proposition* of inference usually uses a form of the verb "to be" and never has a significant modifier. For example, the following proposition is one of inference: *Resolved, that liberal education is obsolete.* The issues in such a proposition are usually restricted to issues of definition. In the example, the meanings of "obsolete" (the key term), "liberal education," and "is" would all be issues. This kind of simple proposition is one of trait inference.

On the other hand, a *complex inference* often uses action verbs and always includes a significant modifier. Further, the modifier is frequently a causal link. These complex propositions are relational inferences. An example of a proposition of relational inference is: *Resolved, that higher education in the United States has sacrificed quality for institutional survival.* A proposition such as this one specifies both an action (sacrifice), and the cause of that action (the motive of institutional survival). Typically, propositions of relational inference raise two kinds of issues—definitional and relational links.

When causality is argued, a number of issues can be predicted. In the example above, the affirmative might argue that whenever college applications declined significantly, then college entrance requirements are lowered to compensate. The introduction of this argument would lead to such questions as these in the debate: Are there other causes of the decision to lower standards? Can the decline in college applications alone explain the lower standards? Thus, causality arguments occur with complex propositions of inference, usually those of relational inference.

The classification of the claim. The kind of claim made by a proposition of inference might also be classified in one of two ways: as an absolute or a general statement. The use of the words "all," "none," "never," or equivalent terms usually indicate an absolute claim. An example of an *absolute proposition* of inference is: *Resolved, that abortion is never a moral act.* In debating this kind of proposition, the existence of any exception to the statement is a major issue. This type of proposition is rare; nevertheless, when such a proposition is debated, two kinds of issues are raised: definitions and exceptions.

A *general proposition* of inference is one in which the overall truth of the claim is a major issue. An example would be: *Resolved, that television is harmful to children.* Although exceptions to the generalization might be important, the issue would not be the existence of exceptions, but rather their significance. A central question, then, in the proposition above would be: "Are the benefits of television enough to deny the general truth of the inference?" Thus, in a proposition of inference expressing a general claim, the major issues would be definitions and the significance of any exceptions.

The use of specific qualifiers. Propositions of inference might also be classified by their use of specific qualifiers. A proposition with specific qualifiers is one that is time- or space-bound by a specific word or phrase. An example would be: *Resolved, that the method of conducting presidential elections in the United States is detrimental to democracy.* The issues in this example will most likely be based on the content designated by the restriction on time or space: in this example issues will be drawn from knowledge of the laws regulating elections in the United States. Thus, after definitions have been considered, the substantive content of the restriction would determine the major issues in a proposition of inference with specific qualifiers.

Propositions of inference without specific qualifiers do not place limits on the location or the time of the subject matter. An example would be: *Resolved, that abortion is immoral.* The issues in this proposition might be drawn from a wide range of examples. It might be more appropriate, however, for such a topic to be developed in terms of relatively abstract or philosophical issues that transcend particular incidents.

Although discovering issues in propositions of inference is dependent upon the above considerations, the overriding issue to be resolved in any non-policy topic is always a question of definition. As indicated in the previous section, the issues dealing with definition are usually developed in the discussion of the criteria. In a proposition of inference, the criteria have a distinct function. Such criteria indicate when the conditions justify the evaluation, which is central to the affirmation of the proposition.

For example, in the previously discussed immigration topic, criteria should indicate how much unauthorized immigration would constitute a detrimental condition to the United States. The criteria would provide the basis for an answer to this question in one of two ways: First, the criteria might suggest a *linear relationship* between the condition and the evaluation. A linear relationship is one that asserts that any amount of the condition justifies, to some degree, the affirmative evaluation. For example, an affirmative debater might claim that any unauthorized immigration constitutes a detriment to some extent (for instance, social costs or moral consequences). Such an assertion would represent a claim of a linear relationship. Accordingly, these issues would be raised: "Would even one unauthorized immigrant be detrimental?" "Would every unauthorized immigrant be detrimental even if employed and paying taxes?"

A second kind of argument would be based on the assumption of a "threshold." A *threshold* is the point at which the condition justifies the evaluation. For example, an affirmative might argue that unauthorized immigrants have become so numerous, and perhaps of a certain nature (for instance, unskilled, unhealthy, dependent upon social services) that they now constitute an economic harm to the United States. When a threshold is argued, the issues raised would include such questions as these: "What is the exact threshold point?" "How do we know that that point has been reached?" "Has it been proven that the threshold has been reached or surpassed?" "How long has this condition existed?"

In summary, the important factors in discovery of the issues in propositions of inference are: (1) structure (simple or complex—trait or relational); (2) the kind of claim (absolute or general); (3) the use of specific qualifiers; and most importantly, (4) the function of the criteria in defining the condition/evaluation relationship.

Issues in Propositions of Value

Discovering issues in propositions of value is very different from finding issues in propositions of inference. The advocate debating a proposition of value faces different kinds of problems due to the different nature of the topics. Nevertheless the starting points are similar—the wording of the proposition and the function of the criteria.

The wording of a proposition of value exhibits a unique complexity, different from that encountered in propositions of inference. Value topics, by definition, feature two values (or valued things) in explicit comparison, and such statements are inherently complex. This complexity results in the introduction of these kinds of issues: "What are the relative advantages of each value?" "What are the relative disadvantages of each value or valued object?"

Relative strengths and weaknesses. Advocates might begin their analysis of propositions of value by considering contrasting strengths and weaknesses. An example of a proposition of value would be: *Resolved, that liberty is more precious than law.* In this example, liberty might be linked to creativity and law might be related to order as possible advantages. On the other hand, liberty might be linked to a risk of disorder and law might be linked to a risk of tyranny. By continuing this process debaters can discover not only the relative merits of each value, but they can also discover the similarities and the dissimilarities of the values.

Exceptions. The wording of most propositions of value also results in general statements rather than absolute claims. Seldom do words such as "all," "never," or "none" appear in value propositions. Thus, the general truth of the claim is usually the focus of the debate.

The existence of a single exception is not usually an issue in this kind of proposition. In the above example that compares liberty and law, the existence of a single exception would not necessarily deny the overall truth of the proposition. A single example, however, could deny the truth of a proposition if worded: *Resolved, that liberty is always more precious than law.* Issues raised concerning exceptions to a general proposition of value are: "How many exceptions are there to the principle?" "Are these exceptions sufficiently numerous or important enough that they cast doubt on the validity of the principle?" "Do the exceptions outweigh the cases in support of the claim?"

Time and place restrictions. Value propositions, like propositions of inference, may be either specific or rather general in terms of place or time restrictions. The following proposition, for example, is location specific: *Resolved, that commercial television is more detrimental than beneficial to American society.* The example is restricted, of course, to American society, and so the analysis must be focused there as well. As with propositions of inference, specific value topics will be debated using issues and evidence pertaining to the particular restrictions.

On the other hand, a proposition such as the liberty/law comparison is not specific to time or place. As indicated previously, such propositions might be more appropriately developed by relatively abstract or philosophical issues rather than by very specific time- and place-bound issues and examples.

The function of criteria. Finally, the function of the criteria in a proposition of value is unique. The criteria dealing with values must specify a method by which the strengths and weaknesses of the values can be mutually and simultaneously evaluated. Weighing contrasting elements, as we have already learned, might be an option in debating propositions of inference, but such a balancing measure is essential in debating value propositions. In the following proposition, a common measure would be necessary to resolve the dispute: *Resolved, that individual rights of privacy are more important than any other constitutional right.* A debater arguing this proposition might suggest that the more important right is the one that provides the greatest freedom for the individual or the one that protects other rights. The selection of such a measure, or criteria, provides the basis for balancing the relative advantages or disadvantages of the competing values.

In summary, the issues in propositions of value may be discovered by examining the following: (1) the relative strengths and weaknesses of the competing values; (2) the number and significance of any exceptions to the general principle; (3) the focus on any time or place restrictions; and finally, (4) the method of weighing the values.

Issues in Propositions of Policy Advocacy

There are two approaches to discovering issues in a policy advocacy debate. The first is the *stock issues approach,* which attempts to identify issues based on the kind of proposition being debated. In other words, the stock issues approach indicates that whenever a policy is being advocated similar questions are raised regardless of the subject matter. An advocate with knowledge of the stock issues on policy topics, for example, would be able to begin the analysis of any advocated course of action.

A second approach attempts to find issues by careful analysis and specific research of an individual subject area. For example, for each proposition debaters might examine possible definition of terms and investigate the subject matter thoroughly before attempting to phrase the issues. The debater using this approach would not attempt to impose any preconceived questions prior to the specific analysis and research.

The merits of each approach have been extensively and vigorously analyzed.[2] The stock issues approach may be criticized in several respects. First, stock issues analysis might be ineffective for certain topics or subjects. For example, a stock issues question for controversies involving policy advocacy is: "Is there a significant problem demanding immediate action?" Yet not all advocated policies are based on the need to solve significant problems. Changes in policy are sometimes motivated by a desire for more efficiency or better results.

Second, the use of stock issues might also bias decision-making towards particular paradigms or philosophies. For example, if stock issues require the discovery of a significant problem, there is an implicit principle established: change can only be justified by serious harmful conditions. That is one way, perhaps even the best way, to justify a change of policy, but there are other points of view.

The above criticisms do not suggest that the stock issues approach should not be used. Stock issues analysis can be an effective starting point for analysis of policy controversies, but advocates who use stock issues must not use them as tools to produce a final analysis. Stock issues should be tools of discovery; they provide a starting point but should not define or limit the thinking about policy changes. Certainly stock issues should be used simultaneously with careful study and thorough research of particular subjects. Finally, the advocate should never consider any analysis final or complete until he or she has considered all possible perspectives.

Specific Stock Issues

Policy changes, particularly those associated with government action to solve societal ills, have traditionally been associated with problem-solving analysis. In particular, John Dewey's "reflective thinking" process and pragmatic philosophy have guided much of the thinking about what constitutes legitimate reasons for changing public policy.

It should not be surprising, therefore, that the stock issues in an advocacy of policy embody much of Dewey's thinking. The logic of the sequence of stock issues parallels the natural sequence of events that the human organism follows when a "felt difficulty" is experienced. The questions that are raised when encountering such feelings are similar to those in the initial stages of policy analysis.

The first questions that should be asked are, therefore:

"What is the nature of the difficulty?"

"Can the situation properly be called a problem?"

"Does the situation pose a significant threat to material well-being, life, health, or values?"

"What is the extent of the condition?"

"Is there an extensive harm?"

"Is the situation serious enough to justify immediate action?"

These kinds of questions illustrate the first stock issue of policy advocacy analysis often referred to as *the significance or harm issue:* **Is there sufficient harm to justify an immediate change in existing policy?**

After answers are offered to the questions above, another set of questions should be asked:

"What are the causes of these conditions?"

"Which causes are most important?"

"What is the nature of these causes?"

"What is the nature of the present policy system?"

"Are there attempts being undertaken currently that have the potential to solve these problems?"

"What level of effectiveness, if any, does the present policy system have?"

"What is the relationship between the present policy system and the causes?"

"Do the causes reside inside or outside the policy system now in force?"

"Do the causes exist in the structure of the present policy system or in the attitudes of the administrators?"

"What other barriers to solutions exist?"

"What is the nature of these barriers?"

"What is the relationship between the barriers and the present policy system?"

"What specific flaws within the present system render it ineffective to alleviate the harmful conditions?"

Such questions seek to discover why the present policy system cannot solve the harmful conditions and whether the system is uniquely or "inherently" flawed. This issue is usually referred to as *the inherency issue.* Thus, the second issue in policy advocacy is: **Can the present system remedy the harmful conditions?**

A third group of considerations would follow these listed above and would focus on the method of solution:

"How might a new policy remove the causes and any barriers to solution?"

"If the causes and barriers cannot be removed, what strategy can be adopted to deal with the problems?"

"Can the symptoms of the problems be treated by a new policy?"

"Will the proposed changes alleviate each and every harmful condition?"

"If the solution is less than comprehensive in scope and less than complete in impact, how much of the problem will be remedied?"

"What available evidence indicates the proposed solution will work?"

"Has the proposed solution been tested previously in an analogous situation?"

"If not, how can the efficacy of the solution be demonstrated?"

These questions suggest a third stock issue, often referred to as *solvency:* **Can a new policy solve the harmful conditions?**

An example illustrates how stock issues might be applied to a specific proposition to generate specific questions for beginning analysis:

Possible Proposition: Resolved, that the university should significantly strengthen the regulation of fraternities and sororities.

First Stock Issue—Significance: Is there sufficient harm to justify an immediate change in existing university policies? Is hazing an extensive and serious problem? Have there been substantial violations of campus alcohol policies by fraternities and sororities? Have fraternal organizations been responsible for significant vandalism or damage to university property? Have other important regulations been violated? Do the problems created by fraternities and sororities require immediate action?

Second Stock Issue—Inherency: Can present university regulations solve any possible harmful conditions? Is there evidence to link the fraternities and sororities to the specific incidents—hazing, alcohol policy violations, property damage, and so on? What are the current university policies to deal with these situations? Are the policies clearly established? Are the policies understood? Are the policies consistently and effectively enforced? Are penalties sufficient to deter violations? What other specific flaws exist in the policies? Are there other barriers to solving these problems?

Third Stock Issue—Solvency: Can a code of conduct or new regulations deal effectively with these problems? Can a new code be established, understood, consistently and effectively enforced? Will any new penalties be sufficient to deter violations? Will the proposed remedy deter all of each of the harmful conditions? If not, how much of the problem can be solved? Can fraternities and sororities be made legally and financially responsible for any problems that are not prevented by the new code? Have any other universities used similar codes or regulations? Were they effective? What other data are available to demonstrate the effectiveness of a new code of conduct?

The three stock issues above will guide the analysis of most propositions of policy advocacy. In a sense it can be said that such propositions require that these three stock issues be discussed. When a debater arguing on the affirmative side of the proposition has satisfactorily answered the questions posed above, then the proposition has been justified. The requirement that a proposition be justified in the first affirmative speech of a debate is called a *"prima facie"* burden. In other words, an affirmative speaker must answer these questions in the first affirmative speech or the affirmative case is not *prima facie.*

In most policy advocacy debates, the debaters opposed to the proposed changes will discuss the adverse consequences of the new policy. These adverse consequences are usually compared with any benefits of the new policy. Thus most advocacy debates will feature a fourth group of vital questions, which can be considered as an additional stock issue. The fourth stock issue poses this overall question: **Do the advantages of the new policy outweigh its disadvantages?**

This stock issue is often referred to as the costs–benefits issue because all of the costs of the proposed policy are balanced against all of its benefits. In the example of the fraternity regulations controversy cited above, costs–benefits analysis might raise these kinds of specific questions:

> **Fourth Stock Issue—Cost–benefits:** What are the additional advantages of a new code or set of regulations? Would any university funds be saved by reducing damage to university property? Would relations with the community be improved? Would adherence to other university regulations be enhanced? What are the disadvantages of the new code? Would student–administration rapport be diminished? Would security costs increase? Would adherence to other regulations be diminished?

In summary, the stock issues of a policy advocacy debate are:

1. Is there sufficient harm to justify an immediate change in existing policy?
2. Can the present policy system remedy the harmful conditions?
3. Can a new policy solve the harmful conditions?
4. Do the advantages of the new policy outweigh its disadvantages?

As suggested previously, these stock issues are only starting points for analysis. Stock issues can generate a beginning case outline for the affirmative and negative advocates. Debaters should also consider the specific wording of the proposition, the findings of their research into the subject matter, and alternative perspectives (such as systems analysis), in developing issues and specific arguments.

Systems Analysis

Another method to guide the initial analysis of policy change propositions is the application of *systems theory.* Systems theory is more a perspective or general method of analysis than a specific theoretical framework. Although there are several possible applications of systems analysis to policy advocacy debate, this text will present one brief version.

To understand systems thinking, a definition of a system is necessary. *A system may be defined as a set of objects that interrelate with one another as a unique whole.* For example, a university may be viewed as a system. A university is made up of several integral components, which may be considered subsystems—colleges, academic departments, a student health service, a security department, fraternities, and many more. Furthermore, a system may be contained in as well as containing other systems. A state university, for example, may be part of a state university system, which in turn is a part of the overall state institutional government. Thus, systems must be understood as usually interdependent with other systems.

From a simple perspective, systems analysis as a tool for discovering issues in policy controversies may be explained by five ideas: system descriptions, goals analysis, component and relationship functions, evaluation, and finally, alteration.

First, *system description* actually includes several distinct tasks. Systems selection can be crucial in the process of discovering issues. For example, the student analyzing the fraternity regulation controversy might have to consider several different systems—fraternities, security department, the university administration, the university community, and perhaps state government. Although deciding which system to study is a choice that will vary with each topic, it is usually desirable to begin the analysis with the largest relevant system. In the previous example, state government might be an appropriate focal point if state government expenditures or time commitment had been seriously affected by fraternity activity. If not, then the university community might be a proper choice for focus.

Another aspect of system description might include system classification. Systems may be classified as either open or closed. *An open system is defined as one that is highly integrated with its environment and contains many channels of communication.* On the other hand, a closed system is not well integrated with its environment and possible communication channels are limited. Closed systems often attempt to maintain their systems by internal means, but they do so at the risk of atrophy and dissolution. For example, a university administration might be classified as closed if student conduct codes were formulated without significant student input. Finally, system description would include a careful examination of how the system is linked with other systems as discussed above.

Second, *goals analysis* may be the most important concept in the application of a systems perspective. A system can perhaps best be understood in terms of its goals—the ultimate objectives it strives to maintain. Systems may have multiple goals, in which case a *hierarchy of goals* is necessary for analysis. Goals also may change over time; a system may have been created for one purpose, only to have new goals evolve as the system operates. Furthermore, goals within a system or among different systems may be discovered to conflict or even to be mutually exclusive.

The purpose of goals analysis is to find these goals, hierarchies, alterations, and possible conflicts. For example, the goals of a fraternity, on its operations level, may shift as a new group of members with different attitudes and priorities takes over. Public service projects might be neglected and the number of social events might be increased. Goals analysis can frequently reveal such shifts and may thereby allow the advocate to discover important issues.

Third, the *components and their relationships* within the system also should be analyzed. The components are the objects within a system and, as indicated above, may include still other systems. The primary steps in such an examination are to identify the components, their functions, and finally their relationship within and to the system. The functions of a component may be closely related to its goals, and the functions may thus be assessed by the application of the goals. Several questions might be raised in this stage, such as: Are the components functioning effectively? Do the relationships within the system help or hinder the functions? If the components include other systems, are the subsystems in harmony with the larger system?

The relationships within the system may deserve special attention. They may be classified as "simple" or "complex." A simple relationship will feature a single task or may even be a one-way relationship. A complex relationship will include many tasks and will involve two-way relationships. Although a single task that involves a one-way relationship might be vital, this is a somewhat rare situation. Usually, the more vital the task, the more complex will be the relationship of the component (which performs the task) with others within the system.

In the fraternity regulation controversy, the components might include any or all of the following: the code of student conduct, relevant university administrators, the campus security department, local police, specific local residents, and fraternities and sororities. Importantly, the facts of the case—the conditions under which the controversy takes place—might determine whether the relationships between components are simple or complex. For example, if a resident of the community complains about a fraternity disturbance that occurs off campus, the relationships with university administrative and campus security components might be relatively simple. There might be reports made by the police to the university (one-way) but little else might occur between the police and university components. On the other hand, if the same incident happened on campus, and local police were requested, then the complexity of the relationship between the same components would be much greater. As you can see, the complexity of relationships among components will vary with differing conditions.

Fourth, *evaluation of a system* should begin with examination of its goals. A system's goals might be criticized based on their merit (their worth) or based on their function (compatability).

If the goals of a system are defensible, then evaluation should focus primarily on the results or the *outcomes* of the system. The outcomes of a system are *the effects produced by the efforts of the system to achieve its goals.* The outcomes may be evaluated on the basis of their impact upon the goals. Questions aimed at determining the system's effects would include: Does the system achieve its goals? Do all of the system's outcomes contribute toward the goals? Are any of the outcomes extraneous or even counterproductive?

In the fraternity regulation topic, such questions might be asked regarding various components or subsystems: Are all of the fraternities' and sororities' activities necessary to meet their goals? Are any of the activities actually counterproductive to meeting those goals? Are all of the enforcement procedures used by campus security necessary to reach their respective goals? Are any of their efforts counterproductive to those ends?

The answers to evaluation questions such as those above will lead to the fifth and final concept of systems analysis of policy advocacy controversies: alteration. *Alteration* of a system should begin with selecting the components that might be manipulated effectively. For example, in the case cited above, the university might choose to revise its code of student conduct.

Systems analysis also recognizes that when one component is altered, then other components will also be affected. The nature of the relationship among the components affected will in part determine the nature of the effects. If fraternities, for example, are attentive to changes in the code of student conduct, they may, with appropriate incentives, alter their behavior. On the other hand, if they do not know or believe that the code affects them in significant ways, then there will probably be no change.

Finally, a genuine systems approach would include provisions in the proposed policy for *monitoring, feedback, adaptation, and fine tuning*. The systems perspective espouses the principle that change, to be successful, must necessarily be complex and dynamic. From this point of view, proposals that are simple and that represent isolated actions will fail.

As indicated above, systems analysis focuses upon policy proposals in a particular way, and may be employed before or after or in place of imposing the traditional stock issues questions. Systems analysis may be either a supplement or an alternative to traditional analysis.

When might the systems perspective be used most productively? First, systems analysis might be employed when there is no clear and compelling need for immediate action. In such situations, change might still be desirable for reasons of greater flexibility or efficiency.

Second, certain kinds of affirmative cases may be more easily constructed within a systems perspective. For example, for a topic in which public policy goals are important, debaters may wish to use a goals-criteria case, discussed later in the text. Given the importance of goals analysis in the systems approach, debaters might be wise to use it in such situations.

It is also clear that systems analysis has great utility in the comparison of policy alternatives. Thus, any advocate who might wish to compare the advantages of policy systems might also use the systems approach productively. Some writers have suggested that systems analysis is especially appropriate for comparative advantage cases.[3]

Finally, systems analysis are an option whenever stock issues seem inappropriate or unclear. However, it should be emphasized once again that neither approach should be attempted without careful analysis of the wording of the proposition and substantial investigation of the topic area. Without these steps, both methods of discovering issues will likely fail, or at best will produce shallow analysis.

Issues in Propositions of Policy Evaluation

Propositions of policy evaluation share some of the characteristics of both non-policy and traditional policy propositions. The central feature common to both policy evaluation and non-policy propositions is the concept of evaluation. Both types of propositions feature a key evaluative term which must be defined. Policy evaluation and policy advocacy are also similar in that they may be developed surrounding similar issues. These similarities are the starting points for discovering issues in propositions of policy evaluation.

The first, and frequently the most important, issue in policy evaluation is the definition of the key evaluative term or phrase. In the following example, "justified" is the key term: *Resolved, that the United States is justified in providing military support to non-democratic governments.* In policy evaluation topics, the key terms are usually such words as "justified," "desirable," "effective," and so on. The affirmative will usually employ criteria to define the evaluative terms. The selection of the criteria should be a major issue; this selection will determine the remaining issues in the debate.

The criteria in policy evaluation controversies will usually consist of those that are selected from traditional stock issues. For example, advocates debating the military support topic above might choose to define *justified* within the context of cost–benefit analysis: If the advantages of the policy concept (military support to non-democratic governments) outweigh its disadvantages, then the policy concept is justified.

As discussed above, the choice of such criteria itself should be a major issue. If the affirmative chooses cost–benefit analysis as the criteria in this example, then the negative might argue that the criteria should also include the significance and solvency issues. The negative might reason that if there is no need for the policy (significance) then the policy will not be justified. Thus, the central issue in this example would be: What does it mean for a policy to be justified?

A statement of criteria might also include the inherency issue, if the policy is not yet in force. For example, the negative could argue that existing arms negotiations will be sufficient to reduce the risks of nuclear war or gain whatever advantages the affirmative might have claimed. Inherency, however, will not be an issue in most policy evaluation disputes because these controversies usually occur within a context in which the policy is already in force.

Propositions of policy evaluation can also be debated in terms of criteria drawn from a systems analysis perspective. In such a case, the issues associated with systems analysis, as discussed previously, would be relevant.

In summary, the primary issues raised in a policy evaluation debate would be: (1) the criteria chosen to define the key evaluative term and (2) the other issues determined by the selection of the criteria. In most policy evaluation debates, these other issues will be selected from the traditional policy issues: significance, solvency, and cost–benefits.

Special Issues in Educational Debate

In educational debate there are several special issues. These issues are *regulatory* in function; in other words, they are devised to ensure that the competitors adhere to the rules of intercollegiate debate. One of the most important of these rules is that the affirmative team should limit their arguments to those that are relevant to the topic selected for the debate. This section will examine two more specific aspects of this important issue: non-topicality and extratopicality.

Non-Topicality

When the negative team in an educational debate raises the issue of non-topicality, they are arguing that the affirmative is not defending the assigned proposition or topic. The issue of non-topicality is a very important one in an intercollegiate debate. Unless the affirmative is defending the assigned proposition, then the truth of their assertions, the quality of their evidence, the importance of the subject matter they raise, and their skill in debating are all irrelevant. If a negative team successfully argues non-topicality then they need not win or even raise other issues in order to win the debate.

In most debates, the issue of non-topicality focuses upon questions of definition. Has the affirmative properly defined the important terms of the proposition? Have they defined the terms by direct definitions, or through a presentation of the affirmative case and plan, or through both? In a non-policy debate, or in a policy evaluation debate, the affirmative will present definitions and/or criteria to define the terms explicitly. In a policy advocacy debate, the affirmative plan sometimes functions as an example which defines the proposition operationally. In all kinds of debate, explicit and operational definitions are supplemented by other arguments that define the meaning of the terms in the context of the particular subject matter.

In many debates the issue of topicality raises the question of whether the affirmative definitions are reasonable ones. Affirmative teams will usually claim that they have a presumptive right to define terms and thereby determine the issues of the debate as long as those definitions are reasonable. On the other hand, negative debaters may argue that "reasonable" is a rather vague term and therefore a poor standard for determining topicality. Further, the negative may claim that the affirmative is obligated to use the "best" definition available in order to assure any reasonability.

Non-topicality is an issue that can be argued in both policy and non-policy debates. However, some theorists believe that the reasonability standard should apply to policy debate, whereas the "best" definition standard should apply to non-policy propositions. Walter Ulrich provides a rationale for such a distinction. Ulrich argues that non-policy propositions are mainly concerned with "meaning" and thus the best definition standard is appropriate. He writes:

> The best definition is also consistent with the purpose of the resolution. If we were asked to support the resolution, we need to ask ourselves what the resolution means, either as a statement to ourselves as to the nature of our beliefs, or as a statement to others as to the probable state of affairs in the world. In either case, precision would be desirable. When philosophers debate over what is the nature of 'good' or 'justice' or other terms, they do not accept the first 'reasonable' definition; they seek to discover the best possible definition. [4]

Both the meanings of the particular terms in any given proposition and the standards that should be used to resolve non-topicality issues are debatable. There are no universal standards that will be accepted by every debate judge. Topicality questions should be treated like any other issue and should be determined by the particular arguments in each debate.

Extratopicality

Extratopicality is an issue usually raised in an educational debate on a proposition of policy advocacy. When a negative team argues extratopicality, they are claiming that some central element in the affirmative analysis is outside (extra) the scope of the proposition. Usually the negative will claim that parts of the affirmative's proposed policy are extratopical. Sometimes a negative team will identify the advantages of the recommended change as extratopical if they are the result of a part of the plan that is not within the proposition's scope.

The primary issue in extratopicality concerns what the affirmative is allowed to propose and still remain within the scope of the proposition. Although most policy propositions do not specify financing or enforcement measures in the proposed policy statement, affirmative teams are allowed to include these items in their proposed changes. However, affirmative teams will be vulnerable to a charge of extratopicality if they claim advantages that are unique to the financing or enforcement provisions. The general principle is that the affirmative should not be allowed to claim advantages that are not directly tied to a policy concept specified by the proposition. Usually the affirmative will be permitted to use measures such as enforcement and funding that are *enabling measures* (practical devices that allow the plan to operate). However, the affirmative generally will not be allowed to claim independent advantages that result from those measures alone.

When an affirmative team loses an extratopicality argument, they do not necessarily lose the debate. The effect of a successful extratopicality argument is to remove the affected parts of the affirmative plan along with any related advantages from the debate. In other words, the judge, if convinced that a feature of the plan and a related advantage are extratopical, will exclude those items from consideration. There may still be sufficient topical arguments left after the exclusion to justify the proposition.

Although there are other kinds of topicality arguments in educational debate, most of those special arguments are either variations of non-topicality and extratopicality or they are developed in similar ways. This discussion of the two major topicality issues should provide starting points for the student interested in intercollegiate debate.

Summary

Issues are the vital questions contained within propositions selected for debate. The nature, kinds, and number of issues in a given topic are dependent upon the kind of proposition, its wording, and the subject matter of the topic.

All non-policy propositions have several elements in common. Such topics always feature a key evaluative term that must be defined. This key evaluative term raises three issues relevant to every non-policy proposition. First, what is the key term? Second, how should the term be defined? Third, do conditions exist such that the evaluation can be confirmed? Finally, the most useful method of defining the key evaluative term is through a set of criteria which specifies how the conditions should be measured.

Propositions of inference may be subdivided as: (1) simple or complex—trait or relational, (2) absolute or general, and (3) with or without specific qualifiers. The nature of the issues that might be discovered in a proposition of inference are dependent upon these classifications. Propositions of inference will often deal with criteria that seek to establish either a linear relationship or a threshold to indicate when conditions exist so as to justify the evaluation of the key term.

Propositions of value are necessarily complex because they are comparisons of values. The wording of most propositions of value usually results in general rather than absolute claims. Value propositions, however, may or may not feature specific time or place qualifiers. The function of criteria in a proposition of value is unique; it must specify a method by which the strengths and weaknesses of the values might be mutually and simultaneously evaluated.

Traditional policy propositions may be analyzed initially through the use of stock issues. Although stock issues should be accompanied by careful attention to the wording of the topic and substantial research, they do provide useful questions for many policy topics. The traditional stock issues are: (1) significance, (2) inherency, (3) solvency, and (4) cost–benefits.

An alternative or additional perspective on policy topics might be provided by an application of systems analysis. Systems analysis might be attempted by applying five concepts to a given policy controversy: (1) system description, (2) goals analysis, (3) component and relationship analysis, (4) evaluation, and (5) alteration. Systems analysis may be productively employed when there is no clear compelling need, or when special case formats (comparative advantages or goals-criteria) seem desirable, or when stock issues are not helpful.

Policy evaluation propositions share the characteristics of both non-policy topics and traditional policy questions. Although policy evaluation topics will include a key evaluative term, they also will usually be debated in terms of some of the issues of policy debate. Thus, the issues in a policy evaluation debate are: (1) issues surrounding the definition of the key evaluative term and (2) one or more of these policy issues—significance, solvency, and cost-benefits.

The special issues of non-topicality and extratopicality are concerns to the student interested in competitive intercollegiate debate. In such educational debates, non-topicality might be argued by the negative team if the affirmative case and plan (policy) or definitions and case (non-policy and policy evaluation) are not legitimate interpretations of the proposition being debated. Extratopicality is an argument usually associated with policy advocacy topics and is raised when either the affirmative plan or advantages are outside the scope of the proposition. Topicality arguments should be debated like any other arguments and should be resolved based on the arguments in a given debate.

Notes

1. See Glen E. Mills, *Reason in Controversy* (Boston: Allyn and Bacon, 1966), pp. 62–65, and Ronald J. Matlon, "Debating Propositions of Value," *Journal of the American Forensic Association,* 14 (Spring 1978): 194–204.
2. See Robert P. Newman, "Analysis and Issues—A Study of Doctrine," *Central States Speech Journal,* 13(1961): 43–54, and Raymond Nadeau, "In Defense of Deliberative Stock Issues," *Central States Speech Journal,* 13 (1962): 142.
3. Bernard Brock, et al., *Public Policy Decision Making: Systems Analysis and Comparative Advantages Debate* (New York: Harper and Row, 1973).
4. Walter Ulrich, "The Nature of the Topic in Value Debate," *CEDA Yearbook,* (Don Brownlee, California State University, Northridge: Cross Examination Debate Association, 1984), p. 2.

Questions and Exercises

1. Select a newspaper or magazine editorial on a controversial subject and answer the following questions:
   a. What was the proposition being debated? Carefully word a proposition based on your understanding of the content of the editorial.
   b. What were the major questions from the perspective of the author?
   c. Are these questions "issues" as defined in this chapter?
   d. Are there any issues that were not discussed in this editorial or article?
   e. If there are issues that were not discussed, why were they omitted? Limited focus? Poor analysis? Poor understanding of the subject matter? Other reasons?
2. Read one of the intercollegiate debates in the appendices of the text and answer the following:
   a. What kind of proposition was being debated?
   b. Did the classification of the proposition determine the issues that were being raised?
   c. Were the major questions that were raised *issues?*
   d. Were there any issues that were not raised?
   e. Why were issues omitted?
3. Select a current campus or community controversy and do the following:
   a. Phrase propositions of inference, value, policy advocacy and policy evaluation from what you know and have read about the controversy.
   b. With each proposition, develop specific issues that should be raised in debates with these propositions.

Suggested Readings

Flaningam, Carl. "Value-Centered Argument and the Development of Decision Rules." *Journal of the American Forensic Association.* XIX (Fall 1982), 107–115.

Matlon, Ronald. "Propositions of Value: An Inquiry Into Issue Analysis and the Locus of Presumption." *Dimensions of Argument: Proceedings of the Second Summer Conference on Argumentation,* edited by George Ziegemueller and Jack Rhodes. Annandale, VA: Speech Communication Association, 1981, pp. 494–512.

Warnick, Barbara. "Arguing Value Propositions." *Journal of the American Forensic Association,* XVIII (Fall 1981), 109–119.

Brownlee, Don. "In Search of Topicality: Definitions and Contexts." *CEDA Yearbook, 1981.* California State University, Northridge: Don Brownlee, 1981, pp. 32–34.

FIVE

The Nature of Reasoning

As Chapter Two stresses, values play a central role in argument. Our discussion of the universal audience underscores this important role; undeniably, persuasive claims are based in large part on the values common to most audiences. Despite the importance of value appeals to successful argument, however, more is usually required.

A string of value appeals without coherence or purpose would perhaps be pleasing to hear, but would probably be unpersuasive. *There must be an ordering of the appeals, a selection of the appeals, and a direction for the argument.*

To achieve this order and direction, a study of reasoning is essential for the successful arguer. How do our thought processes lead us to certain claims? It is one thing to possess skill in *presenting* argument; it is another and perhaps more essential skill to be able to "invent" argument, or to "discover" argument. One accomplishes the latter through reasoning. In this chapter we will discuss (1) the nature of inductive reasoning and its function in argument, (2) the use of example and analogy, (3) the concept of contrast and dissociation, (4) the nature of deductive reasoning, and (5) the nature of fallacies.

Inductive Reasoning

Induction is a cognitive process of *moving from specific observations or instances to a generalization.* Suppose that Professor Gonzales walked into his physics class at the regularly scheduled time and found puddles of water on the floor. Suppose further that he noticed that the ceiling was water-stained and was dripping. Also noting that it was not raining outside and had not rained for several days, Professor Gonzales concludes that the air conditioning must be leaking. Professor Gonzales has engaged in inductive reasoning. He has observed several conditions (puddles on the floor, ceiling water-stained, water dripping from the ceiling, and the absence of rain), and from them has drawn a conclusion. He has moved from specific observations to a generalization.

Perfect and Imperfect Induction

Inductive reasoning elevates experience or observation to paramount importance in gaining understanding. Induction is invaluable, for that reason, to scientific discovery. A scientist will observe nature and from these observations will attempt a generalization to explain them. The generalization recognizes in the various observations a coherent or sensible pattern.

In science, these generalizations are sometimes called *theories*. Most inductive reasoning involves a limited number of observations, and because of this may lead to faulty or incorrect generalizations. Unless one can observe all possible instances or examples, induction deals in probabilities, not certainty.

Perfect induction occurs when all possible instances are observed. For instance, if one were to discover that all professional golfers earn in excess of $200,000 per year, then a perfectly safe conclusion would be that professional golf is a lucrative profession.

Chapter Outline

Imperfect induction, of course, is when all instances cannot be observed or considered before generalizing. Imperfect induction is possible at virtually any time. Perfect induction, on the other hand, is rarely possible or practical.

Suppose Senator Jones maintains that since military assistance to Brazil, Mozambique, Argentina, and Mexico has been a failure, military aid is generally a failure. Senator Jones has engaged in imperfect induction—he has not considered all countries that receive U.S. military aid. Just because the induction is imperfect does not invalidate the conclusion, however; nor does it mean that the generalization is not persuasive. It simply means that it is not certain.

If an induction is not certain, the probability of the generalization should be as strong as possible, and there are several ways to ensure this strength. The first method of ensuring the strength of induction is to base the generalization on *typical examples.* The number of examples is relatively unimportant so long as the examples cited constitute a fair representation of the whole of which they are a part. Upon examining the example above, one notices that only four countries were cited: Brazil, Argentina, Mexico, and Mozambique. In order to determine the strength of the induction we should ask the following questions: "Are these countries typical of all countries that receive our aid?" "Are they typical by region?" "Are they typical by size or population?" "Are they typical in the amount of aid received?"

A cursory review of the examples cited would probably lead one to make a negative assessment on all of the above questions. Three of the four examples are from Central or South America, and none are from Europe or Asia. They might be somewhat typical in size or population, but certainly not in the amount of aid received. Therefore, the conclusion is not reliable.

A second way to ensure the strength of an induction is to be certain that the examples cited are *consistent with other possible examples.* The question of consistency is related to but not the same as the question of typicality. Typicality deals with the representativeness of the examples; consistency deals with the absence of major exceptions.

For example, we might observe that World War I began under a Democratic administration, and that World War II and the Korean War also began under a Democratic administration, and we could conclude that Democratic administrations are more likely to lead the nation into war than are Republican administrations. Even if the examples cited were typical of all U.S. wars, our conclusion could still be criticized for not being consistent. Our opponents could reject the conclusion based on *major exceptions.* The Civil War is a major exception: it began under a Republican administration. The Spanish-American War also began under a Republican administration, as did the Vietnam War. Thus, it is possible for the observations to be typical, and yet not be able to withstand the recognition of major exceptions.

On November 20, 1969, then-Vice President Spiro Agnew spoke in Montgomery, Alabama in criticism of the press. He argued:

> A single company in the nation's capital holds the control of the largest newspaper in Washington D.C., and one of four major television stations, and an all-news radio station, and one of three major national news magazines—all grinding out the same editorial line—and this is not a subject that you've seen debated on the editorial pages of the Washington Post or the New York Times.
>
> For the purpose of clarity, before my thoughts are obliterated on the smoking typewriters of my friends in Washington and New York, let me emphasize that I am not recommending the dismemberment of the Washington Post Company. I'm merely pointing out that the public should be aware that these four powerful voices hearken to the same master.
>
> I'm raising these questions so that the American people will become aware of—and think of the implications of—the growing monopoly that involves the voices of public opinion, on which we all depend for our knowledge and for the basis of our views.[1]

Agnew claims that major newspapers enjoy excessive power over public opinion and cites the *Washington Post* and indirectly refers to the *New York Times* as the basis for those claims. Speech critic Karlyn Kohrs Campbell complains of faulty reasoning stemming from inconsistent examples in the Agnew speech. She writes:

> At Montgomery, Agnew singled out the *Washington Post* for attack, a newspaper that exists in one of the three remaining large cities with more than one major newspaper under separate ownership. He attacked the *Washington Post* ownership of WTOP–TV and radio but neglected to mention that there are four major television stations, three UHF stations, and 35 radio outlets in Washington D.C. He also failed to mention the obvious examples of news media concentration surrounding him as he spoke. The *Montgomery Advertiser* and the *Alabama Journal* are both owned by Multi-media, Inc. In Alabama, the Newhouse newspaper chain owns both dailies in Huntsville and Mobile, WAPI–TV, AM and FM radio stations in Birmingham, and CATV in Anniston. Newhouse and another giant chain, Scripps–Howard, share ownership of the daily papers in Birmingham. In nearby areas Newhouse owns the dailies in New Orleans and Pascagoula, Mississippi, and Scripps–Howard owns the newspapers and WMC–TV in Memphis. Agnew also neglected to mention a major media conglomerate generally well disposed to the President's Vietnam policy.[2]

Campbell recognized faulty induction in the Agnew speech. There were major exceptions to the examples Agnew cited, and the recognition of those exceptions weakens the persuasive force of the argument.

Connecting and Disconnecting Observations

Reasoning through connecting and disconnecting, or through comparison and contrast, is a common tactic, and is at times effective and compelling.

These forms of inductive reasoning are used when two observations, examples, or conditions are involved in the reasoning process.

Comparison or the use of analogy indicates an *indirect* resemblance of one observed object to another object not observed. Such an observation moves from the known to the unknown, from the certain to the uncertain, from an actual observation to a predicted similarity in an unobserved object.

Two examples from a speech by Ronald Reagan illustrate reasoning through analogy. In a speech delivered in January of 1984, Mr. Reagan said:

> We can't predict how the Soviet leaders will respond to our challenge. But the people of our two countries share with all mankind the dream of eliminating the risk of nuclear war. It is not an impossible dream, because eliminating these risks is so clearly a vital interest for all of us.
>
> Our two countries have never fought each other. There's no reason why we ever should. Indeed we fought common enemies in World War II. Today our common enemies are poverty, disease, and above all, war.[3]

Reagan began with actual observations: (1) the Soviet Union and the United States have never been at war; (2) we have fought against common enemies. He then moved to predicted similarities in unobserved future conditions: (1) there is no reason why we ever should fight a war against each other, and (2) there is every reason why we should again fight against common enemies. Reagan is clearly comparing the conditions which were favorable to peace between the Soviet Union and the United States during World War II with conditions in the immediate future. The conclusion is, of course, that peace with the Soviet Union in the future is a reasonable prediction.

In the same speech Reagan again utilizes analogy. He says:

> Just suppose with me for a moment that an Ivan and an Anya could find themselves, oh, say, in a waiting room or sharing a shelter from the rain or a storm with a Jim and Sally. And there was no language barrier to keep them from getting acquainted.
>
> Would they debate the differences between their respective governments? Or would they find themselves comparing notes about their children and what each other did for a living? Before they parted company they would probably have touched on ambitions and hobbies, and what they wanted for the children and problems of making ends meet.
>
> And as they went their separate ways, maybe Anya would be saying to Ivan: "Wasn't she nice? She also teaches music." And Jim would be telling Sally what Ivan did or didn't like about his boss. They might even have decided they were going to get together for dinner some evening soon.
>
> Above all they would have proven that people don't make wars. People want to raise their children in a world without fear and without war. They want to have some of the good things over and above bare subsistence that make life worth living. They want to work at some craft, trade, or profession that gives them satisfaction and a sense of worth. Their common interests cross all borders.[4]

In this analogy Reagan utilizes an observation, an assumed trait of human behavior that the audience will likely accept, and compares those traits to the dynamics of international politics. The analogies above illustrate how the use of comparison can serve as an effective reasoning tool.

Contrast and dissociation deals with observation and prediction, as did comparisons and analogies. There is a fundamental distinction, however. Analogy observes conditions in something familiar and links them to similar conditions in something unfamiliar. Contrast and dissociation moves from the observation of the disparate conditions of two objects to a prediction of the reasons underlying the difference. In other words, dissociation is the attempt to reconcile two inconsistent observations.

Suppose you are watching a magician perform. As his assistant lies in a box, the magician appears to saw the poor victim in half. You also observe, to your amazement, that the "victim" seems to be unaffected by the apparent dismemberment. The observations are absolutely incompatible. The observations (that the assistant has been sawed in half, and that the assistant is not injured) cannot *both* be true. The assistant has either been fatally injured by the ordeal, or in truth was never sawed in half. By separating or dissociating the two observations and reconsidering them individually within the context of their occurrence, the inconsistency might be reconciled.

Let us look at the first observation, that the assistant has been sawed in half. By reviewing the context of the performance several conclusions should be forthcoming, including (a) a magician is not likely to purposely injure his assistant, and (b) considering society's severe restrictions against murder, a performer is not likely to saw someone in half in full view of a large audience. It is not likely that the magician actually did what he appeared to do.

If we now look at the second observation—that the assistant was not hurt—within the same context, we will probably conclude that this observation is the more likely of the two. Given the context in which both observations occurred, and considering that (a) the magician needs an assistant for other shows, and (b) the nature of a magician's performance is to create illusion, the second observation is more reliable.

Inductive reasoning, if followed carefully, can be a reliable and effective method of "inventing" argument. Whether perfect or imperfect, induction can be compelling. By connecting or disconnecting observations, induction can assist us in making sense of our experiences and thus can be a useful persuasive tool.

Deductive Reasoning

Controversies involving public issues necessitate a demonstration of *probability.* The various forms of inductive reasoning that we discussed above may be used to establish such probabilities, as may other forms of reasoning. Deductive reasoning or deductive logic, if used correctly, can be a powerful tool for establishing the probabilities that underlie most controversies. We will focus on deductive reasoning in this section.

Deductive reasoning moves from a general assumption to a specific conclusion. The general assumption, known as the *major premise,* leads to the conclusion through a *minor premise,* usually an observation. These components make up the tool of deductive reasoning called the *syllogism.*

The syllogistic process begins with the major premise or general assumption. There are two sources for the major premise: (1) the product of inductive reasoning, and (2) first principles.

Often the major premise is provided through inductive reasoning. In fact, this is the source of most deductions that we make daily, perhaps unaware that we are engaged in the reasoning process. Consider the following observations:

1. Pete Rose is a professional baseball player and is wealthy.
2. Nolan Ryan is a professional baseball player and is wealthy.
3. Phil Garner is a professional baseball player and is wealthy.
4. Steve Carlton is a professional baseball player and is wealthy.
5. Steve Garvey is a professional baseball player and is wealthy.
6. Jose Cruz is a professional baseball player and is wealthy.
7. Dale Murphy is a professional baseball player and is wealthy.
8. Tim Wallach is a professional baseball player and is wealthy.
9. Ricky Henderson is a professional baseball player and is wealthy.
10. Dave Winfield is a professional baseball player and is wealthy.

Based upon these observations, a logical conclusion would be that professional baseball players are wealthy. This conclusion, of course, is a result of inductive reasoning—moving from specific instances to a generalization. This generalization might then serve as a major premise in deductive reasoning. If our inductive reasoning leads us to conclude that professional baseball players are wealthy, and sometime in the future we hear of someone who is a professional baseball player, say John Doe, then we might conclude that he is also wealthy. An illustration of that reasoning would look like this:

MAJOR PREMISE: Professional baseball players are wealthy.
MINOR PREMISE: John Doe is a professional baseball player.
CONCLUSION: John Doe is wealthy.

In the above examples, induction has provided the major premise for the deductive scheme.

Another source for the major premise is *first principles,* or deeply held beliefs which are widely accepted. For instance, the belief that "all people are created equal," is a first principle. Other examples would include: "all humans are mortal," and "money is the root of all evil." A deduction based upon a first principle as the major premise would look like this:

MAJOR PREMISE: No class of people is better than any other class of people. (Based on the first principle that all people are created equal.)

MINOR PREMISE: Europeans and Asians are classes of people.

CONCLUSION: Neither Europeans nor Asians are better than the other.

Whether the major premise is formed from induction or from first principles, the major premise, the minor premise, and the conclusion form a syllogism. We will now discuss the three major types of syllogisms, which are (1) categorical, (2) disjunctive, and (3) hypothetical.

Categorical Syllogisms

The categorical syllogism is the most widely recognized syllogism, and is perhaps the easiest to understand. It is easy to recognize because its name accurately describes the major premise: the major premise of the categorical syllogism contains a categorical or universal term. Such a term is said to be *distributed.* Examples of universal terms would be "all," "every," "each," and "none." Consider the following syllogisms:

MAJOR PREMISE: *All politicians* are corrupt.

MINOR PREMISE: Senator Bribe is a politician.

CONCLUSION: Senator Bribe is corrupt.

MAJOR PREMISE: *Every freshman* is required to live on campus.

MINOR PREMISE: Sylvia is a freshman.

CONCLUSION: Sylvia is required to live on campus.

MAJOR PREMISE: *Each hourly employee* was paid a Christmas bonus.

MINOR PREMISE: Jose is an hourly employee.

CONCLUSION: Jose was paid a Christmas bonus.

MAJOR PREMISE: *No* untenured faculty member may hold a second job.

MINOR PREMISE: Professor Bramble is an untenured faculty member.

CONCLUSION: Professor Bramble may not hold a second job.

Notice that in each example above, the major premise contains a categorical or universal term. The categorical term indicates "belonging" or "inclusiveness." The diagram below indicates the relationship between the statements. If the middle term encompasses the minor term (1 within 2), and the major term encompasses the middle term (2 within 3), then the major term also en-

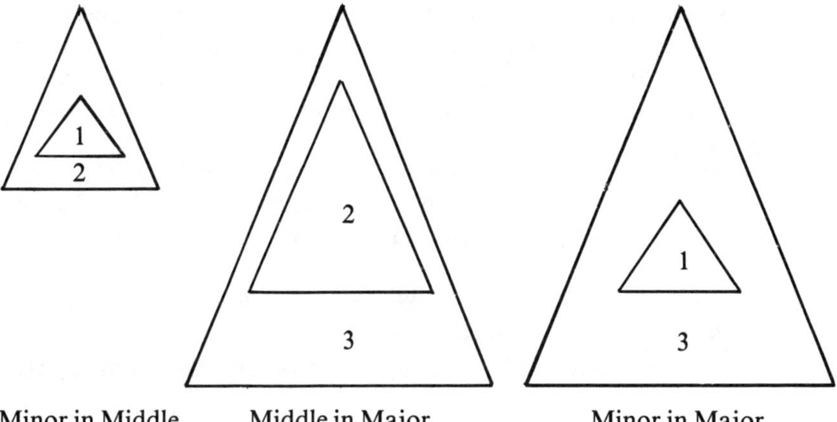

Minor in Middle   Middle in Major   Minor in Major

FIGURE 5–1

compasses the minor term (1 within 3). These terms are defined in more detail below.

In addition to containing a universal or distributed term, a categorical syllogism must satisfy three other requirements:

1. There are three statements, but no more than three (major premise, minor premise, and the conclusion).
2. There are three terms, but no more than three terms (the major term, the middle term, and the minor term).
3. Each term must be repeated, but no more than once.

In the following example each of the terms and its use is illustrated:

MAJOR PREMISE: [All politicians] (middle term) are [corrupt] (major term).

MINOR PREMISE: [Senator Bribe] (minor term) is a [politician] (middle term).

CONCLUSION: [Senator Bribe] (minor term) is [corrupt] (major term).

MAJOR TERM = corruption

MINOR TERM = Senator Bribe

MIDDLE TERM = politicians

You will notice that in the above example all of the necessary antecedents are met. There are three statements, three terms, and each term is repeated once. In addition, note that (1) the middle term appears in the major premise and the minor premise, (2) the major term appears in the major premise and the conclusion, and (3) the minor term appears in the minor premise and the conclusion. For obvious reasons, the terms must be repeated in precisely this fashion. If the middle term does not appear in both the major and minor premises, no valid conclusion is possible. Likewise, if the minor term does not appear in both the minor premise and the conclusion, the conclusion would make no sense. Finally, for the conclusion to be valid, it must contain the major term.

Three rules govern the conclusions of categorical syllogisms. The first is that **if both the major premise and the minor premise are positive, then the conclusion must also be positive.** Consider the following illustration:

MAJOR PREMISE: All debaters are intelligent. (positive)

MINOR PREMISE: Erika is a debater. (positive)

CONCLUSION: Erika is intelligent. (only a positive valid conclusion is possible)

Secondly, **if one of the premises is negative, then the conclusion must also be negative.** For example:

MAJOR PREMISE: No senior level course is held on Tuesdays and Thursdays. (negative)

MINOR PREMISE: Advanced Thermodynamics is a senior level course. (positive)

CONCLUSION: Advanced Thermodynamics is not held on Tuesdays and Thursdays.

Finally, **if both premises are negative, then no valid conclusion is possible:**

MAJOR PREMISE: No senior level course is held on Tuesdays and Thursdays. (negative)

MINOR PREMISE: Argumentation and Debate is not a senior level course. (negative)

CONCLUSION: No valid conclusion is possible.

Disjunctive Syllogisms

A disjunctive syllogism is one in which alternatives are offered in the major premise. Usually such a syllogism can be recognized by the presence of the word "either-or" in the major premise. The major premise sets forth two absolute alternatives. The minor premise either denies one or the other alternative, or it affirms one or the other alternative. The following are examples:

MAJOR PREMISE: John will either travel to Texas this summer or he will attend summer school.

MINOR PREMISE: John will travel to Texas this summer.

CONCLUSION: John will not attend summer school.

MAJOR PREMISE: The president has either vetoed the bill or it has become law.

MINOR PREMISE: The president has not vetoed the bill.

CONCLUSION: The bill has become law.

In the first example, the minor premise affirms one of the alternatives. In the second example, the minor premise denies one of the alternatives. The following diagram illustrates the function of the disjunctive syllogism:

MAJOR PREMISE

There are but two alternatives: either A or B

MINOR PREMISE

There are four possibilities:
1. A is affirmed
2. A is denied
3. B is affirmed
4. B is denied

CONCLUSION

There are four possibilities:
1. If A is affirmed, then B is rejected.
2. If A is denied, then B is confirmed.
3. If B is affirmed, then A is rejected.
4. If B is denied, then A is confirmed.

The necessary conditions for the disjunctive syllogism are obvious. First, the two alternatives offered in the major syllogism must be absolute, and there can be no more than two possible alternatives. Second, the alternatives must be mutually exclusive. Alternatives A and B cannot exist at the same time.

Hypothetical Syllogisms

A third type of syllogism suggests cause and effect. This cause and effect relationship, suggested in the major premise, is called *hypothetical.* The hypothetical syllogism is identified by a rather complex major premise which contains a *consequence;* the occurrence of this consequence is dependent upon a given condition (antecedent). Usually the words "if" and "then" will appear in the major premise. The following is a hypothetical syllogism:

MAJOR PREMISE: If it rains (Antecedent), we will hold the ceremonies in the ballroom (Consequent).

MINOR PREMISE: It will rain.

CONCLUSION: We will hold the ceremonies in the ballroom.

There is an obvious but important condition necessary for a valid hypothetical syllogism. The major premise should be structured so that the affirmation of the antecedent leads to the consequent as a valid conclusion. Conversely, the denial of the consequent should lead to the denial of the antecedent as a valid conclusion (see below for the discussion of hypothetical fallacies).

The following diagram illustrates the function of the hypothetical syllogism:

MAJOR PREMISE

A consequent X results when an antecedent Z is present.

MINOR PREMISE

There are two possibilities:
1. The antecedent is affirmed.
2. The consequent is denied.

CONCLUSION

There are two possibilities:
1. If the antecedent is affirmed, then the consequent is also affirmed.
2. If the consequent is denied, the antecedent is rejected.

Fallacies

Fallacies are instances of faulty reasoning. An important characteristic of fallacies is that they are deceptive: they appear to be logically sound when, in fact, they are flawed. Fallacies can occur by design or as a result of faulty thinking. Sometimes speakers attempt to shroud a weak argument with a veil of logic, attempting to deceive their listeners. At other times speakers produce fallacies unintentionally; they are themselves deceived.

It is important for the speaker to be familiar with fallacies so that they can be avoided. It is equally important for listeners to be aware of fallacious reasoning in order to guard against being "taken in" by deceptive arguments.

There are many different kinds of fallacies and available space allows for only a brief discussion of them. The following discussion, however, includes examples of those fallacies that are most common and the most harmful if accepted by listeners.

Semantic Fallacies

These fallacies are deceptive in that the meaning of words shifts in the course of the reasoning process, or an improper meaning is given to a key term in the reasoning process. Consider the following reasoning:

> Only adults are allowed to sign contracts. Since I am employed, and possess an automobile, and have never been arrested, and have earned a drivers license, I am an adult. I should therefore be allowed to sign a contract.

The reasoning above is faulty because the meaning of "adult" is not the same in the first statement as it is in the second statement. "Adult" as it is used in law, concerning contracts, refers to age and not mature behavior. The second usage, however, deals with maturity and not age. The speaker has either intentionally shifted the meaning of the word "adult" or s/he applied an improper meaning of the word unintentionally. Consider another example:

> All men are created equal, and are endowed by their creator with certain inalienable rights, that among these are life, liberty and the pursuit of happiness. Since Ezmarelda is a woman, she has no right to life, liberty, or the pursuit of happiness.

The meaning of the word "men" in the example above clearly does not refer to gender but to all human beings. When the proper meaning of the word is considered, the conclusion in the example is absurd.

Hasty Generalization

Hasty generalization is a fallacy of inductive reasoning. It occurs when partial or distorted facts are considered in the reasoning process. It occurs when the examples cited are not typical or consistent (see the discussion of perfect and imperfect reasoning at the beginning of this chapter for examples). Simply put, a hasty generalization is reached through careless or intentionally truncated reasoning.

Post Hoc Ergo Propter Hoc

This fallacy, which means "after this therefore because of this," is faulty causal reasoning. Consider the following reasoning:

> In 1985, I donated $5,000 to the alumni fund at Quintilian College. For the first time in 30 years, the college won the football championship of their conference. If it were not for that donation, the college may never have tasted the joy of being a champion.

Obviously the speaker's conclusion is faulty. Just because the football team won a championship after a donation does not mean that one was caused by the other.

Hypothetical Fallacies

These are fallacies associated with hypothetical syllogisms. As you learned, the only valid conclusions possible in hypothetical reasoning are: (1) denial of the consequent, or (2) affirmation of the antecedent. Sometimes, speakers attempt the opposites: (1) to affirm the consequent, or (2) to deny the antecedent. When this occurs, the resulting conclusions are not valid.

Consider the following example:

> If an apple is falling from that tree, then there is gravity in our environment. An apple is not falling from that tree. Therefore, there is no gravity in our environment.

Or this example:

> If an apple is falling from that tree, then there is gravity in our environment. There is gravity in our environment. Therefore, an apple is falling from that tree.

The conclusions in both of these examples are obviously faulty. In the first example, there are other more plausible explanations to explain the absence of the falling apple. In the second example, there is no necessary relationship between gravity and falling apples—just because it is true that gravity is present, there is no guarantee that apples are falling.

Circular Thinking

This fallacy occurs when the reasons given for a particular conclusion are the same or are similar to the conclusion itself. The following example, taken from Richard Whately's *Elements of Logic* is illustrative:

> Every particle of matter gravitates equally; "why?" because those bodies which contain more particles even gravitate more strongly, i.e. are heavier; "but those which are heaviest are not always more bulky;" no, but they still contain more particles, though more closely condensed; "how do you know that?" because they are heavier; "how does that prove it?" because all particles of matter gravitating equally, that mass which is specifically the heavier must [needs] have the more of them in the same place.[5]

It is obvious that the conclusion in the above example is scarcely different than the statement that initiated the line of reasoning. It is circular—it ends where it begins.

Mistaking Sign for Cause

This fallacy occurs when one argues that the eradication of a symptom solves the problem that caused it. Consider the following exchange:

Carl: Pornography helps support organized crime. So, by restricting pornography we can help stop organized crime.

Janet: Even if you could eradicate pornography, wouldn't organized crime turn to other forms of support?

Carl: They depend on pornography.

Janet: They do now, but the motivation is profit isn't it? I mean, organized crime would just turn to some other profit-making scheme, wouldn't they?

Carl: All I know is that organized crime depends on pornography to exist.

Janet: Carl, don't they exist on profit, and pornography is just a way to make money?

Carl: Oh, I don't know.

What Carl has done is to mistake a sign (a symptom of organized crime—pornography traffic) for its cause (profit). Eliminating a symptom, in this case pornography, will not necessarily solve the problem of organized crime.

Syllogistic Defects

Syllogistic defects lead to faulty reasoning. Such things as the "undistributed middle term" in a categorical syllogism will lead to invalid conclusions. Syllogisms that have more than three terms, or terms that are not repeated, or terms that are repeated more than once are also faulty and lead to invalid conclusions. Invalid conclusions also result when the alternatives presented in disjunctive syllogisms overlap, or when they are not absolute.

Summary

Even though the presentation of argument is essential, the discovery of argument through reasoning is also essential. Selecting the appropriate value appeals, or the most advantageous organizational structure, or even the strongest supporting evidence will be insufficient without a firm grasp of the logical foundation of argument. Indeed, effective argument and reasoning are inseparable.

Inductive reasoning, moving from the observation of specific instances to a generalization, elevates experience to paramount importance in the discovery process. Although perfect induction results in a generalization which is certain, most inductive reasoning is imperfect and leads to probable conclusions. For induction to be sound the observations must be both typical and consistent. Analogy and dissociation are other ways to reason inductively.

Deductive reasoning moves from a generalization, gained either through induction or from first principles, to a specific conclusion. The vehicle of deduction is the syllogism, structured with a major premise, a minor premise, and a conclusion. There are three different kinds of syllogisms: (1) categorical, (2) disjunctive, and (3) hypothetical.

Finally, errors in reasoning, either by design or through ignorance, are called fallacies. Fallacies are deceptive. Some speakers design arguments to appear logical when, in fact, they are not. Some speakers present flawed arguments unintentionally because they themselves are deceived.

Notes

1. *New York Times,* November 21, 1969, Sec. I, p. 22.
2. *Critiques of Contemporary Rhetoric,* (Belmont, CA: Wadsworth, 1972), p. 96.
3. *Vital Speeches of the Day,* Vol. 50, February 1, 1984, p. 227.
4. *Vital Speeches,* p. 229.
5. *Elements of Logic,* (Boston: James Munroe and Co., 1859), p. 221.

Questions and Exercises

1. What role does reasoning play in the development of argument?
2. Define inductive reasoning.
3. What is the difference between perfect and imperfect induction?
4. Identify and discuss the ways in which one can ensure that conclusions gained through imperfect induction are sound?
5. What is analogy and how is it used in argument?
6. What is dissociation and how is it used in argument?
7. Define deductive reasoning.
8. Name and diagram the function of the three types of syllogisms.
9. Identify the following fallacies:
   a. semantic fallacies
   b. hasty generalization
   c. *post hoc ergo propter hoc*
   d. hypothetical fallacies
   e. circular thinking
   f. mistaking sign for cause
10. Identify the defects, if any, in the following syllogisms:
    a. All dogs have four legs
       My cat has four legs
       Therefore, my cat is a dog
    b. All people need nourishment
       Fish need nourishment
       Josh needs nourishment
       Therefore, Josh is either a fish or a person
    c. Either Jim is angry or he is asleep
       Jim is awake
       Therefore, Jim is angry

d. If it rains we will hold the ceremonies in the ballroom
   It will not rain
   Therefore, we will not hold the ceremonies in the ballroom
e. If it rains we will hold the ceremonies in the ballroom
   We will hold the ceremonies in the ballroom
   Therefore, it will rain

11. Select a speech from a recent issue of *Vital Speeches of the Day.* Identify an argument and determine the type of reasoning it reflects. Is it sound? If so, explain. If not, why not?
12. By looking through speeches, debates, campaign literature, and so on, find at least one fallacious argument. Identify the type of reasoning attempted and why it is fallacious.

Suggested Readings

Berube, David. "Debating Hasty Generalization." *CEDA Yearbook, 1984.* California State University, Northridge: Don Brownlee, 1984, pp. 65–73.

Herbeck, Dale and Katsulas, John. "The Affirmative Topicality Burden: Any Reasonable Example of the Resolution." *Journal of the American Forensic Association,* XXI (Winter 1985), 133–145.

Rhodes, Jack and Pfau, Michael. "Resolution or Example: A Reply to Herbeck and Katsulas." *Journal of the American Forensic Association,* XXI (Winter 1985), 146–149.

SIX

Searching for Evidence

Searching for evidence is one of the most important tasks of the advocate or the intercollegiate debater. The student interested in being an effective arguer will also need to become an effective researcher.

Sources of Evidence

To find evidence for arguments, an advocate must learn to research. If a debater is already a skilled researcher, then he or she will have an advantage over other beginning debaters. This section will guide the beginner as well as more experienced researchers through the steps of effective research in the following subdivisions: (1) beginning research, (2) using the card catalog and periodical indexes, (3) using computer research, (4) using government documents, (5) finding legal documents, and (6) other sources of evidence.

Beginning Research

Any advocate or any college debater who wishes to be thoroughly prepared should begin research as soon as possible. For example, as soon as the precise wording of the topic or proposition being debated is known, a letter to a U.S. Congressperson or Senator may help you obtain much information. Every year various government agencies make information available to college debaters on the intercollegiate debate propositions. The Congressional Research Service (CRS) prepares a compilation of readings annually on both the high school and college policy debate topics. The compilation for the college policy topic is not available until very late in the year and debaters usually have discovered most of the articles selected by the time it is available; however, CRS books from previous years may be useful for future topics. It should be noted that these are now printed in very limited numbers. The congressional or senatorial staff can check with the CRS and other agencies for available information. In addition, once contact is established with a helpful staff member, then future requests for specific government publications not available at local libraries may be much more quickly handled. If there are several debaters at a college desiring such assistance, it would be wise to work through the debate coach or director of forensics to obtain such material.

Private institutions, foundations, and other organizations can also provide significant amounts of information. After the topic has been announced, then the appropriate groups can be contacted to provide information. For example, the national offices of organizations such as automobile clubs, insurance companies, insurance research institutes, and other similar groups have provided bibliographies, reprints of articles, and their own research on topics dealing with mandatory seat belt laws and installation of air bags. Some groups contacted might, of course, have vested interests in promoting certain views. Students should be cautious about using information from pressure or lobby groups. Much of the information provided by such groups may be credible and very useful; however, students should avoid in-house publications where there is a strong indication of a significant bias.

Students should begin their own library research by compiling a list of key topics for using the card catalog, indexes, and other library resources. The way to create this list is by analyzing the precise wording of the topic and by brainstorming. Brainstorming is a quick method of generating ideas for arguments, affirmative cases, and negative strategies. (See *Steps in Effective Brainstorming,* below.) After the list of key topics is composed, then the list needs to be "translated" into terms and topics used by the library resources. An examination of some of the popular indexes listed a little later in this section will help convert the list into more useful terminology.

Chapter Outline

Steps in Effective Brainstorming

Brainstorming is a method of generating ideas quickly for evaluation after the session.

Prior to Brainstorming:

1. Announce the topic or problem □ Although brainstorming is informal and partially impromptu, advance thinking usually is necessary to produce a quantity of ideas.
2. Limit the size of the group □ Brainstorming works most effectively in small groups (15 or under).
3. Limit the time for the session □ Brainstorming sessions are most effective when limited to an hour or less. If more time is allotted, the discussion will probably shift to evaluation of proposals, which is counterproductive to the objective of the session.

Rules for Brainstorming:

1. All group members should participate □ A teacher, coach or experienced debater can serve as a leader to encourage all to offer ideas or add to and develop ideas offered by others.
2. No pattern or order is followed □ Brainstorming needs to be spontaneous to be effective. Although brainstorming is often chaotic, such disorganization is better than suppressing idea-generation, which an organized discussion can do.
3. No criticism or evaluation is permitted □ Criticism and evaluation also discourage contributions at the idea-generation stage. Often brainstorming is done prior to extensive research and uninformed participants may offer both good and bad ideas. However, if there is immediate evaluation of bad ideas, good ideas may also be discouraged.
4. All ideas are recorded □ The leader of the discussion may wish to record the ideas on a blackboard if the meeting is held in a classroom. Or, a group member may wish to volunteer to list the ideas during the session.

After Brainstorming:

1. A post-brainstorming discussion is essential □ Without any follow up of brainstorming, participants often feel as if the session was a waste of time. The post-session meeting should put the information gathered to use and also indicate future benefits of the information gained. This meeting should be more organized with the leader exercising more control.

2. Evaluation and criticism are encouraged □ In the discussion that occurs after brainstorming, the list of ideas is thoroughly analyzed. Ideas that clearly are not worth further attention are discarded and ideas that require additional explanation and discussion are pursued.
3. Follow-up action is planned □ At the end of the post-brainstorming discussion the future use of the information is planned. This may take the form of research assignments or a final discussion of future uses of the ideas.

Using the Card Catalog and Library Indexes

After the key terms have been translated into useful topics, the next task for the debater doing research is to prepare a bibliography of books, periodical articles, and other materials available in the library they will be using. The best place to start is with the library's main card catalog. Most students who have done any research in a library of any kind are familiar with the card catalog. However, very few students take advantage of all the information that can be found simply by looking in the card catalog.

Although libraries sometimes have several card catalogs, some of which are relatively small and specialized, almost all libraries use one central card catalog. Many students think that the library's "check-out" books are the only items listed in the card catalog, but this is almost always incorrect. A main card catalog is a record of all the circulating and reference books and other materials in the library. While the card catalog may not list individual magazine and journal articles, it will provide access to all the periodical titles. After using the indexes discussed below, students may need to return to the card catalog to check for the availability of the material in the indexes.

Card catalogs will usually be indexed so that a researcher can locate a work by author, title, or subject matter. Card catalogs will of course list the call numbers of the material, but the cards contain other information useful to the beginning researcher. As one example, the card for a work will usually alert you to any significant bibliography contained in the work, which can be a valuable clue to other sources on the research topic. Students should become familiar with the card catalogs at their own libraries and take advantage of the information available.

The periodical indexes are an important resource for debaters seeking current information on controversial topics. Beginning debaters might start with the *Reader's Guide to Periodical Literature,* which indexes popular magazines and a few well-known journals. Almost every college and public library carries this index. Though the *Reader's Guide* is a useful research tool, this index deals primarily with materials of interest to the general reader,

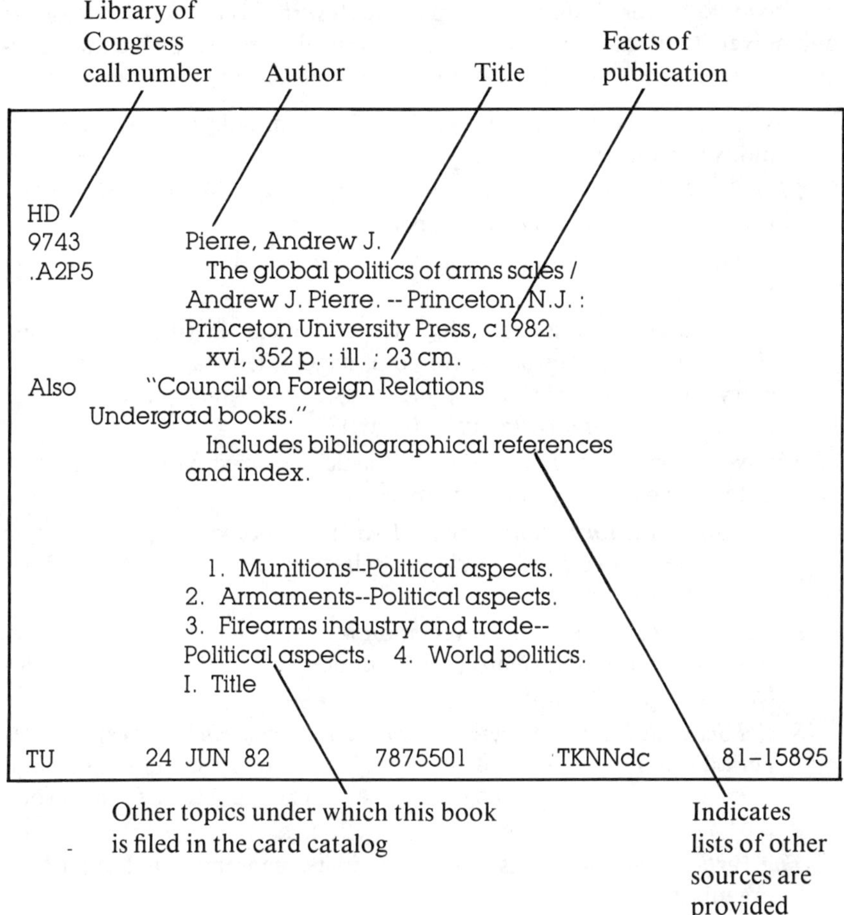

This card catalog card indicates a significant amount of useful information. It indicates where the book can be found using the Library of Congress classification system and that additional sources are listed in the book's bibliographical references. Further, the topics indicated on the author card provide other key words and phrases for researching this subject in the card catalog and other sources.

Card from the University of Tennessee main library card catalog.

FIGURE 6–1 Sample card catalog card.

and it would be very limiting to stop research with this index. Many college and university libraries will also have the following indexes, which will provide debaters access to more substantial materials on controversial topics:

Business Periodicals Index lists articles from periodicals in business and industry from 1958 to date.

Christian Science Monitor Index covers the available issues of this national and international newspaper.

Education Index includes educational periodicals, books and pamphlets from 1929 to date.

Humanities Index contains listings for periodicals in such fields as archaeology, classical studies, folklore, history, language, literature, literary and political criticism, philosophy and religion. (Formerly titled *Social Sciences and Humanities Index.*)

The New York Times Index covers all articles carried by the newspaper. Subject and author (if any) are indexed.

Public Affairs Information Service (PAIS) lists books, pamphlets, some government documents, periodicals in economics and public affairs from 1915 to date.

Research in Education, prepared monthly by ERIC (Educational Resources Information Center; see computer searches also), covers educational research reports.

Social Sciences Index (formerly *Social Sciences and Humanities*) includes periodicals in the fields of anthropology, economics, environmental science, law and criminology, medical science, political science, sociology.

The Vertical File Index lists in monthly issues pamphlets and publishing organizations.

The Wall Street Journal Index indexes the articles carried by subject, author (if any), and company or corporate name.

Many college and university libraries will have numerous other specialized indexes in a variety of fields. Students should check with the reference librarian for information on specialized subject indexes. Use of these indexes will provide lists of articles with more detailed and substantive treatment of topics being researched.

Computer Searches

Major universities and many smaller colleges currently have computer search services. Computer search services can access hundreds of databases, or online information files, offered by commercial vendors such as Lockheed Dialog, System Development Corporation, Bibliographic Retrieval

A GENERAL WORKS
(General encyclopedias, reference books, periodicals, etc.)

B PHILOSOPHY-RELIGION
- B-BJ Philosophy, including BF Psychology
- BL-BX Religion

C AUXILIARY SCIENCES OF HISTORY

D HISTORY: GENERAL AND OLD WORLD
- DA Great Britain
- DD Germany
- DK Russia
- DT Africa

E-F HISTORY: THE AMERICAS

G GEOGRAPHY, ANTHROPOLOGY, FOLKLORE
- G Geography (General)
- GB Physical geography
- GN Anthropology
- GR Folklore
- GV Recreation, Physical Education

H SOCIAL SCIENCES
- HA Statistics
- HE Transportation and communication
- HF Marketing, management, accounting, and advertising
- HG Finance
- HM Sociology
- HQ Marriage and family
- HV Social pathology, public welfare, and criminology

J POLITICAL SCIENCE
- JC Political theory
- JF Constitutional history (General and comparative)
- JK U.S. Constitutional history

K LAW

L EDUCATION

M MUSIC AND BOOKS ON MUSIC

N FINE ARTS
- NA Architecture
- ND Painting
- NK Decorative arts and interior design

P LANGUAGE AND LITERATURE
- PA Classical languages and literature
- PE English language (including dictionaries)
- PN General and comparative literature, film, theater, journalism, etc.
- PQ Romance literatures
- PR English literature
- PS American literature
- PT Germanic literatures

Q SCIENCE
- QA Mathematics
- QC Physics
- QD Chemistry
- QE Geology
- QH Natural history, biology, and ecology
- QK Botany
- QL Zoology
- QP Physiology and biochemistry

R MEDICINE
- RA Public health, forensic medicine and toxicology
- RC Internal medicine, psychiatry, sports medicine
- RT Nursing

S AGRICULTURE
- SB Plant culture
- SD Forestry
- SF Veterinary medicine
- SH Fisheries

T TECHNOLOGY
- TA General engineering
- TH Building construction
- TJ Mechanical engineering
- TK Electrical engineering
- TP Chemical engineering
- TR Photography
- TT Arts and crafts
- TX Home economics

U MILITARY SCIENCE

V NAVAL SCIENCE

Z BIBLIOGRAPHY AND LIBRARY SCIENCE

The Library of Congress classification system arranges books, periodicals and other materials according to a letter and number code system. The brief outline above shows some of letter classifications and the corresponding subjects. A reference librarian should be able to provide a more specific number for a particular subject interest.

FIGURE 6–2 Brief Library of Congress Classification.

Services, Pergamon Infoline, and Mead Data Central Nexis, as well as the federally subsidized files of the National Library of Medicine (Medline) and the Department of Energy (Recon).

Online data bases, which are continually increasing in number, include a great variety of topics in science, health, technology, business, social sciences, education and the humanities. The most frequently cited kind of source in databases are journal articles, but other kinds of resources are also listed, including books, newspapers and conference proceedings. Many of the periodical indexes listed above are accessible through some kind of computer search. In fact, almost all databases correspond to a printed index which may also be available in the library. There is usually a fee for computer searches so they should be carefully planned in advance. In addition, many libraries require that appointments be made to do a computer search.

Preparing for an Effective Computer Search

1. Discover if a computer search is the best way to do the research. If needed indexes are available and the scope of the particular research question is relatively narrow, it may be simpler to search the indexes in a traditional way.
2. Find out the special rules, uses, and limitations of the computer search service that is available. For example, libraries may require appointments and students will want to know about the approximate costs of the search.
3. Prior to going to the library, write a statement defining the topic of the research. If this is preliminary debate research, the proposition might provide an adequate statement. Make certain that the research statement is expressed in a good, grammatical sentence and that any of the relationships between concepts are expressed clearly.
4. Go to the library before the search. List the key words or phrases of the proposition or topic. If the computer database being searched has a special thesaurus, such as ERIC does, or a special list of subject headings, such as can be found in the *Medical Subject Headings,* then it will be useful to use the sources for the key words or phrases list.
5. If there is a printed (paper) index of the database being searched, it is usually helpful to look at a recent year's accumulation of subjects. Try to find materials in the index using the selected key words and phrases. It may be necessary to add, delete, or change some of these words and phrases.
6. Check one of the articles listed in the printed index using these key words and phrases. If these terms help locate a very relevant article, then they may also be useful in the computer search.

One very useful computer search service is available through ERIC. The Educational Resources Information Center is a nationwide information system supported by the National Institute of Education. The various ERIC clearinghouses are located at universities and with professional organizations throughout the nation and focus on specific academic fields. A variety of information, including abstracts of many academic convention papers, is available through the ERIC computer database. ERIC also has its own thesaurus (*Thesaurus of ERIC Descriptors,* 9th edition, 1982), which is the key to locating terms with which to index ERIC materials. ERIC is a unique way to access materials which otherwise are very difficult to obtain, such as academic convention papers. This and other aspects make ERIC a very useful resource on a variety of topics.

Overall, computer research services can supplement or even replace the traditional bibliography search. Students should check with a reference librarian to determine the usefulness of a computer search on specific topics.

Government Publications

Government publications are documents produced by local, state, federal, or international government agencies. Such government agencies "produce" documents directly by issuing or indirectly by financing. Due to the great variety of such publications, it is often helpful to check with the librarian to determine the kinds of government documents available.

Federal government documents are often the most useful resources for college debaters. There are two main distributors of federal government publications:

Government Printing Office
Superintendent of Documents
Washington, D.C. 20402
202-783-3238
202-275-3030 (Congressional Publications)

The Government Printing Office sells through mail orders and government bookstores more than 25,000 different items from various government agencies.

National Technical Information Service
Department of Commerce
5285 Port Royal Rd.
Springfield, Va. 22161
703-487-4699

NTIS is the central source for the public sale of U.S. and foreign government-sponsored research, development and engineering reports, and other analyses prepared by national and local government agencies, their contractors or grantees, or by Special Technology Groups.

Many of the items available from these sources may be available free and much more quickly through either the publishing agency or department or through a Congressperson or Senator, as we mentioned at the beginning of this chapter.

Federal government documents are distributed or "deposited" to certain libraries. The depository library system is based on three principles: (1) depository libraries will be located in each state and Congressional district; (2) all government publications will be made available to depository libraries; and (3) government publications shall be available for the free use of the general public. Although all government documents are available to depository libraries, libraries will not usually receive all of the available documents. For example, if a university is the site of a depository library, the library will usually select those documents that support the university's programs of study and research.

Students are often reluctant to use government documents because of the perceived difficulty in finding them. The major print source for access to non-Congressional documents is the *Monthly Catalog of United States Government Publications.* This index gives access to agency annual reports, pamphlets, proceedings, and similar documents in several ways: (1) author (corporate or personal), (2) title, (3) subject, and (4) series number.

For Congressional publications, students should consult the Congressional Information Service (CIS). The CIS Index has a unique feature in the personal name index for Congressional hearings: researchers can locate both the name of the person who testified and on which side of the issue the person stood.

In addition, the federal government publishes many journals that are indexed in the *Index to U.S. Government Periodicals.* This index, begun in 1970, is a "reader's guide" to government periodicals.

Statistical information is available from two government sources. The *Statistical Abstract of the U.S.* is the best one-volume annual work, and the *American Statistics Index* (ASI) covers U.S. statistics from the late 1960s to present with detailed, descriptive abstracts of the citations. *ASI* is also indexed by subject, name, category, and title.

Another special source of information is the *Federal Register.* Published daily, the *Federal Register* provides information about public regulations and legal notices issued by federal agencies. These include presidential proclamations, executive orders, and federal agency documents. This is an important source on recent changes by the federal government.

Almost every college and university and even many public libraries will receive some kinds of government documents, even if the library is not a federal depository library. For example, many small community libraries will receive and keep recent issues of the *Congressional Record,* which is indexed by subject and by the name of the congressperson or senator. Students should check with the local libraries in their area for the best sources of government documents.

Legal Resources

Law libraries can be very valuable resources for the college debater. Debaters may wish to find court decisions, copies of laws, articles in law reviews, and other materials available in a law library.

A standard index of law reviews available in law libraries is the *Index to Legal Periodicals.* This index covers legal periodicals published in the United States, Canada, Great Britain, Ireland, Australia, and New Zealand. Yearbooks, annual institutes, and annual reviews of the work in a given field or on a topic are also included. Articles are indexed under subject and author. In addition, there is an index of cases, statutes, and book reviews. The "Table of Cases" lists cases alphabetically under both the plaintiff's and defendant's name. The "Table of Statutes" lists statutes by jurisdiction. Statutes are then cited alphabetically by name. Finally, book reviews are listed under the name of the author, or under the title of the work if the author is unknown.

Locating a court decision often seems to be a difficult task for the beginning researcher. *Court digests* can provide case citations, the name of the court deciding the case, the name and date of the case, and a brief abstract about the case. Digests are published in either a geographical or a jurisdictional format. All published cases will appear in one of the following digests, depending on the court in which the case was decided.

COURT	DIGEST
U.S. Supreme Court	*U.S. Supreme Court Digest*
U.S. Court of Appeals and/ or U.S. District Courts	*Federal Digest* (cases prior to 1939); *Modern Federal Practice Digest* (1939–1961), *Federal Practice Digest* (1961 to present)
Any State	Digest for the state or the *American Digest System* (either *Decennial Digest* or *General Digest*)

The information in a digest will be arranged alphabetically by subject matter (legal topics), and the subject matter will be subdivided into the different components that make up the whole of the subject matter. Case opinions in the abstract paragraph form will be arranged under the different components.

Most frequently debaters will need to find the text of the opinion of a court case, especially U.S. Supreme Court opinions. Either the name of the case or the case citation is required to find an opinion. If the name of the case and the court that decided the case is known, then the digest for that court system will assist in locating the opinion. The digests (see above) give the case citations that indicate the volume and the sources in which the opinions are published. For example, if the case is *Baker* v. *Carr* and was decided by the U.S. Supreme Court, then the case will be cited as follows:

Baker v. *Carr,* 369 U.S. 186, 82 S.Ct. 691, 7 L.Ed.2d 663.

This citation provides information on three different sources where the opinion in *Baker* v. *Carr* can be found. Translating this citation is not difficult. Each part of the citation after the name of the case consists of three items: (1) volume number, (2) abbreviation for the source and (3) page number where the opinion begins. For example, 369 U.S. 186 specifies volume 369 of the *United States Reports* with the opinion beginning on page 186. As this citation indicates, this opinion can also be found in the *Supreme Court Reporter* and in the *Lawyers Edition–Supreme Court Reports–Second Series.* All of these sources will contain the complete opinion of the court, but different additional materials may also be provided.

Common Abbreviations for Court Reporter Sources

U.S.L.W.	*United States Law Week*
U.S.	*United States Reports*
S.Ct.	*Supreme Court Reports*
L.Ed.2d	*Lawyers Edition–Supreme Court Reports–Second Series*
F.2d	*Federal Reporter, Second Series*
F. Supp.	*Federal Supplement*

For other abbreviations of regional and state reporters consult law librarian reference sources.

If only the name of the case is known, then it will be necessary to consult *American Digest System,* which contains tables of cases for all published cases. It should be noted that many opinions are not published. For example, trial opinions generally are not published, while appellate opinions usually are published. The *American Digest System* is divided into ten year segments titled *Decennial Digests,* with the latest ten years titled the *General Digests.* Therefore, when the date of a case is unknown, several volumes need to be checked.

Information on very recent Supreme Court cases and the full text of some opinions and excerpts from other opinions are published in *United States*

Law Week. This is the only widely available source that publishes the text of important cases before the preliminary printing in *United States Reports*.

Even if students do not have access to a law library, many college and university and even many community libraries will have at least one source of information available on United States Supreme Court decisions. In addition, many libraries will also subscribe to a few of the outstanding law reviews.

Other Sources of Information

There are many other sources of information, and these will vary in usefulness with each library and in particular with the programs or community being served by the library. Students should check the vertical or pamphlet files and other special sources at their particular libraries. There is no substitute for being thoroughly familiar with all the resources of a library, even a library on a small college campus or one serving a relatively small city or community. What may not be available at a given library may be available through inter-library loans and other special programs.

At some point in the research process students will want to, and should, browse through library resources. If the library has an open-stacks policy, then browsing can be very effective for locating materials missed in bibliographical searches or those few items (especially periodicals) that may not have been listed in the bibliographical sources consulted. Browsing can be effective if the library's organizational plan is understood. Almost all college and university libraries use the Library of Congress Classification System, and using the code "letters" students can browse through the relevant holdings on the library shelves. Often a reference librarian can provide a more specific "number" for browsing the particular subject areas. Browsing can be useful, but it should not be a substitute for planned research.

Reading Research to Discover Evidence

After preparing a beginning bibliography and obtaining some of the articles, students can begin reading to become familiar with the topic and discovering a few possible affirmative case ideas and negative strategies. After some reading, students should brainstorm again and with the help of a teacher, coach, or experienced debater develop lists of affirmative and negative arguments that should be researched. This list should be viewed as representing the kinds of statements that debaters might want to document. These arguments should not be viewed as either a "script" or a "shopping list" for research.

At this stage the student can begin *reading to research*. Such reading is different from reading for familiarity or general understanding. Such reading is focused and purposeful. The debater's goal is to search for supporting materials for possible argumentative claims in a debate. In the beginning stages of research the debater may wish to copy all evidence that supports all possible argumentative claims on the proposition selected for debate. Later research will be more selective and will possibly be coordinated with other students by a teacher or coach.

When reading an article, a student may see the same argument expressed in several different ways. It will probably be unnecessary to record numerous different versions of the same statement. In selecting which evidence to record, the student should consider the criteria for effective evidence discussed above, the conciseness of the evidence, and its credibility (see Chapter Seven).

The issues associated with the proposition also might provide the researcher with some guidelines for choosing evidence for research. First, the debaters should consider what kind of research questions are posed by the proposition. Does the proposition pose descriptive, analytical, comparative or prescriptive inquiries? Next, the proposition for debate can be classified. Based on the kinds of inquiries posed, the proposition can be classified as a proposition of inference, value, policy, or policy evaluation. Finally, the issues might then be listed, perhaps during a brainstorming or analysis session led by a teacher or coach. For example, if debaters are researching a policy question, they might raise the key significance, inherency, solvency and cost-benefits issues.

Effective and efficient reading of research to discover supporting material is a skill that requires practice and experience.

Recording Evidence

It is very important that evidence be recorded properly. The following guidelines for recording evidence are especially for intercollegiate debaters, but they also represent sound practices for any advocate researching controversial topics.

1. Evidence should be recorded verbatim. In a debate evidence is used formally, much in the same way that testimony, documents, and physical evidence are used in a trial. Thus, the authenticity of evidence is an important concern. Word-for-word transcription and presentation of evidence in an intercollegiate debate is the rule rather than an exception.

Except in very rare circumstances, *debaters should not paraphrase evidence.* Such an exception might be if an idea is expressed throughout several paragraphs, and might be difficult to record as a concise word-for-word citation. Before paraphrasing evidence, debaters should check with their coach or teacher to discern if the paraphrasing is necessary. If it is ever necessary to paraphrase evidence, then the debater should indicate that the evidence is paraphrased on the index card on which the evidence is recorded. In addition, when that evidence is presented in the debate, the speaker should indicate orally that it is paraphrased. Finally, the debaters must have the original document or a photocopy of the evidence to be provided upon demand by the opposing team during the debate and by the judge after the debate.

Debaters should also avoid the use of ellipses in recording evidence for reasons suggested above. If ellipses is used in the recording of evidence, then

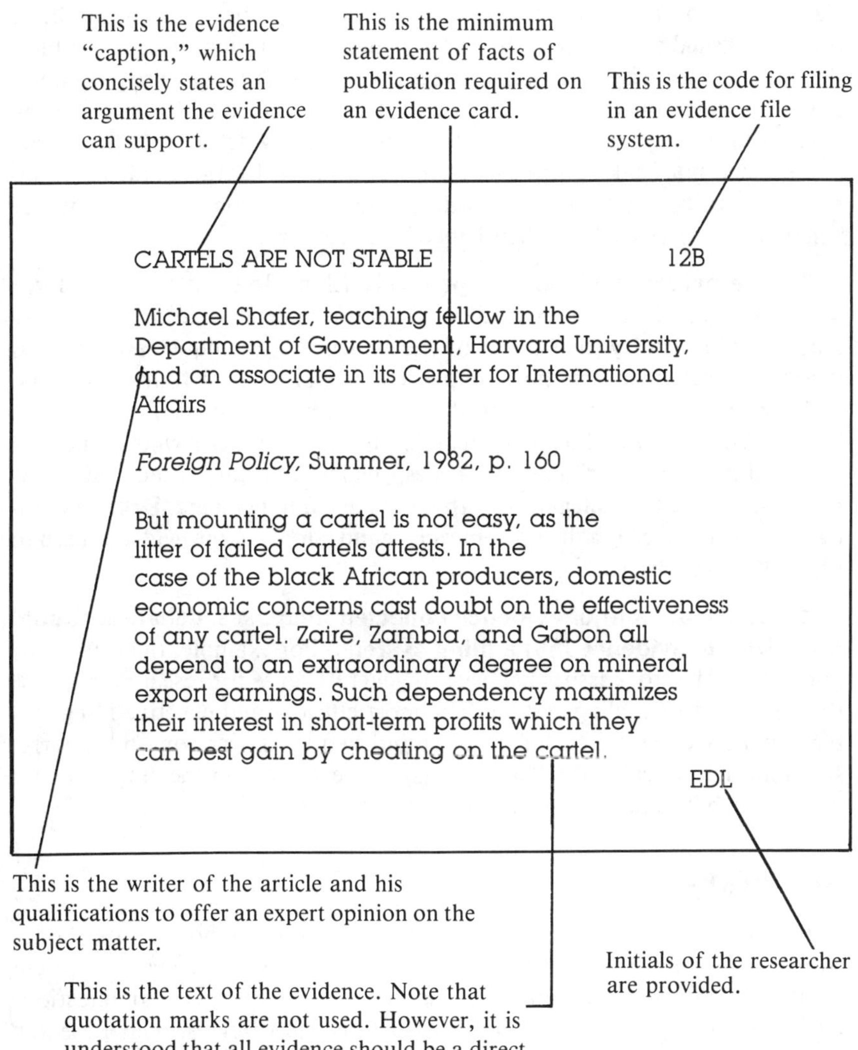

FIGURE 6–3 Sample evidence card.

the debater should also have the original or a photocopy of the evidence available for inspection upon request.

2. The complete facts of publication must be available for every item of evidence used in a debate. When evidence is recorded, this basic information must be provided: (1) the name of the person being quoted, (2) the qualifications of the person being cited (for example, position, experience, and so on), (3) the precise title of the magazine, journal, book, or other published document in which the evidence was found, (4) the complete date of the last revised publication or edition, and (5) the precise page number(s) on which the evidence was found. Failure to record this information may result in the judge of the debate excluding the evidence from the debate and the decision making process. Again, the reason for this guideline is authenticity. Information must be available that allows opposing advocates to verify for themselves the authenticity of the evidence.

3. The evidence should be properly identified. At the top of the 4 × 6 (suggested size) index card on which the evidence is recorded, the debater should identify the subject of the evidence in a unique caption. This "caption" may be a very short simple sentence of three or four words, and will assist the debater later in identifying each item of evidence.

The evidence should also be identified by the researcher who found and recorded it from the original. This is especially important if the evidence is being shared with a colleague or other debate team members. Debaters' initials often are placed in the bottom right-hand corner of the evidence card to identify the researcher.

4. As the amount of evidence collected increases, debaters should organize the evidence into a filing system. For example, the lists of arguments or the stock issues list used to generate ideas for research might be the beginning of a filing system. The most efficient and effective filing systems will have every item of evidence indexed by its caption and a corresponding numerical code. This will assist the student in locating evidence during a debate and refiling it afterwards.

Summary

Finding evidence is a process that involves knowing how to use the resources of the library as well as other information sources. Research might begin with contacting a Congressperson or Senator for special publications available from government agencies, such as the Congressional Research Service. Students should also learn to use the card catalog, various library indexes and other standard library guides. Computer search services can also supplement research in traditional indexes. Government publications are especially valuable resources and can be accessed through several different indexes.

Legal publications, including court opinions and law reviews, are also useful to debaters. Most libraries will have at least some information available on U.S. Supreme Court cases and many libraries will have at least one source that allows students to find the texts of the Court's opinions.

Other sources of information include pamphlet files and systematic browsing.

Reading research to discover evidence is a focused activity that requires practice. Recording evidence should follow specific guidelines so that the authenticity of evidence may be verified.

Questions and Exercises

1. *Group Exercise:* Using a current or recent intercollegiate debate proposition, go through the steps suggested in "Beginning Research" to create a list of ideas, arguments, key words and phrases for initial library research.
2. Using a current or recent intercollegiate debate proposition, translate the terms of the resolution into key words and phrases that would be useful in one or more of the following indexes:
   a. *Business Periodicals Index*
   b. *Christian Science Monitor Index*
   c. *Education Index*
   d. *Humanities Index*
   e. *The New York Times Index*
   f. *Public Affairs Information Service* (PAIS)
   g. *Research in Education*
   h. *Social Sciences Index*
   i. *The Wall Street Journal Index*
   j. *The Vertical File Index*
3. List the different indexes available for government documents in your college or university library.
4. List the different ways to find the text of U.S. Supreme Court opinions in your college or university library.
5. Find the text of these U.S. Supreme Court Cases:
   a. *Brown* v. *Board of Education* (1954)
   b. *Haig* v. *Agee,* 453 U.S. 280
   c. *New York Times Company* v. *United States* (1971)
   d. *Olmstead* v. *United States* (1928)
   e. 410 U.S. 113

Suggested Readings

Captor, Renee. *Library Research for the Analysis of Public Policy.* (PS–19) Croton-on-Hudson, NY: Policy Studies Associates, 1979.

Cohen, Morris. *Legal Research in a Nutshell,* 3rd ed. St. Paul, MN: West Publishing Co., 1978.

Coplan, William and O'Leary, Michael. *Analyzing Public Policy Issues.* (PS–17) Croton-on-Hudson, NY: Policy Studies Associates, 1978.

SEVEN

Using Evidence

Aristotle identified two basic components of a persuasive argument—the statement of the argument and its proof. Although more recent theorists, such as Toulmin, see the structure of an argument as more complex, the proof for an argument is nevertheless an indispensable element. Proof in an argumentative situation may consist of either the reasoning or the evidence an advocate provides to support a claim. Thus, an argument may be supported by either reasoning or evidence or both.

The Role of Evidence

Although evidence functions as the support for an argument it is also the raw data that "starts" an argument.[1] Unless the advocate finds evidence or reasons, then there is no basis for a claim. Although as a form of proof evidence is similar to reasoning, evidence also has unique characteristics. Evidence, unlike reasoning, comes from outside the speaker's own immediate and personal resources. Evidence is not produced by an arguer's intellectual creativity. Instead, evidence is either known or discovered by an advocate and presented to a judge or an audience. *Evidence, therefore, can be defined as facts, inferences, statistics, examples, interpretations, or judgments known or discovered, but not created by the advocate.*

The role of evidence in argumentation is complex. As the Toulmin model indicates (see Chapter Two), evidence or data is one of the three necessary elements for an argument. The evidence is linked to the claim by a warrant, which allows the leap or connection to be made between the evidence and the claim. For example, suppose there is evidence that Professor Church's classes are always full; the student might then claim that Professor Church is a good teacher. The warrant would be that full classes are a sign that the teacher is good. The evidence would provide *indirect* support for this argument.

Suppose a student found evidence that Professor Church's student critiques showed that he was consistently rated as a good teacher. The warrant for this argument would now change and would be that student critiques of good teaching are indications that the teacher is good. The warrant for the argument is now much closer in wording and concept to the claim. Thus, in a sense the "leap" from the data to the claim is less difficult. Such evidence is *direct* support for your argument. *Evidence may, thereby, be classified as either direct or indirect depending on how close a connection there is between the data and the claim.* However, direct and indirect evidence are both acceptable and usable forms of evidence. The advocate frequently must rely on much indirect evidence to substantiate the claims in a debate.[2]

The first function of evidence is to provide proof for an argument. Some kinds of evidence serve to illustrate an argument as well as acting as proof. Still other kinds of evidence function primarily as illustrations and have little power as proofs. For example, if a student cites a particularly effective lecture that Professor Church has given, such a case may serve to illustrate the professor's effective teaching techniques, but it does not prove overall that he is a good teacher.

Evidence functions in argumentative situations complex ways, many of which will be discussed in this chapter. This chapter will also discuss kinds of evidence and the presentation of evidence.

Kinds of Evidence

Observations

Evidence can be classified in two general categories, as observations or as evaluations. We will discuss evaluations later in this chapter. *Observations are descriptions of events, objects, persons, places, or other concrete and empirically verifiable phenomena.* This category of evidence is a large one and can be subdivided as into four groups: (1) facts, (2) inferences, (3) statistics, and (4) examples.

Facts

The word "fact" is a very commonly misapplied term. In everyday conversation people tend to use the term *facts* to identify their beliefs. This use of the word is, of course, very imprecise and misleading. *Facts can instead be defined as indisputable descriptions of events, objects, persons, places, or other concrete and empirically verifiable phenomena.* Although there may be many facts, there are usually relatively few facts that can function as *direct* evidence in an argumentative situation. If facts were available to serve as direct evidence for many claims in a debate, then those claims would tend to be indisputable. Furthermore, if those claims were crucial to the defense of the proposition being debated, then there would be only one arguable side in the debate and the proposition would be undebatable.

Facts, when they are used by arguers, often function as *indirect* evidence. For example, when a murder case goes to trial, the facts that the prosecuting attorney might present are often circumstantial or indirect evidence. They might include such items as where the weapon was found, the fingerprints found on the weapon, the condition of the victim, the position of the body, and the presence or absence of such physical evidence. The attorney's case might consist entirely of facts and other kinds of indirect or circumstantial evidence. The arguer should note that indirect evidence is not necessarily ineffective evidence. Many persons have been convicted of crimes based on such evidence.[3]

Arguers using and confronting facts should be certain that the evidence is factual. Facts, as indicated above, are often confused with other kinds of evidence, such as inferences.

Inferences

Facts are most often confused with inferences. *Inferences can be defined as descriptive statements about events, objects, persons, places, or other concrete and empirically verifiable phenomena that are gained by reasoning from something known or assumed.* As discussed previously (Chapter 3), inferences may deal with (1) traits or characteristics, (2) relations among phenomena (e.g., causality), (3) history, and (4) the future. Although there may be many similarities in the wording of facts and inferences, the distinction lies in whether or not the observation is disputable. For example, the claim that President John F. Kennedy is dead is for most reasonable persons indisputable and therefore a fact. However, the claim that Lee Harvey Oswald alone killed President Kennedy is an historical inference that is disputable.

Inferences, unlike facts, are more likely to function as direct evidence in argumentative situations. Arguers, therefore, often seek inferences to support their claims in a debate. In many debates where the arguers have a significant amount of direct evidence much of that evidence consists of inferences.

Statistics

Statistical evidence is very similar to an inference in that both kinds of evidence can document characteristic, relational, historical, or future conditions. However, statistical evidence is distinctive in that it always empirically quantifies the conditions. *Statistical evidence can be defined as empirically quantified descriptions of events, objects, persons, places, or other phenomena.*

Statistics may come from either public or private records. Public records tend to be "archival" in nature. In other words, data is produced over long periods of time for purposes other than academic study. For example, birth and death records are kept as part of most local government archives. Although they might not be prepared in anticipation of study, a sociologist or an epidemiologist, for example, might find such records useful for social scientific or scientific studies.

Private records tend to produce data that is episodic in nature. In other words, data is produced for short periods of time for specific purposes. For example, an industry may keep records of production, employment, employee sick days, and so on. Such data is usually produced for internal purposes and is not prepared in anticipation of outside study unless there is some local, state or federal regulation that compels the compilation of such data.

Records may also be produced in the public or private sectors in which there is anticipation of study. As indicated above, laws may compel companies to keep records. For example, federal anti-pollution laws might compel industries to keep records of air, water, noise, or other forms of pollution. Or, public or private groups may study phenomena for the purposes of examining possible relationships. In such situations as these, statistics will be produced, usually sporadic in nature, and there will frequently be problems in the credibility of such information. It is important that the advocate knows what kinds of records were used to produce the statistical evidence that is used for an argument so that the nature of the evidence and its credibility might be understood.

Statistical evidence may also be either factual or inferential and either direct or indirect. Statistical evidence that is factual will most likely be dealing with concepts and measurements that are agreed upon and non-controversial. For example, the claim that the distance between the earth and the sun is 93 million miles is factual and statistical evidence. However, factual and statistical evidence will usually function only as indirect evidence in a debate. On the other hand, the claim that there are over 25 million Americans living in poverty is inferential and statistical evidence. Such evidence is disputable since both the concept and the measurement of poverty are controversial subjects.

Statistics can present hundreds or thousands of cases in a single figure. Advocates can demonstrate trends, show the general picture, or draw comparisons and contrasts over time. Statistical evidence also may attempt to establish complex relationships. Depending on the area of research, statistics may attempt to illustrate causal types of relationships—although the word *causality* will seldom be used. Clearly, there are certain relationships in science where causality can be demonstrated or approached. Certain diseases, for example, can be causally linked to certain conditions.

In the social sciences, however, statistical relationships are much more complex and less certain. A social scientist may start with the task of attempting to demonstrate that two variables are at least *not* independent. After this is determined the social scientist may attempt to study the way in which the two variables "co-vary" or *vary together.* Variables also may be directly or inversely related. If variables directly co-vary, then as one variable increases so does the other. If variables are inversely related, then as one variable increases, the other decreases. Of course, when there are more than two variables involved in a relationship, then such multivariate relationships are even more complex. Despite the presence of even very strong relationships, the words "causal relationship" will seldom appear in statistical evidence, especially if the field of study is in the social sciences.

Advocates who use statistical evidence will be more effective if they understand the meaning of the statistics and what kind of relationships, if any, are being described in the evidence. Such understanding will be produced by the knowledge of basic concepts in statistics as well as by familiarity with the entire context of the statistical evidence that has been chosen for an argument.

Examples

Examples are defined as descriptions of individual events, objects, persons, places, or other concrete and empirically verifiable phenomena. As such, examples have limited use in terms of their ability to function as proof for generalizations. An example is an *illustration* rather than proof of an argument. Although an individual example may suggest that a generalization is true, a great number of examples would be required to demonstrate the truth of most generalizations.

The time constraints upon most advocates in either public or educational debates usually prohibit the use of examples as a form of proof for a broad generalization. Examples might be more effectively used in combination with factual, inferential, or statistical evidence so that a generalization might be illustrated as well as proven.

When advocates use examples, they should take care to use examples that are typical. In other words, the examples used should reflect the usual rather than the unusual case. The typicality of an example should not be confused with its significance. An example may be very important, but thereby may also be very atypical. For instance, if advocates were debating whether or not the United States should give military aid to foreign countries, they might choose to talk about the example of arms sales to Saudi Arabia. During the early 1980s Saudi Arabia was the recipient of one of the largest arms sales provided by the United States. Since this was one of the largest sales, the Saudi Arabian transfer was one of the most significant; by the same standard it was also one of the most atypical. Thus, examples must be used carefully if the credibility of the evidence is to be preserved.

Evaluations

The second major category of evidence consists of evaluations. *Evaluations are defined as statements that consist primarily of interpretations or judgments of descriptions or other evaluations.* All evidence is influenced by the perception of the author and thereby in a sense reflects an "evaluation." The evidence included in the category of evaluations, however, is evidence in which the author *intentionally* makes either an interpretation or a judgment.

In both sub-categories of evaluations (interpretations and judgments) the credibility of the author is even more important than in other kinds of evidence. With evaluations, the value of the evidence is dependent primarily upon the quality of the perception of the author. Unlike evidence that is primarily descriptive (observations), there is more than a mere reporting function for the author to perform.

Interpretations

The starting point for interpretative evidence is a description—a fact, inference, statistic, or example. *Interpretative evidence can be defined as authoritative data that analyzes or explains an event, object, person, place, or other concrete and empirically verifiable phenomenon.* Interpretative evidence adds to the meaningfulness of observations by analysis or explanation. Furthermore, the authoritativeness of the source should further enhance the effectiveness of the evidence as support for an argument. For example, statistical evidence might indicate how much military assistance was provided to Saudi Arabia, but interpretative evidence could analyze and explain the nature of that assistance and its relative importance compared with other examples of military assistance. Again, an important issue in the credibility of interpretive evidence is often the authority of the source.

Judgments

The starting point for evidence that presents a judgment is either a description or an evaluation. Evidence that "judges" attempts to make *conclusive* statements about the meaningfulness of descriptions or other evaluations. *Judgments can be defined as authoritative evidence that presents a conclusive determination of the significance of observations (descriptive evidence), interpretations, or of other judgments.* Unlike interpretative evidence, judgments do not just add to the meaningfulness of descriptions; instead, judgments determine the essential meaningfulness of a description from the source's perspective. For example, a judgment of the sale of military assistance to Saudi Arabia would explain its contribution to providing stability in the Middle East and any other significant consequences.

Judgments may also make claims about other evaluations. For example, one authority may judge the Saudi Arabian arms sale to promote stability whereas another source might declare the sale to threaten world peace. Such evidence would depend upon its authoritativeness for much of its effectiveness.

These categories of evidence discussed above designate specific tasks or functions. Advocates may discover evidence that combines these tasks. In other words, evidence might fit two or more categories at once. A debater arguing about Saudi Arabia, for example, might present evidence that documents the statistical size of the arms sale there as well as judges its importance. These categories, then, are designed to indicate the purposes that evidence might fulfill and thereby provide standards for determining whether evidence achieves those purposes.

Characteristics of Effective Evidence

Evidence that is presented in argumentative situations should have certain qualities in order to be effective. First, evidence should be from a sufficiently reputable authority depending upon the task of the evidence. For example, if the evidence is reporting an event, then a newspaper or popular magazine account may be sufficient. On the other hand, if the evidence presents an interpretation or judgment of the significance of that event, a more authoritative source may be desirable.

Second, evidence should present *the basis* for a conclusion as well as the conclusion itself. The basis may be reasoning, data, or other forms of evidence—facts, inferences, statistics, examples, or the evaluations of other authorities. Without the basis of a conclusion, evidence becomes totally dependent upon the authoritativeness of the source. Reliance on such evidence takes much of "the reason-giving nature" of argumentation out of a debate.

If the advocate must choose between evidence that provides a basis and no conclusion and evidence that provides a conclusion and no basis, then the evidence that provides the basis is the preferred kind of supporting material.

Third, it is important that the evidence presented in argumentative situations be accessible to the advocates and to the audiences or judges. This means that evidence should be from public statements. It also means that the materials from which the evidence is taken should be available. In a public debate evidence from secret or unapproachable sources should be avoided. Why, for example, should a legislator or the public base an important policy decision on evidence that cannot be verified? Even in cases of legitimate national security concerns, key senators and representatives have been given access to evidence that serves justifications for important decisions.

In an educational debate there should be no evidence that is not published. All evidence should be accessible to the participants once it has been presented. After the conclusion of an educational debate, the judge(s) may wish to see evidence in order to make their decision. If this request is made, then the debaters should provide the evidence at the conclusion of the debate.

Other guidelines for the recording of evidence and the presentation of evidence are discussed elsewhere in the text.

Presenting Evidence in a Debate

When an advocate wishes to introduce evidence into a public or an educational debate, the evidence may be introduced either informally or formally. Informal introduction of evidence involves the citing of substance of evidence without indicating a source for that evidence. Austin Freeley terms this method of introducing evidence as *judicial notice.*[4] This method of introducing evidence is suitable for presenting facts, common knowledge, and universally-held assumptions. The informal method of substantiating claims is used frequently in public debates and in less competitive kinds of educational debates, such as parliamentary and informal classroom debates. However, it should be noted that informal introduction of evidence is always appropriate if the evidence being submitted is genuinely indisputable. If the opposing advocate chooses to dispute the evidence and the audience or judge agrees that the evidence is disputable, then formal introduction of the evidence is required.

Formal introduction of evidence requires that evidence be presented with great precision, and certain guidelines should be carefully followed. First, the advocate should properly attribute sources. As we have emphasized, whenever a speaker relies on the ideas or evidence of others, then that source should be properly identified. The minimum amount of identification that the speaker should present is the name of the source and the date of the statement. It is also desirable for the speaker to cite the qualifications of the source as an authority. In addition, as you know, intercollegiate debaters are required to present upon demand the full citation of any evidence.

Second, evidence that is presented in a debate should be quoted precisely. In intercollegiate competition evidence should be quoted word for word as well as being recorded word for word. In public debates verbatim presentation of evidence is the exception rather than the rule. Nevertheless, challenges often occur in public debates that can be settled effectively by verbatim presentation of evidence.

Third, evidence should not be distorted. Evidence can be distorted in a number of ways. Evidence might be misinterpreted so as to change its meaning, or words might be added or deleted from the original so as to change the meaning. Another way of distorting evidence is to misrepresent the context of evidence. For example, if an author were explaining a point of view prior to attacking it, it would be a misrepresentation of the context of that evidence if a debater were to quote the explanation of the evidence as if the author were espousing that point of view. Such distortions are very serious matters. An intercollegiate debater who violates these standards can suffer serious consequences.

There are no formalized rules for the advocate in a public debate such as those for the intercollegiate debaters; nevertheless, these are practical guidelines that all ethical speakers should follow when presenting evidence in argumentative situations.

Summary

Evidence can be defined as facts, inferences, statistics, examples, interpretations, or judgments, known or discovered but not created by the advocate. The role of evidence in argumentation is complex. Evidence provides a starting point as well as support for arguments. Furthermore, evidence can represent a direct or indirect relationship with argumentative claims, depending on the similarity of the warrant to the claim.

Evidence can be divided into two major categories—observations (descriptive evidence) and evaluations (opinion evidence). Observations consist of facts, inferences, statistics, and examples. Facts are indisputable events, objects, persons, places, or other concrete and empirically verifiable phenomena. Inferences are disputable claims about these same phenomena that deal with traits, relationships, history, or the future.

Statistical evidence consists of empirically quantified descriptions of events, objects, persons, places, or other phenomena. Statistical evidence is complex and students should be familiar with basic concepts when using statistical data to support arguments.

Examples are individual events, objects, persons, places, or other concrete and empirically verifiable phenomena. As such, an example usually functions as an illustration of rather than as proof of a generalization or an argument.

The second major category of evidence consists of evaluations. Evaluations are defined as statements that consist primarily of interpretations or judgments of descriptions or other evaluations. Although all evidence is influenced by the perception of the author and thereby reflects an "evaluation," the evidence that falls into this category is that in which the author intentionally makes either an interpretation or a judgment.

Interpretative evidence is authoritative data that analyzes or explains an event, object, person, place, or other concrete and empirically verifiable phenomenon. Interpretative evidence adds to the meaningfulness of observations by analysis or explanation.

Judgments are authoritative evidence that present a conclusive determination of the significance of descriptive evidence interpretations, or of other judgments. Unlike interpretative evidence, judgments do not just add to the meaningfulness of descriptions; instead, judgments determine the essential meaningfulness of a description from the source's perspective.

Finally, the presentation of evidence should follow similar guidelines so that evidence is ethically introduced into debates.

Notes

1. See also George Ziegemueller and Charles Dause, *Argumentation: Inquiry and Advocacy,* (Englewood Cliffs, NJ: Prentice-Hall, 1975), p. 49.
2. Austin Freeley, *Argumentation and Debate: Reasoned Decision Making,* 5th ed., (Belmont, CA: Wadsworth, 1981) uses the terminology of direct and indirect evidence but the terms are defined differently on pp. 74–75.
3. Freeley makes a similar point on p. 75.
4. Ibid., p. 76.

Questions and Exercises

1. Find several different kinds of articles (e.g., reports and editorials) on a current controversy from a newspaper or a magazine. Select several items of evidence from these articles and write down in short simple sentences the arguments that the evidence supports.
2. Classify the evidence found above as:
   a. direct or indirect
   b. observations or evaluations

3. Classify the observations or descriptive evidence found in exercise #1 as facts, inferences, statistics, or examples.
4. Classify the evaluations or opinion evidence found in exercise #1 as interpretations or judgments.
5. Could any of the evidence found in exercise #1 be introduced informally in a debate? Explain.

Suggested Readings

Brownlee, Don. "The Consequences of Quantification." *CEDA Yearbook, 1982.* California State University, Northridge: Don Brownlee, 1982, pp. 29–31.

Spiker, Barry, Daniels, Tom and Bernabo, Lawrence. "The Quantitative Quandry: The Use and Abuse of Statistical Evidence." *Journal of the American Forensic Association,* XIX (Fall 1982), 87–96.

EIGHT

Credibility in Argumentation

Credibility is a frequently used term, especially in the discussion of public affairs. For example, several recent United States presidents have been concerned about "credibility gaps." To be credible, in this popular use, means to be believed or to be telling the truth. However, there is a great deal of difference between these two notions of "being believed" and of "telling the truth." Pollsters can measure whether or not the public believes what an advocate says, but whether or not the advocate is telling the truth often seems to be a matter of individual opinion.

For credibility to be a useful term for the student of argument, the public advocate, or the intercollegiate debater, it needs to be described in meaningful ways. The pollster whose study reveals that Senator Chang is credible or not credible does not tell very much about the substance of credibility. Furthermore, an individual opinion about a speaker's truthfulness also indicates very little.

The Nature of Credibility

To formulate a meaningful definition of credibility, it is necessary to understand that there are different kinds of credibility; this chapter will identify and discuss these types of credibility in the first section. And for the definition of credibility to be meaningful, it also needs to focus on the sources or characteristics of credibility. *This chapter defines credibility as the condition of possessing a sufficient quantity of certain specific characteristics so as to merit belief.* In other words, credibility can be described in terms of other subsidiary qualities. In the remaining sections of this chapter the qualities of credible evidence and how they might be used as guides to building credibility and to testing credibility will be the major focus.

Kinds of Credibility

Credibility can be classified according to the particular source being discussed. For example, you can evaluate the credibility of the speakers, their arguments, or their supporting materials. This chapter, therefore, identifies three kinds of credibility: (1) the credibility of arguers, (2) the credibility of arguments, and (3) the credibility of evidence. Although the credibility of the arguer is in part dependent upon the credibility of his or her ideas and his or her supporting materials, there nevertheless are several significant and independent considerations associated with each. Since the evaluation of each of these sources involves different and important considerations, each is treated separately.

The Credibility of Arguers

The credibility of arguers deals with how general audiences make decisions about whether a particular speaker should be believed. Such audiences are often influenced by factors that are seemingly unrelated to the content of the speaker's messages.

Twenty-three centuries ago Aristotle identified a speaker's *ethos* as an important source of persuasion. Aristotle categorized ethos as one of the kinds of artistic proofs that are invented by the speaker himself. Ethos may be defined as the special relationship or rapport that a speaker establishes with an

Chapter Outline

audience as a person of character, intelligence, and good will. The sources of ethos include both the prior knowledge that an audience has about a speaker and what the speaker says in the message.[1] Public advocates are frequently reminded by audiences that significant incidents in their past continue to affect their credibility.

More recent research, including numerous experimental studies, has identified six major sources of personal credibility: attraction, competence, delivery and organization, similarity, sincerity, and trustworthiness. Examination of each of these sources provides some insights into the kinds of speakers that audiences perceive as credible.

First, *attraction* or *source attractiveness* is an important factor. Pace, Boren, and Peterson note that attractiveness is difficult to define: "Source attractiveness, like other complex concepts, has several dimensions, perhaps some that have not been identified."[2] However, research has shown that physical appearance can be a significant factor in influencing attitudes. Mills and Aronson showed that communicators who are attractive in their personal appearances are much more effective in influencing attitudes than unattractive communicators.[3] However, many factors can cause attraction, including familiarity, similarity (discussed below), and liking.[4] Speakers should be aware that not all audiences will find the same factors attractive.

Second, *competence* is defined as perceived knowledge of the subject matter. The concept of competence is similar to Aristotle's idea of intelligence as a factor in ethos. Although actual knowledge of the topic and intelligence can contribute to competence, listeners may decide that a speaker is competent even if s/he only seems to know what s/he is speaking about.[5] Speakers can do a number of things to enhance their competence—such as citing high ethos sources in persuasive messages. However, high ethos sources are not persuasive in all circumstances.[6] If a speaker can determine which attributes will enhance his or her perceived competence in a particular situation, then s/he should consider developing those attributes. Such attributes can be important since research has shown that competence may be the most important factor in ethos and that ethos may be the most important factor in influencing attitudes and behaviors.[7]

Third, *effective delivery and organization* can also contribute to a speaker's credibility. In a study of disorganization and noninfluencies (vocalized pauses and repetitions) McCroskey and Mehrley discovered that well-organized and fluent speeches were significantly more effective in influencing attitude change. They also found that the use of sources was perceived as more authoritative in such speeches.[8] Although there is some conflicting research on the effectiveness of organization and a fluent delivery, most studies tend to support that they contribute positively to personal credibility.[9]

Fourth, *similarity of attitudes* or other characteristics between a speaker and the audience can also enhance credibility. Kenneth Burke asserted this principle when he declared: "You persuade a man only insofar as you can talk his language by speech, gesture, tonality, order, image, attitude, idea, *identifying* your way with his."[10] Empirical research has shown that similarity can be an even more important factor than expertise.[11] This finding would seem to indicate that even the most knowledgeable speaker should attempt to identify with the audience and demonstrate significant areas of similarity.

Fifth, *sincerity* is an effective factor in credibility when perceived by audiences as a speaker characteristic. Previous research has shown that sincerity is a highly regarded trait both in interpersonal and public speaking situations.[12] Sincerity can be more important than similarity, at least in some cases. For example, *Time* observed that Ralph Nader, who wore his hair short and dressed very conservatively, was very popular with very dissimilar college students of the early 1970s because he was perceived as sincere.[13] However, there is no evidence to suggest that most audiences can judge between real and apparent sincerity.

Sixth, the final factor of credibility is *trustworthiness.* Listeners tend to judge speakers as trustworthy if they are truthful, fair, and impartial. Much research on trustworthiness indicates a variety of factors that might be perceived as trustworthiness.[14] If speakers have no apparent self-interest or if speakers argue in apparent opposition to their own self-interest, they will be perceived as worthy of trust. In a study of messages from a convicted criminal, researchers showed that even a low-ethos source could be viewed as highly credible because he was speaking against his apparent self-interest.[15] This would seemingly suggest that speakers may enhance their credibility by indicating that they are not advancing their own interests in their attempts to persuade audiences.

As the above discussion suggests, these factors can individually or together enhance the credibility of speakers with general audiences in significant ways, even if they are not relevant to the actual truthfulness of the messages. This discussion, however, is not meant to suggest that arguers can or should use these factors instead of rational appeals. Rather we suggest that the arguer must understand that being truthful, logical, using good evidence, and other rational appeals is not always enough to persuade general audiences.

The Credibility of Arguments

General audiences often make judgments about the credibility of arguments as well as about arguers. How do they decide if an argument is credible? Aristotle said, "A statement is persuasive and credible either because it is directly self-evident or because it appears to be proved from other statements that are so." What, then, is a self-evident statement? Aristotle answers, "In either case it is persuasive because there is somebody who it persuades."[16] In other words, the audience determines whether or not a statement is self-evident.

When audiences make a decision about whether a statement is self-evident, usually they will automatically accept the statement without giving much thought to the need to verify its truth. When audiences accept statements without much thought, they will usually do so for one of several reasons. First, audiences tend to accept what is consistent with their own experience as self-evident. This is probably the reason that identification with audience experiences, discussed by Burke, is very effective. This is also probably a reason why audiences are more easily persuaded by speakers who have first-hand knowledge of a subject.[17]

Second, audiences tend to accept statements that are consistent with their values. This idea is related to the concept of similarity discussed above. Thus, identification on the level of values will probably also be effective with such audiences.

Finally, when audiences view a statement as indisputable they will tend to accept it automatically. Such statements may be facts or what the audience perceives to be factual. When audiences must supply reasons before accepting statements as self-evident, they will usually supply a self-evident type of statement.

The general audience will often not demand evidence for claims, especially if the statements are seemingly self-evident or can easily be linked to such statements. Sometimes, as discussed above, audiences will perceive the speaker as credible and will accept his or her statements based on the personal credibility of the speaker. However, other audiences, such as highly educated audiences or specialized listeners such as debate judges and critics, will demand that statements be well supported.

The Credibility of Evidence

Although audiences do not always demand evidence from an advocate before they accept his or her claims, they should. Further, although speakers do not always offer evidence for the claims they assert, they should. As discussed in previous chapters, evidence is crucial to the support of arguments and rational decision making. The advocate also has an ethical obligation to offer support for his or her claims.

Advocates should not offer just any evidence and audiences should not accept just any evidence to verify a claim. The evidence must be credible. The remainder of this chapter examines the specific characteristics of credible evidence, and these characteristics are examined as general tests of evidence. (This chapter will also discuss specific tests of evidence.) In order to use many of these tests of evidence, the advocate will need to be able to find substantial information about the writers and researchers they will be attempting to evaluate. Intercollegiate debaters will find it helpful to become familiar with the many reference books in their libraries that provide information about current writers and researchers. For examples, publications such as *Current Biography, Who's Who,* and *Directory of American Scholars* will often be very useful in discovering background information about sources. In addition, book reviews will often provide substantial information about the author, especially if the book being reviewed is a first or first major work.

General Tests of Evidence

When advocates search for evidence to support a claim or when they look for possible flaws in the evidence offered by their opponents, they might choose to evaluate it in terms of the *characteristics of credibility* or the general tests of evidence. These general tests of evidence are examined in the following categories: (1) environmental factors, (2) perceptual characteristics, and (3) characteristics of testimony.

Environmental Factors

The environment in which evidence is both gathered and used is crucial to its credibility. Newman and Newman note that "The situation in which evidence is generated is certainly one dimension on which it may be evaluated."[18] However, this text suggests that the environment in which evidence is used should also be examined. This analysis suggests that at least three environmental characteristics should be examined: (1) stress, (2) access, and (3) freedom to report.[19]

Stress

When evidence is gathered in stressful situations or is used by advocates in stressful situations, it is possible that the stress will be so great that there will be either unintentional or intentional distortion. Newman and Newman call this principle the tension test: "In general, *the lower the tension associated with an event, the higher the credibility of reports about that event.*"[20]

We do not suggest that all researchers and advocates using evidence in all high tension situations distort. However, in general, the higher the stress of a situation, then the higher the risk of distortion. For example, both hot and cold wars often generate propaganda which by definition is information with minimal credibility. Of course, certain individuals may abuse evidence at relatively low levels of stress. Advocates should, therefore, raise this question about evidence: Was there sufficient stress present when the evidence was gathered or reported to cause distortion?

Access

When evidence is gathered in situations in which the access is significantly restricted to either the researcher or the general public, then the credibility of the evidence, based on the knowledge of the situation, is unknown. Newman and Newman see the lack of access as somewhat more important. They state: *"The more accessible the situation being reported on, both to the reporters and to the consumers of reports, the more credible the reports."*[21]

We do not suggest that limited access necessarily means low credibility, but it does mean that a judgment that the evidence is credible cannot be made based on the situation. However, there may be other reasons for finding the evidence either credible or incredible such as those discussed later in this chapter. For example, during the Watergate crisis President Nixon claimed that there was nothing incriminating on the White House tapes prior to releasing them. Since at that time there was no access to the tapes, there was no way to make a judgment about the credibility of that statement unless Nixon's credibility was evaluated in terms of other factors, such as his past history of truth telling. Advocates should, therefore, raise this question about evidence: Did the source's or the public's access to the situation make the evidence less credible?

Freedom to Report

When there is either a formal or informal restraint on telling the truth, then that restraint significantly and adversely affects the credibility. Newman and Newman state the principle slightly differently: *"The more freedom a witness has to report things as he sees them, the greater his credibility."*[22]

We suggest that there are two kinds of possible restraints on the freedom to report. First, formal restraints or formal gag orders that carry the force of explicit institutional policy or even the force of law can limit freedom to report. For example, if a chemical company is accused of polluting, the company may have a policy that only the designated spokesperson should make any statements to the press. Or, a judge may impose gag orders on the participants in a trial not to make public statements until a certain time.

A second kind of restraint is an informal gag rule, which operates only in certain environments. This kind of gag rule is an implicit understanding that subordinates should not dissent from company policy as stated by the boss, and this kind of restraint will vary in importance with the personality of the boss. Advocates should, therefore, raise this question about evidence: Did either formal or informal gag rules significantly limit the source's credibility?

Perceptual Characteristics

Perceptual characteristics make up another major category of tests of evidence. The credibility of evidence, especially of interpretations and judgments, is often dependent upon the quality of the perception of the authority. Indeed, the perceptual characteristics of evidence may be the most important tests of evidence. This section examines three major perceptual factors: (1) proximity, (2) accuracy, and (3) stance.

Proximity

When there is great distance, in terms of either time or place, between a source and the subject, then there is a significant risk of low credibility. The issue of proximity or nearness of the source to the subject matter has at least three possible dimensions.

First, a source may be an eyewitness. The use of eyewitness testimony poses a dilemma. Noted legal scholar Elizabeth Loftus explains: "Whether we are concerned with the identification of persons or the accurate recounting of the details of an event, there can be problems posed by evidence of eyewitness testimony. The problem can be stated rather simply: on the one hand, eyewitness testimony is very believable and can wield considerable influence over the decisions reached by a jury; on the other hand, eyewitness testimony is not always reliable."[23]

Although being an eyewitness by no means guarantees high credibility, at least eyewitness reports about an event do not rely on the perception of another. From this standpoint, there is less filtering of the information and thereby less risk of perceptual distortion due to filtering. On the other hand, eyewitnesses are probably exposed to greater stress. Being an eyewitness, therefore, may actually be a negative factor. Eyewitness testimony is also subject to other problems that are discussed below.

Second, a source may be contemporary with the event being reported upon. Newman and Newman state this principle: *"The more contemporaneous the report of a witness, the more credible his testimony."*[24] Writers, even if they are not eyewitnesses to events, are more likely to be accurate reporters if they are contemporaneous to an event. They will understand the environment and they will probably have access to a large number of eyewitnesses. At a later point in history such an understanding and choice of eyewitnesses will not necessarily be available.

Third, a source can also be evaluated by his or her choice of other sources. At least two questions are related to this kind of evaluation: (a) Are the sources used primary or secondary? Newman and Newman state: *"The more discerning a writer's selection of primary sources, the more credible his testimony."*[25] Primary sources are usually viewed as better sources because of the reasons discussed above. There is less filtering and there is a greater probability of material being based on either eyewitness or contemporaneous accounts. (b) What is the quality of the sources used? For example, the quality of the sources might be assessed by applying the general tests of evidence discussed in this chapter, and advocates should therefore raise these questions:

Was the source's proximity to the situation detrimental to the credibility? If the source was an eyewitness, did being an eyewitness benefit or hurt the credibility of the report? If the source was contemporaneous with the event being reported upon, did that status benefit the credibility of the report? Was the source's selection of sources beneficial or detrimental to the credibility of the report?

Accuracy

Accuracy is a major and complex issue in finding credible evidence. Several factors are used in determining accuracy.

Citation. First, is the evidence accurately cited? Newman and Newman state: *"The more accurate the citations of a writer, the more credible his testimony."*[26] As we have discussed, there are a variety of ways in which the context might be distorted. For example, if a college debater were to quote a position that was being summarized or even attacked by a source as if the source were advocating that position, that would be a significant misrepresentation of the context of the evidence. Other methods of inaccurate citation would be deleting, adding, or altering words. Sometimes in using ellipses or in integrating quoted material into other materials, such as might be done in an argumentative essay or in a manuscript speech, words might be deleted, added or altered for legitimate reasons without changing the meaning. However, this must be carefully done so that the reader or audience knows what is being quoted directly. Intercollegiate debaters who desire to do this should seek assistance from their coaches. Advocates should, therefore, raise this question about evidence: Are there any inaccuracies in the citation of the evidence that damage its credibility?

Accuracy Record. A major way of judging the credibility of a source is to assess the past history of that source's truthfulness. Newman and Newman explain: *"The more accurate the description and prediction record of a source, the higher the credibility of his testimony."*[27] Intercollegiate debaters will, of course, avoid notoriously inaccurate sources. However, all advocates should be aware of the accuracy record of all their sources, and should raise this question about evidence: Does the accuracy record of the source indicate any problems in credibility?

Training. A major way of assessing the credibility of a source is to evaluate the source's education, training, or equivalent experience such as experience in the field. Newman and Newman use the concept of expertise: *"The greater the relevant expertise of an author, the higher his credibility."*[28] The advocate testing the source should ask such questions as these: What kind of training does the source have? What kind of training does the source need to make the claim being asserted?

Training is often relevant to testing the reliability of eyewitness testimony. Eyewitness observation is subject to many factors, including accuracy of perception and stress. John Kaplan explained some of the factors affecting eyewitness evidence in criminal cases: "Of course the reliability of eyewitness accounts is affected by many variables—stress, cross-racial aspects of identification, and the effect of intervening observations and events."[29] To a certain extent, training may make eyewitness testimony more reliable. For example, a general's observation of a battle would most likely be more reliable than that of a civilian because the general knows what to observe and can handle the stress of a military conflict more effectively. Advocates should, therefore, raise this question about evidence: Does the source have sufficient training or equivalent experience to make a credible report?

Stance

A very important issue in the credibility of evidence is the stance or perspective of the source. A source may be objective, biased, or reluctant in offering testimony.

Objectivity. To be objective towards a topic means to have no vested interest in a particular resolution. Objectivity does not mean that a source is uninterested in the subject matter; the objective writer is interested in a subject because of the merits of the subject matter. Complete objectivity is almost never achieved, and some bias towards a position does not necessarily indicate that the source should not be trusted. For example, a very good source may be biased towards a certain solution to a problem because it is the best solution. Nevertheless, advocates should raise this question about evidence: Does the source have sufficient objectivity to make a credible report?

Objectivity is often difficult to discern. Often the most effective way to find objectivity is to search for bias. Thus, understanding bias is a key to finding objectivity.

Bias. As suggested above, bias is not necessarily a disqualifying characteristic. Bias should be a serious concern when it is so great that it adversely affects the perception of the source. One method of identifying bias is to examine the quality of the writing, discussed below.

To understand the nature of a disqualifying bias, the researcher should attempt to identify possible reasons for bias. Such bias is usually the product of either economic or ideological motivation. If a speaker has an economic stake in advocating a certain position, then the credibility of his or her testimony should be doubted. For example, if a new General Motors car is criticized as being unsafe, the General Motors spokesperson will probably defend the car. Needless to say, such claims are not very credible because of the economic interest of the speaker.

Ideology can have a serious adverse impact upon the credibility of evidence. Ideologies can be defined as systems of beliefs. The kinds of ideologies that pose the greatest threat to credible reporting are those that attract a certain kind of intensely dedicated follower. Such followers are so intensely dedicated that their perception becomes distorted or they willfully distort their statements in a misguided effort to serve their particular causes. Newman and Newman write: "Ideologies are the most potent of the many factors which distort perception."[30] Ideologies are sometimes revealed by the author's affiliation with extremist groups or by the use of loaded language. Advocates should, therefore, raise this question about evidence: Does the source have sufficient bias to damage the credibility of his or her reports?

Reluctance. The third possible stance is reluctance. Newman and Newman state the reluctance principle: *"The greater the damage of his own testimony to a witness, the more credible it is."*[31] This principle suggests that when a witness testifies against his or her own interest the testimony is true. It is clear that such evidence is very persuasive. Walster, Aronson, and Abrahams showed in the previously cited study of testimony from convicted criminals that such testimony was persuasive because it was reluctant.

However, we suggest that such evidence should be viewed more cautiously. Such evidence probably is true, but the reluctant witness may not be making a complete disclosure. For example, if the Secretary of Defense testifies before a congressional committee and admits that the defense budget could be cut by $5 billion, this statement probably should be viewed as true. However, it may be that the Secretary has failed to disclose that the budget could be cut by as much as $20 billion. Advocates should, therefore, raise these questions about evidence: Does any reluctance in the stance of the source enhance his or her credibility? If his or her credibility is enhanced, to what extent should the source be believed?

The advocate using evidence should be sensitive to all of these characteristics of perception—proximity, accuracy, and stance—in order to be able to identify the most credible evidence.

Characteristics of the Testimony

Another way of evaluating credibility is to examine the nature of the statements that writers make. In particular, this section focuses upon three characteristics: (1) authenticity, (2) consistency, and (3) quality of the writing.

Authenticity

Authentic testimony is of course evidence that is actually of the supposed author or origin. Evidence that is not authentic is fabricated or fake. Obviously, evidence that is not authentic has no credibility. Newman and Newman apply this concept only to documents, but we suggest that it also applies to other kinds of materials.[32] For example, several years ago the *National Enquirer* published on the front cover a picture of Raquel Welch and Freddie

Prinz, along with a caption suggesting a special relationship. The CBS program *60 Minutes* then exposed the photograph as a fake, further damaging the credibility of the infamous publication. When an intercollegiate debater fabricates evidence, he or she also risks permanently losing his or her credibility.

However, it is often difficult to detect evidence that is not authentic. Newman and Newman suggest that the presumption of authenticity is what should be examined. They state: *"The greater the presumption of authenticity, the higher the credibility of a document."*[33] Thus, advocates should be cautious about any evidence that seems to lack authenticity, and should raise this question about evidence: Are there any indications that the source's statements are inauthentic and thereby incredible?

Consistency

When an advocate is inconsistent, his or her credibility may be seriously damaged. Others apply the concept of consistency only to documents, but consistency is also important in other situations.

Audiences and debate judges expect advocates to be consistent in most situations. Of course, advocates may change their minds on important issues over time. However, within an individual argumentative essay or speech and even within a relatively short period of time on the same topic, consistency is expected. When advocates are not consistent, their credibility is seriously challenged. The expectation of credibility may even extend to public advocates who join together for a common cause. For example, during the 1984 presidential campaign President Reagan and Vice-President Bush took different positions on whether taxes might be raised in the next term. This inconsistency caused problems for the Reagan–Bush campaign until it was resolved. When two students debate together as a team, they are also expected to be consistent. Although there are exceptions to any principle, including this one, researchers, writers, and advocates are generally expected to be consistent. Advocates should, therefore, raise these questions about evidence: What is the expectation of consistency for the source in the particular situation? Does any inconsistency damage the source's credibility?

Quality of Writing

Examination of the quality of the writing of evidence might provide some clues to the credibility of the source. As indicated above, the quality of the writing may indicate the presence of serious bias. Extreme positions may reveal themselves in a writer's word choice, especially in the author's conclusions. Newman and Newman state: *"The more careful the generalizations of a witness, the higher the credibility of his testimony."*[34] However, we suggest that the researcher should examine all aspects of the writing for indications of problems in the source's credibility. As suggested above, examination of loaded language might also indicate an ideologically motivated bias. Newman and Newman provide several examples of how this kind of analysis might be done.[35] Advocates should, therefore, raise this question about evidence: Does the quality of the source's writing indicate any possible problems in his or her credibility?

In summary, the general tests of evidence include environmental factors, perceptual characteristics, and characteristics of testimony. These tests are important for all rational advocates and decision makers to use in determining the credibility of their own as well as their opponent's evidence. The intercollegiate debater should find these tests of evidence especially useful. The general tests of evidence may be less effective for general audiences, who often focus on those factors dealing with the credibility of the speaker and of the arguments.

The advocate who is committed to rational decision making should use these tests, even with general audiences, and should attempt to persuade audiences that these are important questions that must be resolved. The obligation to make this attempt is an ethical obligation for the rational advocate who realizes the importance of these issues.

Although evidence might not satisfactorily meet all of these tests of evidence, it might still be sufficiently credible to be valuable in a debate. The advocate who plans to use such evidence should carefully apply these tests to discover if any problems exist that could disqualify the evidence as uncredible.

General Tests of Evidence

1. Was there sufficient stress present when the evidence was gathered or reported to cause distortion?
2. Did the source's or the public's access to the situation make the evidence less credible?
3. Did either formal or informal gag rules significantly limit the source's credibility?
4. Was the author's proximity to the situation detrimental to the credibility?
   a. If the author was an eyewitness, did being an eyewitness benefit or hurt the credibility of the report?
   b. If the author was contemporaneous with the event being reported upon, did that status benefit the credibility of the report?
   c. Was the author's selection of sources beneficial or detrimental to the credibility of the report?

5. Are there any inaccuracies in the citation of the evidence that damage its credibility?
6. Does the accuracy record of the source indicate any problems in credibility?
7. Does the source have sufficient training or equivalent experience to make a credible report?
8. Does the source have sufficient objectivity to make a credible report?
9. Does the source have sufficient bias to damage the credibility of his or her reports?
   a. Is there an economically motivated bias that might damage the source's credibility?
   b. Is there an ideologically motivated bias that might damage the source's credibility?
10. Does any reluctance in the stance of the source enhance his or her credibility? If credibility is enhanced, to what extent should s/he be believed?
11. Are there any indications that the source's statements are inauthentic and thereby incredible?
12. What is the expectation of consistency for the source in the particular situation? Does any consistency damage the source's credibility?
13. Does the quality of the source's writing indicate any possible problems in his or her credibility?

Specific Tests of Evidence

The tests above can be used to evaluate almost all kinds of evidence. In addition to using these tests, the advocate should ask questions that are important in determining the credibility of certain kinds of evidence. This section examines these questions relating to the following areas: (1) facts, (2) inferences, and (3) statistics and methodologies.

Facts

As discussed in Chapter Six, facts are indisputable descriptions of events, objects, persons, places, or other concrete and empirically verifiable phenomena. The tests of a fact, therefore, deal with whether or not it meets the characteristics specified in the definition. An advocate testing an asserted fact asks: Is the asserted fact a genuine fact?

1. The testing of the genuine nature of a fact can be accomplished by answering the following questions. Is the asserted fact truly indisputable? Or is there substantial and serious argument over the claim? For example, the statement that John F. Kennedy was president of the United States is not arguable and is factual. On the other hand, it would be improper to classify the statement that Kennedy was a good president as factual because it is a disputable claim.

2. Is the fact empirically verifiable? Or is the fact a matter of interpretation or judgment? For example, the claim that a certain number of casualties occurred in a specific war may be empirically verifiable. However, the claim that the war was caused by a certain series of events probably could not be empirically verified. In this example, the first claim might be a fact but the second claim could never be so classified.

3. Can the asserted fact be verified by numerous observations and observers? If a claim can be checked only by one or a few persons in either one or a few situations, it probably is not a fact. For example, numerous reporters could verify the events of the Vietnam War because of their almost unlimited access. On the other hand, relatively few individuals could verify the operations of U.S. forces in the Reagan administration's 1983 invasion of Grenada because there was almost no press access to the actual battlefield events.

4. Is the asserted fact consistent with other known facts? Some asserted facts should be doubted because they are contradicted by a large body of other facts. For example, if Mrs. Garcia claims that laetrile cured her cancer and all other factual evidence indicates that laetrile cannot cure cancer, then Mrs. Garcia's claim cannot be considered factual.

5. Is the asserted fact completely reported? Sometimes a full disclosure of information about an event is necessary to classify it properly. For example, if Mrs. Garcia was also receiving chemotherapy for cancer, then that information would also need to be supplied to have sufficient information to verify any claim about her alleged cancer cure.

By attempting to answer these questions, the advocate can determine whether or not a claim can be properly identified as factual.

Inferences

Inferences, as previously defined, are descriptive statements of events, objects, persons, places or other concrete and empirically verifiable phenomena. Inferences are gained by reasoning from something known or assumed. We previously identified four kinds of inferences: (1) trait, (2) relational, (3) historical, and (4) future or predictive. Inferences might be tested by asking questions dealing with each kind of inference.

1. Trait inferences might be tested by asking the following question. Is there substantial evidence that the trait is present? For example, to test the in-

ference that Ronald Reagan is a good president it would be necessary to ask if there are sufficiently numerous indications of his accomplishments. Depending on the wording of the trait inference other questions might need to be posed, but the major question deals with the sufficiency of evidence for the inference.

2. Relational inferences should be tested by asking questions that focus upon the verifiability of the relationship, which is usually a causal relationship. Thus, the questions that should be posed are those that test causal reasoning, such as those discussed in Chapter Five. Example: When the asserted cause is present, is the asserted effect also present? When the asserted cause is absent, is the asserted effect also absent? Does a variation in the asserted cause also produce a variation in the asserted effect? Are there any other possible causes that might also produce the effect?

3. Historical inferences are often either trait or relational inferences. Therefore, the questions above often test historical inferences also. In addition, questions might also be posed about the accuracy of the historical sources that are available. For example, if a source claims that the issue that started the war between the states was slavery, the source might be questioned as follows: Did the source understand the historical milieu of that period? Was the source influenced by attitudes and values of a different period of history? Was the source possibly influenced by his or her own attitudes and values?

4. Predictive inferences are also usually trait or relational inferences. Therefore, the questions above can test such inferences. In addition, questions might be posed about the ability of the source to predict the future. For example: What is the basis for prediction? Did a recurrent pattern exist in the past that is likely to be repeated in the future? Or, are there other equally possible but mutually exclusive events that might occur?

Testing inferences is more complex since there are many possible wordings. Thus, additional questions to test a specific inference might arise from its wording. The advocate who tests inferences will have to consider each individual claim very carefully.

Statistics and Methodologies

Chapter Six defined statistics as empirically quantified descriptions. As such, statistics often make comparisons or show relationships. Audiences are often impressed by statistical evidence and many general audiences tend to look upon statistical evidence as factual. However, statistics often involve important interpretations and judgments and in reality might be quite subjective.

Statistics are often used in and produced by scientific studies, and a related aspect of scientific studies and statistics is *methodology.* Methodologies are the sets of steps or procedures that studies use to examine and process data. Methodologies may specify the kinds of statistical processes that will be used.

Advocates using or evaluating statistics or methodologies need to understand the basic issues that surrounded the generation of the information. The following questions raise some of these basic issues and can also be used to test the soundness of statistics and methodologies.

1. Was the source committed to an objective scientific study? This is the same perceptual question raised above by the question of stance, but here the situation is clearly either/or: Is the source objective or biased? Does the source seem to be interested in a certain outcome? For example, if a scientist is studying the health hazards of cigarette smoking and the research is funded by tobacco companies, there is substantial risk that the researcher will be interested in an outcome that minimizes the harms of smoking. Studies that are not committed to objective inquiry are of course not credible.

2. Are the key concepts or terms accurately defined? Often researchers will deal with very subjective concepts. For example, if statisticians are studying poverty, the fundamental concept of poverty must be defined. If the study uses a standard definition that has been used by numerous other studies or by government agencies, then there may be no cause for concern. On the other hand, if the study uses an unusual definition without a sound justification, then that might be a sign that the source was not committed to an objective study.

3. Are units that are being compared really comparable? As suggested previously, statistics are often used to show comparisons. For example, if statistics are used to show differences in foreign aid from one time period to another, the question of comparability can be significant. If the amount of expenditures is expressed in dollars, then the amount should be expressed in dollars adjusted for inflation; otherwise, the amounts of expenditures might not be comparable.

4. Are the statistics or methods completely explained? Often statistics and studies will be cited without sufficient explanation. For example, advertisers will cite such statistical recommendations as "4 out of 5 experts recommend" their product, but they will not indicate the size of the sample surveyed. Or, an intercollegiate debater may name the methodology of a study without explaining what that methodology actually does. Without an explanation the study may not be meaningful to any of the participants, including the audience or the judge. Often the starting point of effective refutation can be a simple challenge to explain the statistics or the methodology. However, it will not be sufficient simply to ask the question. The advocate will need to explain why it is necessary to have the requested information.

5. Are statistics from different bases mixed together? Advocates will sometimes attempt to take data from one study and combine it with informa-

tion from another study. This kind of mixing of statistics usually results in misleading conclusions. For example, if an advocate uses a definition of poverty from one study and a statistic on the extent of poverty from another, the result might be completely inaccurate. Only if the two studies are based on the same definitions and have other important similarities can there be any combining of the data. In general, such combination of statistics should be avoided.

6. Are the statistics gathered over a sufficient period of time? Often writers will attempt to use statistics to indicate a trend. For example, if an author is discussing unemployment, then a significant rise in unemployment might be claimed. However, the advocate who desires either to use this evidence or to refute it, might pose such questions as the following: How long has unemployment been increasing? Is the period of time over which there has been an increase long enough to constitute a trend? If not, what period of time would be sufficient to constitute a trend? Without the answers to questions such as these, it will be difficult for an advocate to defend such statistics. On the other hand, raising challenges such as these can be part of an effective refutation of the author's argument.

7. Is the sample size sufficient? Most studies will focus upon a certain population, but samples of that population are selected because it is either impossible or undesirable to study the entire population. The advocate should carefully read the discussion of the sample size in the original study. Most studies should specify the size of the sample and provide criteria for judging whether the size is sufficient to make generalizations. This is a fairly basic methodological question and unless the issue of sample size is properly handled, most reputable journals will not publish the study. If there is no information provided on sample size, the advocate should be very cautious. If the advocate doubts that the study is correct in its claim of adequacy, s/he will need to have a detailed understanding of statistics and methodologies to judge the adequacy of the sample size.

8. Is the sample representative of the population? Most studies will also explain the method of choosing the sample, and it should be clear how the sample is representative of a certain population. Again, if the study does not explain how the sample was selected, the advocate should be very cautious. For example, many social science studies performed on college campuses use students as sample populations. Yet, depending on the study and subject matter, college students may not be representative of the general population. Many studies attempt to use random samples. If this is the case, the advocate examining the study should try to determine if the subjects have actually been randomly selected. Questions concerning samples and how they are chosen can become complicated; a student may need to learn much more about sampling and the design of studies simply to know what questions to

ask. However, it is almost always relevant to ask about the representativeness of the sample.

9. Are the statistics or the concepts being studied really an index to what the researchers or the advocates want to know? Sometimes researchers cannot study directly what they desire to know about. For example, if researchers want to study voting behavior, they cannot enter the voting booth. They may study instead the voting intentions prior to the election or reports about voting behavior after the election. However, if the statistics do not measure what the researcher or the advocate wants to know, then the study no matter how well executed otherwise is irrelevant. Raising this kind of question can often be very effective in refuting a study.

10. Are the results of the study externally valid? External validity means that the results of the study can be generalized to the population being studied. For example, one kind of threat to external validity is an unrepresentative sample. A special kind of problem with samples and external validity is known as *subject effects,* which result when subjects for a study are poorly selected. For example, if subjects are eager to please the researcher, then there is an adverse subject effect. Advocates should examine studies carefully for other kinds of threats to the external validity. A lack of external validity can mean that the conclusions of a study, perhaps effectively executed otherwise, have no application beyond the group being examined.[36]

11. Are there any threats to the internal validity of the study? Internal validity means that the researcher can be sure that the change in the dependent variable was the result of the experimental change in the independent variable. For example, if a researcher is studying the effect of public service announcements on students' perceptions of drunk driving (the independent variable), then she wants to be sure that any attitude changes in the students (the dependent variables) who view these announcements are the results only of the announcements.

Two types of problems can damage internal validity—experiment effects and experimenter effects. Experiment effects occur when the experiment is poorly set up or conducted. For example, if the researcher poorly designs a questionnaire on voting attitudes so that its biases lead the subjects to give certain responses, then there is an adverse experiment effect. Experimenter effects result when the experimenter influences the outcome of the study. For example, an experimenter's attractiveness or nonverbal behavior during a study may distract or influence a subject's choices. Threats to internal validity mean that the relationship under study cannot be properly examined and this can make the entire study incredible.[37]

12. Is the measuring device or the study reliable overall? For example, if a chemical analysis (measuring device) is designed to measure the amount of pollution in drinking water, then it should produce the same results every

time it is used to test the same water supply. If it does, then the measuring device is reliable. Also, if a study can be repeated or replicated under similar conditions and produce similar results, then the study is reliable overall. If a measuring device is not reliable, then the internal validity of the study is in danger. And if the study overall is not reliable, then the credibility of the study's conclusions is not very high.

These are only a few of the questions that might be used to evaluate statistics and the methodologies of studies. If the advocates are very knowledgeable, they might pose even more difficult questions. For example, if two social scientists are debating the merits of a particular study, one might raise the question of whether a particular methodology was appropriate for the study. However, questions involving such sophisticated considerations will rarely be raised in a public debate and probably will not be raised in very many intercollegiate debates.

Tests of Statistics and Methodologies

1. Was the source committed to an objective scientific study?
2. Are the key concepts or terms accurately defined?
3. Are units that are being compared really comparable?
4. Are the statistics or methods completely explained?
5. Are statistics from different bases mixed together?
6. Are the statistics gathered over a sufficient period of time?
7. Is the sample size sufficient?
8. Is the sample representative of the population?
9. Are the statistics or the concepts being studied really an index to what the researchers or the advocates want to know?
10. Are the results of the study externally valid?
11. Are there any threats to the internal validity of the study?
12. Is the measuring device or the study reliable overall?

Summary

This chapter defines credibility as the condition of possessing a sufficient quantity of certain specific characteristics so as to merit belief. There are three kinds of credibility: (1) the credibility of arguers, (2) the credibility of arguments, and (3) the credibility of evidence. Aristotle identified ethos as crucial to the credibility of arguers. More recent research, including numerous experimental studies, has identified six major sources of personal credibility: attraction, competence, delivery and organization, similarity, sincerity and trustworthiness.

Arguments also may have credibility with audiences, especially if the audiences identify the arguments as self-evident statements. Audiences tend to identify personal experiences and statements that are consistent with their own values as very persuasive.

The credibility of evidence is very important to highly educated audiences, to rational decision makers, and to students and judges involved in intercollegiate debate. Debaters will need to know how to find information about the researchers and writers of evidence in order to be effective in testing evidence.

The general tests of evidence fall into three major categories: (1) environmental factors, (2) perceptual characteristics, and (3) characteristics of testimony. Environmental factors include Newman and Newman's issues of stress, access, and freedom to report.

Perceptual characteristics include the issues of proximity, accuracy, and stance. Proximity deals with primary and secondary sources, eyewitness testimony, and whether or not a writer is reporting upon contemporary events. Accuracy is a major consideration and includes such factors as the accuracy of the citation of evidence, the accuracy record of the source, and the researcher's or writer's training and qualifications. The stance of a source may be either objective, biased, or reluctant. Advocates need to understand the sources and the degrees of biases in order to determine whether or not a source is too biased to be credible.

Characteristics of testimony include authenticity, consistency, and the quality of the writing. These characteristics can also be very important in determining the credibility of evidence.

Finally, this chapter examined the specific tests of certain kinds of evidence, including (1) facts, (2) inferences, and (3) statistics and methodologies.

Notes

1. See Lester Thonssen, A. Craig Baird, and Waldo W. Braden, *Speech Criticism,* 2nd ed. (New York: Ronald Press, 1970), pp. 65, 434–36, 458–60.
2. R. Wayne Pace, Robert R. Boren, and Brent D. Peterson, *Communication Behavior and Experiments: A Scientific Approach* (Belmont, CA: Wadsworth, 1975), p. 100.
3. Judson Mills and Elliot Aronson, "Opinion Change as a Function of the Communicator's Attractiveness and Desire to Influence," *Journal of Personality and Social Psychology,* 1 (1965): 173–77.

4. See Pace, Boren, and Peterson, pp. 100–101.
5. Jack L. Whitehead, Jr., "Factors of Source Credibility," *Quarterly Journal of Speech,* 54 (1968), p. 60.
6. See Pace, Boren, and Peterson, pp. 94–95.
7. See Douglas G. Bock and Thomas J. Saine, "The Impact of Source Credibility, Attitude Valence, and Task Sensitization on Trait Errors in Speech Evaluation," *Speech Monographs,* 42 (1975): 235; and Pace, Boren, and Peterson, p. 95.
8. James C. McCroskey and R. Samuel Mehrley, "The Effects of Disorganization and Nonfluency on Attitude Change and Source Credibility," *Speech Monographs,* 36 (March 1969): 13–21.
9. See Pace, Boren, and Peterson, pp. 96–97.
10. Kenneth Burke, *Rhetoric of Motives* (New York: Prentice–Hall, 1950), p. 55.
11. See Timothy C. Brock, "Communicator Recipient Similarity and Decision Change," *Journal of Personality and Social Psychology,* 1 (1965): 650–54.
12. See N. H. Anderson, "Likeableness Ratings of 555 Personality-Trait Words," *Journal of Personality and Social Psychology,* 9 (1968): 272–79; and W. K. Clark, "A Survey of Certain Audience Attitudes Toward Commonly Taught Standards of Public Speaking," *Speech Monographs,* XVIII (March 1951): 62–69.
13. *Time,* May 10, 1971, p. 18.
14. See Wayne N. Thompson, *Quantitative Research in Public Address and Communication,* (New York: Random House, 1967), pp. 54–59; and Pace, Boren, and Peterson, pp. 93–102.
15. Elaine Walster, Elliot Aronson, and Darcy Abrahams, "On Increasing the Persuasiveness of a Low Prestige Communicator," *Journal of Experimental Social Psychology,* 2 (1966): 325–42.
16. Aristotle, *Rhetoric,* trans. W. Rhys Roberts (New York: The Modern Library, 1954), p. 27.
17. See Terry Ostermeier, "Effects of Type and Frequency of Reference upon Perceived Source Credibility and Attitude Change," *Speech Monographs,* 34 (1967): 137–44.
18. Robert P. Newman and Dale R. Newman, *Evidence* (New York: Houghton Mifflin, 1969), p. 74.
19. These categories are based on Newman and Newman's situational tests of evidence with some modifications, pp. 74–76.
20. Newman and Newman, p. 74–75.
21. Ibid., p. 75.

22. Ibid., p. 76.
23. Elizabeth Loftus, *Eyewitness Testimony* (Cambridge, MA: Harvard University Press, 1979), pp. 6–7.
24. Newman and Newman, p. 84.
25. Ibid., p. 84.
26. Ibid., p. 85.
27. Ibid., p. 82.
28. Ibid., p. 80.
29. John Kaplan, "Foreword," in Loftus, *Eyewitness Testimony* (Cambridge, MA: Harvard University Press, 1979), p. vii.
30. Newman and Newman, p. 60.
31. Ibid., p. 79.
32. Ibid., p. 77.
33. Ibid., p. 77.
34. Ibid., p. 78.
35. Ibid., pp. 78–79.
36. See Dale Leathers, *Orientations to Researching Communication* (Chicago: Science Research Associates, 1978), pp. 28, 31, 33.
37. Leathers, pp. 28, 31, 33.

Questions and Exercises

1. Attend a persuasive public speech on a controversial contemporary issue and analyze the credibility of the speaker according to:
   a. Aristotle's concept of ethos
   b. Any or all of the six factors of personal credibility
      1. attraction
      2. competence
      3. delivery and organization
      4. similarity
      5. sincerity
      6. trustworthiness
2. Find the text or transcript of a persuasive public speech on a controversial contemporary issue and analyze the credibility as indicated above in exercise #1. Do you feel that your analysis can be as accurate in examining the text as it would be if you viewed the speech? Why or why not? Explain in detail.
3. Find a magazine article in a magazine with a clear bias (for example, *Nation, New Republic,* or *National Review*) on a contemporary controversial issue in which the author takes a clear position. Analyze the credi-

bility of the arguments as discussed in this chapter from your own point of view. What statements does the author make that you tend to accept without very much consideration? What kinds of statements are these? Facts? Personal Experiences? Statements that agree with your values? When you disagree with a statement made in the article, is the statement either inconsistent with your personal experience or contrary to your values?

4. Using several evidence cards prepared for an argumentative speech or a debate, examine the information provided about the sources carefully. List as many questions as you can think of that need to be answered to defend the credibility of the source or the statements made by the source. How many of these questions can you answer? How many questions would require additional research for you to answer? What kind of research would need to be done? Would you need to go back to the original article? Would you have to look up additional information about the author?
5. Do a complete credibility study of evidence prepared by another student. Use all the relevant categories and tests of evidence discussed in this chapter. Do additional research as necessary to verify the original context, accuracy of citation and to find additional information about the source. Indicate in your conclusion how credible the evidence is. For example, does the source have sufficient training to make the statement?
6. Idea for a term paper or class project: Do a credibility study of a major book or a newspaper's coverage of an event or issue over a period of time.

Suggested Readings

Wenzel, Joseph. "Ethical Proof: A Re-examination of Aristotelian Theory." *Argument in Transition: Proceedings of the Third Summer Conference on Argumentation,* edited by David Zarefsky, Malcolm Sillars, and Jack Rhodes. Annandale, VA: Speech Communication Association, 1983, pp. 43–53.

NINE

Building an Affirmative Case

What does it mean to be on the affirmative side in a debate? What does it mean for an advocate to affirm or defend a topic or proposition? The answers to such questions as these are the initial guides to building an affirmative case.

When a speaker affirms a proposition, he or she says "yes" to the question or inquiry implicit in the proposition. For example, if a student is on the affirmative side on the topic, *Resolved: That the United States should significantly increase its foreign military commitments,* then the student is answering "yes" to the question "Should the United States significantly increase its foreign military commitments?"

From one perspective, when an advocate defends a proposition, whether it is a policy or a non-policy claim, then he is also putting forth or advancing an idea. In so doing, he desires that an audience or a judge will believe that the idea is true based on his arguments. Thus, the advocate who defends the proposition usually has the burden of proof for defending that proposition.

Initial Considerations

The ways in which a speaker chooses to say "yes" and to advance ideas are the starting points for an affirmative case. *An affirmative case is defined as the organized collection of arguments that a particular advocate constructs to defend a specific proposition.* Advocates in public debates as well as in educational debates both do and should prepare cases in order to be effective. However, advocates involved in public controversies have much more flexibility both in the kinds of cases they construct and in changes that they might decide to make during a debate.

Advocates dealing with policy questions may advance or evaluate "plans." *A plan is defined as the outline of the specific changes in law and public policy that affirmative advocates are either recommending or evaluating.* For example, if debaters are defending a proposition of policy advocacy, they will construct an outline of the changes they desire to make in the laws and public policies. This outline will constitute the affirmative plan. On the other hand, if debaters are dealing with a question of policy evaluation, then they may choose to discuss the policy on the conceptual level without actually identifying or constructing a specific plan of action.

Building an affirmative case is also dependent upon the format of the debate. A public advocate may begin or join a debate at almost any point. Furthermore, she may begin with an incomplete case or she may modify her position as the debate progresses. In public argument it is common for policy proposals to emerge much later or to change during the controversy, which may last days, months or even years. On the other hand, students involved in educational debates are required to present a complete or *prima facie* case in the first speech. Moreover, in most traditional educational formats the debate will last no longer than one and two hours, and the affirmative speakers will both begin and end the debate.

This chapter will examine the major methods of building affirmative cases and plans for policy and non-policy debate resolutions. In particular, this

Chapter Outline

chapter will focus upon: (1) cases in policy debate, (2) cases in non-policy debate, (3) policy evaluation cases, (4) preparing the first affirmative speech and (5) the affirmative speaker's responsibilities.

Cases in Policy Debate

Case building should begin only after debaters have done substantial research and have a clear understanding of the issues. Advocates cannot effectively choose their case formats until they have the knowledge provided by research and the focus provided by an analysis of the issues.

This section will focus upon four basic kinds of affirmative cases: (1) the needs case, (2) the comparative advantage case, (3) the goal-criterion case, and (4) the alternative justification case. In addition, this section will examine the basic considerations in constructing an affirmative plan.

The Needs Case

The starting point of *the needs case* calls for the presence of a specific condition in the present policy system; this condition is a clear, compelling, and present need for a change in policy. There must be a significant "felt difficulty." Traditionally, needs cases focus upon significant amounts of human suffering. For example, if students analyze the nature of pollution in the United States, they might find evidence which indicates that existing levels of pollution create life-threatening conditions by causing various diseases, such as cancer. Such evidence and argumentation might provide the basis for the beginnings of a needs case. Thus, the significance issue in a needs case is usually one that can be developed as clear, compelling, concrete, and contemporaneous threats to human health and life.

For a needs case to be effective the present policy system must be ineffective. In other words, the debaters should be able to document that the present policy system no longer functions. Usually the needs case is not appropriate if the present system is simply inefficient or is failing to achieve some potential. In the pollution example, students would probably examine the effectiveness of the Environmental Protection Agency (EPA) as one of the relevant policy systems. If they found that the failures of the EPA constituted a complete failure of the system to function, then a needs case would probably be appropriate. The affirmative advocate would also be expected to demonstrate strong linkages between the failures of the EPA and the persistent inability of the present system to solve the harmful conditions documented in the significance issue. Thus, the inherency issue in a needs case is usually developed in an argument that the present system has failed to function.

In any policy debate case, the affirmative is required to demonstrate *solvency.* Solvency is sufficiently demonstrated when the advocate shows that his/her proposed course of action (the plan) can work and can produce the desirable effects or advantages. At one time in intercollegiate debate, especially in discussions of need cases, the term solvency was narrowly interpreted to mean total eradication of a problem. However, this interpretation was eventually viewed as unreasonable since few affirmative advocates could meet such a burden of proof for any affirmative plan. When affirmative debaters use the needs case format today, they are usually expected to demonstrate that a specific amount of the need will be solved by the proposed plan. For example, an advocate arguing about pollution will be expected to indicate the amount and kind of pollution that will be solved and the corresponding reductions in disease and deaths that will accrue due to the plan. The specific means of demonstrating solvency are discussed later in this chapter, in the section on the construction of affirmative plans.

In summary, there are three basic units in the needs case: (1) a clear, compelling, and present need, (2) present policy systems that have failed to function, and (3) solvency that is demonstrated in a specific amount or quantity. Importantly, these three units should be carefully linked together by the case: the evidence of need should be related directly to the failures in the present policy systems; the solvency should be based upon reforming or solving the failures of the policy systems; and the problems solved should be those identified in the need analysis. Finally, the presentation of the needs case is usually organized in terms of the issues presented above, and a simple outline might be as follows:

I. Need arguments
II. Arguments about present system failures
III. Plan outline
IV. Solvency arguments

If students are to debate the topic, *Resolved: That the federal government should implement a program that guarantees employment opportunities for all United States citizens in the labor force,* then a needs case might be outlined as follows:

I. Unemployment is a serious national problem.
   A. A large class of unemployed exists with special characteristics.
      1. This class has experienced long periods of unemployment.
      2. Their job skills are not relevant to the contemporary economy.
   B. Unemployment is a serious threat to the individual and to the nation.

1. Individual Harms
    a. stress related disease
    b. alcoholism
    c. mental illness and suicide
2. Societal Harms
    a. lost tax revenues
    b. welfare costs
    c. undeveloped human potential

II. Present system policies are innately inadequate to solve the unemployment problem.
  A. The present system is committed to economic growth as the solution to unemployment.
  B. The unemployed population is beyond the aid of economic growth.
    1. They are not skilled in the areas of economic revitalization.
    2. Economic growth is limited.
  C. Programs that could help are being reduced or eliminated.
    1. Federal job training has declined substantially.
    2. States follow federal lead in cutting state retraining programs.

III. [Plan outlined in detail, including . . . new federal job training programs designed to retrain the target population with relevant job skills for the present and future economy.]

IV. The affirmative plan will significantly reduce unemployment.
  A. The affirmative plan provides appropriate job training for the target population.
  B. Job opportunities and increased income will reduce the harms of unemployment.

In summary, the needs case is distinctive because it reflects the view that a policy change is essential because of the fundamental breakdown of the present system.

The Comparative Advantage Case

As with the choice of the needs case, the choice of *the comparative advantage case* format should be made only after substantial study, research, and analysis of the issues. The starting point of the comparative advantage case is *acceptance of the purposes of the present policy system.* The advocate of the comparative advantage case proposes that a new policy can better achieve the purposes of the present system—thereby producing comparative advantages. For example, suppose students are analyzing present system policies towards unemployment. They might find that they are in argeement with a present purpose of reducing unemployment to a certain specified level. However, they might find that the present programs are inefficient in accomplishing this purpose. In such a situation, debaters might consider using a comparative advantage case.

The issues in a comparative advantage case are the same as in the needs case—significance, inherency, and solvency. However, they are developed very differently, and the perspective of the comparative advantage case is quite special. The difference in perspective is partially reflected in the wording of the arguments; in particular, the wording of the significance issue in the comparative advantage case is positively worded and future-oriented. Instead of focusing upon the present needs, deficiencies, or harms of the present policy system, the debater examines the future advantages of the proposed system.

In addition, the significance issue should be developed by analyzing the comparative efficiencies of the two policy systems—the present and the proposed policy systems. For example, if debaters are analyzing unemployment and federal policy, the significance issue might be developed by focusing upon the unemployment that is not solved by the present system that would be solved by the proposed system. The affirmative arguing this case would probably want to show why this specific level of unsolved unemployment is undesirable.

The inherency issue should also be developed comparatively. In this issue both the characteristics and the effectiveness of the two policy systems are compared. For example, in the unemployment controversy the advocate might examine the differences in present and proposed programs (e.g., how they are administered, target populations, skills taught, and so on) and the consequences. These differences might be classified as differences in the nature of the programs or as differences in the degree of effectiveness. If the programs are different in their natures, they will probably produce qualitatively different results. Advantages produced by qualitatively different programs are unique advantages. *Thus, a unique advantage is defined as one that can be produced only by a particular program.* As an example, if present training programs teach skills that are either insignificant or produce short-term jobs, and the proposed programs would teach significant skills and produce long-lasting employment opportunities, then the proposed program would produce unique advantages.

Although an affirmative debater might successfully defend a proposal with advantages that are only quantitatively different, the proposal that yields unique advantages is usually the preferred approach because it is strategically stronger.

Demonstrating solvency in this kind of affirmative case again requires comparative analysis. The advocate must compare the relative effectiveness of the two systems. If the affirmative plan is superior to the present policy system because of quantitative differences, then the quantitative difference must be proven. On the other hand, if the affirmative advantages are unique to the proposal, then the affirmative must demonstrate the advantages that result are of a significantly different nature from those that can be produced by the present system. The kinds of affirmative advantages that might be offered in a comparative advantages case are varied. Advantages might deal with alleviating harmful conditions, such as in the needs case, or they may deal with areas of philosophical or value superiority as justification.

Comparative advantage cases often deal with more than one significance issue. For example, after outlining a proposal to provide jobs with a public works project, an affirmative team might argue that two advantages would result: significant numbers and kinds of jobs would be provided and worthwhile public works projects might be accomplished. If the advantages argued are produced by different parts of the proposed policy change, then the advantages are independent. On the other hand, if one advantage is dependent upon another, then the advantages are concomitant. In the example of the employment and the public works proposal the advantages are concomitant because the employment produces the public works.

The organization of the presentation of the comparative advantage is very different from the needs case. The first step in the analysis is to outline the proposed policy changes. Then the advocate demonstrates the advantages that would result, with each advantage developed in terms of the three primary issues—significance, inherency, and solvency. A simple outline of a comparative advantage case follows.

Plan Outline

I. Advantage
   A. Significance
   B. Inherency or Uniqueness
   C. Solvency

II. Advantage
   A. Significance
   B. Inherency or Uniqueness
   C. Solvency

If students were to argue the resolution on employment opportunities discussed above, then a comparative advantage case might be outlined as follows:

Topic: RESOLVED, that the federal government should implement a program that guarantees employment opportunities for all United States citizens in the labor force.

[Plan outlined in detail including . . . a negative income tax which decreases federal subsidies to the poor to only 50 cents for every dollar earned.]

I. The affirmative plan will more effectively stimulate economic growth.

- A. The federal government is committed to using fiscal policies to stimulate the economy.
  - 1. Legislation commits the federal government to this principle.
  - 2. Past and recent presidents have pursued this policy.
    - a. Roosevelt
    - b. Kennedy
    - c. Johnson
    - d. Reagan
  - 3. Federal commitment to economic stimulation is based on the desirability of economic growth.
- B. Present federal government policies are innately inadequate.
  - 1. Present policies feature a commitment to utilize tax reductions to stimulate economic growth.
  - 2. Tax reductions are inefficient in stimulating economic growth in the sectors of the greatest need.
    - a. Tax reductions favor the middle and upper income groups in terms of immediate impact.
    - b. Tax reductions may be saved rather than spent, thereby diminishing the immediate impact upon economic growth.
- C. The affirmative plan will more effectively stimulate the economy.
  - 1. The negative income tax will reach the sectors of greatest need immediately—the poor and the near poor.
  - 2. Economic stimulation to these sectors will more likely be spent rather than saved, thereby enhancing the immediate impact upon economic growth.

II. The affirmative plan will provide a superior response to poverty caused by underemployment.

- A. The present system is committed to the reduction of poverty.
  - 1. Legislation commits the federal government to the eradication of poverty.
  - 2. Past and recent presidents have espoused this principle.
- B. Underemployment is a significant problem.
  - 1. The transition from an industrial to a service economy has shifted workers from high and moderate income jobs in heavy industries to low income jobs in the service industries.
  - 2. The shift will increase these problems in the future.
  - 3. Underemployment is a major cause of poverty.
- C. Present system policies to combat underemployment are inadequate and counterproductive.
  - 1. Programs for the underemployed are a low priority.
  - 2. Welfare programs discourage work in the private sector.
  - 3. Minimum wage increases destroy job opportunities.
- D. The affirmative plan is a superior response to underemployment.
  - 1. The negative income tax plan will raise the incomes of the underemployed above poverty.
  - 2. The negative income plan encourages rather than discourages work.

In summary, the comparative advantage case is very different from the needs case, because it suggests that a policy change is desirable rather than essential.

Goal-Criterion Case

The starting point for the goal-criterion case is similar to the comparative advantages case. Both begin with the acceptance of assumptions of the present system. Whereas the comparative advantage case generally accepts the general purposes of the present system, the goal-criterion case accepts a goal or very specific policy objective. The goal will probably be identified and discussed at length in the first affirmative presentation. In addition, the affirmative utilizing the goal-criterion format also states a criterion for measuring achievement of that goal. For example, if a speaker chooses a goal of full employment, then s/he will need to identify the point at which full employment will be achieved. An economist might be cited who defines full employment at a certain percentage point of transitional unemployment depending upon economic conditions.

In developing issues, the goal-criterion case is very similar to the comparative advantage case. Significance in both cases is measured by the admitted failures of the present system. For example, if the goal of full employment is defined as an unemployment rate of 5% and present unemployment is 7%, then the affirmative might specify a level of significance at 2% unemployment. Similarly, the harms that the affirmative might cite for unemployment, such as adverse health effects, could also be quantified at levels indicated by the gap.

The inherency issue in the goal-criterion case has an additional obligation that the needs and the comparative advantage cases do not have. The inherency issue in the goal-criterion case consists of two subissues—the commitment of the present system to the goal and the innate flaws that make the present system unable to achieve the goal. Unless the affirmative debaters prove that the present system is committed to the specified goal, there can be no inherent problem since the problem is defined as the failure of the present system to achieve its goal.

The solvency issue in the goal-criterion case is measured by the criterion. If the proposal meets the criterion, then complete solvency is achieved. Often the goal-criterion case is combined with the comparative advantage case and the debater only claims that the proposal will achieve the goal better than the present system.

In summary, the goal-criterion case is similar to the comparative advantage case in terms of the starting point and the development of the issues. However, the goal-criterion case is usually more explicit and concrete in its assumption of specific present-system objectives. A simple outline of the goal-criterion case illustrates how the issues might be organized.

I. The present policy system is committed to the goal of ________________.
   A. Goal and criterion are defined.
   B. Legislation commits the present system to the goal.
   C. The goal is desirable.

II. The present system does not meet the goal.
   A. A significant gap exists between the present system and the goal.
   B. This gap is undesirable.

III. The present system inherently cannot meet the goal.

Plan Outline

IV. The affirmative proposal is more effective than the present policy system in achieving the goal.
   A. The gap is reduced.
   B. Reduction of the gap is advantageous.

If the employment opportunities topic were being debated, then a goal-criterion case might be outlined as follows.

Topic: RESOLVED, that the federal government should implement a program that guarantees employment opportunities for all United States citizens in the labor force.

I. The present policy system is committed to the goal of full employment.
   A. The goal and the criterion are defined as follows:
      1. The goal of full employment is defined at that point at which all those desiring a job have one.
      2. The criterion for measuring full employment will be expressed in terms of the percentage of unemployment that represents transitional unemployment.
   B. Legislation commits the present system to the goal.
   C. The goal is desirable.
      1. Economic advantages result with full employment.
      2. Social advantages result with full employment.

II. The present system does not meet the goal of full employment.
   A. A significant gap exists between the present levels of employment and full employment.
   B. This gap is undesirable.
      1. Unemployment is a serious threat to the individual.
         a. stress-related disease
         b. alcoholism
         c. mental illness and suicide
      2. Unemployment is a serious threat to society.
         a. lost tax revenues
         b. welfare costs
         c. underdeveloped human potential

III. The present system inherently cannot meet the goal of full employment.
  A. Present mechanisms to generate economic growth consist of reducing taxes.
  B. Reducing taxes cannot achieve full employment.
    1. Tax reduction strategies put income into the hands of middle and upper income groups.
    2. Money to middle and upper income groups will not generate sufficient jobs for unemployed.

[Plan outlined in detail, including . . . federal job training and federal government becoming the "employer of last resort."]

IV. The affirmative proposal is more effective than the present policy system in achieving the goal.
  A. Federal training will provide significant numbers of job opportunities.
  B. Employment opportunities are guaranteed by the federal government becoming the employer of last resort.

In summary, the goal-criterion case is similar to the comparative advantage case in the acceptance of assumptions of the present policy system. However, the goal-criterion case is distinctive in its acceptance of a specific goal that both the present and the proposed policy systems strive to obtain.

The Alternative Justification Case

The alternative justification case is simply a way of presenting more than one affirmative case in a debate. The words "alternative justification" suggest the strategy of this case; the case format presents two or more different rationales to justify the resolution. Lichtman, Garvin, and Corsi explain that "the alternative-justification affirmative extends the logic of the parallel advantages case. An affirmative team employing this approach explicitly recognizes that a given proposition is sufficiently broad to encompass different policy systems. It offers in a single debate, two or more parallel affirmative plans, each of which is a legitimate, if narrow, interpretation of the debate resolution."[1]

Each rationale is presented as an independent and complete case and plan sufficient to prove the resolution. The strategy is designed to allow the affirmative the option of pursuing certain cases while dropping others depending on the strength of the negative attack. However, the affirmative burdens for presenting a *prima facie* case exist for each case within the alternative justification case. These obligations may be difficult for the first affirmative speaker to meet while still maintaining a coherent first presentation.

The alternative justification case might combine several of the formats discussed above. However, the alternative justification format most frequently uses a variation of the comparative advantage format. For example, the following outline represents how an alternative justification case might be organized:

Plan I Outline

I. Advantage
   A. Significance
   B. Inherency or Uniqueness
   C. Solvency

II. Advantage
   A. Significance
   B. Inherency or Uniqueness
   C. Solvency

Plan II Outline

Advantage
   A. Significance
   B. Inherency or Uniqueness
   C. Solvency

Plan III Outline

Advantage
   A. Significance
   B. Inherency or Uniqueness
   C. Solvency

Lichtman, Garvin, and Corsi outlined how this case might have been argued on a previous intercollegiate debate topic:

Topic: RESOLVED, that the federal government should establish a system of compulsory wage and price controls.

I. The resolution will guard against the ravages of inflation.
   Plan: Setting a percentage ceiling on all wage and price increases.
   A. Inflation generates harmful distortions in the economic system.
   B. Current efforts are incapable of halting inflation.
   C. Strict controls can effectively halt inflation.

II. The resolution will protect the poor from economic discrimination.
   Plan: Outlawing excessively high food prices in ghetto areas and establishing higher minimum wages.
   A. Unreasonably low wages and high prices afflict the American poor.
   B. No mechanism exists to curb this ghetto-gouging.
   C. Federal controls can stop ghetto-gouging.

III. The resolution will minimize the suffering of the chronically ill.
   Plan: Lowering the prices of patent medicines and regulating pharmacists' wages.

A. Millions of chronically ill cannot afford necessary prescription drugs.
B. Present controls on prescription costs are ineffective.
C. Federal wage and price standards will guarantee lower prescription costs.[2]

In summary, the alternative justification case is an attempt to organize in a strategic manner some combination of two or more cases. The alternative justification case frequently resembles a comparative advantages case with a separate plan for each advantage.

Plan Construction

The construction of an affirmative plan can never be separated from the particular resolution being debated, or more especially from the specific affirmative justifications that the affirmative advocates choose to argue. Furthermore, the affirmative plan should always be the last step in the analysis regardless of the case format being utilized. The reason for building the plan last is that the plan is dependent upon all of the prior steps in the analysis—significance, inherency, and solvency. These steps must be accomplished before the particular plan can be created. For example, unless the specific harms of unemployment that will be argued are understood, then there is no effective way to construct a plan to solve or reduce them. The affirmative advocates must also know conceptually how they will solve and specifically how they will document solvency prior to building the plan. The plan cannot solve the problem unless the concept of solvency is clearly placed in the plan.

Even if the debaters choose a comparative advantage case format, the final construction of the plan should be constructed after the affirmative advantage areas have been chosen. The comparative advantage plan may come first in the presentation of the first affirmative speech, but the plan can only be constructed after the other parts of the case have been decided. Despite the very specific nature of every affirmative plan, certain concepts and characteristics are important to almost every plan that might be constructed in a policy debate. This section considers these concepts and characteristics.

First, the wording of policy advocacy propositions gives affirmative plans a special status in an educational debate. Policy advocacy resolutions are always worded in terms of an action that *should* occur. The word *should* in an educational debate is interpreted to mean that an action ought to occur even if political opposition or the lack of political support would make it impossible. This interpretation focuses an educational debate of a policy advocacy proposition on the rational motivations, such as those arguments that represent enlightened self-interests, socioeconomic considerations, or national interests. This focus gives the affirmative debaters what is known in an educational debate as *fiat power. Fiat power is the assumption that for purposes of debate the plan is assumed to come into existence once it is justified by rational motivations.*

Fiat power makes arguments concerning the impossibility of the plan coming into existence irrelevant in an educational debate. For example, suppose students are debating the proposition, *Resolved, that the federal government should own and operate the basic manufacturing industries in the United States.* A negative team might be able to develop substantial arguments indicating that powerful political lobbies both would and could stop Congress from passing such a proposal. However, the affirmative could respond to such arguments by indicating that such argument addresses not whether the proposed policy change *should* be enacted but whether or not it *would* be enacted.

Fiat power does not allow the affirmative to construct either unreasonable or unworkable proposals. The affirmative debaters always have to prove the workability of their proposals and genuinely unreasonable proposals are frequently unworkable or so disadvantageous that the affirmative team will find them indefensible.

Second, the wording of the policy advocacy proposition also limits what may legitimately be included in the affirmative plan. The wording of the topic functions both to designate the subject matter and to limit the debate. The affirmative plan should enact the central concept of the resolution being debated. With a few exceptions discussed later in this section, the affirmative cannot enact a different concept or additional concepts that are not in the wording of the proposition. If the affirmative enacts a concept other than the one contained in the proposition, then the affirmative plan will not be topical, and if the affirmative creates additional concepts not in the proposition, then the affirmative plan will be extratopical.

Third, despite the complexity of affirmative plans in many educational debates, the construction of an affirmative plan on most policy advocacy resolutions need begin with only four basic elements. These basic elements are: (1) administration, (2) essential functions, (3) enforcement, and (4) funding.

Administration is usually the first part or "plank" in an affirmative plan. Administration may take the form of a government board or agency with procedures for appointing and removing administrators. For example, an affirmative team might specify that the board members be appointed by the president and confirmed through the appropriate congressional process. Depending on the complexity of the proposal, the administration plank may be more detailed. However, the affirmative team is not expected to give the wording of a law in the outline of its proposal. The time limits of an educational debate do not permit complete description of this or any part of the plan, and only the major concepts should be included.

Plan functions or "mandates" are usually the second and always the most important part of the affirmative outline. These are the concepts of the proposition in operational form. For example, suppose the resolution being debated was: *Resolved, that the federal government should grant annually a specific percentage of its income tax revenue to the state governments.* The plan mandates might include the specific percentage of the federal revenues that would be shared and to what branches or units of state governments these funds might be provided.

Enforcement is often the third part of the affirmative outline. Although enforcement might sometimes be very complex, enforcement can often be explained very simply with phrasing such as "specific civil and criminal penalties will be legislated and enforced through the federal court system." However, specific resolutions may require different kinds of enforcement.

Funding is the final essential element of most policy proposal outlines. The importance of the funding will vary with the topic. Most policies advocated will require at least some financing for administration. However, topics that call for the reduction of actions or the abolition of policies may actually save money. In those policy topics where there is substantial need for new funds, it will be important for the affirmative team to select a method of funding that is not significantly disadvantageous.

The administration, enforcement, and funding are the basic elements in affirmative plans and are usually referred to as *enabling planks.* In other words, these elements are typical of the operations necessary for most new policies to come into existence. It should be noted that the wording of policy advocacy propositions itself does not include these elements. In a sense, they may seem to be extratopical parts of the plan since they are outside the designated concepts of the resolution. However, in educational debates these kinds of elements are not only allowed, but are usually considered essential. Additional elements may be included in a plan if they are designated by the concepts of the resolution or if they are other types of enabling planks.

I. Administration
II. Functions
    A.
    B.
    C.
    . . . .
III. Enforcement
IV. Funding

FIGURE 9–1 Simple outline of the components of an affirmative plan.

Cases in Non-Policy Debate

As in policy debate, case building for a non-policy proposition should begin only after debaters have done substantial research and have a clear understanding of the issues. In non-policy debate the wording of the particular proposition has probably even more influence on determining the particular case format. Several general guidelines can assist in the construction of cases on non-policy propositions.

This chapter will consider the following methods of building affirmative cases: (1) the criteria fulfillment function, (2) case building for inferential propositions, and (3) the value justification case.

The Criteria Fulfillment Function

As indicated in Chapter Four, the three starting points for discovering the issues in most non-policy propositions can be found in the answers to these three questions:

1. What is the key evaluative term or phrase?
2. How should the key evaluative term or phrase be defined?
3. Do conditions exist such that the evaluation can be affirmed or denied?

The use of a criterion or set of criteria is one method of answering the second of these major questions—the definition of the key evaluative term or phrase. The criterion or set of criteria can also be an important starting point for organizing an affirmative case on a non-policy topic. An additional starting point to a case may be provided by the answer to the third of these questions—do existing conditions meet or fulfill the criteria for the key evaluative term?*

Any affirmative case on a non-policy proposition will answer these questions. Therefore, the answers to these questions may also be used as a method of outlining an affirmative case. Such an outline emphasizes two essential parts—justification of the criteria and proof that existing conditions fulfill the criteria. Therefore, a criteria-fulfillment format will be appropriate for an affirmative case in which the affirmative desires to focus the debate on these two elements and wishes to organize the presentation of the case accordingly. The following outline indicates how this outline might be used.

---

*If the wording of the proposition is in the past or future tense, then the wording of this question will also change accordingly as follows:

Past Tense: Did conditions exist that met or fulfilled the criteria for the key evaluative term?

Future Tense: Will conditions exist that meet or will fulfill the criteria for the key evaluative term?

I. The key evaluative term is effectively defined by the criteria of ______________.
   A. These criteria are defined and explained as follows:
      1. Criterion of . . .
      2. Criterion of . . .
   B. These criteria constitute good definitional standards.
      1. Philosophically. . .
      2. Pragmatically. . .

II. Existing conditions fulfill the criteria.
   A. Philosophically. . .
   B. Pragmatically. . .

It should be noted that if the criteria themselves are not significant issues, then the criteria fulfillment outline format will probably be inappropriate. Or, if the focus of the debate should be mainly on the existing conditions, then this case format will again be less effective.

In summary, the criteria fulfillment function is the basic pattern for case building on all non-policy propositions. Ziegemueller and Dause distinguish between a criteria establishment case and a criteria application case, but the concepts are very similar to each other and to the criteria fulfillment outline described above.[3] The following sections of this chapter will include examples that illustrate the various uses and modifications of the criteria fulfillment outline.

Case Building for Propositions of Inference

Building a case for propositions of inference is especially dependent upon research and upon analysis of the wording of the individual topic. However, there are some general guidelines for case development, based on the kind of inference and how issues are developed with that kind of inference; these will be discussed in the subsections that follow.

First, *trait inferences* deal with claims about things known or assumed. This kind of inference is very similar to the category of non-policy propositions that David Zarefsky has discussed, indicating that this kind of proposition "is one which concerns whether or not to bestow a given value judgment on an object, event, person, or act. Here the question is . . . whether or not a *particular* value is appropriate to characterize a given object."[4]

The Needs Assessment Case

When the *criteria* for the value judgment is not a major issue, the affirmative case will usually focus on the *appropriateness* of the judgment for a particular situation. If this is the focus, the development of the case may resemble the development of the significance issue from a policy advocacy proposition, and proceed without the burden of developing the other issues. Such a case might be called a *needs assessment case*. Because of the narrowness of the focus in such a case, other questions may then arise and become issues. For example, the significance of assigning the trait may become a major question. (Of course, this kind of issue raises the question of the worth of the proposition, which the Affirmative might also defend.)

If students were to debate the topic, *Resolved, that the Supreme Court exercises excessive power,* then a needs assessment case for this trait proposition might be outlined as follows.

I. The powers of the Supreme Court are defined by the U.S. Constitution.
  A. The Constitution allocates only judicial power to the Supreme Court.
    1. Article III designates only judicial powers to the Supreme Court.
    2. Other powers are vested in other branches or remain with the states.
      a. Article I awards legislative power to the Congress.
      b. Article II awards executive powers to the president.
      c. Amendment X delegates unawarded powers to the states and to the people.
  B. These definitions constitute good criteria for judging the abuse of power.
    1. Strict adherence to written constitutions is necessary to protect democracy.
    2. The founding fathers intended that the Constitution be strictly observed.
    3. Abuse of power by the Supreme Court occurs when the Court exceeds the role of judiciary as strictly defined by the Constitution.

II. The Supreme Court has assumed legislative power.
  A. Legislative powers are clearly defined by Article I of the Constitution.
  B. Examples illustrate various areas in which the Supreme Court has acted as a legislative body.
    1. *Plessy* v. *Ferguson*
    2. *Brown* v. *Board of Education*
    3. *Roe* v. *Wade*
    4. *Obscenity Cases*

III. The Supreme Court has assumed executive power.
  A. Executive powers are clearly defined by Article II of the Constitution.

B. Examples illustrate various areas in which the Supreme Court has acted as an executive body.
   1. *Youngstown Sheet and Tube Co.* v. *Sawyer* (The Steel Seizure Case)
   2. *United States* v. *Nixon*

In summary, the affirmative case-building process for a proposition of trait inference can usually be based on the criteria fulfillment outline with little or no modification.

The Action–Motive Case

Because any case that focuses on a causal relationship automatically indicates numerous other issues, the criteria fulfillment outline is not as well-suited to building a case on a proposition of relation inference. The issue of causality would probably dictate a significant modification of the case format. For example, such questions as the following are frequently raised by causal arguments: How will causality be demonstrated? Is the association between the assumed cause and effect a consistent one? Is the association between the assumed cause and effect a strong one? Was the assumed cause sufficient to bring about the assumed effect? Do the assumed cause and effect occur in a proximate and appropriate time sequence? Can a third causal factor explain the appearance of the assumed cause and effect relationship? How can other possible causes be explained?

The affirmative debater may be able to specify how causality will be demonstrated, and perhaps other aspects of causality, in the statement of the criteria. In dealing with propositions in which causality may be a controversial matter, this can be an effective way of handling the causality issue. The following outline illustrates this kind of case format.

I. The following definitions provide criteria for the key terms and causal relationship of the resolution.
   A. These criteria are defined and explained as follows:
      1. Criterion of . . .
      2. Criterion of . . .
   B. These criteria constitute good definitional standards.
      1. Philosophically. . .
      2. Pragmatically. . .

II. Conditions illustrate that the causal relationship exists.

One type of relational case is called the *action-motive* case. The action-motive case focuses only on the motivations or reasons for the specified action. For example, if students were to debate the topic, *Resolved, that higher education in the United States has sacrificed quality for institutional survival,* then an action-motive case on this proposition of relational inference might be outlined as follows:

I. The following criteria define the key terms in the resolution:
  A. Quality in higher education refers to the following:
    1. Student quality as measured by scores on standardized tests.
    2. Quality of curriculum as determined by quantitative and qualitative measures of course content.
    3. Standards for graduation and degree requirements as measured both quantitatively and qualitatively.
  B. Institutional survival refers to maintaining enrollments at comparable levels.
  C. Sacrificed is a causal relationship that can be measured by John Stuart Mill's canons of causation.
  D. These criteria constitute good definitional standards.
    1. Philosophically. . .
    2. Pragmatically. . .

II. Conditions illustrate a clear decline in the quality of higher education due to attempts to maintain enrollments.
  A. Public and private colleges have been forced to lower entry requirements to bolster enrollments.
  B. The inclusion of less-qualified students has led to weaker curriculums and a necessary lowering of degree requirements and graduation standards.
  C. The education of traditional students has suffered because of the entry of the new students with fewer abilities and skills.

Construction of a *prima facie* case on a relational inference proposition requires that the causal relationship be demonstrated in the first affirmative presentation. The affirmative debaters might also wish to include arguments dealing with a causal relationship, such as those listed above, as an effective pre-emptive refutation.

The Historical Criteria Case

An historical inference formulates conclusions about something known or assumed that existed or took place in the past. The criteria fulfillment format might again be useful for this kind of proposition but the first affirmative speaker may need to address additional issues. These issues deal with the appropriateness and the relevance of the criteria and the data used in analyzing and verifying inferences about historical situations.

For example, if a student attempts to support the inference that Abraham Lincoln was an effective president, the standards for assessing effectiveness will require careful consideration. As an example, it might be argued that the standards for assessing Lincoln's effectiveness should be based only on the knowledge that was available to Lincoln at the time, and that data not available to Lincoln at the time of a decision should not be considered in assessing his action.

As the above example illustrates, the appropriateness and relevance of both criteria and data might be especially important issues in debating propositions of historical inference. With this in mind, the criteria fulfillment outline might be modified as follows.

I. The historical situation is effectively assessed by the criteria of ________________.
   A. These criteria are defined and explained as follows:
      1. Criterion of . . .
      2. Criterion of . . .
   B. These criteria are appropriate standards for assessing this period in history.

II. Available and appropriate data confirms the assessment.
   A. Data supports the assessment.
   B. Use of this data is appropriate for analyzing this situation in this period of history.

If students were to debate the topic, *Resolved, that the atomic bombing of Nagasaki, Japan was unnecessary,* then a case for a proposition of historical inference might be outlined as follows:

I. Military actions during wartime might effectively be assessed by the criterion of the minimum necessary force.
   A. The criterion of the minimum necessary force is defined and explained as follows:
      1. Minimum necessary force means the efficient use of military force during wartime.
      2. Minimum necessary force means the least violent force necessary.
   B. These criteria are appropriate standards for assessing this period in history.
      1. Minimum necessary force was standard military principle and practice.
      2. Much of World War II was conducted based on this principle.

II. The bombing of Nagasaki was unnecessary by the principle of minimum necessary force.
   A. The destructive power of the bombing of Nagasaki constituted excessive military force.

B. Japan had already lost the war prior to the bombing of either Hiroshima or Nagasaki.
C. Internal politics in Japan made surrender and peace inevitable prior to the bombing.
D. President Truman was informed of the destructive force of the atomic weapons prior to the decision to bomb both Hiroshima and Nagasaki.
E. Even if the atomic bombing was necessary to end the war quickly and save lives overall, the bombing of Hiroshima should have been sufficient.

In summary, cases for propositions of historical inference can usually be based on a slight modification of the criteria fulfillment format.

The Predictive Criteria Case

The criteria fulfillment format may be modified in yet another way to conform to the proposition of predictive inference. As with propositions of historical inference, issues might arise that question the relevance of the criteria and data to the task of dealing with a different time and situation.

The affirmative case for a proposition of predictive inference must also deal with the issue of whether or not prediction is possible. For example, if students were to debate the topic, *Resolved, that a space-based anti-ballistic missile system will be feasible by the year 2000,* the affirmative advocates might deal with the issue of predictiveness either in the criteria or in the data; they might define feasibility in such a way as to lessen the burden of prediction, or they might be able to discover evidence that supported the possibility of the prediction.

The following outline indicates how the criteria fulfillment case might be modified for a proposition of predictive inference.

I. The future situation is effectively assessed by the criteria of ________________.
   A. These criteria are defined and explained as follows:
      1. Criterion of . . .
      2. Criterion of . . .
   B. These criteria are appropriate standards for assessing this future situation.
   C. These criteria make predictions possible.
II. Available and appropriate data confirms the prediction.
   A. The data supports the prediction.
   B. The data is appropriate and relevant to the prediction.
   C. The data makes the prediction possible.

If the anti-ballistic missile system topic were being debated, then the affirmative might outline the following case for this proposition of predictive inference.

Topic: RESOLVED, that a space-based anti-ballistic missile system will be feasible by the year 2000.

I. The future feasibility of a space-based anti-ballistic missile system can be effectively determined by the criteria of available and sufficient information.
   A. These criteria are defined and explained as follows:
      1. The criterion of availability of information means that the scientific community will possess the necessary knowledge.
      2. The criterion of sufficient knowledge means that the scientific community will know which technological options might be most productively pursued.
      3. Feasibility does not mean an operable system will be functioning.
      4. Feasibility does not specify a certain degree of effectiveness.
   B. These criteria are appropriate standards for assessing the state of scientific knowledge.
   C. These criteria make predictions possible.
      1. Rate of knowledge growth has always outstripped predicted growth rates.
      2. Although specific technologies have been difficult to predict, scientific communities have been able to predict what knowledge they will have.

II. Multiple sources will provide the necessary information.
   A. President Reagan's research programs will yield results.
      1. Significant funding exists now.
      2. Congressional support will increase in the future.
   B. Other space programs will provide information.
      1. Space shuttle research will be significant.
      2. Other research will contribute.
   C. Allies will provide significant information.
   D. Scientific communities will share valuable information.
   E. Natural growth in information will provide any other necessary information.

In summary, affirmative cases on propositions of inference are highly dependent upon research and discovery of the issues associated with particular topics. However, modifications of the criteria fulfillment case format will usually provide guidelines for building case outlines.

The Value Justification Case

As indicated in Chapter Three, a proposition of value is a comparison of one value to another, one valued thing to another, or a comparison of the benefits and the detriments of an idea or object. Such comparisons present conflicts and value claims seek to resolve these conflicts.

The value justification case is a very effective method for building cases on this kind of proposition. This case format is a slight modification of the value benefits analysis developed by Raymond Zeuschner. Zeuschner himself notes that this kind of case is very similar to the comparative advantages case used to build cases on policy propositions. "In this vein, Value Benefits would offer the value claim—usually the resolution or a defined subset thereof, and then offer decision makers a rationale which would support some sort of expected benefit(s) to be derived from the new value."[5] Furthermore, as Zeuschner indicates, this approach seems relevant to the real-world decision-making process: "People do make decisions, do weigh judgments on the basis of perceived benefit."[6]

The development of the value justification case includes four issues that help to resolve the conflict between the values or things being compared. (1) What are the criteria for the comparative evaluation? (2) What are the benefits of the value(s) or thing(s) being evaluated? (3) What are the benefits of the alternative value or thing being compared? Or, if the benefits and the detriments of a single idea or thing are being weighed, then what are the detriments of the idea or thing? (4) What is the evaluation based upon the answers to these questions? The outline for this kind of case might be as follows:

I. The comparative evaluation can effectively be made by using the criteria of ________________.
  A. The criteria are defined and explained as follows:
    1. Criterion of . . .
    2. Criterion of . . .
  B. These criteria constitute good standards for comparative evaluation.
    1. Philosophically. . .
    2. Pragmatically. . .

II. The benefits of ________________ are:
  A.
  B.
  C.
  . . .

III. The benefits or detriments of ______________ are:
   A.
   B.
   C.
   . . .
IV. The comparative evaluation reveals . . .

If advocates were to debate the value topic, *Resolved, that commercial television is more detrimental than beneficial to American society,* then a value justification case might be outlined as follows.

I. Comparative evaluation of commercial television can effectively be accomplished by using the criteria of cost–benefits.
   A. Costs–benefits is defined and explained as follows:
      1. Assessing the costs includes all of the adverse impacts of commercial television.
      2. Assessing the benefits includes all of the positive impacts of commercial television.
      3. Completing costs–benefits analysis requires that the costs be compared with the benefits.
   B. Cost–benefits criteria constitute good standards for comparative evaluation.
      1. Cost–benefits analysis is a logical extension of the reflective thinking process.
      2. Cost–benefits analysis is a traditional tool of decision making.
      3. Cost–benefits establishes clear burdens for affirmative and negative ground.
II. Commercial television exposes children to significant amounts of negative stimuli.
   A. Commercial television results in significant amounts of the following:
      1. television violence
      2. manipulative advertising
      3. misleading nutritional information
   B. High levels of television violence encourage negative attitudes and behaviors in children.
   C. High levels of manipulative advertising is harmful to children.
   D. High levels of misleading nutritional information is harmful to children.
   E. The impact of television on children is the most important consideration in evaluating commercial television's impact.
III. Commercial television's benefits to children are minimal.
   A. Education on commercial television is insignificant in quantity.
   B. The quality of education on commercial television is poor.
IV. Overall, commercial television's disadvantages exceed its advantages.

In summary, the value justification analysis case is the non-policy counterpart of the comparative advantages case in policy debate. Furthermore, it is especially useful for organizing a case for a proposition of value and can be easily developed by answering the questions posed by the four issues that are innate to every proposition of value.

Policy Evaluation Cases

As indicated in Chapter Three, policy evaluation propositions are claims that make an evaluative judgment about a course of action. This kind of proposition may deal with the desirability of a particular policy, but such topics do not advocate that the policy be implemented. Since policy evaluation propositions are in many ways similar to both policy advocacy and non-policy propositions, the case building process will also be similar.

Although the issues of policy evaluation topics vary with the wording of individual resolutions, certain issues will be common to all propositions of policy evaluation. First, policy evaluation propositions require the use of definitions or criteria to provide standards for the evaluation being proposed. For example, if the topic, *Resolved, that a flat tax is desirable* were being debated, then the concept of a desirable tax policy would need to be specified by definition or by a set of criteria for a productive debate to occur.

Second, depending upon the wording of the topic and the issues specified by the criteria, the remaining issues will probably be drawn from the issues traditionally associated with policy debate. In most propositions of policy evaluation these other issues will be any or all of the following: Is there a significant problem or potential advantage area that justifies the existence of the policy system? Does the policy solve a significant problem or yield a significant advantage? Do the advantages of the policy system outweigh its disadvantages? All of these issues would probably be relevant if the flat tax topic were being debated. For such a case, the question of cost–benefits (advantages and disadvantages) will not need to be developed in the first affirmative presentation; the criteria may be cited as the traditional policy analysis issues. This kind of case might be outlined as follows:

I. Policy evaluation can be effectively accomplished by the criteria of policy analysis.
   A. Policy analysis issues include:
      1. Is there a significant need or potential advantage that justifies the policy?
      2. Does the policy solve the problem or yield the advantage?
      3. Do the advantages of the policy outweigh the disadvantages?

B. If the answer to these questions is positive, then the policy is favorably evaluated.

II. There is a significant need or potential advantage that justifies the policy.

III. The policy solves the problem or yields the advantage.

If the flat tax resolution were being debated, then the outline for a specific policy evaluation case might be as follows:

Topic: RESOLVED, that a flat tax is desirable.

I. Criteria: A flat tax system should be evaluated by the issues of policy analysis.
   A. Policy analysis issues include:
      1. Is there a significant need or potential advantage that justifies the policy?
      2. Does the policy solve the problem or yield the advantage?
      3. Do the advantages of the policy outweigh the disadvantages?
   B. If the answer to these questions is positive, then the policy is desirable.

II. The present tax system is unjust.
   A. Significant tax loopholes create an inequitable system.
   B. Present system inequities constitute an unjust system.
   C. Injustice threatens democracy.

III. A flat tax restores justice to the tax system.
   A. A flat tax consists of the following elements:
      1. No or few deductions.
      2. Lower rates.
      3. Fewer tax brackets.
   B. A flat tax eliminates the cause of the injustice in the present system—tax loopholes.

It should be noted that the policy evaluation affirmative case will not usually deal with the issue of inherency since the existence of the policy system or alternative policy systems will not usually be relevant to the evaluation.

In summary, policy evaluation topics feature the issues and the case characteristics of both policy and non-policy propositions. Usually the issues of policy evaluation debates concern the criteria for evaluation, the need or advantage of the policy, the effectiveness of the policy in solving the need or yielding the advantage, and finally, the cost–benefits of the policy. A policy evaluation case can be easily developed by constructing arguments on the first three of these issues. The cost–benefits issues can also be discussed, though this issue does not need to be presented in the first affirmative presentation.

Preparing the First Affirmative Constructive Speech

In the first constructive speech the affirmative team's most important task is to provide a rationale sufficient to justify the proposition. This rationale is the previously discussed *prima facie* burden of the affirmative team. In addition, the first affirmative speech poses other obligations and provides other opportunities.

First, the first affirmative speaker should present an introduction, state the proposition being debated, and provide definitions of the key terms or phrases. As we have discussed, definitions are important for several reasons. Definitions not only clarify the meaning of the resolution, they also limit the scope of the topic. The affirmative has the right to define the terms of the proposition as long as their definitions are reasonable. However, there are some argumentation theorists who believe debaters arguing non-policy propositions should use the best definitions available.

The affirmative team may choose from a number of methods to define terms. The most common methods of definition for a proposition of policy advocacy are *operational definitions* and *definition by example*. Debaters can use operational definitions by explaining the function or "operation" of the term in a specific context. For example, when an affirmative team outlines its policy proposal or plan they are providing an operational definition of the topic being debated.

The second common method of definition is the use of an example or several examples. If, for instance, debaters were arguing the topic, *Resolved: that any and all injury resulting from the disposal of hazardous waste in the United States should be the legal responsibility of the producer of that waste,* they might decide to focus their case upon the example of the waste from nuclear power plants. This would be the use of definition by example.

In non-policy debate the most common method of definition is *definition by authority*. Debaters may effectively use *specialized* dictionaries, encyclopedias and authoritative publications which define key concepts. General dictionaries and encyclopedias will be much less helpful and less effective in defining terms. Frequently, debaters will rely on such legal sources as *Black's Law Dictionary* or *Words and Phrases*. However, these sources, while frequently more specific in the wording of definitions, may be inappropriate and sometimes less helpful than even general sources. If debaters rely on authoritative definitions, they should be certain that the definitions are from respected authorities in the particular field and are relevant to the specific context of the topic.

Other methods of definition include the use of definitions based on history, derivation, and negation. Definitions based on the history of the concept and derivation of the terms are very similar. To define a concept historically involves discussion of the origin, history, and evolution of the concept. An authority may provide an historically-based definition of a concept. The definition of a term based on its derivation focuses on the etymology of the word. For example, examination of the Latin roots of a term might be useful in explaining the origins of a concept. Definitions might also be provided by negation—in other words, by explaining what words or phrases do not mean.

As indicated above, definitions are often crucial in educational debates. Definitions not only provide a common basis for understanding and argument, often they will also be the basis for the legitimacy of a particular interpretation of the resolution being debated. Given this function, definitions are often the basis for an affirmative team's argument that its interpretations of the proposition are topical. Definitions are even more important in non-policy debate, because they usually provide the criteria for making the evaluation that is the central task in debating most non-policy topics.

Second, after providing definitions the first affirmative speaker should preview the arguments or contentions that make up the affirmative case. This preview is often referred to as the *signposting step* since it indicates to the audience or judge what is "ahead" in the rest of the speech.

Third, the affirmative should develop the contentions with appropriate analysis and evidence. The first affirmative speech presents special opportunities for the debater to support his or her arguments. For example, the first affirmative speech is the only speech that can be completely prepared before the debate begins; as such, it is usually a manuscript speech. The wording of the speech can be carefully considered and the evidence can be more carefully selected and explained than in any other speech in the debate. The first affirmative speech is also an opportunity for the affirmative to use longer pieces of evidence, or evidence that requires explanation and context to be effective.

In the development of an affirmative case, intercollegiate debaters should take into account that they will probably wish to use their case for an extended period of time—for an entire tournament or for an entire debate season. In such circumstances, the analysis and the evidence should be able to withstand the intense scrutiny of their opponents and judges not once but possibly several times. Therefore, the first affirmative should consist of the best arguments and the best evidence that is available to support the resolution.

Fourth, after the case has been developed the first affirmative speech should summarize and have an appropriate conclusion. The first affirmative speech is an opportunity for good persuasive speaking as well as an opportunity for intelligent argument.

INTRODUCTORY MATERIAL	Introduction Statement of the Proposition Definitions Plan (in policy debate) Signposting Step
CASE DEVELOPMENT	Contention I Contention II Contention III etc.
CONCLUDING MATERIAL	Summary Conclusion

FIGURE 9–2 The organization of the first affirmative constructive speech.

Affirmative Speaker Responsibilities

In the traditional organization of a debate, the affirmative team will have four speeches. Each of the two team members will have the opportunity to speak twice—one constructive speech and one rebuttal speech. Three guiding principles can help the affirmative debaters in each speech fulfill the responsibilities associated with that speech. First, each debater must fulfill the burden of rejoinder or rebuttal. Although the affirmative team usually has the burden of proof, both teams in a debate have a burden of rejoinder or rebuttal. In other words, after the first affirmative speech, each debater has the obligation to respond to the previous advocate's arguments. A debater should never ignore an opponent's arguments even if they are clearly irrelevant. S/he always has at least the obligation to explain why arguments are irrelevant or to give other reasons why s/he will not respond to specific arguments.

Second, each debater should always set priorities in responding to the opposing arguments. Usually the first priority is to respond to arguments that have not been dealt with previously. After these arguments are discussed, then the debater can proceed to issues that have been previously argued. The second priority is to answer the most important issues remaining in the debate. It may seem unusual that dealing with the most important issues is a secondary priority; however, in intercollegiate debate an argument that is not dealt with at all is usually awarded to the team that raised it. Therefore, all arguments should be discussed or the importance of an unanswered argument may overshadow the more important issues.

Third, the affirmative has an additional obligation: to re-establish the affirmative case. Since the affirmative case is the basis for the verification of the proposition, the affirmative must always re-establish its affirmative case.

Since much of an intercollegiate debate will deal with the specific affirmative contentions, usually the affirmative debater can re-establish the case as s/he fulfills the burden of rejoinder.

In most intercollegiate debates the duties of each speaker are predictable. The obligations of the first affirmative speaker are explained above and will vary depending on the kind of proposition and the kind of case the affirmative team has chosen. If the first negative fulfills his or her obligations in a traditional way, the second affirmative speaker will be responding to direct argumentation against the case outlined by the first affirmative speaker. Thus, the second affirmative speaker will be able to both respond and rebuild the affirmative case simultaneously.

The first task of the second affirmative speaker, however, is to identify a theme or state a perspective or philosophy that will refocus the debate on affirmative ground. Since the previous negative speaker has focused on the case from the negative point of view for a substantial period of time, the second affirmative speaker should indicate to the judge or audience the theme that will both organize and join his or her speech to the first affirmative presentation.

Next, the second affirmative speaker should preview or signpost the arguments of his or her speech. Speakers will generally try to use the same organizational pattern throughout as much of the debate as possible. Whenever possible, the first affirmative case outline is used as a basic outline for each of the first three speakers in a debate. When this is done, each speech will

SECOND AFFIRMATIVE CONSTRUCTIVE	FIRST AFFIRMATIVE REBUTTAL	SECOND AFFIRMATIVE REBUTTAL
Statement of theme Signposting step	Signposting	Theme
Refutation of first negative	Responses to second negative Constructive speaker's arguments	Signposting Step
&		Off-Case or Plan Issues
Rebuilding of affirmative case	Signposting	Signposting
Additional affirmative justifications	Responses to first negative Rebuttal speaker's arguments	Case Issues Theme Conclusion
Summary Theme Conclusion		

FIGURE 9–3 Affirmative speakers' responsibilities.

serve as a frame of reference for the next speech and the debate will be relatively easy to understand and to follow for both experienced debate judges and audiences. This pattern of organization also makes the signposting step of the second affirmative a relatively simple statement. For example, the second affirmative speaker might simply say, "I will answer Kris's arguments in the order of the affirmative case outline." Since Kris followed the first affirmative outline, it will be easy for the second affirmative to do the same without any elaborate explanation.

As indicated above, the main task of the second affirmative is to respond and rebuild. However, the second affirmative may also wish to add new justifications for the resolution in this last constructive speech, presenting the new arguments at the end of the responding and rebuilding process. If these new arguments are to function as independent justifications for the resolution, they must possess all the characteristics of a *prima facie* case. This may be difficult to accomplish if the first negative speaker is an effective debater.

The final task of the second affirmative speaker is to summarize and conclude. With this step the affirmative should once more remind the listeners of the theme that unifies his or her arguments.

The first affirmative rebuttal is often a turning point in an intercollegiate debate. This can be a very difficult speech since it must deal with the arguments of two previous negative speakers. However, if the first affirmative rebuttal speaker follows the priorities listed above, s/he will be successful. The first task will be to deal with those arguments that have not yet been discussed, usually the arguments made by the second negative constructive speaker. If the negative uses the traditional division of labor, the second negative will deal with a group of arguments very different from those that his partner dealt with. Usually, these arguments will consist of either "plan attacks" (e.g., disadvantages) in policy debate or "off-case arguments" (e.g., countervalues) in non-policy debate. Thus, the first task of the first affirmative rebuttalist is to respond to these arguments.

The next responsibility of the first affirmative rebuttalist is to answer the arguments made by the first negative rebuttal speaker. In most debates these arguments will deal with the same issues raised by the first negative and second affirmative debaters in their constructive speeches. In this situation selectivity should be the principle—the speaker should choose the major issues.

The final speech in the debate is the second affirmative rebuttal. S/he should discuss all the remaining issues in the debate. If possible, the second affirmative should begin this speech by re-iteration of the affirmative theme or philosophy. Also, this speech should feature a clear signposting step. This speech will need to deal with all of the negative issues as argued by both the first and second negative speakers. This means that the second affirmative rebuttal speaker will probably be dealing with both the "case" issues—the same issues she dealt with in her constructive speech—and the plan attacks of off-case issues—the issues that her partner dealt with in his rebuttal. The fundamental question about organizing this speech usually concerns where to begin. The second affirmative might most effectively begin with the off-case or plan issues and then finish the debate talking about the issues from the perspective of the affirmative case. The last task of this speaker is to summarize and conclude, and an appropriate and often effective way to conclude is to focus once more on the theme that unifies the affirmative arguments.

Throughout both affirmative rebuttals there should be frequent signposts to make certain that the listeners are following the argumentation.

In summary, the responsibilities for the affirmative debaters in an educational debate should be guided by the burden of rejoinder and the priorities for dealing with arguments.

Summary

An affirmative case consists of those arguments that justify or verify the proposition. The kind of case used to affirm a proposition is dependent upon the kind of proposition being debated, the particular topic, and any discoveries or strategic considerations produced by the affirmative debaters during research and the analysis.

The majority of cases in policy advocacy debate fall into the categories of the needs case, the comparative advantage case, the goal-criterion case, and the alternative justification case. The construction of the affirmative plan for all of these cases will usually include at least four common features: (1) administration, (2) functions or mandates, (3) enforcement, and (4) funding.

The majority of cases in non-policy debate use the criteria fulfillment function with various modifications, such as the needs assessment action-motive cases, and the value justification case. Policy evaluation cases feature the characteristics of both policy and non-policy cases.

This chapter also summarizes the organization of a debate, the preparation of the first affirmative speech, and the responsibilities associated with each of the other affirmative speeches.

Notes

1. Allan Lichtman, Charles Garvin, and Jerry Corsi, "The Alternative-Justification Affirmative: A New Case Form," *Journal of the American Forensic Association,* X (Fall 1973): 60.
2. Ibid., p. 61. Reprinted by permission of the American Forensics Association.

3. George W. Zeigemueller and Charles A. Dause, *Argumentation: Inquiry and Advocacy* (Englewood Cliffs, NJ: Prentice–Hall, 1976), pp. 169–70.
4. David Zarefsky, "Criteria for Evaluating Non-Policy Argument," *CEDA Yearbook 1980* (Don Brownlee, California State University, Northridge, 1980), p. 11.
5. Raymond Zeuschner, "Value Benefits Analysis as an Affirmative Paradigm," *CEDA Yearbook 1982* (Don Brownlee, California State University, Northridge, 1982), p. 16.
6. Ibid., p. 17.

Questions and Exercises

1. What is a case?
2. What is a plan?
3. Select a recent controversy. After some preliminary reading, formulate a proposition and, based on the classification of cases in this chapter, outline as many different kinds of cases as possible.
4. Check the *Congressional Record, Vital Speeches, Congressional Digest* and other sources for several recent speeches by different congresspersons or others advocating new programs. Identify the characteristics of their arguments that are similar to the characteristics of different kinds of affirmative cases. What kinds of cases do they seem to be presenting? Do these advocates ever seem to combine the elements of the different kinds of cases? If so, why do you think this occurs? If not, why do you think it does not occur?
5. Read the first affirmative speech of one of the debates at the end of the text, identify the characteristics of the case, and classify the case as one of the kinds of affirmative cases discussed in this chapter.

Suggested Readings

Flaningham, Carl. "Concomitant Vs. Comparative Advantages: Sufficient Vs. Necessary Conditions." *Journal of the American Forensic Association,* XVIII (Summer 1981), 1–8.

Young, Gregory and Gaske, Paul. "On *Prima Facie* Value Argumentation: The Policy Implications Affirmative." *CEDA Yearbook, 1984.* California State University, Northridge: Don Brownlee, 1984, pp. 24–30.

Jones, M. Anway and Crawford, Stephen. "Justification of Values in Terms of Action: Rationale for a Modified Policy-Making Paradigm in Value Debate." *CEDA Yearbook, 1984.* California State University, Northridge: Don Brownlee, 1984, pp. 11–15.

TEN

Negative Strategies

Simply stated, the task of the negative in any debate is to deny the proposition. There are numerous ways in which advocates can accomplish this. In this chapter we will present, first in general terms and then more specifically, the methods of negative argument.

The Position

A necessary starting point in developing negative arguments is to determine a negative position. The negative position is a general "game plan." It is not a collection of specific arguments but an "idea" of how the negative team will select the specific arguments they will use. Negative teams that advance negative arguments randomly and without any discernable purpose may ultimately fail to adequately deny the proposition. The advocates may sustain many random, individual arguments that, collectively, do not undermine the affirmative claim. Another danger of proceeding without a negative position is the tendency toward contradiction. Without a clear idea of the direction of the negative case, there is great danger of contradicting what has been argued earlier. As a result, legitimate but contradictory negative arguments might be argued inadvertently.

In order to develop the negative position, attention must be paid to (1) the nature of the proposition, (2) the structure of the affirmative case, and (3) the strength of individual affirmative arguments. Suppose that two teams are debating a proposition of trait inference: *Resolved, that victimless crime laws are outside the legitimate function of government.* As you learned in Chapter Four, a trait inference will lead to a consideration of the following issues:

1. The definition of key terms.
2. The criteria for judgment:
   Does the criteria suggest a linear application?
   Does the criteria suggest a threshold?
3. What are the affirmative burdens?

After determining how the negative ought to view the meaning of the key terms in the proposition, we would turn to a consideration of the second issue, the function of the criteria.

Suppose that an affirmative team supporting the above proposition presents their case as presented in Figure 10–1.

A general question the negative must ask is whether the affirmative arguments, if sustained, support the proposition. If they do, then the affirmative has presented a *prima facie* case and the negative must analyze the case further. In looking at the structure of the case the following questions should be asked and answered:

1. Are the data reasonable?
2. Are the data adequately supported?
3. Do the data actually lead to the claim suggested?
4. Is the warrant reasonable?
5. Can the warrant actually be applied to the data presented?

Chapter Outline

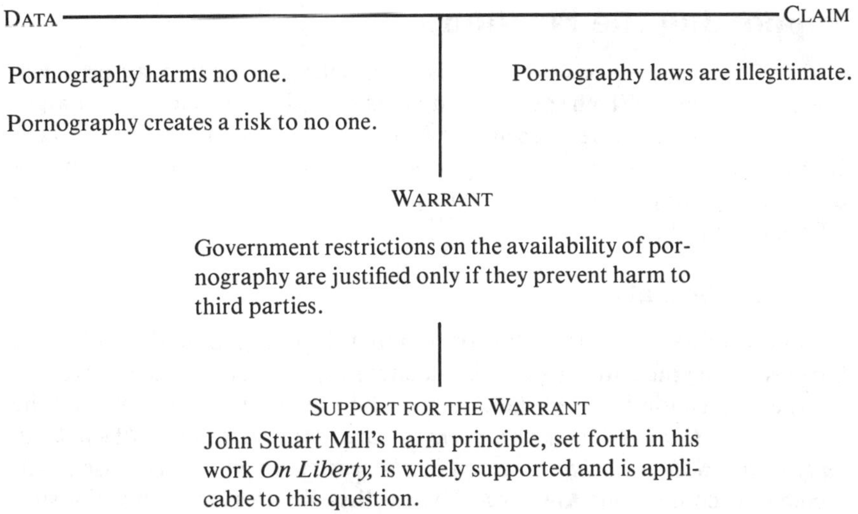

DATA — CLAIM

Pornography harms no one.

Pornography creates a risk to no one.

Pornography laws are illegitimate.

WARRANT

Government restrictions on the availability of pornography are justified only if they prevent harm to third parties.

SUPPORT FOR THE WARRANT

John Stuart Mill's harm principle, set forth in his work *On Liberty,* is widely supported and is applicable to this question.

FIGURE 10–1

Finally, individual arguments should be considered and their strength determined. In the above example, a negative team would have several options open to them in developing a negative position. One of the most obvious choices would be to deny the data. That is, to argue that pornography *does* harm third parties. If this strategy or "game plan" is successful then it would not be necessary to deny the warrant.

On the other hand, a negative team might wish to deny the warrant. They might determine that the data cited by the affirmative team is adequately supported and cannot be denied, but that the warrant is flawed or inappropriate and its application to the data would not be valid. For example, the negative team might argue that while it may be accurate that pornography harms no one, the government has a legitimate legal right to restrict behavior disliked by a majority of citizens. Or they might argue that the government has the right to restrict that which it considers immoral or which is contrary to prevailing societal values. Both of these are appropriate alternative warrants which, if sustained, would diminish the impact of the data.

Either of the above options would undermine the affirmative claim. Of course, a negative team might decide that the best strategy would be to deny the data as well as question the validity of the warrant. If time constraints prevent pursuing both options with equal force, the emphasis of one over the other while attempting both might be the answer. These and other position options will be considered in the following section.

Supporting the Position

Once the negative position is chosen, specific arguments may be developed and applied. Which specific arguments are to be used and how the arguments are to be supported depend, of course, on the negative position taken. In this section four basic negative positions will be discussed: (1) denying the data, (2) rejecting the warrant, (3) disputing jurisdiction, and (4) attacking affirmative insufficiency.

Denying the Data

A negative team can take the position that the data is flawed; this is done by questioning the authority of the evidence supporting the data or by rejecting the connection between the evidence and the observation. Consider the proposition: *Resolved, that producers of hazardous waste should be held legally responsible for injuries caused by the waste.* An affirmative case might include the contention: **Abandoned waste disposal sites are deadly.** For support, suppose the affirmative team offered the following evidence:

> Howard Rishel, Terrance Boston, Curtis Schmidt, and Oscar Albrecht. "EPA Project Summary: Cost of Remedial Response Actions at Uncontrolled Hazardous Waste Sites." March 1983.
>
> WASTES AT UNCONTROLLED AND ABANDONED DISPOSAL SITES CONTAIN TOXIC, REACTIVE, IGNITABLE, CORROSIVE, AND PERSISTENT HAZARDOUS SUBSTANCES THAT POSE SIGNIFICANT RISKS TO PUBLIC HEALTH AND THE ENVIRONMENT.

The authority of the evidence above could be questioned on a number of grounds. First, one could indict the evidence for being dated. It has now been several years since the source was printed; in that time improvements might have alleviated the problem. Second, the qualifications of the sources were not mentioned. Were they administrators of the EPA? Were they investigators? Were they in a position to know the facts? Since the information has not been provided the authority of the evidence is in doubt.

An additional complaint might be levied against the authority of the evidence in that the Environmental Protection Agency might be biased. Since it is a regulatory agency, its interests might be fostered by an overstatement of the problem. An assessment of an environmental problem made by an agency whose own existence depends on public concern about the problem might well be overstated.

Finally, one might question the methodology used to arrive at the conclusion stated in the evidence. How does the source know that wastes at abandoned sites pose significant risks to the public? The following considerations would be important:

1. Were the risks determined through scientific studies?
2. If so, were these studies conducted by the sources themselves?
3. If conducted by someone else, were the researchers qualified?
4. What methods did the experimenters employ?
5. Did the methods control for other possible causes of the harms?

The answers to these questions could strengthen the negative position. If the statement about public health harms was made without benefit of experiment, then the conclusion it touts might well be flawed. If the conclusion was based on experiments or studies that were not controlled, then the public health risks could be caused by something other than the toxic wastes.

By questioning (1) the recency of the evidence, (2) the source's bias, and (3) the methodology utilized to arrive at the conclusion, the authority of the evidence can be undermined. If the evidence used to support the data is undermined, the negative position is strengthened significantly.

Besides questioning the authority of the evidence, a negative team may deny the connection between the evidence and the observation. Using the example above, the denial of such a connection can be accomplished through the claim of flawed reasoning or through a more careful reading of the evidence. A negative team could argue that the evidence represents a hasty generalization. They might say that, while some abandoned sites are dangerous, not all are harmful, and the evidence does not claim that all sites are harmful. If all sites were considered, the conclusion might be different.

A negative team might also propose that other factors exist which mitigate or diminish the impact of the harm. For example, they might claim that the Comprehensive Environmental Response, Compensation, and Liability Act of 1980 reduces any harm that might exist. In view of the harmless abandoned sites and the mitigating federal law, the evidence simply does not support the contention.

A more careful reading of the evidence might also weaken the connection between the evidence and the observation. In the example above, a close look at the evidence reveals that it specifically says that wastes at "uncontrolled and abandoned" disposal sites are hazardous. The observation or contention is confined only to abandoned sites, however. How much of the problem is caused by the sites being uncontrolled? Are there sites that are abandoned but controlled? Are there uncontrolled sites that are not abandoned? Since the observation deals only with abandoned sites, the evidence really does not directly support it.

Also notice the specific wording of the contention: **Abandoned waste disposal sites are *deadly*.** The harm claimed from the sites is that they are "deadly." Nowhere in the evidence, however, does the word "deadly" appear; it is not even suggested. The evidence says that such sites "pose significant risks to public health." Significant risks to public health might not include life-threatening harms.

By (1) claiming that the connection between the evidence and the data has been drawn by faulty reasoning and (2) being certain that the evidence reads as it is claimed by the affirmative, the data in this case can be challenged effectively. That, of course, strengthens the negative position.

DENYING THE DATA

1. Question the authority of the evidence:
   a. recency
   b. bias of the source
   c. methodology
2. Question the links between evidence and observations:
   a. flawed reasoning
   b. more careful reading of the evidence

Rejecting the Warrant

Another position a negative team can take is to reject the validity or the application of the warrant. This position can be supported by (1) establishing that the warrant is unreasonable, (2) indicting the support for the warrant, or (3) offering an alternative warrant.

Consider a debate on the proposition *Resolved, that the method of conducting presidential elections in the United States is detrimental to democracy.* An affirmative team might argue that if the method of presidential elections undermines majority rule, then democratic values will be threatened and the method will be detrimental to democracy. This is the warrant or standard by which the data will be evaluated.

One negative approach would be to establish that the warrant is unreasonable. The affirmative thinking behind the standard of majority rule is undoubtedly that it is an essential element of democracy. The negative could argue that (1) majority rule is neither essential nor particularly important to the maintenance of a democracy, (2) there are other elements or characteristics of a democracy and that restricting the standard to majority rule is a characteristic of a perfect democracy, and (3) no democracy is or ever has been perfect and that perfection is an unreasonable standard. In this way, the negative would undermine the legitimacy of the warrant.

If the warrant is unreasonable, then the data cannot be interpreted properly. If the data cannot be interpreted properly, then the validity of the affirmative claim is in doubt and the negative position is strengthened.

In other cases it may be determined that the warrant is not inherently unreasonable, but that support for the warrant is weak. Consider the above example once again. The proposition that majority rule is essential to democracy might be supported by reference to certain political theorists. In such a case the warrant might not be invalid, but the authority of the theorists cited to support the concept might be called into question. If the affirmative cites Richard Nixon to support the claim of the essential nature of majority rule to democracy, the negative team could question the validity of Richard Nixon's qualifications to set standards of democracy. They could claim that politicians are poor sources for such determinations. The negative could also present authorities of equal or greater qualifications who directly dispute the standard the affirmative offers. This strategy would at least establish that other standards deserve consideration, thus weakening the validity of the affirmative warrant.

REJECTING THE WARRANT

1. Establish that the warrant is unreasonable.
2. Indict the support for the warrant.
3. Offer an alternative warrant.

Disputing Jurisdiction

Jurisdiction deals with establishing the ground on which the debate takes place. It centers on issues that determine the meaning of the proposition. The negative team should scrutinize the affirmative definitions of the proposition's key terms and dispute them if there is reason. (See Chapter Four for a general discussion of definitions as issues.)

Assume that there is a debate on the proposition: *Resolved, that victimless crime laws are outside the legitimate function of government.* The key terms in this proposition are "victimless crimes," "outside," "legitimate," and "function of government." If the negative has a problem with the affirmative definition of any of these terms, it will be an important issue in the debate.

Suppose that the affirmative team defines "legitimate" as "conforming to established rules, standards, and principles."[1] If their definition is accepted, the affirmative team will have to prove only that certain victimless crimes fall "outside" accepted principles or standards. The negative team will probably wish to establish an alternate definition of "legitimate"—one that would restrict the latitude the affirmative has in supporting the proposition. In order to limit this latitude, the negative will challenge the definition, and offer an alternative. The negative team might want to limit the affirmative to a definition of legitimate as "that which is lawful, legal, or recognized by law."[2] The impact of this jurisdictional dispute is great.

The affirmative team's definition of legitimate as "conforming to principles" would allow them to argue that in the instance of pornography laws, for example, such restrictions violate the principle of free expression. If such an argument is sustained, the law's illegitimacy has been supported. If the negative definition of the term prevails, however, then the issue of free expression becomes less important because a different standard has been applied. The definition of legitimacy offered by the negative narrows the relevant discussion to what is legal or lawful, and this restriction makes the task of the affirmative much more difficult.

In non-policy debate, these jurisdictional disputes are extremely important because often warrants are established through the definition of key terms of the proposition. Thus, a dispute of these definitions, as in the case above, may end in undermining the warrant. Although warrants are important in debates on any proposition, they are particularly crucial for non-policy topics.

Another way in which the negative can claim jurisdictional differences is to accept the warrant offered by the affirmative team, but with an alternative interpretation of it. Suppose that an affirmative team argues that government restrictions are legitimate only if they protect third parties from harm. To show that victimless crime laws are not legitimate, the affirmative team might demonstrate that certain victimless crimes, pornography for example, hurt no one but the perpetrator. Since pornography hurts no third parties, it might be argued, then pornography laws are not legitimate.

The negative could accept the harm principle but dispute its meaning. The negative could interpret "harm" as inconvenience, or nuisance, or psychological harms. These kinds of "harms" might be easier to establish, and if sustained, this interpretation would weaken the affirmative case. These issues and choices will help to establish the ground upon which the debate rests: What does the proposition mean? What standards should be used? Exactly how do we apply the standards? These basic issues can serve as a foundation for a negative position.

DISPUTING JURISDICTION

1. Dispute the definition of key terms
2. Dispute the meaning of the warrant

Attacking Affirmative Insufficiency

This negative approach questions the adequacy of a key portion of the affirmative case. The nature of the approach will depend on whether the proposition is one of policy advocacy or one of non-policy.

Policy Propositions

Affirmative insufficiency in propositions of policy advocacy centers on the inadequacy of the affirmative solvency. If the affirmative presents a needs case, the negative can argue that the plan offered will not solve the problem that has been presented. This is typically called a *Plan-Meet-Need argument* or PMN. Plan-Meet-Need arguments usually focus on three affirmative plan deficiencies: (1) conceptual errors, (2) structural inadequacies, or (3) barriers to implementation.

Conceptual Errors are claimed when the affirmative team misanalyzes any fundamental part of their case, which prevents the solvency of their proposal. Consider the following proposition: *Resolved, that the federal government should implement a program that guarantees employment opportunities for all U.S. citizens in the labor force.* Suppose further that the affirmative presents the following needs case:

I. Unemployment is a serious national problem.
  A. A large class of unemployed exists.
    1. They are the long-term unemployed.
    2. Their job skills are not relevant to the contemporary economy.
  B. Unemployment is a serious threat to the individual and to the nation.
    1. Individual harms
      a. stress related disease
      b. alcoholism
      c. mental illness and suicide
    2. Societal harms
      a. lost tax revenues
      b. welfare costs
      c. undeveloped human potential

II. Present system policies are innately inadequate to solve the unemployment problem.
  A. The present system is committed to economic growth as the solution to unemployment.
  B. The unemployed population is beyond the aid of economic growth.
    1. They are not skilled.
    2. Economic growth is limited.
  C. Programs that could help are being reduced or eliminated.
    1. Federal jobs training has declined substantially.
    2. States follow federal lead in cutting state training programs.

III. Plan
   A. A Board of Vocational Rehabilitation and Training will be established.
   B. Funding will be provided by a fifty cent surcharge on the purchase of tobacco products.
   C. Enforcement will be provided through the Federal Bureau of Investigation according to existing statutes and compliance mechanisms.
   D. Mandates of the Board will be:
      1. to establish a comprehensive program of vocational rehabilitation for those whose skills are no longer suited for modern economic realities.
      2. to provide training for those without any skill relevant to the present or future economy.

Notice that the affirmative argues that one of the fundamental reasons for unemployment is poor training, the other is slow economic growth. The negative could object to this analysis, arguing that unemployment is caused not by a lack of training but by large federal deficits. Thus, the negative will attempt to argue that the affirmative has analyzed the cause of the problem inaccurately, and if this is so, it is likely that the proposed plan will not work. In this way, objection of conceptual errors supports the argument that the affirmative plan fails to meet the need set forth in the affirmative case. If deficits and not lack of training cause unemployment, the affirmative analysis suffers from conceptual error.

This kind of objection is not easy to sustain, but if a conceptual error can be proven it is very effective. One might design the objection this way:

I. The affirmative misanalyzes unemployment.
   A. The affirmative assumes that the cause of unemployment is a poorly skilled workforce.
      1. The cause of unemployment is shrinking capital for business expansion.
      2. The cause of shrinking capital is slow economic growth.
      3. The cause of slow economic growth is the huge federal deficit.
         a. leads to an excessively strong dollar
         b. which leads to large balance of trade deficits
         c. which indicates less demand for domestic products

If the negative is successful in sustaining this line of attack, then they can claim the present system will solve unemployment since even the affirmative agrees that present programs are aimed at achieving that goal. It would also be clear that the affirmative plan could not solve unemployment, given the negative objection. Exactly why the plan would fail to solve the problem will be clear when a second type of objection is made—that of structural inadequacies.

Structural inadequacies include such deficiencies as missing mandates, or lack of key mechanisms (such as funding or enforcement). Consider the above example again. In considering any plan-meet-need argument, the negative asks, "Is the affirmative proposal adequate to solve the problems they present?" According to the example above, the question specifically would be, "Is a program of vocational and basic skill training sufficient to solve the problem of unemployment?" The objection outlined in the section above, focusing on conceptual error, actually provides a basis for an answer to this question.

If the cause of unemployment is the large budget deficits, then the mandates provided in the affirmative plan will not address the cause. Thus the objection of conceptual error above can be continued to support the objection of structural inadequacies:

II. Affirmative mandates address only training.
  A. Better training will not solve the problem.
  B. Training programs will worsen the problem.
    1. Training programs do not solve the deficits.
    2. The cost of training programs will increase the deficits.
  C. There are no mandates that guarantee employment. At best, the affirmative plan provides training for possible employment, but does not guarantee it.

III. Affirmative funding mechanism is inadequate.
  A. Training programs are expensive.
  B. The fifty-cent tobacco tax is inadequate to pay for such programs.
  C. So, even if training would solve unemployment the affirmative plan would not be adequately funded.

Either of these objections, if sustained, would be a potentially fatal blow to the affirmative case. If the plan cannot solve the problem presented, for whatever reason, then it matters little whether the affirmative sustains the other portions of their case. If the affirmative cannot solve the problem, they cannot prevail.

Barriers to implementation typically involve psychological impediments to the implementation of the affirmative proposal. This objection is that the affirmative plan will not be implemented because of some barrier or barriers within the present system that cannot be overcome. These can include: (1) psychological barriers, or (2) circumvention.

The negative can show that there is significant opposition in the present system to the kind of reforms that the affirmative suggests, and that this opposition will prevent enforcement mechanisms from working. Using the above example, the negative might argue that the people who would likely implement and enforce the suggested training programs are adamantly opposed to them, it is thus reasonable to assume that they would not implement or enforce them properly.

A circumvention argument is one that points to a "loophole" which allows the mandates of the affirmative plan to be avoided. The example above offers an illustration: according to the affirmative plan, the states are not obliged constitutionally to cooperate with the federal program. There is no provision in the affirmative case which compels them to do so. It could be argued, then, that the states would not cooperate. Thus, the plan is circumvented. The argument could be designed this way:

I. The states will circumvent implementation.
  A. States are needed for implementation.
    1. the unemployed need to be identified
    2. deficient skills need to be identified
    3. only the states have the resources for identification
  B. States are opposed to training programs.
  C. The plan has no mechanism to force states to comply.
  D. The states will not comply.

As other plan-meet-need (PMN) objections, barriers to implementation point to the insufficiency of the affirmative plan to solve the problem it was designed to solve.

Plan-meet-advantage arguments, or PMAs, are similar to plan-meet-need arguments: both question the sufficiency of the affirmative plan. However, PMNs apply to needs cases, and plan-meet-advantage arguments apply to other policy cases such as comparative advantages or alternative justifications. The needs case outlined above can be revised into a comparative advantages case such as this one:

I. [Same plan as before]
II. The plan will alleviate stress.
  A. Unemployment is linked to stress.
  B. Stress is harmful.
    1. stress causes disease
    2. stress causes alcoholism
    3. stress leads to mental illness and suicide

III. The plan will reduce the budget deficit.
   A. Increased employment will increase tax revenues.
   B. Increased employment will decrease welfare costs.

A plan-meet-advantage argument would question the adequacy of the plan to achieve the two advantages claimed by the affirmative. The same conceptual objections and barriers for implementation can be made for this case structure, too. Only the structural inadequacies would have to be argued differently since, of course, the structure is different.

At least two PMAs would be possible in the above example. First, that the affirmative plan will not alleviate stress. This PMA is built upon the previous argument that training programs will not increase employment. If unemployment is not reduced, then no advantage can be claimed. A second PMA might be that since job training will not decrease unemployment, the deficit could not possibly be reduced by the plan.

In policy advocacy debate, plan-meet-need and plan-meet-advantage arguments are important considerations for the negative team. If sustained they can significantly strengthen the negative position.

Non-Policy Propositions

Affirmative insufficiency in non-policy propositions usually centers on the adequacy of the generalization the affirmative draws from the examples they present. As with policy propositions, the aim of the attack is to question the sufficiency not of single issues or evidence but of a key portion of the affirmative case. Whereas this approach focused on the *plan* in policy debate, it will focus on the adequacy of the generalization for non-policy debate. Assume that students are debating: *Resolved, that U.S. military support to nondemocratic governments is justified.* The key generalization will be made based on the examples of nondemocratic governments offered by the affirmative team to support the proposition. Suppose an affirmative team presents this case:

I. U.S. military support for Taiwan is justified.
   A. Taiwan is strategically located.
      1. strategic for commerce
      2. strategic for defense
   B. Support for Taiwan stabilizes the region.
      1. Taiwan is important to Japan
      2. Taiwan is important to South Korea

II. U.S. military support for El Salvador is justified.
   A. El Salvador is strategically located.
      1. strategic for defense
      2. serves as a buffer to communism

B. Support for El Salvador protects Mexico.
   1. Mexico strategically crucial
   2. Mexico strategic for commerce
      a. trade
      b. energy

The question that the negative should ask is, "Do the affirmative examples sufficiently represent all nondemocratic governments?" In the above example, "Do the examples of Taiwan and El Salvador sufficiently support the proposition?" To answer the question, the negative should consider two things: typicality and consistency.

Nontypicality is a determination that the affirmative examples are not typical of all possible examples. In reference to the illustration above, several considerations are possible. One could consider the land size of the country, distance from the U.S., their proximity, their population, their military strength, type of government, location, available resources, and so on. Which of these characteristics is important will be determined by the particular case the affirmative presents. If by some standard the negative determines and can demonstrate that the examples are not typical, then the generalization will not be valid.

Taiwan and El Salvador can be viewed in a number of ways. In terms of location, they are perhaps as typical as two examples could be, one in Asia and the other in Central America. These two regions do represent a good many nondemocratic governments. The negative could argue, however, that examples from South America and Africa would make the generalization more acceptable and that the two examples are not very strong.

The negative could also consider the size of the countries cited as examples. It could be argued that both countries are very weak militarily and thus are not typical of nondemocratic governments. Any characteristic which makes the examples appear to be unrepresentative of other possible examples calls into doubt the inference or generalization gained from them.

Inconsistency is a determination that the examples used by the affirmative are not consistent with other major examples. This consideration is similar to nontypicality, but there is a difference. Typicality is the *representativeness* of the examples. Consistency is the *absence of major exceptions.* It is possible for the examples to be representative of the whole, but counter to some major exceptions.

Consider the example above. A negative team might agree that Taiwan and El Salvador are typical of nondemocratic governments in most ways, but that there are other typical examples which, if considered, would not support the proposition. For instance, the negative might point out that South Africa is also nondemocratic, it is also a typical example, but support for their government is not justified. These kinds of arguments are sometimes called *counter-warrants.* Considered by themselves, they "warrant" the rejection of the proposition.

Objections based on either typicality or inconsistency weaken the affirmative case. If sustained, these arguments will significantly strengthen the negative's position.

ATTACKING AFFIRMATIVE INSUFFICIENCY

1. Policy propositions
   a. plan-meet-need deficiency
      conceptual errors
      structural inadequacies
      barriers to implementation
   b. plan-meet-advantage deficiency
      conceptual errors
      structural inadequacies
      barriers to implementation
2. Non-policy propositions
   a. typicality
   b. consistency

Other Negative Arguments

In addition to the arguments above, other negative arguments are available to advocates debating policy propositions. These are: (1) disadvantages, (2) inherency, (3) minor repairs, (4) counterplans, and (5) counter-warrants.

Disadvantages

A disadvantage argued by the negative is an objection that the proposition, if adopted, will lead to certain harmful effects. A disadvantage can be directed toward the proposition, or it may be directed toward the particular affirmative proposal. Either way, the negative must be prepared to prove that the disadvantage will absolutely occur if the affirmative proposal is adopted.

It is possible for a negative team to concede that the identified problem will be solved by the affirmative proposal, but that other more significant disadvantages will accompany it. Considered together, it could be reasoned, the disadvantages outweigh the advantages and the proposition should not be adopted.

With the introduction of disadvantages by the negative and advantages by the affirmative, the debaters engage in the conflict that surrounds the *weighing of values*. In a policy debate involving these issues, the judge must weigh the benefits of reducing unemployment, for example, and the disadvantages of inflation. If the affirmative plan will solve unemployment, but cause inflation at the same time, the judge must decide if the trade-off is advisable. A disadvantage can be constructed in this way:

I. The affirmative proposal will increase inflation.
   A. The affirmative calls for job training programs.
      1. training programs are expensive
      2. revenue cannot meet their cost
      3. the government will borrow to pay for the programs.
   B. Government revenue shortfalls lead to inflation.
   C. Inflation is devastating.
      1. inflation hurts the elderly
      2. inflation hurts our defense
      3. inflation hurts the farmer
   D. The present system is inflation free.

Finally, to be valid a disadvantage must also be unique. If the disadvantage that the negative argues will happen anyway, no matter what policy is implemented, then the disadvantage is not unique and is not valid. In the above example, if inflation will occur in the present system or any other system, then the disadvantage should not be argued.

Inherency

Inherent means intrinsic or endemic. Something that is inherent is firmly established or is an essential part of a system or thing. In debate, the term *inherent* usually refers to an inseparable condition, component, or effect of a system of public policy. For instance, we might say that party primaries are inherent to the system of presidential politics. This example indicates an inherent component of the system. Effects can also be inherent. One could argue that large financial commitments are inherent byproducts of the system of presidential politics.

Inherency is an important issue in any policy advocacy debate. If a component or effect is inherent to a system, then to eliminate the component or to alter the effect requires a fundamental change. Usually propositions of policy advocacy call for significant or fundamental revision of the status quo. In order to justify this fundamental change, the affirmative team has to prove that the disadvantageous components or effects are an essential part of the system. They must be prepared to argue that no less than a fundamental alteration of the system will alleviate the deficiencies.

Suppose a debate took place on the following proposition: *Resolved, that the power of labor unions should be significantly reduced.* The affirmative would identify a component or effect of labor unions that is both harmful and inherent to the system. The affirmative team might argue that labor unions, through their wage demands, cause high inflation. The affirmative plan would reduce the power of labor unions to negotiate wages; therefore the affirmative would claim the advantage of suppressing inflation.

A negative team would want to consider the endemic nature of wage negotiations to labor unions. Can wages be controlled and not significantly reduce the power of labor unions? In other words, can the problem be solved through a nonresolutional remedy? If it can, the affirmative has not presented a justification for fundamental change. If an affirmative team fails to demonstrate an inherent need for change, they cannot prevail in a policy advocacy debate.

Minor Repairs

If the affirmative team has identified a legitimate problem, it might be solved through a nonresolutional and nonfundamental remedy. In other words, minor repairs are not indications of a breakdown of the present system, but simply a recognition that minor improvements in the status quo might be beneficial. These remedies are called minor repairs. In the above example, the affirmative team has identified inflation as a significant problem caused by labor union wage demands. The negative might suggest wage and price controls as a remedy. These, it could be reasoned, would check inflation, solve the high wage demands, and do so without significantly reducing the power of labor unions.

The use of a strategy suggesting minor repairs can be very effective for the negative team. If the problem identified by the affirmative can be solved and disadvantages prevented, then there is certainly no justification for the adoption of the proposition.

Two conditions are usually required of minor repairs. First, the negative must be somewhat specific as to the nature of the repairs. Since the suggestion is made in response to an affirmative proposal, it is perhaps unreasonable to demand as much clarity as demanded of the affirmative proposal; however, it should be specific enough to allow an affirmative defense.

Second, the negative should demonstrate that the improvements they claim will result from the repairs are probable. Using the previous example, the negative should prove that wage and price controls would likely reduce inflation.

Counterplans

Repairs, such as those we just discussed, and *counterplans* may seem similar at first, but they are in fact different. Negative teams who argue minor repairs essentially *accept the desirability of the status quo.* They deny that there are problems inherent to the present system but acknowledge problems that can be solved within the system without fundamental changes.

Teams who argue counterplans, on the other hand, *acknowledge problems that are endemic to the system and propose changes to the status quo;* these suggested changes act as a nonresolutional alternative to the affirmative proposal. Wayne Thompson has identified several categories of arguments to which most counterplans lead.

1. The negative proposal solves the needs assessed by the affirmative:
   a. Negative solves Need One in that: [solvency analysis]
   b. Negative solves Need Two in that: [solvency analysis]

   or

   The negative proposal accrues certain advantages the affirmative proposal does not:
   a. Negative achieves Advantage One in that: [advantage analysis]
   b. Negative achieves Advantage Two in that: [advantage analysis]

2. The negative proposal solves additional needs which the affirmative has not claimed:
   a. Need One is solved in that: [solvency analysis]
   b. Need Two is solved in that: [solvency analysis]

3. The negative avoids the disadvantages accrued by the affirmative proposal.[3]

Usually a counterplan is a risky strategy for the negative to employ, for several reasons. First, with the suggestion of a counterplan, most judges feel that the negative assumes the burden of proof. Some judges maintain that in such cases the burden does *not* shift from the affirmative and others believe that a counterplan neutralizes the burden of proof; in any case, the presentation of the counterplan drastically changes the responsibility of each side.

Second, the counterplan must be mutually exclusive of the affirmative proposal. If the judge can accept both plans, then the resolution will be adopted and the affirmative will prevail. If carefully considered and soundly constructed, the counterplan is a legitimate negative strategy.

Counter-Warrants

Many negative arguments require very specific knowledge of the particular affirmative case being attacked or refuted. However, at least one negative approach requires no specific negative application. This is the use of *counter-warrants,* used in both policy and non-policy debating.

Counter-warrants are premised upon certain important principles. First, counter-warrants are based on the assumption that the focus of the debate should be the resolution. Although an affirmative approach might examine a particular example of the resolution, the focus of the debate nevertheless should be the resolution. Second, the use of counter-warrants is based upon an assumption about a crucial link between the particular affirmative case and the resolution being debated. Counter-warrant theory assumes that if the affirmative uses an example of the resolution, then that example must support the entire resolution. Counter-warrants are designed to test whether or not the affirmative case is sufficient *inductively* to prove the resolution. In other words, counter-warrants are designed to force the affirmative to show a significant or representative relationship between the resolution and the particular affirmative case.

A counter-warrant may be defined as a negative constructive argument which denies or refutes the proposition being debated without directly clashing with the specific affirmative analysis. For example, if the affirmative is debating the topic, *Resolved: That the United States should significantly reduce its foreign policy commitments,* an affirmative team might interpret this resolution and argue against the United States involvement in El Salvador. The negative using the counter-warrant approach might argue that withdrawal from Vietnam was disastrous. According to the rationale for counter-warrants the affirmative's ability to answer this argument would test the significance and the representativeness of the affirmative's case.

James Paulsen and Jack Rhodes describe the logical requirements of a counter-warrant on a resolution: "(1) that the area of counter-warrant is a legitimate topical area, i.e., a plausible example of the resolution, and (2) that action of the nature suggested by the resolution would be—or in the case of a past example, was—disastrous."[4] This suggests that counter-warrants that apply to topical cases that the affirmative is not defending might also be viewed as disadvantages.

Paulsen and Rhodes discuss counter-warrants in the context of intercollegiate tournament debate on propositions of policy advocacy, and the use of counter-warrants in policy advocacy debate is the subject of much controversy.[5] However, counter-warrants may also be argued on non-policy propositions. In fact, some argumentation theorists find counter-warrants a more effective strategy in non-policy debate than in policy debate. Walter Ulrich explains:

> While there are numerous arguments against counter-warrants in policy debate, it is unclear that these arguments apply to counter-warrants in value de-

bate. Initially, the resolution in value debate would seem to have a different function than the resolution in policy debate. In policy debate, by tradition, we have allowed debaters to select a single policy to defend. Even though there may be other ways to view the topic, by convention it is assumed that the entire topic is not debated. The result is that NDT tends to use broad topics that cannot be debated in their entirety.

This is not the case in CEDA. If anything, there is a dominant viewpoint that the entire resolution should be debated in CEDA, not just a part of the resolution. Many individuals feel that CEDA was created, at least partially, as a reaction to unusual cases that focused on one corner of the resolution. Thus, the view of the community toward the topic is different in CEDA than in policy debate, suggesting that the entire topic should be debated in CEDA. This would legitimize counter-warrants in CEDA.[6]

The debater who uses the counter-warrant strategy will need to be able to defend the strategy as theoretically legitimate. Greg Tolbert and Steve Hunt summarize some of the objections against counter-warrants:

> Many have criticized the use of counter-warrants in debate: First, they suggest that counter-warrants decrease clash. Second, critics argue that counter-warrants promote superficial analysis. Finally, opponents contend that counter-warrants give an unfair advantage to the negative team.[7]

Tolbert and Hunt, however, argue against these common objections and make a case for the use of counter-warrants in non-policy debate. The debater who wants to be well prepared to either refute or defend the counter-warrant strategy should be familiar with these and other critiques of counter-warrant theory.

A final consideration is how to utilize counter-warrants in the debate format. The current practice in non-policy intercollegiate debate is for the second negative speaker to use counter-warrants either alone or in combination with other arguments. However, this division of labor simply reflects the current practice and does not necessarily represent a theoretical perspective.

Negative Speaker Responsibilities

Traditionally there have been certain responsibilities that each speaker in a debate has been expected to fulfill. Some of those responsibilities are as a result of convention and others are required by the nature of the proposition. The responsibilities of the negative speakers in a debate will depend primarily upon the nature of the proposition.

Policy Propositions

Negative speakers on propositions of policy advocacy have an additional task which debaters on other propositions do not. This is the issue of solvency.

The division of labor in such debates is crucial, for without a sound plan of division the task might become unmanageable.

The first negative constructive speech should be aimed primarily at the stock issues other than solvency: significance and inherency. This responsibility is to some degree based on convention, but it does have a logical justification. If the affirmative cannot establish that there is a fundamental need to significantly alter the present system, then there is no reason to discuss issues of solvency. If there is no need to change in the first place, then the nature of the change is unimportant.

The second negative speaker, then, is left with the issue of solvency and comparative worth of the proposal. Arguments aimed at the sufficiency of the affirmative's proposal are paramount in this speech. In addition to the attacks on affirmative insufficiency, the second negative constructive might deal with the comparative worth of the affirmative plan. For instance, the affirmative proposal, if adopted, might lead to certain disadvantages that would not occur if the present system was retained.

The discussion of solvency is crucial because even if the affirmative establishes a need for fundamental change, they also have the obligation to prove that their particular proposal will meet that need. If affirmatives fail in that regard, they cannot prevail.

Rebuttals offer a unique opportunity for the negative team in any debate. According to the traditional and widely-used cross examination format, the negative team delivers their first rebuttal immediately after the presentation of their second constructive speech and the cross examination period. This succession of speeches is called the "negative block." The negative has a substantial amount of time to present nonrefuted argument. The "block" is followed by the first affirmative rebuttal, which is considerably more brief than the two consecutive negative speeches.

The first negative rebuttal will handle the same issues that were included in the constructive speech. In addition, the first negative rebuttalist will attempt to respond to any new arguments presented in the second affirmative constructive.

The second negative rebuttal has a very important function, which is to identify the voting issues for the judge and explain why the negative team has prevailed on those issues. The second rebuttal is also the first and only chance for the negative to respond to the affirmative arguments on solvency and disadvantages. Therefore, most of the second rebuttal should center on those issues.

Non-Policy Propositions

Because non-policy propositions differ from those of policy, speaker responsibilities also differ. The importance of the division of labor, however, is no different. Success in debating non-policy propositions will largely depend on an effective division of responsibilities. As with policy propositions, the responsibilities of each speaker are based both on convention and upon the nature of the task.

The first negative constructive speech will center on issues of jurisdiction, denying data, and criteria. These attacks can fairly be described as *direct refutation.* The first negative speaker will respond to the arguments of the affirmative, and the speech will respond directly to the affirmative case.

The second negative constructive will generally focus discussion on other reasons to reject the proposition. As we learned earlier in the chapter, these are called counter-warrants, which do not directly respond to affirmative arguments. The second negative will also deal with any new arguments presented by the second affirmative speaker.

The first negative rebuttal will respond to affirmative case arguments and attack, the second affirmative case responses. The first negative rebuttal completes the negative block, so care must be taken to ensure that this advantage is utilized to its utmost.

The second negative rebuttal has the same unique obligations in non-policy debate as in policy debate. The second rebuttal is the first and last opportunity for the negative team to respond to affirmative counter-warrant arguments. Most of the rebuttal should probably focus on those issues. In addition, the second negative should identify the voting issues for the judge and explain why the negative should prevail on those issues.

POLICY PROPOSITIONS	NON-POLICY PROPOSITIONS
First Negative Constructive:	First Negative Constructive:
Significance	Jurisdiction
Inherency	Denying Data
Topicality	Criteria
Second Negative Constructive:	Second Negative Constructive:
Solvency	Counter-Warrants
New Affirmative Arguments	New Affirmative Arguments
Cost–benefits	
First Negative Rebuttal:	First Negative Rebuttal:
Significance	Jurisdiction
Inherency	Denying Data
Topicality	Criteria
Second Negative Rebuttal:	Second Negative Rebuttal:
Solvency	Counter-Warrants
Issues Clarification	Issues Clarification

FIGURE 10–2

Summary

The task for the negative team in any debate is to deny the proposition. There are numerous ways to accomplish this, including general negative positions and specific ways of supporting those positions. A negative team develops a general negative position in order to argue with purpose and to avoid contradiction. In developing a position, negative teams should consider the nature of the proposition, the structure of the affirmative case, and the strength of individual affirmative arguments.

Negative teams can choose to (1) deny the affirmative data, (2) reject the warrant, (3) dispute jurisdiction, or (4) attack insufficiency.

If denying the data, the negative may challenge the authority of the evidence, or question the links between the evidence and the observations. If rejecting the warrant, negatives can establish that the warrant is unreasonable, indict the support for the warrant, or offer an alternative warrant. If disputing jurisdiction, the negative team can dispute the definition of the key terms or challenge the meaning of the warrant.

If attacking affirmative insufficiencies in policy advocacy debates, the negative team might point to conceptual errors, structural inadequacies, or barriers to implementation. For debates on other propositions, affirmative insufficiencies may be argued through a demonstration of nontypicality or inconsistency in the examples used by the affirmative.

Other negative arguments take the form of (1) disadvantages, (2) inherency arguments, (3) minor repairs, (4) counterplans, and (5) counter-warrants. No matter which position or specific argument the negative team chooses to put forward, extreme care should be taken in the development, support, and presentation.

Notes

1. *Webster's New World Dictionary of the American Language* (New York: Simon and Schuster, 1980), p. 807.
2. *Black's Law Dictionary*, 5th ed. (St. Paul: West Publishing, 1979), p. 811.
3. Thompson presents these arguments in a different manner and in a slightly different context. For Thompson's treatment see *Modern Argumentation and Debate* (New York: Harper and Row, 1971), pp. 90–91.
4. James W. Paulsen and Jack L. Rhodes, "The Counter-Warrant as Negative Strategy: A Modest Proposal," *Journal of the American Forensic Association* XV, No. 4 (Spring 1979): 207.
5. See Marjorie Keeshan and Walter Ulrich, "A Critique of the Counter-Warrant as a Negative Strategy," *Journal of the American Forensic Association* 16 (Winter 1980): 199; Pat Ganer, "Counter-Warrants: An Idea

Whose Time Has Not Come," in *Dimensions of Argument: Proceedings of the Second Summer Conference on Argumentation,* ed. by George Zeigemueller and Jack Rhodes (Annadale, Va: Speech Communication Association, 1981), pp. 476–84; and Rich Simon, "The Case Against Counter-Warrants in Value Proposition Debate," in *CEDA Yearbook, 1984,* (Northridge, CA: Don Brownlee, California State University, 1984), pp. 48–53.

6. Walter Ulrich, "The Nature of the Topic in Value Debate," in *CEDA Yearbook, 1984,* (Northridge, CA: Don Brownlee, California State University, 1984), p. 4.
7. Greg Tolbert and Steve Hunt, "Counter-Warrants: A Method for Testing Topical Justification in CEDA Debate," in *CEDA Yearbook, 1985,* (Northridge, CA: Don Brownlee, California State University, 1985), p. 24.

Questions and Exercises

1. What general factors should be considered in developing the negative position?
2. How does an advocate, while on the negative, deny the data?
3. What are the four basic negative positions?
4. What issues are involved in rejecting the warrant presented by the affirmative team? What are the alternatives available to the negative team to reject the warrant?
5. How does a negative team dispute jurisdiction?
6. Why is recognizing conceptual errors important to the negative team in attacking affirmative insufficiency?
7. What are plan-meet-need arguments?
8. What are plan-meet-advantage arguments?
9. How do structural inadequacies support PMNs or PMAs?
10. What is nontypicality?
11. What is inconsistency?
12. What are disadvantages and how are they constructed?
13. What does inherency mean? Why is it an important issue for the negative team to understand?
14. What are minor repairs?
15. How do minor repairs differ from counterplans?
16. What are the requirements of counterplans?
17. What are the speaker responsibilities of the first negative constructive in a policy debate? In a non-policy debate?

18. What are the speaker responsibilities of the second negative constructive speaker in a policy debate? In a non-policy debate?
19. What are the responsibilities of the rebuttal speakers in a policy debate? In a non-policy debate?
20. Read the non-policy debate transcript in Appendix B. Identify the general negative positions taken. Identify the specific arguments used to support those positions. Evaluate the strength of the positions and their supporting arguments.
21. Select a transcript of an intercollegiate debate on a policy topic. Identify the general negative positions taken. Identify the specific arguments used to support those positions. Evaluate the strength of those positions and their supporting arguments.

Suggested Readings

Cirlin, Alan. "On Negative Strategy in Value Debate." *CEDA Yearbook, 1984.* California State University, Northridge: Don Brownlee, 1984, pp. 31-39.

Gotcher, Mike and Biggers, Thompson. "An Alternative Approach to Negative Speaker Duties in CEDA Debate." *CEDA Yearbook, 1984.* California State University, Northridge: Don Brownlee, 1984, pp. 40–48.

Herbeck, Dale. "A Permutation Standard of Competitiveness." *Journal of the American Forensic Association,* XXII (Summer 1985), 12–19.

Hynes, Thomas. "Study: Hope or False Promise." *Journal of the American Forensic Association,* XVI (Winter 1980), 192–198.

Kaplow, Louis. "Rethinking Counterplans: A Reconciliation with Debate Theory." *Journal of the American Forensic Association,* XVII (Spring 1981), 215–226.

Shelton, Michael. "In Defense of Study Counterplan." *Journal of the American Forensic Association,* XXI (Winter 1985), 150–155.

ELEVEN

Refutation

When advocates debate, they must consider one another's claims. If two speakers present opposing arguments without reference to their opponent's ideas, there is no clash and, in a sense, no debate. Refutation provides the tools for, or the means of, dealing with opposing arguments.

What Is Refutation?

Refutation may be defined as *the act of proving an argument either erroneous or false, or both.* Refutation differs from constructive argument in that the first purpose of refutation is to remove an idea from the listener's consideration rather than to persuade the listener to accept a new idea. The effective debater will use refutation and constructive argument together.

Speakers employ refutation in both public and educational debates. For example, when a lawyer cross-examines a witness she often attempts to destroy the witness's credibility. She may do this by formulating her questions to reveal a motive for lying or by revealing inconsistencies in the testimony. This is refutation in the courtroom.

When Congress considers a new law, legislators will usually devote time both to defeating opposing legislation and to promoting their own bills. Similarly, when presidents propose new policies or justify existing policies, it is not unusual for them to refute their critics.

In educational debate both affirmative and negative teams may use refutation throughout the debate. The first affirmative speaker may even choose to refute a possible argument before the negative team has had the opportunity to speak. This is *pre-emptive refutation.* Under the traditional division of labor for the negative team, the first negative speaker refutes the affirmative case arguments and the second negative speaker presents constructive arguments. It is not unusual for the first negative speaker to use refutation exclusively. As you will see later in this chapter, however, some forms of argument refute and construct simultaneously.

In educational debate, refutation is the means of fulfilling the burden of rebuttal. *The burden of rebuttal, also referred to as the burden of rejoinder, is the obligation of any debater or team to respond to the argument or to concede that argument.* Regardless of the merits of the argument, if it is not answered then it is conceded. Even if the argument is, in the view of the advocate, "unworthy of response," that advocate must explain the reason that the argument deserves no response.

This chapter will review the traditional means of refutation, forms of counter argument, the criteria for choosing among methods of refutation, the steps for organizing refutation, and the preparation of briefs and blocks.

Direct Refutation

Refutation does not always require authoritative evidence, but it does require an informed understanding of the issues, effective listening, quick thinking, and analytical ability. Refutation that makes use of these abilities is often referred to as *direct refutation.* There are four methods of direct refutation: (1) attack the credibility of the source, (2) attack the content of the evidence, (3) attack the logic of the argument, and (4) attack the relevance of the argument. Consider each method and its applications.

1. Attack the credibility of the source. In listening to a debate, each speaker should try to note the sources of the evidence and their qualifications. This is especially important if the opposing advocate relies heavily on one source or if one crucial piece of evidence supports a vital link in the opponent's argument. The debaters may use cross-examination to gain additional information about sources and to test the opposing team's ability to

Chapter Outline

defend their source's credibility. Once the debater identifies potentially vulnerable sources, s/he can consider how to challenge the source. Are the source's qualifications known? Are the qualifications less than substantial? Does the opinion offered by the source require special areas of expertise? Does the source possess these special areas of expertise? Does the source have any ideological commitment or vested economic interest that would prejudice his or her testimony significantly?

Often debaters attempt to cite evidence from specific government administrators defending the quality of their institutions. A proposition that might engender such an attempt is: *Resolved, that higher education in the United States has sacrificed quality for institutional survival.* If the opposing team attempts to defend the quality of such an institution by using a quote from the institution's administrator, a credibility challenge would probably be made, such as: "The evidence is biased. What would you expect the administrator to say? He cannot afford to denigrate the quality of his institution."

A thorough knowledge of the principles of credible evidence will enable the debater to make effective challenges. Any successful credibility indictment will require that the disputed source be defended, or that the disputed evidence be replaced or lose the support it would otherwise have given.

2. Attack the content of the evidence. This method of refutation assumes that there may be problems in the content of the evidence. As indicated previously, every piece of evidence should contain a conclusion and the reasons or data to support the conclusion. Even though debaters should of course analyze and reason independently when presenting evidence, evidence that presents only a conclusion or generalization is often vulnerable to the attack that it is conclusionary. Therefore, debaters should question their *own* sources, and make sure that there is a basis in documentation for any conclusions drawn by the source or by the presenter of the evidence. Superior evidence will present the supporting reasons and data for a conclusion. *All* evidence should present at least an indication of the reasons behind the claims.

A challenge of incomplete evidence may be worded in the form of a question: "How did Wilbanks reach this conclusion?" or as a statement: "Church did not indicate any reasons for his findings." Inconsistencies in evidence or between different sources, or between two or more pieces from the same source might be possible areas for refutation on the content of the evidence.

Evidence from different sources should be consistent if used to support the same argument or line of reasoning. For example, in debating the education topic used above, affirmative teams would be required to prove that the quality of higher education programs has declined. One case approach might be to discuss the decline of liberal arts programs. If the affirmative team does not make sure that all their supporting evidence discusses the same concept of liberal arts, this flaw will make the evidence vulnerable to attack. An opposing speaker might demand: "The affirmative must prove that all the evidence is based on the same concept of liberal arts. If this is not done, then we do not know where quality has declined." When the content of the evidence is effectively refuted, that evidence must be either replaced or removed from consideration. In the above example, successful refutation by the negative team would have made it difficult, if not impossible, for the affirmative to repair the damage.

3. Attack the logic of the argument. This method of refutation involves identifying problems in reasoning or in the logic of the argument. For example, advocates should certainly examine opposing arguments for problems in any causal relationships that are claimed. A debater may be able to challenge the logic of an argument when there is no apparent "causal link" or when there is "a confusion of correlation with causality." Effective refutation of the logic of an argument requires a thorough knowledge and understanding of how arguments are structured and the common problems in reasoning.

A disagreement often occurs regarding arguments making relational inferences, such as an argument that claims harms from pornography. Advocates of banning pornography will commonly argue that exposure to pornography will lead certain individuals to commit sexually oriented crimes. The evidence used to support this argument might show that areas where pornography is sold also have high levels of sexually oriented crime. This would be a *post hoc* fallacy. A debater attempting to refute such an argument might say, "No causal link is shown between exposure and the commission of these crimes. Just because they occur in the same localities does not prove the causal relationship. This may be coincidental, or there may be other factors causing the crimes—poverty, alcoholism, or unemployment, for example."

When the logic of an argument is effectively refuted it is often impossible to repair the damage. Because effective responses to such refutation require more than just replacing evidence, attacking the logic may remove an argument or an issue permanently from the debate.

4. Attack the relevance of the argument. A very effective method of direct refutation is to attack the relevance of the argument or issue. The debater attempting to assess the relevance of the argument should pose this question: If the argument is valid, then does the argument support the overall position it is supposed to support? For example, when a debater argues that a case is not topical or that an affirmative advantage stems from an extratopical plank in the plan, the affirmative case or that advantage need not be considered by the judge because they are irrelevant to the proposition being debated.

Sometimes proving the irrelevance of an argument is dependent upon first demonstrating another argument, which may require documentation. In debating U.S. involvement in Central America, for example, that involvement might be justified in that it supports the goal of stopping communism from spreading into that region. If an advocate can establish that the goal of stopping communism is either impossible or counterproductive, then that goal becomes irrelevant.

However, proving the irrelevance of an argument is not always dependent upon documentation. Often, showing that an argument or issue is irrelevant requires a demonstration that the argument simply is not related to the position being proposed.

When the relevance of an argument is effectively refuted, that argument is permanently removed from the debate. This is especially true if the refutation is based on relationships rather than documented assertions.

These four methods of direct refutation require careful listening, analytical skill, the ability to think and organize quickly, and an understanding of the topic. The debater who learns to effectively use these methods of direct refutation will be well prepared in many argumentative situations on many different topics.

Counter Argument

Another method of refutation is counter argument. *Counter argument* may be defined as *the substantive denial of the particular arguments and issues of the arguments being forwarded by the opposition.* For example, when one speaker argues that poverty has increased, the opposing advocate might counter argue and respond, "the increases are incidental and do not necessarily constitute a trend."

Effective counter argument requires a thorough knowledge of the topic and authoritative evidence to counter the opposing speaker's specific claims and evidence. Counter argument also allows a debater to prove an opposing argument false while simultaneously advancing an idea to displace the false argument. Counter argument, then, both removes an argument and adds vital positions for the judge or audience to consider. The several modes of counter argument include direct denial, re-analysis, changing the perspective, and turn-arounds.

1. Direct denial. This is one of the most common modes of counter argument and the most common mode of refutation. Direct denial requires the contradiction of the opposing claim. In its simplist form, direct denial is responding to a hypothetical statement of "x is y" with "x is not y." As the 1984 elections approached, various Democratic opponents and critics of

President Reagan criticized his cuts in domestic spending. To refute this claim, administration spokespeople and other defenders cited statistics that reflected real increases in the spending for certain social programs—thus denying that cuts were as severe as the critics claimed.

Direct denial does not always involve a *complete* contradiction. For example, if an advocate proposes that "unemployment is increasing among minority groups," the opposing speakers might argue that "the increases are small." This response is not a complete contradiction, but it diminishes the significance of the claim.

2. Re-analysis. Re-analysis, the second mode of counter argument, is adding new information to allow the original argument to be re-examined by the audience or the judge in a new context. If a speaker argues that state funding for higher education has been cut, the opposing speaker might counter with, "private funding for education has increased." The impact of this argument changes the context of the original argument and communicates two important points: (a) the original analysis was not complete because it did not include all potential funding sources, and (b) when the new information is considered, the conclusion about the adequacy of funding has to be revised. The effectiveness of re-analysis as a form of refutation depends upon both the debaters' understanding of the topic and the quality of the evidence provided.

3. Changing the perspective. Counter argument based on changing the perspective involves a more radical form of re-analysis. When a debater effectively changes the perspective of an argument, s/he adds information that makes the original position offered by the opponent seem irrelevant. For example, an advocate might argue that federal government programs designed to help the poor are inadequate, basing the argument on flaws in three major programs—AFDC (Aid to Families with Dependent Children), CETA (Comprehensive Employment Training Act), and unemployment compensation. The opposing speaker might respond by arguing that there are dozens of federal programs to help the poor and numerous state and local programs not even discussed. When such information is added to the debate, the failure of three programs, however large they are, seems less damaging. Changing the perspective is a very effective means of refutation and depends upon a very thorough knowledge of the topic area and superior evidence.

4. The "turn-around." A final mode of counter argument is the "turn" or "turn-around," which concedes the principle of an argument and then re-analyzes or changes the perspective so that the re-analyzed argument supports the opposing side of the debate. In educational debate, if an affirmative team "turns" a negative disadvantage or countervalue offered by the negative team, the "turned" argument becomes either an advantage or a value that supports the affirmative interpretation of the topic.

Consider the following proposition: *Resolved, that censorship is justified to defend the national security of the United States.* In debating this proposition, negative teams will commonly argue that the "right to know" is more valued than censorship. An affirmative team might respond that having judges determine when we have a "right to know" is a more dangerous form of censorship than the one the proposition suggests. Most turn-arounds require evidence, as would this particular argument. Affirmative teams might document such a position by citing evidence such as this piece from David O'Brien in the 1980 *Villanova Law Review:*

> Judicial articulation of such a right to know might prove particularly pernicious in two ways. First, the right to know inevitably leads to judicial determinations of what the public does and does not have a right to know, and thus invites restrictions on freedom of speech and press in the form of prior restraints. Moreover, judicial creation and construction of the contours of a directly enforceable right to know usurp Congressional power to determine the wisdom, need, and propriety of public and press access to government information and facilities.[1]

If the affirmative was justifying a Congressionally legislated form of censorship, then they could argue that the negative countervalue of the right to know actually justifies the affirmative position; thus the term "turn-around."

All four methods of counter argument—direct denial, re-analyzing, changing the perspective, and turn-arounds—share a common feature. All attempt to refute while simultaneously proving an argument false and replacing the disproven claim with an alternative claim. In order to answer such refutation the advocate is compelled to deal with the new claim before re-establishing the original argument.

Choosing Methods of Refutation

In most debates, whether public or educational, speakers are able to choose among several methods of refutation. However, advocates are usually required to limit choices because of time constraints or because they do not want to present contradictory arguments. Given both the availability of choices and the necessity of making choices, how should the advocates choose among the methods of refutation?

First, in public debates the audience should be a major consideration. What method of refutation will be effective with a given audience? Before many audiences, for example, pointing out that an opponent has used a *post hoc* fallacy will be meaningless. Consideration of audiences requires thorough analysis of their backgrounds, attitudes, socioeconomic characteristics, and many other variables. The debater who argues frequently before general audiences would be wise to study persuasion as well as argumentation and debate. Adapting to particular audiences may also require the debater to consider the content of arguments before considering the method of refutation.

Second, in educational debate students should also consider their audience—the judge. As debaters become more experienced they will become more familiar with a variety of debate judges and the types of arguments and methods of refutation they prefer. For example, debaters will discover that some judges place greater emphasis on direct refutation while others are more easily persuaded by counter argument that is documented by authoritative evidence. Coaches and more experienced teammates will be able to guide the beginning debater in making choices for judge adaptation.

Third, in both public and educational debates the lasting impact of the refutation should be a major consideration. Is the method of refutation likely to permanently dispose of the argument or issue? Or, will the opposing advocate be able to re-establish his or her argument with ease? The methods of direct refutation discussed earlier in this chapter were presented in order of the least effective to the most effective, from the least permanent to the most lasting. It is much easier to respond to refutation on source credibility, for example, than to respond to refutation on the inherent logic of an argument. In the case of answering a credibility challenge, the damage can be repaired by providing new evidence from a reliable source; re-establishing the logic of an argument is much more difficult.

The listing of the methods of counter argument also reflects the order of effectiveness, as mentioned above. For example, a viable turn-around is generally more difficult to answer than an equally viable direct denial. An affirmative turn-around has the potential of utilizing a large portion of the negative's argumentation and evidence as justification of the affirmative position. A direct denial, on the other hand, may be refuted by a single argument and a single piece of evidence. Of course, if the judge does not like turn-arounds as a form of refutation, then the use of a turn-around would be poor audience analysis and would be an unwise choice on that basis.

Speakers in both public and educational debates have to consider listener preferences and the lasting impact of the refutation when making choices regarding the methods of refutation.

Organizing Refutation

Even the best argument will be ineffective if it is not understood. Organization will add clarity to arguments so that they will be understood and thereby more effective. To refute an individual argument six steps are required: (1) state the opposing argument, (2) state the refuting argument, (3) explain the refuting argument, (4) provide supporting material for the refutation, (5) restate the refuting argument, and (6) state the importance of the refutation. We will consider each step.

1. State the opposing argument. This is the argument that will be refuted. The tasks in this step are twofold—location and identification. The listener, whether an audience member or a college debate judge, needs to know where and in what context the opposing argument existed. Of course, the listener needs to know what the argument was.

In an educational debate, the speakers will often use "signposts" or outlining symbols, such as "contention one" or "subpoint a." A debater can assist the judge in locating an argument in the judge's notes by providing the signpost as well as the argument wording: "Chris and Kevin argue in their second point that unemployment results in adverse societal consequences".

In referring to an argument, it is often desirable to use the key words to remind the judge of the concept being argued. For example, if the argument being refuted used the words, "adverse societal consequences" then the debater should use the same terms. This will also assist the judge in locating the original argument. However, in most situations *it is not necessary* to re-explain an opposing argument. (If for some reason this re-explanation is desirable, it should not be done in this step.) There is also no need to summarize the opponent's evidence.

In educational debate, step (1) is often further condensed, and the intercollegiate debater might simply say, "Consider contention one, subpoint a, societal consequences." With these few words the argument is located and identified. Although a few judges may prefer a more complete identification of the argument, this concise kind of oral style is acceptable to most experienced debate judges.

The ethical advocate will make certain that s/he does not misrepresent the opposing argument or position. For example, the ethical debater should not intentionally oversimplify the opposing argument by using circular thinking or the *post hoc* fallacy. The objective of step (1) is to present the argument so that it can be refuted; the objective is not to present the argument in such a way that it is refuted by the way it is stated.

2. State the refuting argument. This is the position the advocate wishes the listener to accept. It should be stated in a single simple sentence with memorable key words. For example, in refuting the argument on adverse societal consequences, the debater might say, "No link exists between unemployment and societal harms." This sentence might be further reduced into a verbal label and become, "No link exists." This choice is partly a question of style and partly a question of judge or audience adaptation. Before more general audiences, more complete explanations will be desirable.

In educational debates an argument stated effectively will be easy to remember and easy to write down quickly. Dramatic, vivid, concrete language and action verbs are also effective, but conciseness should not be lost. Debaters should not attempt to *explain* their arguments in this step. When the statcment and explanation are combined, judges often have difficulty writing down the argument. Clarity and memorable wording are the primary objectives in this step.

3. Explain the refuting argument. This step allows the speaker to explain his or her argument and, if necessary, the opponent's argument. As indicated above, in most debates the advocate will not need or want to explain an opposing argument, but it is usually necessary and desirable to explain the refuting argument. Terms or concepts may require explanation, or a qualification may be necessary for a conclusion.

Even the most effectively supported generalizations are invalid in some applications, and one important way to qualify a conclusion is to explain when it is not true. Using the unemployment example again, the conclusion might be qualified by detailing the link between unemployment and societal harms. The speaker might say:

> The affirmative team is talking about massive levels of unemployment and social disruption. Small amounts, such as the level we are now experiencing, are not likely to cause the kinds of harms the affirmative indicates. If the affirmative could document a 30 to 40 percent unemployment rate, then there would be social chaos and some of the harms they suggest. But the affirmative cannot prove such a level and therefore there is no link.

Thus the negative is arguing that there is no causal link except in cases of massive unemployment.

This is also the step for reasoning, analysis, and the establishment of premises and links that give arguments maximum effectiveness. In educational debates, this is often the most neglected step even among very experienced and effective debaters, even though it is also the step that helps to make supporting material or evidence effective. Too many advocates in both educational and public debates attempt to let the evidence speak for itself.

4. Provide supporting material for the refutation. This is the step for the material that proves the refuting argument. Such material may be analysis, reasoning, authoritative evidence, or some combination of those. It should be noted that authoritative evidence is not always required for this step; it is only one possible form of support. If the speaker is using one of the methods of direct refutation, authoritative evidence will not normally be used. If, for example, a debater is refuting the content of the evidence, the opposing evidence should be cited and the flaws in it should be explained.

As previously indicated, when the debater does use authoritative evidence, then the name of the authority, his or her qualifications as an expert, and the date of the statement should be cited as the *minimal* information to support its authoritativeness. In addition, the debater should have available the complete title of the magazine, journal, or book, the facts of publication, and the page number. This information should be in the proper form on an evidence card. If either the opposing team during the debate or the judge after the debate should ask to see the evidence, then all of this information should be made available to them in the proper form. As you already know, the evidence should be directly quoted and never paraphrased. Ellipses should be avoided, and if used, the team should have the original document or photocopy available.

Occasionally there may be a basis for attacking the authenticity or proper citation of an opposing debater's evidence. If falsification, alteration, or distortion of evidence is ever charged, then it should be done with great consideration, caution, and care. The charge should be worded very clearly and the debater making the charge should have the original document or complete photocopy of the original document as proof for the charge. Of course, falsification of evidence is a very serious breach of educational and competitive debate ethics, and such a breach should be treated as such. Likewise, the charge of falsification, if made without consideration and support should also be taken as a serious breach of proper conduct.

This step of providing the supporting material will usually require the most time and the most attention if the refutation is to be effective.

5. Restate the refuting argument. The restatement of the argument should be in similar, if not identical, wording to the original statement in step (2). The same key words should certainly be used again. This will reinforce the central concept of the argument, and in educational debate will allow the opponents and the judge to write down the argument if they missed it previously.

6. State the importance of the refutation. An individual argument might be important for a variety of reasons. For example, if an argument determines an issue, then the speaker might want to identify the issue. In educational debate, the speaker might indicate an argument's relative importance by identifying the stock issue it supports. A debater refuting the unemployment argument discussed previously might say, "Unless the affirmative shows that unemployment does have a link to substantial societal harms, they have not shown significance." However, the debater should not end the refutation at that point, because s/he has not identified the importance of the issue of significance. S/he could continue, "Therefore, there is no compelling need for the adoption of new federal employment programs." This final step is vital for refutation to have its maximum effectiveness.

It should be noted that many successful advocates will not utilize all six steps in refuting their opponent's arguments. Especially in some educational debates, high school and college debaters often attempt to increase the quantity of arguments by decreasing the amount of time given to the presentation of individual arguments. In such refutation, the debaters will often reduce the steps to three: (1) locating the opposing argument, (2) giving a statement or short caption for the refuting argument, and (3) supporting the refutation. When the argument is so reduced, however, the debater risks losing the argument. This is so because the judge might not understand as well or might not realize why the argument is important. In reducing the argument in such a fashion, debaters sacrifice quality for quantity of arguments.

Preparing Briefs and Blocks

The student involved with educational debate will commonly be refuting a large number of arguments in a short period of time or will be refuting arguments with very little preparation time, or both. In such situations, the debater will need to prepare "briefs" or "blocks" of arguments in advance of the debate. Briefs or blocks are sets of arguments designed as either attacks or responses to other specific arguments. Effective briefs and blocks will usually contain both constructive and refuting arguments and will aid all participants in enhancing the quality and in increasing the quantity of arguments while maintaining the organization of the debate. Both affirmative and negative teams are able to prepare briefs or blocks to increase their effectiveness in educational debate.

Early in the debate season debaters begin their preparations, and they may wish to prepare briefs at that time. *Briefs are comprehensive sets of arguments and evidence that may be given in response to a specific argument or issue.* The first step in the preparation of any kind of debate is for the advocates to predict the arguments that they will frequently oppose. They will then prepare possible responses with the appropriate supporting material. In any specific debate, the advocate will usually select the brief that is most applicable to a particular opposing argument, and then adapt that brief to the argument. The debater using a brief wisely will never simply read the prepared arguments, but will select the parts that will be most effective against the opposing argument at the time. Since a brief is comprehensive, individual arguments on the brief may sometimes appear to be contradictory. A debater must therefore choose the arguments from the brief carefully to avoid internal inconsistencies.

A block is a specific set of arguments that are coherently organized and/or analytically linked. A block is also designed to refute a specific argument or group of arguments and may contain both refutation and constructive arguments. When a debater uses a block, it is commonly used in its entirety. Blocks are often prepared later in the debate season when debaters feel more confident about the specific arguments opponents will make and how best to respond to those arguments. A block is not comprehensive; the less important, weaker, or inconsistent arguments have been discarded before its preparation.

Blocks and briefs may be prepared on 8½ × 11 inch sheets of paper (see Figure 11–1) or on groups of 4 × 6 inch index cards (see Figure 11–2). In general, briefs and blocks can be more quickly revised when they are on groups of index cards. On the other hand, lengthy briefs or blocks on index cards can be unwieldy. Debaters may find one method easier to use than another and should choose individual methods of preparation accordingly.

Neg. Supreme Court is bad.

Thesis: Sup. Ct. should not be used as a basis for decision rule.

1. Court opinions are poorly supported.
   Leonard Levy, Chairperson, Graduate Faculty, Claremont College, formerly the Earl Warren Professor of American Constitutional History at Brandeis "History and Judicial History," in *Hugo Black and the Bill of Rights,* 1978, p. 12
   The Court artfully selects historical facts from one side only, ignoring contrary data, in order to give the appearance of respectability to judgements resting on other grounds.

2. Court uses opinions as basis for decisions.
   A. Not always right
      Mary C. Dunlap, Visiting Professor, Field Studies Program, University of California at Berkley, *Lincoln Law Review,* 1981, p. 53
      To pretend that this body of decision is fully and satisfactorily explicated by reference to some "neutral principles" is to disguise the very nature of litigation, to mask the complex humanness of courts and to deceive ourselves about the challenging distance between our mortal steps and Justice
   B. Take Constitution out of context
      Jennifer Jordan Tachera, Associate Editor *Pacific Law Journal,* 1980 p. 103
      The Supreme Court has emphasized that only certain fundamental rights are deserving of constitutional protection, but cases where this has been found are illustrative rather than definitional

3. Court is indecisive.
   Thomas Emerson, Professor of Law, Yale University Law School, *The System of Free Expression,* p. 15–16
   At various times the Court has employed the bad tendency test, the clear and present danger test, an incitement test, and different forms of the ad hoc balancing test. Sometimes it has not clearly enuciated the theory upon which it proceeds. Frequently it has avoided decision on basic First Amendment issues by invoking doctrines of vagueness, overbreadth, or the use of less drastic alternatives.

4. Court is overloaded.
   Chief Justice Burger, *U.S. News and World Report,* Feb. 14, 1983 pp. 38–39
   I do not monitor my colleagues, but I would estimate that the justices are working at least 60 hours a week and some of them more. My own work week is 70 to 80 hours.

Some arguments might be used individually.

Sometimes a brief may contain a block.

FIGURE 11–1 Partial view of a sample brief on 8½ × 11 sheets.

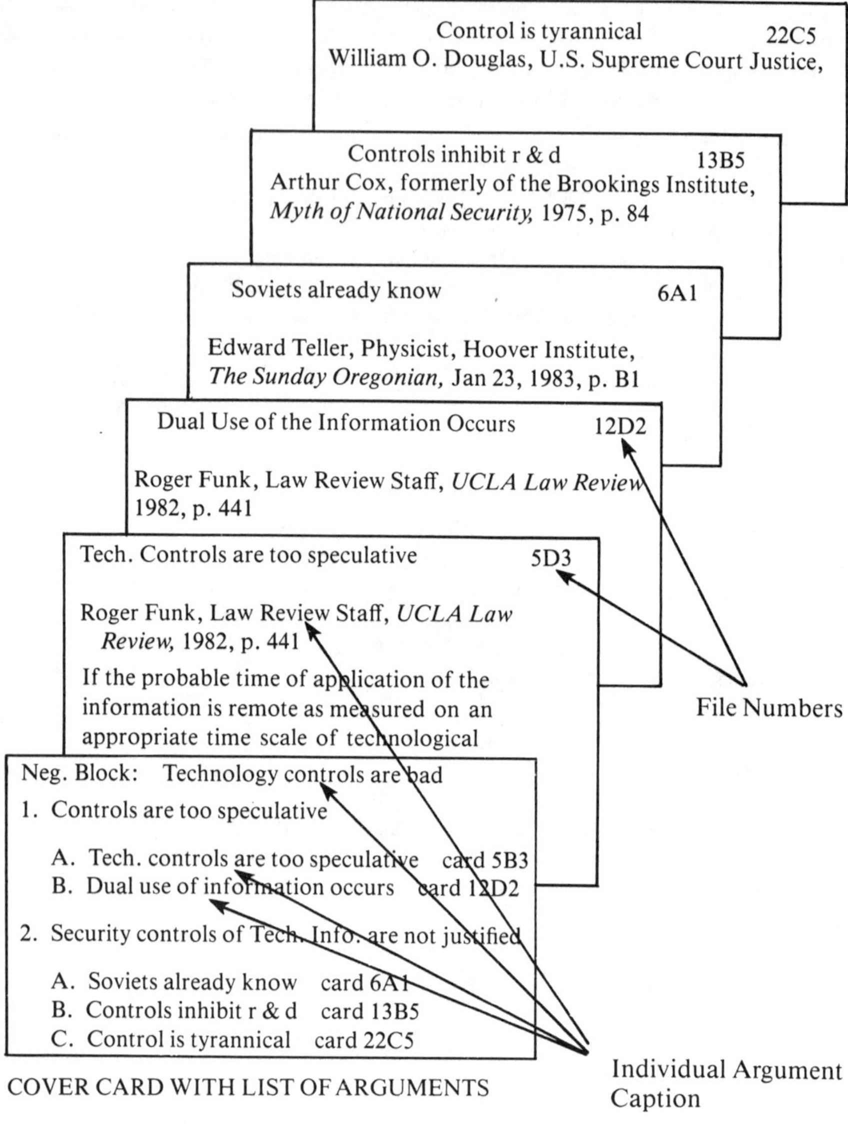

FIGURE 11–2 A block on 4 × 6 index cards.

Summary

Refutation is the art of proving an argument erroneous or false. Refutation occurs in both public and educational debate and allows an advocate to fulfill his or her burden of rebuttal. Traditional methods of refutation include: (1) attacking the credibility of the source, (2) attacking the content of the evidence, (3) attacking the logic of the argument, and (4) attacking the relevance of the argument. Counter argument allows a debater to both deny an opposing idea and advance a new idea for the judge and audience to accept. Four modes of counter argument are: direct denial, re-analysis, changing the perspective, and turn-arounds.

Effective organization of refutation requires six steps in the presentation of an argument: (1) state the opposing argument, (2) state the refuting argument, (3) explain the refuting argument, (4) provide supporting material for the refutation, (5) restate the refuting argument, (6) state the importance of the refutation.

Finally, it is of paramount importance that debaters be prepared to respond to opponent's arguments, and certain devices enable the debater to do this with more facility. Briefs and blocks are such devices. They not only help the debater to recall evidence and lines of argument; they facilitate the organization of refutation.

Notes

1. David M. O'Brien, "Reasoning, the First Amendment, and the Public's Right to Know in Constitutional Ajudications," *Villanova Law Review,* 26(November 1980), p. 7.

Questions and Exercises

1. What is refutation? What role does it play in a debate?
2. Use the editorial page or section of a major newspaper for the following exercises:
   a. Find an effectively argued editorial or letter to the editor and identify the methods of refutation that it employs.
   b. Find an effectively argued editorial that features refutation as opposed to constructive argument and identify the steps of organization the writer has used. Which steps of organizing refutation seem to be vital in an effective written argument?
   c. Find an ineffectively argued editorial and analyze what role the lack of refutation or the poor quality of refutation played in weakening the argument. Did poor organization of refutation lead to the editorial's ineffectiveness?

3. Use recent issues of the *Congressional Record* to locate legislative debates and argumentative speeches. Use the exercises in assignment 1 above to analyze refutation in the legislative forum.
4. Prepare for an in-class argument clash through the following steps:
   a. With the aid of your instructor, word a proposition on a recent controversy with two equally arguable opposing sides, or use the proposition that will be debated in class.
   b. Gather at least 50 pieces of evidence on the proposition reflecting an equal number on each side.
   c. In class, make short speeches (2–3 minutes) with the following ground rules:
      (i) All students must make at least one constructive argument.
      (ii) All students must make at least one refuting argument.
      (iii) All students must use no more than one evidence card in any one speech.
      (iv) All students must make at least one refuting argument without using any evidence.
      (v) Speakers should begin with one argument and alternate, each refuting the previous speaker until that argument is exhausted, and then begin the process again with a new argument.

Suggested Readings

Verch, Stephen and Logue, Brenda. "Increasing Value Clash: A Propositional and Structural Approach." *CEDA Yearbook, 1982.* California State University, Northridge: Don Brownlee, 1982, pp. 25–28.

TWELVE

Cross-Examination

In 1926, J. Stanley Gray proposed that short cross-examination periods be included in the format of intercollegiate debates.[1] The plan was never regularly used until the Cross Examination Debate Association was formed in 1971. CEDA is the largest organization that sanctions intercollegiate debate tournaments, and CEDA has utilized the cross-examination format since its inception. In 1976, the National Debate Tournament used the format for the first time and today virtually all intercollegiate and high school debates include cross-examination in the format.

The cross-examination periods usually come at the end of the constructive speeches, with a member of the opposition questioning the speaker who has just ended the speech. Although there are variations to the format, the following is usually the structure and sequence of the questioning:

First Affirmative Constructive

(Second Negative speaker questions first Affirmative)

First Negative Constructive

(First Affirmative speaker questions first Negative)

Second Affirmative Constructive

(First Negative speaker questions second Affirmative)

Second Negative Constructive

(Second Affirmative speaker questions second Negative)

Cross-examination is a very important part of any debate. It is not an opportunity to be wasted with meaningless and unconnected questions. As with constructive speeches and rebuttals, it is an opportunity to strengthen one's position and to increase one's credibility. An effective cross-examination period can focus the debate on the issues one considers important and clarify any ambiguity that lingers after the opposition has spoken. With the time constraints in place during most debates, any additional opportunity to accomplish these goals should not be squandered.

Functions of Cross-Examination

Specifically, cross-examination serves five functions in the debate. These are: (1) information gathering, (2) clarification of issues, (3) clarification of judgment criteria, (4) building foundations for arguments, and (5) advancing positions.

Information Gathering

This is an essential function of the cross-examination period. One cannot argue against a case that is not understood. For this reason, a debater should take the opportunity offered by the cross-examination period to gather any information missed or missing from the opponent's constructive speech. Most debates move quite rapidly and are concerned with rather complex issues. Therefore, it is not unusual that additional information is needed to fully understand the opposition's arguments.

Such information gathering can save needless and perhaps embarrassing constructive arguments in response to a case not completely comprehended. The following exchange is an example of cross-examination aimed at information gathering:

Q: You said that unemployment contributes to child abuse. Is that right?

A: Yes.

Chapter Outline

Q: What percentage of child abuse cases are attributable to unemployment? Did you say?

A: No, I didn't, but it's about 5%.

Q: Do you have specific numbers? What is 5% in total numbers?

A: I have no idea.

This line of questioning was aimed at gathering more information about the link between unemployment and the incidence of child abuse. What the questioner or her partner can do with the information depends upon the exact nature of their opponent's case and the quality of their own evidence.

Sometimes information is missed in the course of the debate. It is better to take time in cross-examination to ask for the information than to continue unaware of significant portions of your opponent's arguments. The following is an illustration of this kind of questioning:

Q: Did you say there are four contributing factors to child abuse?

A: No. Five.

Q: I didn't get four or five. Could you repeat them?

A: Sure. The fourth was family size.

Q: And the fifth?

A: The fifth was social isolation.

Q: Social isolation? Did you define that?

A: It's just lack of contact with non-family members.

Q: Is the evidence talking about the isolation of the children or the parents?

A: The whole family.

Q: Oh, I see.

For some reason, the questioner failed to get all the information during the constructive speech. It is certainly more sensible to use the cross-examination period to get the information than to continue in the dark.

Clarification of Issues

This function differs markedly from information gathering. An advocate wishing to clarify issues already possesses the information but does not fully understand it. In the following exchange the questioner is attempting to clarify the precise issue his opponent is discussing:

Q: You argued that unemployment contributes to child abuse. Can you explain that?

A: Sure. Unemployment causes stress, and stress has been found to be a leading contributor to child abuse.

Q: So, is the problem stress or unemployment?
A: Since one leads to the other, they are both problems.
Q: O.K. But just because someone is unemployed that doesn't mean that they are going to abuse their children, right?
A: That's right, but they have more of a chance if they are unemployed.
Q: How is that?
A: Because unemployment causes stress.
Q: Certain jobs cause stress too, don't they? Like air traffic controllers and policemen?
A: I guess so.
Q: Then if policemen lose their jobs, they would be less likely to abuse their children?
A: Generally, unemployment increases the risk.
Q: But it's the amount of stress that is the key?
A: That's right.

The questioning has clarified the issue. The questioner has clarified the link between unemployment and child abuse, and perhaps more importantly, the link between stress and child abuse. The strategy the questioner and his partner will want to pursue can now be developed with more certainty. More time can be used discussing stress and less time discussing unemployment since we have discovered in cross-examination that that is where the issue lies.

Clarifying Judgment Criteria

Sometimes it may be unclear how the data presented by an opponent should be evaluated. If there is ambiguity in this criteria, cross-examination is an opportunity to clarify it. Consider this exchange between debaters discussing military support to nondemocratic governments:

Q: You claim that El Salvador is undemocratic. How do you determine that?
A: It is an oppressive government.
Q: Don't they have elections?
A: Yes, but the elections don't mean anything.
Q: Why not?
A: Because they are rigged. Only the government-supported candidates win.
Q: What would it take for them to be democratic?
A: The main thing is equality of rights.

Q: So, elections are not important so long as the people are afforded equality of rights?

A: That's exactly right.

The questioner has clarified the criteria for judging the data. If the data suggests that El Salvadorans are not treated equally by the government, then El Salvador is not democratic. The questioner, however, still does not know exactly what the criteria is and might wish to request more clarity. It is important to establish the most precise ground your opponents are willing to grant you. The ground may be accepted if it suits you or you may reject it and argue other ground if it does not.

A line of questions such as the one below would be aimed at clarifying exactly what each team must prove to prevail on a particular issue, or perhaps even prevail in the debate, depending on the issue at stake. Consider the following:

Q: So, if we can't demonstrate perfect equality then the country is undemocratic?

A: That's right.

Q: Isn't that unfair? Are there *any* perfect democracies?

A: I don't know. I mean to be a true democracy, a country would have to allow significant equality.

Q: What is significant?

A: Well, in Central America, the right to own property and full religious freedom.

Q: So, if we show that a country allows citizens to own property and to worship freely, then it's democratic?

A: I guess so.

Q: Thank You.

Now the questioner and her partner know exactly what their opponents want. To prove a country democratic, they must show that rights exist to own property and to worship freely. That is much clearer than "equality of rights." This clarification saves time in constructives and rebuttals and focuses in the judge's mind a clear standard for evaluating the arguments. Of course, the questioner is under no obligation to accept the criteria, but at least she knows more precisely the position of her opponents.

Building Foundations for Arguments

Building foundations for future arguments is a crucial function of the cross-examination. This preparation for future arguments requires cooperation between partners. A questioner must know exactly what her partner will argue if she hopes to build the foundation for those arguments. If, for instance, your partner were going to argue that pornography should not be restricted because it is an exercise of free speech, you may want to build a foundation for that argument in cross-examination. Consider the following questioning:

Q: You said in Contention II that pornography is a slur to women. Would you consider a slur an expression of opinion?

A: I guess.

Q: You also argued that pornography encourages behavior which is objectionable. Isn't that encouragement an expression of opinion?

A: I suppose.

Q: Why shouldn't opinions be protected by the free speech provision of the First Amendment?

A: Not all opinions are protected. The First Amendment is not absolute.

Q: When is it not applicable?

A: When it harms other people.

Q: O.K. Thank you.

The questioner has claimed three very important accomplishments. First, the respondent has admitted that in certain ways pornography is an expression of opinion. Second, the questioner has prepared the judge for the argument that is to come from her partner. Third, the questions lead the respondent to offer some hint as to the probable response his team will have to the argument —in this case, that the First Amendment is not absolute.

Advancing Positions

Cross examination can also be used to advance positions. This can be done in two ways: (1) by pointing out deficiencies in the opponent's case or evidence, and (2) answering your opponent's attacks.

Pointing out deficiencies. If you feel that your opponent's arguments are flawed, you can point to those deficiencies in cross-examination. Many times, getting an opponent to admit to deficiencies is more effective than direct refutation in constructives or rebuttal speeches. Suppose you want to point out the flaw in your opponent's argument that there is a necessary relationship between pornography and organized crime. You might do that in this way:

Q: When you argue that pornography fuels organized crime, do you mean that without pornography organized crime would vanish?

A: Well, no. But one of the major sources of revenue for organized crime is pornography.

Q: Isn't that just a convenience? If they couldn't depend on pornography, wouldn't organized crime turn to some other activity—like prostitution, or gambling, or drugs?

A: But right now pornography is funding it.

Q: But if pornography were gone tommorow, organized crime would still be here wouldn't it?

A: It wouldn't be as strong.

Q: O.K.

The questioner has made the point. The relationship between pornography and organized crime is weak. Any advantage of reducing organized crime by restricting pornography has been called into question.

Deficiencies in your opponent's case can also be identified by pointing to faulty evidence. Consider this exchange taking place after an argument that pornography leads to violence:

Q: I want to talk about the Thomas card.

A: O.K.

Q: Thomas says that pornography might cause aggression under certain conditions and for certain individuals. Is that correct?

A: Yes, Thomas says that.

Q: But doesn't he go on to say that those conditions rarely exist?

A: He says it has happened occasionally.

Q: And doesn't he say that in those instances where aggression occurs, that it rarely manifests itself in violence? That these people are rarely violent?

A: He implies that. But he clearly says that aggression is possible. And we know that aggressive people can become violent.

Q: Is it probable that these people will become violent?

A: Thomas doesn't say anything about probability.

Q: O.K.

The questioner has clearly undercut the impact of this piece of evidence. It is unlikely now that the judge will consider the evidence further. The questioner has been successful in advancing an argument (that pornography does not lead to violence) by pointing to the faulty evidence of the opponents.

Answering attacks. Sometimes it becomes necessary to weaken an opponent's attacks, and this can be effectively done in cross-examination. Of course, the attacks may be answered in some of the ways already discussed, such as pointing out deficiencies in your opponent's arguments and demonstrating that the evidence used by your opponent is faulty.

You may also answer these assaults by pointing to the strength of your evidence. Suppose that an opponent has argued that, despite your argument to the contrary, pornography causes aggression. We have already discussed an example of pointing out deficiencies in that argument. You may also focus on the strength of your position, as the following example illustrates:

Q: We argued that pornography does not cause aggression. We cited five studies which support that. Did you ever deny those studies?

A: The Thomas card denies the studies.

Q: So, we have five studies in support of the argument and you have one conclusionary card against it. Does that one card outweigh the impact of the five studies?

A: It's a real good card.

Q: But Thomas never mentions the studies does he?

A: Not specifically.

Q: The Thomas card was 1982, right?

A: Yes, I think that's right.

Q: Two of the studies we cited were in 1985 and one was in 1986. All of them are more recent than your "real good" Thomas card. How does the Thomas evidence deny the studies?

A: Well, the conclusion of Thomas is still valid.

Q: All right, thanks.

The questioner has accomplished two things: (1) she has focused a comparison of evidence (which she believes favors her position) and (2) she has forced the respondent to make a rather weak defense, thereby reducing his credibility. The questioner can also design questions to defend against the attack by pointing to the strength of her team's argument. Such as this:

Q: If pornography leads to aggressive behavior, then in the communities where it is restricted, there should be a decrease in aggressive behavior, right?

A: Unless other factors intervene.

Q: You haven't demonstrated any other factors have you?

A: No.

Q: So, unless you can show a decrease in aggressive behavior or the existence of other intervening factors, then can't we assume that pornography does not cause aggression?

A: No, we can't assume that because it isn't that easy to determine those effects. There is always the risk.

Q: Thanks.

The questioner has led the respondent into somewhat of a dilemma. He must either admit there is no causal link between pornography and aggression or recognize that a demonstration of that link is difficult. Either way, the questioner's argument appears to be stronger than the respondent's.

Guidelines for Presentation

Cross-examination can be an effective tool for any team on either side of the proposition. The five functions of cross-examination are crucial ones in determining the outcome of the debate. Even if debaters have a clear vision of the functions of cross-examination, they may nevertheless fail because of the improper manner in which they conduct the questioning. In this section we will present several guidelines of conduct for both questioners and respondents.

The Questioner

Certain suggestions, if followed, will make a cross-examination period more effective for the questioner. These suggestions are:

1. Control the questioning.
2. Organize the questions.
3. Make the questions concise.
4. Know when to stop.

Control the questioning. Sometimes a respondent will attempt to take control of the cross-examination period and lead the questioner astray of his or her purpose. Be on guard and stick to your line of questions. The following example illustrates how a respondent might sidetrack an unsuspecting questioner:

Q: Your standard for evaluating the effectiveness of labor unions is success in wage negotiations?

A: Yes.

Q: Isn't that narrow? Aren't there other functions of labor unions?

A: None as important as wages. Have you shown the importance of any others?

Q: Our entire first constructive talked about three major functions of unions.

A: But they were assertions. I didn't hear any evidence to support any of them. Did you have any?

Q: Well, certainly we did on Contention II, B.

A: Who was that from?

Q: Wilson and Torres, I believe.

A: What qualifications do they have?

The questioner has completely lost control of the cross-examination. The respondent has taken the initiative and has actually reversed roles and has begun to question the questioner. The questioner could have prevented this from happening. Consider the difference between the exchange above and the one that follows:

Q: Your standard for evaluating the effectiveness of labor unions is success in wage negotiations?

A: Yes.

Q: Isn't that narrow? Aren't there other functions of labor unions?

A: None as important as wages. Have you shown the importance of any others?

Q: Sure we have. Don't you agree that job security is a crucial function of unions?

A: Not as important as wages. You haven't presented any evidence to deny that have you?

Q: Answer my questions. What good are wage guarantees if the job itself is in jeopardy? Isn't job security more fundamental than wages?

A: You haven't proven that.

Q: It is logical isn't it? What good are wage guarantees if you have no job?

A: You still have to prove it.

This is a much better performance by the questioner. Despite the attempt to sidetrack the questioner, the respondent was forced to follow the intended line of questions. The persistence of the respondent to divert discussion from legitimate questions probably reduced his credibility, and the questioner got the better of the exchange.

Organize the questions. For the questions to be effective, they must follow a pattern. Asking random questions rarely has any benefit and might confuse the judge or damage the questioner's credibility. One question should build upon the one before it and lead to the question that follows. After the cross-examination period, the judge ought to be able to identify specific "lines" of argument and make a judgment about them.

Ask concise questions. Since cross-examination periods are relatively brief, you will want to ask questions that are as concise as possible. This will allow for more issues to be discussed and more arguments to be advanced, and build a stronger foundation for future arguments. The following question would not be concise:

> Isn't it true that besides stress, social isolation and economic status have a direct relationship to the incidence of child abuse, thereby reducing the importance of stress as a contributing factor?

The question could be asked in a much more concise way without losing meaning or impact. Consider the following change:

> You argue that stress is a major factor in causing child abuse. Aren't there many other causes?

This question, depending on how it is answered, may be followed by other concise questions. The latter example would serve better than the first as a foundation of such a series of questions.

Know when to stop. There are occasions in cross-examination when continuing to press an issue creates no benefit. When a respondent is being evasive, or clearly cannot answer the question, there is no reason to keep pounding away. The following exchange is an example of a questioner who continues questioning far beyond any reasonable hope of gain:

Q: You say that pornography finances organized crime. Is that true?

A: Yes.

Q: Isn't pornography only a convenience. If pornography were eliminated completely wouldn't organized crime simply find alternative resources?

A: Perhaps, but none is as important as pornography.

Q: Maybe now it is the most important. But if it wasn't available wouldn't organized crime turn to other sources of revenue?

A: But pornography is the key. It is the leading source of revenue for organized crime.

Q: But isn't it just a convenience?

A: All I know is that the evidence is clear, pornography supports organized crime.

Q: I don't deny that. What I want to know is—do you think that organized crime would disappear if pornography was eliminated?

A: I don't know.

Q: Then how can you claim that restrictions on pornography check organized crime?

A: Because they depend on pornography to finance their activities.

Q: But aren't there other possible sources to which organized crime would turn for money?

A: Maybe, but none of them are as important as pornography.

Q: O.K. Let me ask something else.

The questioner should have shifted from this line of questioning much earlier. It was obvious very early that the respondent was not going to say what the questioner had hoped. The point had already been made and nothing was to be gained by continuing. The questioner should have recognized this and moved ahead.

The Respondent

There are also certain guidelines that the respondent should follow in order to ensure that the cross-examination period is meaningful. These are:

1. Do not be evasive.
2. Listen carefully.
3. Do not defend untenable positions.

Do not be evasive. There are few things as irritating to a judge than for a respondent to be intentionally evasive. The respondent should answer the question succinctly and directly. There is nothing to be gained by evasive responses. In fact, the likely outcome will be a loss of credibility and lost opportunities to clarify and to advance your positions. Notice the likely impression the respondent is projecting in the following exchange:

Q: Most of your evidence deals with economic support of nondemocratic governments doesn't it?

A: It deals with support.

Q: Economic support right? Instead of military support?

A: Which evidence?

Q: All of it.

A: The evidence deals with the U.S. support of nondemocratic governments and that is what the proposition is about.

Q: Can't you answer the question? What evidence deals specifically with military support? It is a simple question.

A: I've answered it.

Q: No, you haven't. Doesn't all of your evidence talk specifically about the impact of economic support.

A: It talks about support and that is all that we have to do.

Q: Never mind.

Listen carefully. A respondent must listen carefully. Be sure of what the question means and exactly what it asks of you. If you answer a question before you fully understand it, it may appear to the judge and to the questioner that you are being evasive. Another reason to listen carefully is so that you might anticipate the direction of the line of questioning. If you understand where the questioner is leading you, you might avoid costly admissions or dilemmas.

Do not defend untenable positions. When debaters continue to defend positions which clearly have been beaten or which were initially flawed, their credibility suffers greatly. The best strategy is to make sure that your arguments are sound in the first place! If, however, an undeniable inconsistency in your case is identified during cross-examination do not deny the obvious. Such a situation might be handled this way:

Q: In the first speech your partner argued that stress was the major factor in child abuse. Didn't you just read evidence that said stress was only the third leading factor?

A: No, I don't think so, which card?

Q: From Torres, I believe.

A: Let's see. He says. . . . Yes, I guess he does say that.

Q: So stress isn't the major cause of child abuse is it?

A: According to Torres, I guess not. But even Torres says that it is a significant cause—attributable to one in every four cases.

The respondent did not deny the obvious. He had read a piece of evidence that was inconsistent with other arguments. In the example above, the respondent recovered as well as he could have. He recognized the inconsistency, but attempted to limit the impact of it. His credibility is thus in better shape than if he had attempted to defend an obvious inconsistency.

Demeanor

Demeanor in cross-examination is important for both the questioner and the respondent. They should both display behavior that is: (1) poised and confident, (2) direct, (3) communicative, and (4) polite.

It is important for both the questioner and the respondent to appear poised and confident. Many times the arguments are presented with equal force regarding evidence, reasoning, and refutation. In such cases the judge might decide such a closely argued issue in favor of the debater who appears to be the more confident and poised.

If one is confident and poised, questions are usually delivered directly, and one's responses are also not evasive. If debaters are well prepared, if their arguments are sound, if their evidence is strong, there is no reason to be vague or ambiguous with questions nor evasive with responses.

Poise and confidence can also be demonstrated through a communicative delivery style. Reading questions is not communicative and does not reflect adequate preparation or confidence. Both the questioner and the respondent should direct their messages to the judge and, if appropriate, the audience. Debate is a persuasive endeavor and the responses and questions should not be aimed exclusively toward your opponent. Your chances of persuading your opponent during the course of the debate are not good. Your chances of persuading the judge are much better. Make sure the judge understands the questions as well as the responses.

Perhaps the most important point regarding demeanor during cross-examination is to be polite. Debaters should be aggressive, but not overbearing. They should be confident but not condescending. They should also be reasonable in allowing respondents sufficient opportunity to respond and in allowing questioners to control the cross-examination period.

When a questioner demands a yes or a no answer to questions that cannot be easily answered yes or no, that is being overbearing. When questioning, allow the respondent to answer fully. When responding, answer the question fully, but succinctly.

Do not become agitated, combative, or defensive. The best way to defend against an aggressive cross-examination period is to be well prepared. If debaters appear combative or defensive, it points to a lack of confidence or a lack of adequate preparation.

Summary

Cross examination is a vital part of any debate. It allows for: (1) information gathering, (2) clarification of issues, (3) judgment criteria, (4) building foundations for arguments, and (5) advancing positions.

Questioners should control the cross-examination and make sure that the questions asked are not random, but reasonably organized. The questions should also be as concise as possible. Finally, a questioner should not pursue a line of questions beyond the chance of gain. A questioner should know when to stop.

Respondents should never be evasive. They should listen to questions carefully, and avoid defending untenable positions. When an inconsistency or conceptual error is obvious, it is best to admit it, attempt to minimize the importance of it, and move on.

Finally, the demeanor of the debaters in cross-examination is important. Debaters, both questioners and respondents, should be poised and confident. They should be direct in both questions and answers and they should be communicative and polite.

Notes

1. J. Stanley Gray, "The Oregon Plan of Debating," *The Quarterly Journal of Speech,* 13(April 1926), 175–180.

Questions and Exercises

1. What are the five functions of cross-examination?
2. What are the guidelines for questioners in cross-examination?

3. What are the guidelines for respondents?
4. Describe the proper demeanor for debaters in a cross-examination period.
5. Select a speech from any recent issue of *Vital Speeches of the Day* and construct approximately fifteen cross-examination questions aimed at refuting the speaker's argument. Also:
   a. identify which function each question serves.
   b. identify the argument for which the questions might serve as foundations.
   c. identify the arguments they advance.

Suggested Readings

Henderson, Bill. "A System of Teaching Cross-Examination Techniques." *Communication Education,* XXVII (March 1978), 112–118.

Miller, Thomas and Camker, Evan. "The Art of Cross-Examination." *CEDA Yearbook, 1982.* California State University, Northridge: Don Brownlee, 1982, pp. 4–15.

Norton, Rob. "Remembering What the C. E. Stands for: Toward a Greater Role for Cross-Examination in CEDA Debate." *CEDA Yearbook, 1983.* California State University, Northridge: Don Brownlee, 1983, pp. 29–31.

Ziegemueller, George. "Cross Examination Re-examined." *Argument in Transition: Proceedings of the Third Summer Conference on Argumentation,* edited by David Zarefsky, Malcolm Sillars, and Jack Rhodes, Annandale, VA: Speech Communication Association, 1983, pp. 893–903.

THIRTEEN

Style and Delivery

Although the focus of argumentation is usually upon the content or meaning of messages, the advocate's style and delivery are also very important.

The Functions of Style and Delivery

Style and delivery are often confused, so definitions are essential. *Style, written or oral, refers to the choices and combinations of words, sentence structure, grammatical decisions, and other language-related choices that mark an individual writer's or speaker's verbal expression.* A speaker's style may be similar to others or his choices may make his expression distinctive or even unique.

Delivery may be defined as the physical communication of the speaker's message. Delivery includes the production of sounds as well as other physical movement, such as facial expressions and gestures. Although style and delivery are different concepts, they can work together to reinforce or add meaning to a speech.

Style and delivery play important and similar roles in both public and educational debating. In both public and educational debates style and delivery can enhance the effectiveness of speakers by making their arguments clearer, more dynamic, more credible, more memorable and more easily associated with the particular advocate. In addition, style and delivery in both kinds of debate can be used to adapt to different audiences or judges.

A critical function of style and delivery in all kinds of argumentation is to assist in the effective communication of *meaning*. Meaning, according to most contemporary communication theorists, resides not in the message so much as in the individual listener or receiver. Thus, perceived meaning is highly dependent upon the receiver's past experiences and the context in which these experiences occurred. The diversity of human experience therefore brings about a variety of "meanings" for a particular message.

Style and delivery can assist the speaker in approaching the re-creation of experience or putting new ideas in a familiar context. For example, if the speaker uses language choices that are understood, familiar, and comfortable for the audience, then the audience will receive the message more favorably. On the other hand, if the style and delivery cause an audience to focus upon something other than the content of the message, then the speaker may fail. This problem can occur even with seemingly experienced speakers, whose style and delivery may even begin to draw attention away from their arguments. Audiences unfamiliar with the principles of effective style and delivery may even evaluate such advocates as "effective public speakers" but may reject their messages.

Another important function of style and delivery in both public and educational debates is to communicate the attitudes of the arguer. A speaker's style and delivery often provide clues to the way a speaker views the other advocates and the audience or judges. For example, if a speaker is contemptuous of her audience or her opponents, she may use insulting language and speak with a sarcastic tone. However, if an advocate respects her audience, then she will not likely offend them either by her style or delivery choices.

In some ways, the functions of style and delivery differ for educational and public debate. For instance, in public debate style and delivery are more likely to differ significantly from speaker to speaker. Further, because speak-

Chapter Outline

ing situations in public debate vary much more than educational debate formats, the situation and the occasion are much more likely to influence the style and delivery choices that public advocates make.

In educational debate speakers will tend to use a more uniform and succinct or concise style. Because there are strict and relatively short time limits in educational debate, word economy is much more important for the competitive speaker. Also, delivery will probably be more rapid in intercollegiate debate, especially if the debaters and judges are experienced and the topic is familiar to all the participants.

This chapter examines the principles of effective style and delivery for a variety of argumentative situations. The chapter also examines the characteristics of style and delivery in particular educational debate speeches—the first affirmative constructive speech and the rebuttal speeches.

Principles of Effective Style and Delivery

There are many principles of effective style and delivery; we will focus on the following, as those most important for the advocate: (1) the nature of effective oral style, (2) the importance of awareness, (3) vivid, dramatic, and concrete language, (4) the effective unit of proof, (5) the role of analogy in argument, (6) methods of delivery, (7) other important factors in delivery, and (8) audience and judge adaptation.

The Nature of Effective Oral Style

The effective oral style is usually quite different from effective written style. For example, when we write argumentative essays, we are likely to use more compound or complex sentence structures; when we speak we will probably speak in shorter sentences. Indeed, good oral style when written in an essay might seem "choppy." John Wilson and Carroll Arnold have identified a number of significant characteristics of effective oral style:

1. more personal pronouns
2. more variety in kinds of sentences
3. more variety in sentence lengths
4. more simple sentences
5. more sentence fragments
6. many more rhetorical questions
7. more repetition of words, phrases, and sentences
8. more monosyllabic words
9. more contractions
10. more interjections

11. more indigenous language
12. more connotative than denotative words
13. more euphony
14. more figurative language
15. more direct quotation
16. more familiar words[1]

Wilson and Arnold note: "If you study this list of differences you should see two things: (1) the differences are differences of proportion rather than differences of form; and (2) the larger number of specific features in the list will tend to make oral style less formal and more closely fitted to particular people in specific rhetorical situations."[2] Although these characteristics may make oral speech seem less formal by the standards of formal writing, even formal oral presentations often utilize many of these same characteristics. For example, a lawyer's final address to a jury or a president's address to a nation are very formal oral presentations which frequently feature many of these factors.

Why are there differences between effective written and oral style? A major reason is that delivery factors can add significantly to the meaningfulness of verbal statements. A pause, a change in inflection, voice quality, volume, facial expressions, gestures, and other factors can add punctuation to a sentence fragment so that it is meaningful. For example, if two workers are discussing recent union negotiations, delivery factors such as those above can change the phrase "a dollar an hour raise" into a question, or a joyful or depressed exclamation.

Advocates need to understand that good written and oral style are quite different and that often a manuscript speech may sound awkward or excessively formal to an audience because the speech has not been delivered in good oral style.

The Importance of Awareness

All speakers need to be aware of both style and delivery. As indicated above, one important area of awareness is to understand the difference between good oral and written style. However, a more important and basic kind of awareness is understanding of self. In other words, advocates need to be aware of their own oral styles and the particular characteristics. Advocates also need to be aware of their own delivery and their strengths and weaknesses.

The best way to gain awareness is through a combination of self-observation and individual coaching. A first step prior to practice and observation is understanding the factors of good oral style and effective delivery, and the student's coach or teacher can help to indicate those factors. If the student and teacher can observe a practice or tournament debate together, the teacher or debate coach can identify examples of good and bad style and delivery. This is frequently the best way to become aware of style and delivery. Some students also find it helpful to be videotaped during a practice speech or debate and then to watch the tape with a teacher or coach. Practicing before a mirror or listening to yourself on a tape recorder, however, are usually not good ways to observe yourself. Such observation is usually not accurate and can be frustrating and counterproductive.

The attitude of the coach and the student should be constructive. Both should attempt to find good and bad characteristics in delivery and style. The perspective of both the coach and student should also be wholistic; style and delivery cannot be isolated from other aspects of the communication transaction. For example, a speaker's interaction with other advocates and the audience should also be observed. If a coach is videotaping a practice debate, the entire debate should be recorded. The student should have the opportunity to observe herself approaching the podium to speak, speaking, during cross-examination, and even listening to the other debaters.

After this initial practice, self-awareness and the development of good style and delivery can also be enhanced by observing other speakers or skilled debaters. After the student knows and has attempted to practice some of the characteristics of good oral style and delivery, then she can again observe others and more effectively choose the good habits she desires to develop.

Vivid, Dramatic, and Concrete Language

The use of vivid, dramatic, and concrete language will make ideas both more memorable and more credible. Words that create images are usually more memorable because the image is easy to remember; the image then recalls the words for the listener or the reader. When readers are asked to identify the most memorable passages from famous novels, they will usually identify descriptive passages.

Imagery can be defined as descriptive language that evokes in a listener the experience associated with the type of description. For example, if a speaker is describing seeing the horrors of a battlefield, then her language would create those kinds of visual images. There are seven major types of imagery, each related to the specific kind of sensation:

1. Visual (sight)
2. Auditory (hearing)
3. Gustatory (taste)
4. Olfactory (smell)
5. Tactual (touch)
    a. heat and cold
    b. texture and shape
    c. pressure

6. Kinesthetic (muscle strain)
7. Organic (internal sensations)

Public advocates will have many opportunities for using imagery and other specific, descriptive, and concrete detail. Intercollegiate debaters will probably want to devote less time to imagery; however, there will be opportunities for imagery, especially in the first affirmative and in selecting evidence to document harmful conditions.

When using imagery and other forms of vivid expression advocates should remember that they are being used *to enhance memory and credibility.* These principles can help speakers make choices about the types of imagery used, after deciding when and if imagery is appropriate in a given situation.

The use of specific and vivid detail is also persuasive. Indeed, it is an innate human tendency to attempt to create belief by vivid, dramatic, and concrete description. When a child attempts to convince his mother that an event has occurred, he will naturally attempt to describe that event in detail. Audiences are often more easily convinced by speakers who use statistics than those who do not. When a policewoman interrogates a suspect, she will often question him about the details of his alibi. All of these examples support the principle that we both believe and test truths based on the presence or absence of detail.

The Effective Unit of Proof

We have discussed effectiveness from a number of perspectives. For example, Chapter Seven discusses several different dimensions of credibility, and notes that in order for a debater to be credible, the debater, his argument, and his evidence all needed to be credible. Just as credibility has several dimensions, so does an effective unit of proof. An effective unit of proof appeals to audiences or debate judges on several levels.

First, an effective unit of proof has an illustrative dimension. This is the dimension that provides understanding, explanation, or explication. This dimension also captures and sustains audience attention by being interesting, vivid, involving, or dramatic. Examples, illustrations, analogies, imagery are the kinds of supporting materials that fulfill the demands of this dimension.

Though this illustrative dimension of proof is an important one, and a few audiences might be satisfied with evidence that is *only* illustrative, the effective and ethical speaker will also supply evidence to meet a rational dimension. Such an advocate knows that his or her audience analysis may be incorrect and s/he also knows that important decisions should be based on rational argumentation.

Some audiences, such as educated general audiences, expert audiences, or experienced debate judges will consciously focus on the rational dimension of the unit of proof. The rational dimension refers to the requirements that must be met in order for an argument to be considered "proved" to the objective listener. When such a listener demands that an advocate be rational, the listener will not accept the advocate's argument unless the support offered for it meets the relevant tests of reasoning and evidence. For instance, if a speaker attempts to support an argument by example, the rational dimension will require that the speaker demonstrate that there are sufficient examples or that an example offered is typical. The rational focus might also lead audiences to ignore or reject an argument based on exclusively emotional appeals or an argument that is perceived as illogical for other reasons.

Although rational audiences may reject some of the kinds of proof that fulfill the illustrative dimension, this does not mean that such proofs are useless with such audiences. Such proofs do capture the attention and provide explanation that may be critical to an audience understanding and accepting other more strictly rational forms of proof.

Thus, an effective unit of proof consists of two dimensions—an illustrative dimension and a rational dimension. This means that each argument advanced by a speaker should be supported in both ways. This may require more than one item of evidence, or an advocate may find a single quotation that fulfills the demands of both dimensions. The effective and ethical advocate will make certain that both dimensions are fulfilled before s/he concludes that argument.

The Role of Analogy in Argument

Public and intercollegiate debaters will frequently use analogies in their debates. Analogies can function on either an illustrative or a rational dimension. Illustrative comparisons function *rhetorically* to explain and to persuade; rational comparisons function *argumentatively* to prove and persuade.

Analogies may also be either figurative or literal. A *figurative analogy* is one that is used to compare things from two different classes of phenomena. Such analogies are poetic or imaginative in nature since they compare things that have no actual similarities. Such figurative analogies can be used to illustrate concepts. For example, in the debates over the nuclear freeze proposals, Senator Mark Hatfield used an analogy to illustrate that the concept of a freeze was necessary to bring about reductions in nuclear weapons. Hatfield stated in a 1982 interview: "We have to first create a freeze to get a change of direction. A freeze would not impair our ability to reverse the current upward arms escalation. Instead, it would stop the arms race so that it could be reversed. You can't throw a freight train coming down the track into reverse until you first stop it."[3] Advocates frequently use this kind of analogy in public debate. Although intercollegiate debaters use figurative and illustrative comparisons less frequently, such uses can nevertheless be effective.

Literal analogies are comparisons between things from the same class or very similar classes of phenomena. Such an analogy might be used in a policy debate to demonstrate that a proposed solution would be workable. For example, in the 1970s James L. Freund, formerly of the Federal Reserve Bank of Philadelphia, argued that wage subsidies would work to reduce poverty in the United States as they had worked in limited areas in this country and in foreign countries. Freund explained:

> Another plan, wage subsidies, would attack the gap from the other end. Recognizing the difficulty of convincing people to accept lower wages, private employers could be paid allowances for hiring the unemployed or for raising wages of very low-paid workers. In effect, the government would be lowering the price of labor to the firm. . . . Such a wage-subsidy program has been attempted on a limited scale both at home and abroad—when dealing with problems of depressed areas and disadvantaged labor.[4]

This is an example of an analogy between things from the same class.

Literal analogies can also be made between things from similar classes. For example, in order to explain the dangers of chemical and biological war, Professors Intriligator and Brito compared these dangers to those associated with nuclear weapons. They wrote: "The situation with respect to chemical and biological weapons may be like that of nuclear weapons in the many-nation case. Any one nation is restrained from using these weapons by the anticipated response of other nations with the same weapons. Chemical and biological weapons are weapons of mass destruction, potentially causing even greater human destruction than nuclear weapons."[5]

When analogies are used in a debate, they should be tested according to their function. If a figurative analogy is used to illustrate a concept, it should be evaluated based on rhetorical principles. Such analogies should not be evaluated based on argumentative principles. For example, it would be pointless for Senator Hatfield's arms race–train analogy to be criticized as having no points of actual comparison since the analogy does not intend to function in that way. On the other hand, analogies intended to function as real and rational comparisons should be evaluated by argumentative and rational standards. For example, if James Freund's analogy between the different wage subsidy programs was being evaluated, a number of evidential and logical tests would be applied: Did the advocate provide enough information to document the comparison? Are the items being compared similar in a sufficient number of respects? Are the items being compared similar in the most significant qualities? Can any differences in the items being compared be accounted for as either irrelevant or insignificant? Are there other ways to prove the same argument?

Thus, analogies are possible ways of illustrating or proving arguments in both public and educational debates.

Methods of Delivery

There are four methods of delivery that speakers, including advocates, might use: (1) impromptu speaking, (2) extemporaneous speaking, (3) manuscript delivery, and (4) delivery from memory.

Impromptu Speaking

Impromptu speaking means speaking without any advance preparation. For example, if you go to your next debate class and without warning the instructor asks you to make a speech defending the United States foreign policy in Central America, you will be speaking impromptu. Unless you have previously studied or perhaps debated this or a similar topic, you will probably have difficulty thinking of arguments and supporting materials and organizing those materials into a coherent and persuasive presentation. On the other hand, if you are very well informed about the topic and you have developed effective organization and delivery skills, you might be able to deliver a very persuasive speech. In this latter situation, you have advance preparation for the speech even though you had not planned to speak; in this sense such speaking is not impromptu.

We feel that such impromptu speaking for advocates in public or educational debating is at best ineffective and at worst unethical, and that students who participate in intercollegiate debates without preparation will not benefit educationally. However, a public advocate, such as a Congressperson, should be able to speak without specific notice on those issues for which he or she is responsible. For example, if Representative Sullivan is visiting his home district in Leeville and he is called upon to speak about a piece of legislation important to his constituents, he should be prepared to speak even if the particular occasion was unpredictable. His role as a Congressperson requires him to be prepared for such situations.

Students who enter an intercollegiate debate tournament should also be sufficiently prepared to debate the assigned resolution. Such preparation is the joint responsibility of the students and the coach or teacher who enters them into the competition. Students can never be *completely* prepared with specific arguments and evidence for every possible case in a debate. However, they should be well enough prepared with specific evidence and arguments on the major cases, knowledge of argumentation theory, and sufficient skills to assure that they are competitive within the division of competition in which they are entered. With such preparation, the students will be able to argue against even unusual cases and arguments.

Although impromptu speaking is not advisable as a method of delivery for either the public advocate or the intercollegiate debater, it can be valuable as a classroom exercise for the developing of organizational and delivery skills for the intercollegiate debater or the future public advocate. Such impromptu practices can help students develop skills for the effective use of extemporaneous delivery.

Extemporaneous Speaking

Extemporaneous speaking, unlike impromptu speaking, involves a great amount of specific preparation. The speech that is delivered extemporaneously, however, is neither read nor delivered from memory. Extemporaneous speakers usually use limited notes such as an outline and key items of supporting material that must be precisely cited—statistics, direct quotations, and similar items. Extemporaneous speaking can therefore be defined as *presentation based on thorough knowledge and understanding of the subject matter with a lively kind of delivery from limited notes.*

Most public advocates and college debaters will use the extemporaneous method in much, if not most, of their speaking. The congressperson campaigning for re-election will frequently use the extemporaneous method as described above. The college debater will usually use an outline of the arguments of the debate and index cards for exact quotation of all evidence.

Extemporaneous is the most advantageous method of speaking for the public advocate or the intercollegiate debater. It is flexible and allows the speaker to adapt to unexpected arguments. It is more spontaneous and therefore more lively than most manuscript or memorized speeches. Although there is more risk of error with extemporaneous delivery than with manuscript speeches, the risk is minimal if the speaker is well prepared and has used notes for crucial arguments and items of support. It is frequently difficult for less experienced advocates, whether in Congress or in an intercollegiate debate, to control their use of time with the extemporaneous method. However, speakers learn with experience how to control time effectively with the extemporaneous method.

Manuscript Speaking

Manuscript speaking involves writing the speech out in full, word for word, and reading it to the audience or judges. Manuscript delivery allows for maximum precision in terms of word choice, clarity of meaning, and precise use of documentary evidence. Public advocates frequently must use manuscript speaking because the nature of the occasion requires such precision. For example, United States presidents use manuscripts for almost all of their major addresses. Debaters also frequently use manuscripts for the first affirmative constructive speech.

Manuscripts, however, are difficult to deliver effectively. It is difficult for beginning and even more experienced speakers to make the printed word come alive for the listener. Too often the manuscript becomes either a physical or psychological barrier between the speaker and the audience. Many college students have endured a lecturer who read to them from a textbook or notes without sufficient enthusiasm to keep them awake. Many college debate judges have heard too many first affirmative speakers who buried their faces and their words in the pages of a manuscript.

When planning a manuscript speech, a speaker should first determine if the manuscript is really necessary to ensure a required precision of meaning. If a manuscript is not necessary, the speaker should probably use the extemporaneous method. When a speaker has determined that a manuscript is necessary, he or she should devote significant time to practice of that speech. For the intercollegiate debater, practice should be with a listener such as a teacher, coach, or very experienced teammate who can provide helpful criticism.

Delivery from Memory

Delivery from memory is a method that was developed and practiced by rhetoricians from ancient Greece and Rome. It was developed primarily because it was either impractical or impossible for speakers to use manuscripts for lengthy speeches. Speaking from memory is a seldom-used method of delivery for contemporary advocates or even students in debate or speech contests. Public advocates usually cannot, and do not need to, devote the time necessary to memorize their presentations. Also most speech contests and all debate competitions allow either unlimited or limited notes.

Speaking from memory is also a disadvantageous method of delivery. It shares some of the weaknesses of manuscript speaking in that it often seems to lack liveliness because the language and the delivery lack freshness and spontaneity. Even experienced speakers frequently forget parts of their speeches when they attempt to deliver them from memory. If a speaker's time to prepare a speech is viewed as a resource, the time necessary to memorize a speech can also be viewed as a poor investment. Speakers might more profitably spend their time doing additional research or working on other aspects of their presentations.

However, speakers may find it desirable to memorize parts of their presentations without suffering these disadvantages. For example, speakers might wish to memorize introductions, conclusions, or key parts of speeches in order to maintain more effective eye contact with audiences or judges. Speakers who do repetitive kinds of speeches, such as campaign speakers and intercollegiate debaters, will begin to remember naturally many of their arguments and phrasings. This kind of memorization usually results in speeches delivered much more effectively than those a speaker consciously attempts to memorize.

In summary, advocates will find extemporaneous speaking to be the most effective method of delivery. However, manuscript speaking is sometimes desirable for both public advocates and intercollegiate debaters when precision is necessary. Memorized or impromptu delivery is rarely recommended as an intentional method of delivery.

Other Important Factors in Delivery

Familiarity with other aspects of delivery, such as characteristics of the voice and nonverbal communication, will help both public advocates and intercollegiate debaters diagnose and correct minor delivery problems.

Characteristics of the Voice

Any speaker in any situation should be aware of the voice and its characteristics. Awareness of the characteristics of the voice will not only assist speakers in solving minor delivery problems—such awareness will also allow speakers to develop vocal variety that will result in more effective delivery. The most important vocal characteristics are pitch, quality, volume, and rate. *Pitch* refers to the high or low sound of the voice. The pitch of an individual's voice is produced by the fundamental frequency of the vibrations of the vocal folds. The faster the folds vibrate, the higher will be the resulting sound. Pitch varies with both sex and age. Speakers can also vary the pitch of their voices for the purpose of emphasis and to provide vocal variety.

Voice quality refers to the general character of the voice. For example, adjectives such as nasal or denasal, strident, husky, harsh, guttural, rich, or thin are frequently used to describe voice quality. Voice quality is produced by a variety of factors, including some physical features and defects. However, only a very few kinds of voice quality are signs of problems or physical defects. If a speaker is concerned about either pitch or quality, then he or she might consider a course in voice or diction. If there is evidence of a serious problem, speech screening at a clinic might be appropriate. Students interested in these possibilities should consult their teacher or debate coach, who may be able to provide additional information.

Volume or loudness is produced by the relative intensity of the vibration of the vocal folds. Advocates frequently raise the volume of their voices either due to excitement or as a form of emphasis. Although some public advocates and many intercollegiate debaters frequently overuse loudness as a form of emphasis, variations in volume can contribute positively to vocal variety.

Rate refers to the rapidity of delivery. How fast and how rapidly you speak will in part determine the intelligibility of your speech. Variations in rate by either slowing down or speeding up can positively contribute to vocal variety. As with volume, advocates will frequently increase their rate of speaking due to excitement or as a form of emphasis. Many speakers, including intercollegiate debaters, will overuse a fast rate as either a form of emphasis or as a form of intimidation. One additional form of variation of rate is the *pause,* which can be a very effective form of emphasis.

Advocates should also be familiar with two other related concepts dealing with the voice—articulation and pronunciation. *Articulation* refers to the clarity of the production of the sounds of syllables and words. Both clear and unclear sounds are dependent upon how the speaker physically modifies the air stream into sounds. If a speaker is lazy or tired, he or she may mumble. On the other hand, a speaker with a great deal of energy is more likely to articulate clearly. There are numerous reasons for poor articulation, but it is important that this problem be overcome; speakers must articulate clearly or they risk not being understood. Speakers should also avoid *over-articulation* of words or their delivery may sound stilted and artificial.

Pronunciation refers to the correct or preferred ways of saying words. When an advocate mispronounces words that are known by the audiences, the audiences may make incorrect judgments about the speaker's knowledge of the subject matter. As a result the speaker's credibility may be diminished. Dictionaries will list preferred and acceptable pronunciations of words. Speakers should realize, however, that there are three major dialect areas in the United States, which means that there are three varying dialects—Eastern, Southern and Standard American. Although television has done much to make Standard American speech the preferred standard for many, some audiences are still more comfortable with speakers who speak the appropriate regional dialect. Speakers interested in checking variations in the preferred pronunciation of words in the different dialect areas can consult a *pronouncing dictionary,* and speakers concerned about articulation or pronunciation might consider a course in voice and diction.

Nonverbal Communication

Nonverbal communication refers to all messages that are expressed by other than linguistic means. The characteristics of the voice discussed above are relevant to both verbal and nonverbal communication, but we will focus here on the use of the body to communicate. Obviously, a speaker's body—through the use of space, facial expressions, gestures, and other movements—sends messages both intentionally and unintentionally.

It is important that public advocates and intercollegiate debaters be aware of appropriate uses of space as they deal with their colleagues, opponents, and audiences. As you have all probably observed, the distance people place between themselves and others communicates attitudes and can significantly affect communication. Edward Hall identified four zones used by most Americans: intimate (from physical contact to approximately eighteen inches), casual (approximately eighteen inches to about four feet), social (approximately four to twelve feet), and public (approximately twelve feet and outward).[6] These zones do not always apply, of course, but in most advocacy situations these zones are significant. The size of the room in which a collegiate debate is held can affect interaction, for instance. Although a casual distance might be quite appropriate in working with colleagues, during the actual debate the opposing team and the judge will probably expect the debater to maintain a social or public distance. The exuberant debater may violate the space of his or her opponents or the judge. After the debate, however, the opposing teams will usually shake hands and may engage in casual conversation, and at this point the casual and social distances are appropriate.

Advocates must try to be aware of both the unintentional and the intentional use of the body. This awareness should include the realization that the audience will make judgments about the speaker and about the speaker's attitudes towards the opponents and the audience itself. Beginning speakers may attempt to plan gestures, and the result may appear awkward or artificial. Such speakers will often find that they are more successful if they do not attempt to plan gestures; as they gain more speaking experience, they will also gain more confidence. Confidence will allow relaxation and more effective use of the body. Gestures will then come naturally, and confident speakers will be able to use gestures effectively, even when planned.

Finally, advocates should be familiar with several important principles of nonverbal communication. First, you cannot avoid communicating nonverbally. As indicated above, even unintentional movements may send a message to your audience—even failing to move during a speech can send a very strong message. Second, nonverbal communication is subject to many interpretations. Gestures and other movements, including the use of space, can be interpreted in many ways. For example, if you clench your fist during a speech, your opponent may think you are angry and your audience may think you are emphasizing your point. Third, some nonverbal behavior is culture bound: the use of space, direct eye contact, and other kinds of nonverbal behavior vary in different cultures and countries. For example, direct eye contact is a sign of trustworthiness and honesty in American culture, but averting the eyes is a sign of respect in other cultures.

Audience and Judge Adaptation

One of the most important principles of effective style and delivery is that a speaker should adapt to specific audiences or judges. For example, when a Senator speaks to her colleagues on a specific subcommittee, she can probably use specific or technical language since the subcommittee has been studying that topic for a significant period of time. However, if the Senator speaks to her constituents on the same topic, she will want to define her terms and use less technical language. College debaters also need to adapt to different kinds of audiences, judges, and situations. For instance, debaters may confront very experienced debate coaches who do not mind rapid delivery. The same debaters may also speak in front of a public speaking teacher who has judged only classroom debates, and the latter judge might find the rapid delivery unintelligible.

Part of adapting to particular audiences is also adapting to the particular situation, taking into account time, place, and occasion. For example, if a college debater is speaking at the end of a ten or twelve hour day of debates, the judge may appreciate a slower delivery or less intense competition. All speakers should also be conscious of place. Excessive use of volume as a form of emphasis is probably not wise in a small seminar room. Finally, the nature of the event or occasion is also important. For example, United States presidents do not use inauguration addresses to attack their opponents.

In summary, public advocates and college debaters should attempt to consider all aspects of the audiences and the situation, and appropriately adapt both the style and delivery of their speeches.

Style and Delivery in the First Affirmative Constructive

Many of the relevant principles for preparing the first affirmative speech have already been discussed in previous chapters. The first affirmative speech offers debaters the opportunity to use longer pieces of evidence, to explain ideas more fully, to improve and to perfect their persuasiveness, and in particular to improve and perfect their language and style.

As indicated in this chapter, the first affirmative constructive will usually be a manuscript speech. Debaters should take care in preparing and writing this speech to remember the principles of good oral style. The debater will not want the speech to sound like an essay read aloud. Vivid, dramatic, and concrete style can also be perfected in this speech. Since the first affirmative will be closely scrutinized by opponents and judges, the debater who writes the first affirmative should make certain that each argument is fully supported with a unit of proof, complete with both the illustrative and rational components. First affirmative speeches also should be delivered in a lively manner. Although they are manuscript speeches, they need to be delivered with the freshness of language and the spontaneity characteristic of good extemporaneous speaking. Since the first affirmative can be practiced, the first affirmative can perfect all other aspects of delivery, such as the characteristics of the voice and nonverbal communication. Debaters should compose the first affirmative so it can be reasonably delivered in the time allotted.

Finally, the first affirmative should be adaptable in a variety of ways, such as those suggested above regarding time, place, and situation. Debaters certainly should be able to adapt to different judges in terms of rate of delivery.

Effective Style and Delivery in Rebuttals

Two principles should guide style and delivery in rebuttals. First, effective organization is essential in rebuttals, and speakers should keep in mind the principles of effective organization discussed in previous chapters.

Second, language economy is also essential in rebuttals. Debaters will need to be able to refer to arguments and key items of evidence presented earlier in the debate. To master such language economy speakers may adapt the concepts of metonymy and synecdoche from literary analysis. *Metonymy* refers in literary analysis to the use of a related symbol for another. For example, if a writer uses the phrase "the bottle" to stand for strong drink, then that is the use of metonymy. Synecdoche refers to the use of a part to stand for the whole. For example, if a poet refers to the "crown" but means the king, then that is the use of synecdoche. Debaters can use these same principles to identify the key words of both ideas and evidence, which will remind the judge of arguments with full explanations and long items of documentation that were presented earlier in the round. To accomplish this, debaters should first identify the key arguments and items of evidence that they will be using most often during their debates. The debater should then develop memorable metonyms and synecdoches for each idea and piece of evidence; sometimes this can be done by underlining the one or two key words that stand out as the card is read aloud. Later, these phrases can be used to identify the ideas and the evidence in rebuttals.

Summary

This chapter has identified numerous principles of effective style and delivery. Style was defined as the choices and combinations of words, sentence structure, grammatical decisions, and other language-related choices that mark an individual writer's or speaker's verbal expression. Delivery was defined as the physical communication of the speaker's message.

This chapter also indicated the characteristics of good oral style important for the advocate. Crucial to the development of good oral style and delivery is self-awareness. Another characteristic of persuasive speaking is vivid, dramatic, concrete language. The effective unit of proof includes two components—an illustrative and a rational dimension. This chapter also discussed how arguers can use analogies both to illustrate and to prove ideas.

Of the four methods of delivery—impromptu, extemporaneous, manuscript, and memorized—the advocate should usually employ either the extemporaneous or manuscript method. Even when manuscripts are used, however, the speaker should strive for a language that is fresh and a delivery that is spontaneous. The speaker should also take into account other important delivery factors, such as voice characteristics and nonverbal communication. In all aspects of style and delivery speakers should be able to adapt to the audience.

Finally, this chapter briefly examined the importance of style and delivery in the first affirmative constructive speech and in rebuttal speeches.

Notes

1. John F. Wilson and Carroll C. Arnold, *Public Speaking as a Liberal Art*, 5th ed. (Boston: Allyn and Bacon, 1983), p. 228.
2. Ibid., p. 228.
3. Mark O. Hatfield, quoted in "Pro and Con: A Freeze on Nuclear Weapons?", *U. S. News & World Report* (April 5, 1982), p. 56.
4. James L. Freund, "Fighting Poverty with Jobs: Public and Private Payroll Weapons," *Federal Reserve Bank of Philadelphia Business Review* (April 1974), p. 29.
5. Michael D. Intriligator and Dagobert L. Brito, "Nuclear Proliferation and Stability," *Journal of Peace Science*, Vol. 3, No. 2, p. 181.
6. F. Steele, *Physical Settings and Organizational Development* (Reading, MA: Addison-Wesley, 1973), p. 46.

Questions and Exercises

1. What is style?
2. What is delivery?
3. What are the characteristics of effective style and delivery?
4. Define the following:
   a. an effective unit of proof
   b. good oral style
   c. role of analogy in argumentation
   d. methods of delivery
5. Select several passages from the following kinds of materials—newspaper articles, newspaper editorials, novels, magazine articles. Read these aloud. Ask the listeners to indicate which if any seem to have the characteristics of good oral style. Which characteristics, if any, do they have? Why do they have these characteristics or not have them?
6. Each student should prepare a proposition on a controversial campus issue. The teacher should collect these topics, and divide the class into debate teams or pairs of students, randomly assigning every other team or person to the affirmative and negative sides. Then, each group of two or four students will draw one topic for an impromptu debate. Constructive speeches should be no longer than 3 minutes and rebuttals should be no longer than 2 minutes.

Suggested Readings

Vasilius, Janet and DeStephen, Dan. "An Investigation of the Relationship Between Debate Tournament Success and Rate, Evidence and Jargon." *Journal of the American Forensic Association,* XV (Spring 1979), 197–204.

McDonald, Daniel. *The Language of Argument,* 3rd Ed. New York: Harper and Row, 1980.

FOURTEEN

Ethics in Argumentation

Ethics can be defined as the principles that guide human choices about what is considered good or bad, right or wrong, moral or immoral. Ethical principles, systems, and codes reflect much about how their makers and users perceive good and bad. Ethical principles or an ethical code for argumentation and debate, therefore, reflect not only the nature of argumentation, but also American society and its traditional principles. In particular, ethical principles are constructed from an analysis of what constitutes desirable attitudes and behaviors in persuasive situations in American society.

The Nature of Ethics in Argumentative Situations

Systems of ethics in American society are usually based upon three assumptions. First, a system of ethics requires that the principles be supported by the particular community; the individual principles should be recognized as morally right by the majority of the members of the community. Nondemocratic societies might have, instead, systems of ethics based on the approval of religious leaders or other authoritative sources. In both systems, an individual principle might be violated by many members of the community, yet still be consistently and strongly espoused by the members of the community. For example, in contemporary American society honesty is still an important value; although many people find it permissible to lie in many social situations, public advocates are expected to tell the truth—especially when discussing vital public questions.

Second, a system of ethics requires that the principles be known and understood. However, the knowledge and the understanding does not necessarily have to be communicated formally and explicitly to the members of society. For example, in American society people learn in many different ways that honesty is a highly valued principle. In the home children are taught that it is not "right" to lie to their parents. In elementary school children learn not to lie to their teachers. As adults we learn that lying is risky socially and that in legal matters lying violates the law. Thus, even though advocates may never have been taught that they should not lie when pleading a case before the public, society would expect them to know and understand the importance of honesty.

Third, a system of ethics requires that sanctions exist to reinforce the individual principles. In some circumstances, violations of ethical principles may also constitute violations of the law. For example, perjury, libel, and slander laws are all related in part to society's espousal of honesty. In many situations the principles are formally stated and enforced by professional associations. Many professional groups have codes of ethics and committees or other bodies to enforce their principles of conduct. For example, the American Bar Association adopted its *Canons of Professional Ethics* in 1908 and the American Medical Association has had its *Principles of Medical Ethics of the American Medical Association* since 1847. Various state legislatures and both the House and the Senate of the U.S. Congress have ethics codes and committees to regulate the conduct of their members, including some aspects of their argumentative behavior. The American Forensics Association, the professional organization of teachers of argumentation and forensics coaches, has its *Code of Forensics Program and Forensics Tournament Standards for Colleges and Universities.*

Chapter Outline

On the other hand, the sanctions may often be informal, especially when the violation is beyond the law and any code or standard. For example, when a public advocate makes a regular practice of distortion, lying, or misrepresentation, he or she is likely to be discovered either by other advocates or the press. The exposure of such acts of dishonesty will not only be embarrassing, but will significantly lower the speaker's credibility with his or her peers and with the public. Not only might dishonesty threaten the public career of such an advocate, it will also greatly diminish his or her ability to influence the course of public affairs. In a sense, then, dishonesty is regulated by the public forum in a democracy. In much the same way, an intercollegiate debater who is flagrantly dishonest will risk discovery by other debaters or by judges. Most proponents of ethical systems believe, however, that such "self-regulation" should not be an excuse for the failure of groups to establish or to enforce ethical standards by more direct means.

This chapter examines the traditional ethical principles that guide public advocates and college debaters in argumentative situations. In particular, this chapter considers the following: (1) theoretical groundings for ethical systems; (2) ethics and the attitudes of arguers; (3) ethical issues in argumentative situations, and (4) ethical guidelines for educational debate.

Theoretical Groundings for Ethical Systems

In a pluralistic society such as ours there are many possible sources for ethical systems. This chapter will briefly examine the following traditional and contemporary origins: (1) Plato, (2) Aristotle, (3) traditional democratic principles, and (4) a transactional concept of communication.

Plato

Plato (431–351 B.C.) was only one of many influential Greeks in a crucial period of western civilization, but his ideas nonetheless spread far beyond the rooms of his school, the Academy. Indeed, Plato influenced western thought more than any other single philosopher in the history of humankind. In particular, Plato is probably responsible for many of the negative attitudes held toward the study of rhetoric. Everett Lee Hunt explained some of the reasons for Plato's disdain of rhetoric: "The art of rhetoric offered to the Athenian of the fifth century B.C. a method of higher education and, beyond that, a way of life. Plato attacked both. He gave rhetoric a conspicuous place in his dialogues because it represented in Athenian life that which he most disliked."[1] Since argumentation and debate are forms of rhetoric, Plato's critique of the art of rhetoric is directly relevant to argumentation and debate. Plato's critiques and views on rhetoric are contained primarily in two philosophical dialogues—the *Gorgias* and the *Phaedrus.*

In Plato's *Gorgias,* the philosopher makes his indictment of rhetoric clear within the context of a statement of ethical principles. The ethical basis Plato promulgates in this dialogue has continued to be used both to condemn rhetoric and, ironically, to form the basis for an ethical system for public advocates. One of Plato's major concerns was the *neutrality of the means of persuasion;* in other words, Plato was concerned that rhetoric would not always be used for good purposes and could be used for evil purposes. Speaking to Callicles, Socrates voices this concern in a question:

> Does it seem to you that orators always speak with an eye on what is best and aim at this: that their fellow citizens may receive the maximum improvement through their words? Or do they, like the poets, strive to gratify their fellows and, in seeking their own private interest, do they neglect the common good, dealing with public assemblies as though the constituents were children, trying only to gratify them, and caring not in the least whether this procedure makes them better or makes them worse?[2]

Plato reveals in the *Gorgias* and other works his distrust of rhetoric and his distrust of the popular will when manipulated by rhetoric. In this dialogue Plato seems to see no proper role for rhetoric in a just and good society, and indeed the *Gorgias* clearly expresses the view that both rhetoric and rhetoric-influenced popular will are threats to advancing the best interests of society.

In the *Phaedrus,* however, Plato seems to have found a place for rhetoric. According to Hunt, Plato's starting point for an acceptable rhetoric is that the speaker know "the truth of the subject on which he is about to speak." In this dialogue Socrates outlines the other qualities of a good rhetoric, including the knowledge of philosophy, logic, organic organization, and a form of audience analysis. Lastly, the "rhetorician will have such a high moral purpose in all his work that he will be chiefly concerned about saying that which is 'acceptable to God.' " Although this dialogue holds no indication that even the best rhetoric would, in Plato's view, be equal to philosophic discussion, there is at least the recognition of the possibility of an ethical rhetoric.[3]

What, then, are the implications of Plato's views for a contemporary ethical system for argumentation and debate? His views are in some ways inconsistent: the view in the *Gorgias* is quite different from that in the *Phaedrus.* This inconsistency, however, reflects the common perspective that rhetoric is an unfortunate necessity. Although rhetoric is subject to abuse, it can serve the advancement of the public good. This perspective suggests that an advocate should begin with a knowledge of the truth of the subject matter and that the other decisions he or she makes in terms of organization, audience analysis, and strategy should reflect choices that effectively advance the truth.

Aristotle

Although Aristotle (384–322 B.C.) was Plato's most famous pupil, the student had very different ideas, especially about rhetoric, than those of his teacher. Aristotle sought to rehabilitate rhetoric, which had so displeased Plato, from its disreputable state. Friedrich Solmsen notes: "Rhetoric's need for rehabilitation was if possible even greater than poetry's, and in his treatise Aristotle actually reforms this subject and gives it a philosophically respectable standing."[4]

Aristotle's ethical assumptions that are relevant to argumentation and debate are outlined in several works, including the *Nicomachean Ethics, Politics,* and the *Rhetoric.* In the *Nicomachean Ethics* Aristotle explains that the end of human striving is happiness. The happiness to which Aristotle refers is a happiness that is based upon an individual's best possible performance of the function for which he or she is particularly suited, and he feels that the greatest happiness is found in an active life of the soul consistent with virtue. Virtue, Aristotle argues, can best be acquired by practice and habit, and a good man is one who chooses to do what is virtuous and good for its own sake.[5]

The *Politics* shows Aristotle's belief that government both can and should be the means of providing the "good life" for the citizenry. In this work Aristotle critiques Plato's *Republic* and reveals himself, unlike his teacher, to be committed to a democratic form of government. Although Aristotle's form of democracy was not egalitarian by contemporary standards, he nevertheless espoused the democratic principle of a citizenry who could act as a check upon societal leaders who might be tempted otherwise towards tyranny.[6] Given this preference for democratic government, it is not surprising that Aristotle would promote training in rhetoric, which would give citizens the ability to discuss intelligently the major deliberative questions of the day.

As explained in the *Rhetoric,* Aristotle's conception of the good aims or justifications of rhetoric differs significantly from Plato's. In fact, Aristotle seems to have been unclear about the precise aims a statesman should have in the use of rhetoric. Solmsen explains: "There is a curious wavering between the 'good' and the 'expedient.' Which of the two does Aristotle really mean to set up as the goal towards which the political orator should direct his efforts? . . . Here he deals with the 'good,' there with the 'expedient,' while at times he actually treats the concepts as identical. . . ."[7] Although the reasons for this treatment are not clear, perhaps Aristotle was foreshadowing a more contemporary notion that the art of politics, and in this case the art of political oratory, can combine in a harmonious fashion both the "good" and the "expedient."

In Aristotle's rival school, rhetoric was a significant subject of study rather than an object of fear and dispute. Aristotle's *Rhetoric* reveals at least one of the reasons why he believed that rhetoric should not be feared: according to Aristotle, rhetoric functions in a "marketplace of ideas" in which the false and the unjust ideas can not compete successfully with the true and just if presented by speakers with equal skills. "Rhetoric is useful," according to Aristotle, "because things that are true and things that are just have a natural tendency to prevail over their opposites, so that if the decisions of judges are not what they ought to be, the defeat must be due to the speakers themselves, and they must be blamed accordingly."[8] Given this view, the supposed neutrality of rhetoric did not make it a skill to be feared. Instead, rhetoric was a necessary art to be mastered so that truth would not lose out to falsehood due to the inadequacies of the speaker.

In other parts of the *Rhetoric* Aristotle seems to confront the issue of the neutrality of the means of persuasion more directly. Aristotle claims that rhetoric is a useful tool in the discovery of the truth, and that argumentative exercise on both sides of a topic is not only desirable but necessary in order to discover the truth of an issue. "We must be able to employ persuasion, just as strict reasoning can be employed, on opposite sides of a question not in order that we may in exercise employ it in both ways (for we must not make people believe what is wrong), but in order that we may see clearly what the facts are, and that if another man argues unfairly, we on our part may be able to confute him."[9] This view was very different from the one expressed by Plato in the *Gorgias*. On the other hand, it might be argued that Aristotle's proposals met the demands for a good rhetoric laid down in the *Phaedrus*.[10]

What, then, are the implications of Aristotle's views for a contemporary ethical system for argumentation and debate? Unlike Plato, Aristotle saw rhetoric as making positive contributions to both the discovery of truth and the advancement of good for society. *Good* was defined in various ways by Aristotle; good for individuals was fulfillment of an appropriate function and leading a virtuous life. Aristotle's view of government was as a source of much of the good life for its citizenry. Aristotle also advocated a democratic form of government in which the people acted as a check upon their leaders. In the *Rhetoric* the good was sometimes equated with the expedient; this possibly implied that through the arts of rhetoric and politics the political orator could make the good also the expedient.

Aristotle also believed that rhetoric could aid the advocate in the discovery of truth by allowing him or her to understand both sides of various issues. Understanding both sides of issues could also help the arguer in refuting false and unjust positions. If all speakers were of relatively equal skill in the art of rhetoric, truth would naturally prevail over falsehood in the marketplace of ideas.

Traditional Democratic Principles

Aristotle's contributions significantly influenced several key principles of modern democracies and, in particular, contemporary American ideology. First, United States democracy is based in part upon a "marketplace of ideas" theory. The marketplace of ideas is based both on a belief in the right of free expression and on the belief that free competition among ideas will result in superior decisions on public questions. A marketplace of ideas has been guaranteed by the First Amendment to the Constitution. In 1969 the U.S. Supreme Court declared: "It is the purpose of the First Amendment to preserve an uninhibited marketplace of ideas in which truth will ultimately prevail. . . ."[11] In order for the marketplace of ideas to function effectively, access to the marketplace must be possible and the competition must be fair. This fairness is related to the next key value of democratic ideology.

Second, fairness is both an intrinsic and an instrumental value in contemporary American ideology. Fairness is basic to almost every aspect of American life. A study by the Public Agenda Foundation recently concluded: "Americans' commitment to the idea of fair play is part of our national character. In politics, sports, business, and interpersonal relations, notions of fairness, a fair deal, and fair play stand near the top of a hierarchy of national values."[12] Furthermore, "People believe that they will not have an accurate basis on which to make decisions, such as voting, unless they have access to news that provides all the information they need. From this perspective, the public's call for fairness serves an instrumental purpose."[13]

Third, individual responsibility is emphasized in contemporary American democracy. The idea that an individual advocate should be responsible for his or her utterances is especially important to an ethical system for argumentation and debate. As indicated above, Aristotle emphasizes that if truth fails, "the defeat must be due to the speakers themselves, and they must be blamed accordingly." Furthermore, the public holds various speakers accountable according to their function. The Public Agenda Foundation, for example, found different levels of accountability for different kinds of information sources:

> In the public's mind, there are different standards for different types of news sources. If a newspaper, for example, positions itself as a major source of objective information—as providing "all the news that's fit to print"—it is held to a higher standard of accountability. A New York administrative assistant compared newspapers to books. "In a textbook, I expect a balanced presentation of all points of view. But I don't expect or want that from every book on the library shelf. That's the way I feel about newspapers too. The *Times* is like a textbook; its coverage should be objective. The *Village Voice* is like a book on the shelf; it can say anything it wants to.[14]

Although the ideas about the kinds of obligations a speaker has vary, there is agreement that speakers generally are responsible and accountable for what they say.

Finally, the truth is emphasized in various ways in contemporary democratic ideology. Plato's insistence that the truth be pursued and that decisions be based on knowledge are certainly key assumptions of contemporary American democracy. Aristotle's emphasis upon proof for a speaker's assertions is also important in American democracy. Truth-telling is an obligation applicable to all speakers in almost all situations. Thomas Nilsen noted that problems arise not in agreeing that speakers should tell the truth, but in agreeing what constitutes the truth in certain situations. "Although we would all agree that truthfulness is important to morally right speech, we would have difficulty in many instances in coming to agreement on what being truthful entails."[15]

A Transactional Concept of Communication

Studies in interpersonal communication examine the nature of communication between persons. Theorists, teachers, and students in this area are especially interested in such topics as informal communication in social situations, family communication, dyadic communication (between two persons), communication games, the role of space, and the nature of healthy communication. Although interpersonal communication studies focus on a very different area than does argumentation and debate, interpersonal theory does provide some applicable concepts for both public advocates and intercollegiate debaters.

First, the concept of a transactional model of communication provides several starting points for ethical principles. Most current interpersonal communication theorists endorse the transactional concept of communication. The transactional concept is wholistic and focuses upon the entire communication event or transaction rather than dissecting it into many variables, and this theory is based on the belief that communication is simultaneous and mutual.[16] Dennis Smith and Keith Williamson are typical of many interpersonal theorists when they claim: "The transactional model presently appears to be the only model capable of describing communication between two perceiving and adapting human beings."[17]

A number of important principles are associated with the transactional concept of communication. For example, the axiom that it is impossible not to communicate is central to much of interpersonal theory and most transactional concepts of communication. Explained simply, the concept means: "Within a transaction, neither person can stop behaving; and each adapts to the other's behavior. Whether they are talking or remaining silent, being active or being passive, they are behaving. Each person perceives the other's behavior and attaches meaning to some of it."[18] Smith and Williamson state: "The principle that one cannot not communicate is probably the most important theoretical advance in nearly half a century of study of human communication."[19]

Second, the concept of healthy communication also provides for starting points for ethical principles. The concept of healthy communication is based on more than just the absence of negative behaviors. Healthy communication also includes the presence of innately desirable qualities. Smith and Williamson note that healthy communication "promotes optimal interpersonal growth with the fewest difficulties in living."[20] As such, the concept of healthy communication clearly relates to the concept of *good* communication and, thereby, to ethical principles of communication.

Healthy communication is based on five principles: acknowledgment, appropriateness, efficiency, flexibility, and gratification. One, healthy communication can occur only when communicators are able to acknowledge in their own communication the content of the communication of the other persons involved in the transaction. Two, healthy communication also requires that the persons in a transaction use communication in ways that are appropriate to the communication situation. Three, healthy communication is efficient when communicators can attain their objectives with the least amount of unnecessary effort. Four, flexibility in adapting to changed roles, behaviors, and objectives as situations and circumstances evolve is also characteristic of healthy communication. Finally, healthy communication benefits all participants in a transaction.[21]

What, then, are the implications of these concepts for a contemporary ethical system for argumentation and debate? The transactional model seems to provide the basis for two principles. First, the nature of the transactional model suggests that an advocate should be sensitive to the whole of the communication transaction and not just the content of the messages. Second, the transactional model also implies that the participants in any communication situation should view all participants as equals.

The principles of healthy communication also have implications for arguers, and argumentation and debate should be healthy communication in a number of respects. One, advocates should respond to each others arguments. Speakers should not either ignore arguments or claim that their opponents have not made arguments. Two, advocates should respond to arguments and to argumentative situations that are appropriate to the specific situation. For example, advocates can disagree about ideas and yet still like and respect one another. Three, advocates should be efficient in their communication. For instance, advocates should not unnecessarily personalize a dispute. To make arguments against the person rather than the ideas of the opposing speaker usually does not strengthen an argumentative position. Four, arguers should be flexible in varying situations. For example, an experienced intercollegiate debater should assume a different role when debating a novice debater than when debating an equally experienced competitor. Five, all parties in an argumentative situation—advocates and judges or audience members—can and should benefit. If the goals of the particular argumentative process are kept in mind, then all will benefit. For example, in a public debate the ultimate goal is the discovery of truth and perhaps a public decision and in an educational debate the ultimate goal is the promotion of understanding and learning particular skills. Regardless of whose ideas succeed, all participants can benefit from the ultimate goals.

The sources discussed above represent only a few of the possible sources for ethical principles that might be applied to argumentative situations. Other sources might provide additional reinforcement of the same or similar principles. However, these sources were selected to provide what we believe to be the major theoretical foundation for ethical systems.

Ethical Guidelines for Arguers

The final sections of this chapter propose ethical guidelines for advocates, based on the theoretical groundwork discussed above. We believe these guidelines represent the best standards for speakers in argumentative situations. This chapter considers guidelines in the following six areas: (1) attitudes, (2) goals, (3) truth-telling, (4) fairness, (5) other participants, and (6) ends-means justifications.

Attitudes

Arguers' attitudes significantly influence the communication transactions in which they participate, whether those transactions are public or educational debates. Although argumentation traditionally focuses on the content of the message, the non-content related factors, such as arguers' attitudes, should be considered. Wayne Brockriede writes: "The nature of the people who argue, in all their humanness, is itself an inherent variable in understanding, evaluating, and predicting the processes and outcomes of an argument."[22] Furthermore, as indicated above, attitudes are crucial starting points for healthy communication and ethical principles.

In order to establish an ethical guideline regarding an arguer's attitudes, the arguer's choices must first be considered. Using a sexual metaphor, Brockriede identified three kinds of stances that arguers might adopt towards other arguers.[23] First, *rhetorical rape* describes advocates who are interested *primarily* in winning a victory. The victory might be to win a jury's decision in a trial or to win a judge's ballot in a debate. For the rhetorical rapist, the transaction is exploitative and one-sided. It is a form of unhealthy communication because it benefits only one or a few of the participants in the transaction; it is also unhealthy because such argumentation is inappropriate communication given the goals of either public or educational debate. Brockriede describes additional characteristics of rhetorical rape: "Some communicators are not interested in gaining assent to warrantable claims. Instead, they function through power, through an ability to apply psychic and physical sanctions, through rewards and especially punishments, through commands and threats." As Brockriede notes, the rhetorical rapist does not view the other persons in the transaction as persons. Instead, they are viewed as objects or inferior human beings. "So the rapist's intent in a transaction with such people is to manipulate the objects or to violate the victims. The rapist wants to gain or to maintain a position of superiority—whether on the intellectual front of making his case prevail or on the interpersonal front of putting the other person down."[24]

Brockriede cites numerous examples of where this kind of attitude might exist, including in an educational debate. "Another place to find the rapist's attitudes and intentions in the adversary situation is intercollegiate debate. The language is symptomatic: 'We killed them last round.' 'We destroyed them.' 'We cut them down.' In all such situations the rapist's attitude toward coarguers is contempt, his intent is to victimize. . . ."[25] Students involved in intercollegiate debate do not need to and should not assume such attitudes. When they do, the debate can become unpleasant and ceases to be healthy communication.

The second kind of attitude that an arguer might assume, according to Brockriede, is described by the term *seduction*. Rhetorical seduction differs in several ways from rhetorical rape. Although rape by its nature is a situation that is known and understood by both the rapist and the victim, seduction may not be recognized by the victim or the object of the seduction. The means used to gain the ends are also different for the rapist and the seducer. Brockriede explains: "Whereas the intent of the rapist is to force assent, the seducer tries to charm or trick his victim into assent." The charm may be rhetorically translated into "the *pathos* and *ethos* of a discourse, the image of the arguers, his style, and his delivery" which "may bedazzle a coarguer into giving his assent in a manner quite analogous to the act of seduction." Rather than using "rhetorical force," the public advocate or intercollegiate debater who is a seducer is more likely to use "such devices as ignoring the question, begging the question, the red herring, appeals to ignorance or to prejudice . . . withholding information, quoting out of context, misquoting an authority or a witness, misrepresenting a factual situation, drawing unwarranted conclusions from evidence" and other conscious uses "of strategems that appear in lists of fallacies."[26]

Despite such differences, the rapist and the seducer may view their victims in similar ways. The seducer may view his or her victim with contempt or with mere indifference to humanness. In any case, the seducer does not respect either the needs or the true wishes of the victim. Brockriede indicates that numerous examples of rhetorical seducers might be found in the fields of advertising and politics. A senator or even a president who seeks to seduce an audience might do so by withholding evidence or manufacturing evidence to advance his or her claims. However, dishonesty is not the only tool of seduction. For example, the intercollegiate debater who advances a weak argument because s/he believes that neither the opposing debaters nor the judge will spot it is also acting as a seducer. Of course, such behavior is also unhealthy communication because it does not benefit all the participants in the transaction, and this behavior is also inappropriate given the purposes of intercollegiate debate.

The third perspective, according to Brockriede, is the true lover. The "arguer as true lover" differs dramatically from rapists and seducers. He seeks an equal relationship with his opponents. His commitment is not to victory for the sake of victory; instead, his commitment is to higher or ultimate goals. The public statesman who is a "true lover" of his public and his fellow advocates is a person who is genuinely dedicated to the public good. An intercollegiate debater who has this attitude is committed first to the fair and honest competition of the debaters and their ideas.[27]

Another characteristic of the arguer-lover is self-risk. The arguer-lover is dedicated to her specific cause, but she is also willing to risk herself in competition with her fellow advocates. The risk she is willing to take is the risk of losing in the competition—whether it is in the marketplace of ideas or in an intercollegiate debate tournament. The rapist and the seducer are not willing to take such a risk, because their first commitment is to immediate personal gain in the victory of a narrowly defined objective. Brockriede believes that there are few true lover-arguers, though he does feel that philosophers and scientists might in certain argumentative situations illustrate the commitment to an arguer-as-lover perspective.[28]

What, then, do these different perspectives suggest as ethical guidelines for the arguer? Obviously, the rapist and the seducer are not desirable roles. These kinds of attitudes result in unhealthy communication and gain assent by rhetorical force, deception, or trickery. The preferred stance is the arguer as lover. Although the public advocate or the intercollegiate debater who is a true lover-arguer may be rare, the position is not an impossible or unknown one. It does require, however, a clear commitment to the goals of the argumentative process and a willingness to risk the self in fair and honest competition.

Goals

As indicated above, if arguers are committed to the goals of the argumentative process, then there is the possibility that an arguer can also act as a "lover." What are the goals of the argumentative process? As indicated above, the public advocate should be dedicated first to the public good. His commitment to the public good must be above and apart from his commitment to a particular public policy. This means, for example, that although he may be firmly committed to a certain policy in order to solve a societal need, his commitment to the policy should not be pursued at the expense of the public good. The public advocate must also be dedicated to the belief that in a democracy the marketplace of ideas is the best method to determine the public good. As suggested above, this requires that the public advocate be willing to risk himself in fair and open competition.

The next level of commitment should be to the particular policy that an advocate has chosen to support. The public advocate must be committed to a particular policy and within the limits posed by the principles of fair and honest competition she must pursue the advocacy of that policy vigorously. This also implies that the public debater should put forth the best case possible. A merely adequate case may not be sufficient to provide the best or even an adequate solution to a societal problem. Karl Wallace writes: "A communicator in a free society must recognize that during the moments of his utterance he is the sole source of argument and information. His hearers know this fact, and they defer to him. He in turn must defer to them. Accordingly, his speech must reveal that he knows his subject, that he understands the implications and issues relevant to the particular time and occasion, that he is aware of essential and trustworthy opinions and facts, that he is dealing with a many-sided, rather than a one-sided, state of affairs."[29] In other words, the public advocate has duty to search and inquire, and then to build the best case possible for the position he or she advocates. For the marketplace of ideas to function effectively, and for truth and wise public decisions to emerge, there must be rigorous competition among the best ideas possible.

This analysis, then, suggests a hierarchy of goals for the public advocate. First, the public good should be his or her highest goal. Second, the public advocate must be dedicated to the determination of the public good through fair and honest competition in the marketplace of ideas. Third, the public advocate should be committed to his or her particular idea. Fourth, the public advocate must be committed to search and inquire and to present the best case possible for his or her particular idea.

Applying the Goals to Educational Debate

What are the goals for the student participating in the educational debate? His or her first goal should be to the educational process innate in argumentation. The *American Forensic Association Professional Relations Committee Code of Forensics Program and Forensics Tournament Standards for Colleges and Universities* (AFA Code) describes the goals of forensics programs as follows: "Forensics programs and tournaments ought to provide environments where students can become intelligent, effective and responsible advocates and communicators." This statement of goals entails no actual responsibility for the student to determine the public good. However, it does require that the intercollegiate debater be dedicated to the same process that best determines the public good in a democracy—the marketplace of ideas. Given such a commitment, s/he must also be dedicated to fair and honest competition.

The next level of commitment should be to present the best case possible on the assigned side of the proposition. The debater should pursue the development of this case in the same way that the public advocate does—by searching and inquiring. With this goal in mind, the intercollegiate debater should be willing to debate either side of the topic. Some students new to intercollegiate debate find this difficult, because they believe that they are being hypocritical if they defend a position that they do not believe. However, students involved in debate should be committed to the educational process that debate provides. As Aristotle indicated, speakers need to learn to employ persuasion on both sides of a given topic in order to learn the facts of a case and to become more effective advocates for the truth. If students are willing to suspend their commitment to a particular side in a debate while they are debating, they will have a better data base for making a decision about what the truth is, and they will also be able to advance the truth more effectively as public advocates.

This analysis suggests two goals for the intercollegiate debater: the debater should be dedicated first to the educational process innate in argumentation and second to the presentation of the best case possible on the assigned side of the topic.

Truth-Telling

At least since the days of Plato and Aristotle, philosophers and rhetoricians have been concerned about the role of the truth in argumentation. Richard Murphy viewed dishonesty as one of the greatest moral offenses and identified prohibitions against falsehood as absolutely essential to a code of ethics for communicators. Murphy wrote: "There must be no toleration of offenses against common decency such as appeals to base motive, falsifying of evidence, the use of slanderous innuendo."[30] Although there have always been differing conceptions of the truth and how it might be discovered or demonstrated, there is an on-going consensus among the ethical, moral, and political philosophers that truth in general is not only desirable, but is an ethical imperative. There have been debates regarding whether and when exceptions to truth-telling are permissible. For example, in some social situations and in areas such as military strategy during wartime, exceptions have been justified. However, in the area of public controversy, such as public policy debate, there is virtually no exception to the ethical imperative that advocates should tell the truth.

In a democracy, the principle underlying this rule is that if the public or the deliberative body is competent to make the decision, then they must know the truth. If the advocate does not believe that the public or deliberative body is competent to make the decision, then he has a problem in terms of his goals. Such a speaker is not truly committed to the marketplace of ideas as the best means to discover the truth. He is therefore essentially anti-democratic in his perspective, and should not be trusted as an advocate.

As indicated above, the major issue among advocates is not whether or not the truth should be told, but the determination of what constitutes the truth. Karl Wallace outlines a definition of the truth from the perspective of an advocate in a democracy:

> The communicator who respects the democratic way of life must select and present fact and opinion *fairly.* One of his great tasks is to help preserve a kind of equality of opportunity among ideas. He must therefore be *accurate* in reporting fact and opinion; he must *respect* accuracy.
>
> Moreover, he must not intentionally warp and distort ideas. Nor must he suppress and conceal material which his audience would need in justly evaluating his argument.[31]

The truth therefore includes fair and accurate reporting of all relevant information to the audience.

Another aspect of truth-telling is the requirement that a speaker reveal his or her sources to the audience so that they may judge them also. Wallace explains:

> The communicator who believes in the ultimate values of democracy will invariably reveal the sources of his information and opinion. . . . A speaker before any audience is by that fact a public person. . . . A communicator, moreover, will help his hearers to weigh any special bias, prejudice, and private motivations which are inherent in source materials. He knows that argument and fact are unacceptable if their springs are contaminated . . . he has had the opportunity of discovering whether private motives, such as those of self-interest, personal prestige, and personal profit, have merely imparted a special flavor to the source or have made it dangerous to drink. Such information he should share with his hearers.[32]

These same standards for truth of course apply to the intercollegiate debater. The intercollegiate debater should reveal her sources. She should also fairly and accurately present all evidence in a debate. Finally, as discussed above, the debater should present the best case possible. This is part of her obligation to search and inquire and to treat the audience as competent. Her obligation to search and inquire also includes that she should do her own research. The AFA Code states: "Forensics competitors are expected to do their own research." It also notes: "Persons other than the forensic competitor (undergraduate students, graduate student or instructor/coaches) are not to be charged with the responsibility for doing a forensics competitor's research."

In following these principles, the intercollegiate debater—like any student of advocacy—should develop, in Wallace's words, "the *habit of justice.* The habit is based on respect for truth and accuracy and respect for fair dealing. Neither can be disassociated from communication in a free society."[33]

The American Forensic Association has promulgated very specific standards for the documentation of claims in the AFA Code. The Code states: "Forensics competitors shall not use fabricated or distorted evidence." In addition, the Code precisely defines *fabrication* and *distortion* and requires that if evidence is challenged, debaters be able to "provide complete documentation of the evidence (name of author(s), source of publication, full date, page numbers and author(s) credentials where available in the original)." The Code provides for very serious penalties if such problems are discovered. The Code and the standards for evidence in particular are recognized by nearly all members of the forensics community as the minimum ethical standards for the activity.

Fairness

Fairness can be thought of in terms of two subsidiary principles—equality of opportunity and appropriateness. In other words, advocates should treat others—and should expect to be treated by others—equally and appropriately.

Many of the principles we have discussed previously are also principles of fairness.

The transactional model of communication implies that all participants in a communication transaction should treat one another as equals. The principle of acknowledgment also implies that speakers should recognize and respond to one another on both the interpersonal and the argumentative levels. The principle of flexibility suggests also that healthy communication should include arguers who are able to adapt to each other. For example, an experienced debater might assume a "teaching" or a "good model" role when debating an inexperienced opponent. The principle that all evidence used in an educational debate should be published also relates to an issue of fairness—all evidence should be equally available to all competitors. The same principle applied in an intercollegiate debate means that after an item of evidence is introduced in a debate, all participants should have the right to examine the evidence. The courts have similar kinds of procedural rules, which in some situations grant access to evidence prior to trial and in almost all cases give the opposing attorney a right to cross-examine a witness.

Karl Wallace indicates another principle that relates to both ethics and fairness.

> A communicator in a democratic society will acknowledge and will respect diversity of argument and opinion. His selection of issues, his analysis of the situation, the style of his address will reflect the attitudes which signify admission, concession, and compromise. Nevertheless, his communication will not sacri-

> fice principle to compromise, and he will prefer facing conflict to accepting appeasement. For such a communicator, the test question will ever be this: Can I freely admit the force of opposing evidence and argument and still advocate a position which represents my convictions?[34]

This single principle also embodies many of the principles of healthy communication—acknowledgment, appropriateness, efficiency, flexibility, and gratification.

The public advocate and the intercollegiate debater can and should follow Wallace's principle in argumentative situations. For example, the public advocate can and should recognize the legitimate objections of opposing advocates and, if appropriate, modify her proposals. If the advocate is committed to the public good first, then her commitment to a particular idea or policy should be modified if there is a conflict with the public good. The situation of the debater is different since she is assigned to a particular side in each debate; however, she can still admit the effectiveness of her opponent's arguments as long as she can otherwise claim sufficient arguments to justify her position in the debate.

The AFA Code also requires that students entered into intercollegiate competitions be treated fairly. The Code states: "Tournament directors must ensure that all participants compete on a more or less equal basis." Furthermore, the Code lists specific standards for equal treatment of competitors, including the way competitors are matched with one another and the ways in which judges are assigned.

Other Participants

The ethical treatment of other participants in argumentation situations should begin with knowing who they are and their roles. The public advocate will likely confront other advocates and an immediate audience in each argumentative situation. Some of the audience members may have specialized roles. For example, an attorney's audience will include audience members with special powers—namely, a judge and jury. However, there are also other important audience members, such as the witnesses, officers of the court, possibly members of the press, and other observers. A public advocate may also have audiences who are not immediately present and yet play significant roles. For instance, when a U.S. Senator speaks in the Senate chamber on the evils of Soviet Union-supported insurgency movements in Central America, she has some very important non-immediate audiences. The press, the Secretary of State, the Soviet Union's governmental representatives, Central American governmental officials, her constituents, and possibly many other audiences may be affected by what she says.

What are the ethical obligations of relating with these audiences? First, the principles of healthy communication indicate how advocates should relate to all immediate audiences, including the opposing advocates. Acknowledgment, appropriateness, efficiency, flexibility and gratification all indicate that other participants in a transaction should be treated as human beings within the specific context. It is very important that the advocate recognize and respect the humanness of these other participants. Such attitudes and corresponding behavior are not only essential to the role of "arguer-lover"; they also constitute an important part of effective rhetorical strategy.

Second, the public advocate should assume similar responsibilities in relating to non-immediate audiences. Although the advocate may not be able to identify all the non-immediate audiences, he should attempt to do so. The advocate may also be unable to accommodate the needs of all the non-immediate audiences, but he should consider carefully how he can promote healthy communication with the most significant of these audiences. Certainly he should attempt to recognize those audiences with whom he will have future direct contact. Again, such considerations are not only important goals of the arguer-lover, but are also effective rhetorical strategy.

The student involved in educational debate should also consider the other participants, though her concerns have a slightly different focus. In most debate tournaments, the only participants in an actual debate round will be the student's debate partner, the debaters from the opposing team, a judge or sometimes several judges, and sometimes observers. A debater, therefore, is usually dealing with a very small immediate audience, and only in rare circumstances will there be any significant non-immediate audiences. What are the ethical obligations of relating with these audiences? First, the intercollegiate debater should treat all audiences according to the same principles of healthy communication. Acknowledgment, appropriateness, efficiency, flexibility, and gratification all apply, indicating that other participants in transactions should be treated as human beings within the specific context. Because of the competitive nature of the activity, debaters sometimes forget that it is important that they recognize and respect the humanness of these other participants.

Second, it is important that the specialized role of the participants be understood and appreciated. As indicated previously, public advocates and intercollegiate debaters should both treat their opponents in a way to promote healthy communication and to promote a pleasant debate. They should realize that an argument over ideas does not have to be personalized, and they should not confuse disagreement with being disagreeable. They should also recognize that the judge of a debate serves a special function; s/he should be an impartial decision maker in the debate round. The judge's function should also be educational—the AFA Code states: "Tournament judges are obliged to provide detailed and constructive criticism of any and all rounds of competition they evaluate. Judges are to provide written comments on the ballots provided by these tournaments." In this regard, the judge should be viewed as a teacher, for that is his or her ultimate purpose in the debate.

Third, the debater should recognize the rights of the other participants in a debate round. This includes the rights of observers, present in almost all situations. The AFA Code states: "All tournament rounds are open on a space available basis to any and all interested observers, who may take notes." In addition, according to the AFA Code, "participants, coaches of the teams involved, judges or authorized researchers (with the tournament director's approval) may tape record any tournament round of competition." It is usually considered appropriate to tell the participants prior to a debate round if the round is being recorded.

Ends-Means Justification

When the ethical standards or behaviors of arguers are questioned, they will sometimes defend themselves by indicating that the goals or ends of their actions justified their behaviors. In many situations, persons will have seemingly laudable goals to justify their behavior. For example, if a police chief exaggerates crime statistics to bring public attention to a real crime problem, then he is behaving as if the end justifies the means. A president may withhold evidence from a prosecutor because it would allegedly threaten national security. A doctor may lie to a patient about her condition for fear that depression will worsen the condition. A legislator may claim to be a good representative because he was able to use his Congressional committee positions to get a lot of government projects for his district.

However, although an individual action such as those identified above may be justified, it is almost never good to justify such actions with the ends-means rationale. The ends-means rationale is an unsound one for numerous reasons. First, the ends-means justification is by its nature a defensive rationale. Rarely do advocates justify their actions by ends-means unless their methods have been convincingly attacked. The ends-means rationale may in some cases seem a "good" rationale, but it is nonetheless almost always regarded as an "excuse" for admittedly unacceptable behavior.

Second, the ends-means rationale in a specific situation is difficult to challenge and almost impossible to verify. A critic cannot easily challenge the noble ends that an individual has chosen to justify her means; in addition, the ends cannot be verified since the test would be the sincerity of the speaker. Karl Wallace explains: "It is easy to assert high-sounding purposes; it is difficult for the listener to assess the sincerity of these assertions."[35] For example, perhaps the real motive of the police chief who exaggerates the crime statistics is to cover up police brutality. Or, perhaps the president who withholds evidence is covering up his or her own crimes. Perhaps, the doctor who does not reveal the condition to the patient is hiding a potential case of malpractice. Further, the Congressman may have gained personally or financially through certain government projects.

Third, the ends-means rationale is especially inappropriate for the public advocate or the intercollegiate debater. The ends of the advocate are to discover the truth in the marketplace of ideas and to be successful in his support of his own claims. If the advocate is dishonest, he attempts to corrupt the marketplace of ideas. Furthermore, he cannot achieve both of his goals with dishonesty: if his claims are victorious in the marketplace, then dishonesty has won and the marketplace is profoundly corrupted. If, on the other hand, truth is victorious as it should be in the marketplace, then his own views will fail because of his dishonesty.

The intercollegiate debater's primary end should be education, and certainly bad means teach only unethical behavior. Winning a debate, a tournament, or a national championship by less than honest means is clearly not an achievement of the ends of educational debate.

Fourth, the ends-means rationale allows the evil advocate to do what she will. Karl Wallace writes: "The worst evil which follows from an indifference to means is that we make easy the intent of the dishonest, insincere speaker."[36] If the ends become the test of acceptable practices, then all practices are good as long as they can be rhetorically linked to some good end. As indicated above, this is easy to do and almost impossible to verify.

Fifth, the ends-means justification is contrary to democratic values. As indicated above, the ends-means rationale rejects the marketplace of ideas theory. The advocate who uses dishonest means indicates that she does not trust the public to make a wise decision. She has decided what the public decision should be and attempts to force that decision by her use of dishonesty. In a sense she usurps the public's right to decide for themselves. Such views are clearly inappropriate for a public advocate and certainly have no place in the education of future advocates in a democracy.

Finally, the ends-means justification allows bad standards to be used to evaluate argument. Bad standards will in turn generate more bad argument. Karl Wallace explains:

> If we give much weight to the immediate success of a speech, we encourage temptation. To glorify the end is to invite the use of any means which will work. The end can be used, for example, to sanction distortion and suppression of materials and arguments. . . . If we give first prize to the speaker who wins the goal, we not only unnecessarily tempt the honest and sincere man; we undermine the character of the communicator. We associate with 'success' such values as popular prestige and personal ambition. We thus give a premium to the man with a compulsive drive, to him who must win at any cost; and we handicap the man who places the welfare of others above his personal gain.[37]

If the ends-means rationale is so corrupting, then how should arguers view ends and means? Obviously, there should be focus upon both the ends of the speaker and her means. However, Karl Wallace advises that the means deserve morc attention. "There is a better ethic than that which justifies the means by the end. It is an ethic which respects the means more than the end. It governs both the selection and the presentation of materials. Above all, the ethic measures the quality of the communicative product in terms of the communicator, rather than according to its immediate effect upon the audience." In considering purpose, Wallace advises that the purpose should not become an overwhelming concern: "Purpose serves to give organization and shape to a speech, the discussion, or the play; it aids in the choice of means, but it should not dominate the moral values of either the product or the speaker."[38]

Summary

This chapter defined ethics as the principles that guide human choices about what is considered good or bad, right or wrong, moral or immoral. Systems of ethics are based upon a number of assumptions. First, a system of ethics requires that there are principles or a set of principles backed by the particular community. Second, a system of ethics requires that the principles be known and understood. Third, a system of ethics requires that sanctions exist to re-inforce the individual principles.

Some of the possible theoretical groundings for ethical principles include the ideas of Plato, Aristotle, and concepts drawn from democratic principles and interpersonal communication. Though Plato's views are not consistent as expressed in his major statements on rhetoric, in the *Gorgias* and the *Phaedrus,* one view is that rhetoric is an unfortunate necessity. Although rhetoric is subject to abuse, it can serve the advancement of the public good. This perspective suggests that advocates should begin with a knowledge of the truth of their subject matter, and that other decisions made in terms of organization, audience analysis, and strategy should be decisions that effectively advance the truth.

Traditional democratic principles also provide a number of ideas for ethical systems. First, American democracy is based in part upon a "marketplace of ideas" theory. Second, fairness is both an intrinsic and an instrumental value in contemporary American ideology. Third, contemporary American democracy emphasizes individual responsibility.

The concept of a transactional model of communication provides several starting points for ethical principles. Most current interpersonal communication theorists endorse the transactional concept of communication, which is wholistic and focuses upon the entire communication event or transaction rather than dissecting it into many variables. The transactional concept is based on the belief that communication is simultaneous and mutual. The principles of healthy communication—acknowledgment, appropriateness, efficiency, flexibility, and gratification—also have direct application to ethical systems for argumentation and debate.

This chapter recommends ethical principles in these areas—attitudes, goals, truth-telling, fairness, other participants, and ends-means justifications. In terms of attitude, arguers should strive to play the role of the lover-arguer. Public advocates should pursue the goal of the public good as determined in the marketplace of ideas. Intercollegiate debaters should be dedicated to principles of educational debate. These principles are expressed in the preamble and the specific sections of the *American Forensic Association Professional Relations Committee Code of Forensics Program and Forensics Tournament Standards for Colleges and Universities.* Truth-telling is an ethical imperative for all arguers. Fairness and treatment of participants can be guided by numerous concepts, including the principles of healthy communication. Finally, ends-means justifications are not a sound basis for behaviors, and arguers should be greatly concerned about such methods.

Notes

1. Everett Lee Hunt, "Plato and Aristotle on Rhetoric and Rhetoricians," *Studies in Rhetoric and Public Speaking.* (New York, 1925), p. 3.
2. Plato, *Georgias* (New York: Bobbs-Merrill, 1952), p. 76.
3. Hunt, pp. 37–38.
4. Friedrich Solmsen, "Introduction," in *Rhetoric* and *Poetics,* (New York: Modern Library, 1954), p. xvi.
5. See Aristotle, "Nicomachean Ethics," in *On Man In The Universe,* trans. by James E. C. Welldon (Roslyn, NY: Walter J. Black, 1943), pp. 84–243.
6. See Aristotle, "Politics," in *On Man In The Universe,* trans. by Benjamin Jowett, pp. 244--415.
7. Solmsen, pp. xx–xxi.
8. Aristotle, *Rhetoric,* trans. by W. Rhys Roberts (New York: Modern Library, 1954), p. 22.
9. Aristotle, p. 23.
10. See Solmsen, p. xvi.
11. *Red Lion Broadcasting v. FCC,* 395 U.S. (1969), 390.
12. John Immerwahr, Jean Johnson, and John Doble, *The Speaker and the Listener: A Public Perspective on Freedom of Expression* (New York: The Public Agenda Foundation, 1980), p. 23.
13. Immerwahr, et al., p. 25.
14. Immerwahr, et al., p. 24–25.
15. Thomas R. Nilsen, *Ethics of Speech Communication* (New York: Bobbs-Merrill, 1966), p. 16.

16. See Dennis R. Smith and L. Keith Williamson, *Interpersonal Communication: Roles, Rules, Strategies and Games* (Dubuque, IA: Wm. C. Brown, 1977), pp. 3–36.
17. Ibid., p. 32.
18. Ibid., p. 61.
19. Ibid., p. 61.
20. Ibid., p. 30.
21. Ibid., pp. 329–52.
22. Material used with permission from "Arguers as Lovers" by Wayne Brockriede, *Philosophy And Rhetoric,* Vol. 5, No. 1, Winter 1972. The Pennsylvania State University Press, University Park, PA. 16802, p. 1.
23. Ibid., pp. 1–11.
24. Ibid., pp. 2–3.
25. Ibid., p. 3.
26. Ibid., p. 4.
27. Ibid., p. 5.
28. Ibid., pp. 5–8.
29. Karl R. Wallace, "An Ethical Basis of Communication," *The Speech Teacher,* Vol. 4, No. 1 (January 1955), p. 6.
30. Richard Murphy, "A Preface to an Ethic of Rhetoric," in *The Rhetorical Idiom: Essays in Rhetoric, Oratory, Language and Drama,* ed. by Donald C. Bryant (New York: Russell & Russell, 1966), p 140.
31. Wallace, p. 7.
32. Ibid., pp. 7–8.
33. Ibid., p. 7.
34. Ibid., pp. 8–9.
35. Ibid., p. 3.
36. Ibid., p. 3.
37. Ibid., p. 3.
38. Ibid., pp. 3–4.

Questions and Exercises

1. Read and analyze one or more of the following articles of the AFA Code, in the appendix. What are the theoretical groundings for the specific standards in the article(s)? Why do you think each individual standard was established?
   a. Article I: Competitor Standards
   b. Article II: Competitor Practices
   c. Article III: Tournament Practices

2. Find the ethics code of another professional organization (doctors, lawyers, etc.) and compare it to the ethical principles for the public advocate and the intercollegiate debater. Do they seem to be based on similar theoretical groundings? What evidence of similarities do you find? Are any specific standards similar?
3. Read one of the articles or books listed below and indicate the similarities and differences you find in the work compared with the ethical principles studied in this chapter.
   a. Lewis, C.S., *Mere Christianity.*
   b. Machiavelli, Niccolo, *The Prince.*
   c. Minnick, Wayne, "A New Look at the Ethics of Persuasion," *Southern Speech Communication Journal* 45 (Summer 1980): 352–62.
   d. Rokeach, Milton, *The Nature of Human Values.*
   e. Rotenstreich, Nathan, *Humanism in the Contemporary Era.*

Suggested Readings

Johannesen, Richard. *Ethics in Human Communication.* Wayne, NJ: Avery Publishing Group, 1978.

FIFTEEN

Foundations of Debate Evaluation

Robert Rowland has written that the "ultimate goal of debate is to teach people how to argue effectively."[1] This chapter will investigate the various methods by which debate evaluators might approach their task and suggest ways in which debaters themselves might increase the learning potential associated with participation in debate.

We will first look more closely at the goals of debate evaluation. Then we will detail various paradigms of debate evaluation that are currently utilized by debate judges. This chapter is meant more as a guide for debaters in adapting to various standards for evaluation than it is a collection of guidelines for judges, although it may well serve the latter function as well.

Goals of Evaluation

We agree with Rowland that the ultimate goal of debate is to teach. We also believe that one of the goals of debate evaluation should be pedagogic. We will, in fact, identify three general goals of debate evaluation: (1) pedagogy, (2) arbitration, and (3) mediation.

Evaluation as Pedagogic

A debate judge is a teacher. When teachers evaluate examinations, or essays, or public speaking assignments in class, students learn from them. They learn what the strengths of their performances are as well as the nature of their deficiencies. Strengths can thus be enhanced and deficiencies remedied.

Students participating in debate learn how to adapt various arguments to different judges. They learn to cooperate with a partner and to work together to present the best case. The judge facilitates this education. The judge is the critic of the effort and if both the judge and the debaters enter into the endeavor with constructive attitudes, the educational objective will be underscored.

Through the critique, debaters learn how to improve argument skills, delivery skills, and audience adaptation. Most intercollegiate debate ballots include areas of evaluation under one or more of these categories.

Arbitration

A debate judge is an arbitrator. In competitive debate, the judge has the task of choosing a winner, and there are only two options: the affirmative wins or the negative wins. In this respect, the debate judge is an arbitrator. The judge weighs the arguments of both sides and then chooses between them—the function of an arbitrator.

Mediation

The debate judge also serves, at times, as a mediator. He or she mediates the resolution of individual issues. The choosing of a winner cannot be mediated, but the resolution of issues can be. A judge listens to arguments from both sides, and may accept either of those positions or may decide the issue for neither side. It is also possible to not consider the issue at all when making the final decision. Judges mediate issues and reach final decisions as arbitors. The issues are mediated from the perspectives of paradigms or models of decision-making.

Paradigms for Evaluation

Judges do not enter into any debate as evaluators devoid of perspectives on decision-making. Most judges have preferred ways of evaluating a de-

Chapter Outline

bate, and at least attempt to consistently follow those guidelines. Just as people are diverse, so are debate judges, and so are paradigms for evaluation.

In this chapter we will identify and discuss six paradigms currently used in intercollegiate debate. These are (1) skills assessment, (2) stock issues, (3) policy choice, (4) hypothesis testing, (5) judicial, and (6) *tabula rasa*.

For purposes of analysis, the following case outlines, one on a policy advocacy proposition and the other on a proposition of trait inference, will be used as references throughout this section:

Case Outline I: Policy Advocacy

RESOLVED: That the federal government should implement a program that guarantees employment opportunities for all U.S. citizens in the labor force.

I. Unemployment is a serious national problem.
   A. A large class of unemployed exists.
      1. They are the long-term unemployed.
      2. Their job skills are not relevant to the contemporary economy.
   B. Unemployment is a serious threat to the individual and to the nation.
      1. Individual harms
         a. stress related disease
         b. alcoholism
         c. mental illness and suicide
      2. Societal harms
         a. lost tax revenues
         b. welfare costs
         c. undeveloped human potential

II. Present system policies are innately inadequate to solve the unemployment problem.
   A. The present system is committed to economic growth as the solution to unemployment.
   B. The unemployed population is beyond the aid of economic growth.
      1. They are not skilled.
      2. Economic growth is limited.
   C. Programs that could help are being reduced or eliminated.
      1. Federal jobs training has declined substantially.
      2. States follow federal lead in cutting state training programs.

III. Plan
   A. A Board of Vocational Rehabilitation and Training will be established.
   B. Funding will be provided by a fifty cent surcharge on the purchase of tobacco products.
   C. Enforcement will be provided through the Federal Bureau of Investigation according to existing statutes and compliance mechanisms.

D. Mandates of the Board will be:
   1. To establish a comprehensive program of vocational rehabilitation for those whose skills are no longer suited for modern economic realities.
   2. To provide training for those without any skill relevant to the present or future economy.

Case Outline II: Trait Inference

I. Definitions
   A. Victimless crimes: crimes that generally involve only the criminal.
   B. Legitimate: reasonable, logically correct, justifiable or justified.
   C. Outside: without, as in "without legitimacy."
   D. Function: proper activities or duties.
   E. Government: the entire system of polity.

II. Criteria
   A. Restrictions on behavior by government are legitimate only if they prevent harms to others.
   B. John Stuart Mill supports the criteria in *On Liberty*.
   C. The criteria can be applied to the proposition.

III. Pornography poses no threat of harm to third parties.
   A. Pornography is not harmful.
      1. no societal harms
      2. can result in benefits
      3. the harm criteria is not met
   B. Restrictions are harmful.
      1. limit freedom
      2. lead to censorship

IV. Observation: Affirmative has presumption.
   A. Presumption is in favor of free speech.
   B. Presumption is in favor of majority opinion.

Skills Assessment

Judges who evaluate debate according to the skills assessment paradigm view debate as a demonstration of several skills associated with communication and argument. These judges categorize the skills broadly and then prioritize their importance. Finally, this hierarchy of skills is applied to the debaters and their relative skills level is assessed. The skills most commonly considered (in no particular order) are:

1. delivery and persuasiveness
2. evidence
3. refutation
4. language and vocal correctness

5. analysis
6. organization
7. character and demeanor[2]

Strengths and weaknesses. The strengths of this approach center on the educational benefits that may be attained. First, the paradigm emphasizes the communicative skills dimension of debate. In other words, it stresses such considerations as delivery, language, and demeanor. These considerations, long held to be important factors in judging other forensic events, are at times deemphasized by some debate judges. So debaters who must face judges with this paradigm must at least consider these factors, and that is instructive.

Moreover, the skills assessment paradigm is not complex and it is easy for judges to explain and for debaters to comprehend. Third, the paradigm seems to afford equal opportunity for the respective sides to prevail. There is no intrinsic advantage of one position over the other.[3] In addition, this paradigm can be applied to debates on any proposition.

The paradigm is not without weaknesses. Even though the categories are distinctive, the application of the specific skills test is sometimes vague. For instance, what are the standards for delivery? How is refutation going to be evaluated? What is acceptable demeanor to one judge might be offensive to another.

It is also possible that the priorities of the skills may remain unclear to the debaters, may prevent appropriate adaptation, and may interfere with the educational benefit of the evaluation.[4] If the priority of skills is ambiguous, then debaters will also be unclear of the burdens they have to meet in the debate.

Unless the judge is explicit in detailing the description of the skills and their hierarchy before the debate begins, adaptation to this paradigm is difficult. To prepare an assessment of one's debating from this paradigm, prior skills development is necessary. This, of course, is beneficial in any event, and should assist the debater in debating before judges of any stripe.

Debater adaptation. The skills scrutinized in the model can be categorized into two broad areas: those dealing with structure and presentation, and those dealing with the conduct of the debate. Those that deal with structure and presentation include delivery and persuasiveness, language and vocal correctness, organization, and character and demeanor. These skills should be developed before the debate begins.

The others, dealing with the conduct of the debate, may be the focus of debaters adapting to judges using this paradigm. Evidence, analysis, and refutation can be important determinants of the decisions made by skills assessment judges.

CROSS EXAMINATION DEBATE BALLOT©

DIVISION ______ ROUND ______ ROOM ______ JUDGE ______

AFFIRMATIVE ______ NEGATIVE ______

CHECK EACH COLUMN ACCORDING TO YOUR EVALUATION — 1 = UNPREPARED 2 = FAIR 3 = GOOD 4 = EXCELLENT 5 = SUPERIOR

1st AFF.	VALUE 1	2	3	4	5	NAME	RANK ( ) IN ROUND
ANALYSIS/ DEFINITION							
EVIDENCE							
AUDIENCE ADAPTATION							
REFUTATION/ REBUTTAL							
DELIVERY							
ORGANIZATION							
CROSS-EXAM.							
COURTESY							
SUM TOTAL (40 Max.) →							

1st NEG.	VALUE 1	2	3	4	5	NAME	RANK ( ) IN ROUND
ANALYSIS/ DEFINITION							
EVIDENCE							
AUDIENCE ADAPTATION							
REFUTATION/ REBUTTAL							
DELIVERY							
ORGANIZATION							
CROSS-EXAM.							
COURTESY							
SUM TOTAL (40 Max.) →							

2nd AFF.	VALUE 1	2	3	4	5	NAME	RANK ( ) IN ROUND
ANALYSIS/ DEFINITION							
EVIDENCE							
AUDIENCE ADAPTATION							
REFUTATION/ REBUTTAL							
DELIVERY							
ORGANIZATION							
CROSS-EXAM.							
COURTESY							
SUM TOTAL (40 Max.) →							

2nd NEG.	VALUE 1	2	3	4	5	NAME	RANK ( ) IN ROUND
ANALYSIS/ DEFINITION							
EVIDENCE							
AUDIENCE ADAPTATION							
REFUTATION/ REBUTTAL							
DELIVERY							
ORGANIZATION							
CROSS-EXAM.							
COURTESY							
SUM TOTAL (40 Max.) →							

(X ONE) TEAM RATINGS (X ONE)

AFFIRMATIVE		NEGATIVE	
☐ UNPREPARED	☐ EXCELLENT	☐ UNPREPARED	☐ EXCELLENT
☐ FAIR	☐ SUPERIOR	☐ FAIR	☐ SUPERIOR
☐ GOOD		☐ GOOD	

BE SURE YOU HAVE CHECKED ALL AREAS

I am persuaded to vote for team: ______

of the ______ side.

______ JUDGE'S SIGNATURE ______ SCHOOL

(tear along here after reading)

NOTE TO JUDGES

Please fill out this ballot completely as the speaker points and team ratings are necessary to match following rounds. Each of the categories is described below:

1.) **Analysis/Definition:** Your evaluation of how clearly the teams present their definition of the terms of the resolution, and how significantly, fairly and completely that understanding of the topic is presented.

2.) **Evidence/Reasoning:** Do the debaters present sufficient, quality evidence to support their arguments? Is the evidence fully cited? Are inferences drawn from the evidence warranted?

3.) **Audience Adaptation:** Do the speakers make an effort to relate their arguments to you directly? Do they use audience analysis? Wit? Humor?

4.) **Refutation/Rebuttal:** Do the speakers clash with opponents' arguments? Are they able to synthesize and narrow the focus of clash during rebuttal time?

5.) **Delivery:** Do the speakers present their ideas at a tone and rate which the audience can follow and respond to?

6.) **Organization:** Are the speakers following a consistent pattern of organization and idea development? Do the debaters use adequate transitions and sign posting to make their ideas clear?

7.) **Cross Exam.:** Do the speakers utilize the cross examination time to clarify the opponents' case? Do they lead opponents through a series of questions designed to build examiners' ethos? Do they make subsequent use of matters raised under cross-examination?

8.) **Courtesy:** Do the speakers exhibit a respect for their opponents and the audience, and the worth of ideas?

SPECIAL NOTE: If this debate is on the "CEDA" resolution, it may be a "Value-oriented" proposition. If so, some specific aspects of "policy" debate, such as plans, traditional disadvantages and inherency arguments, may not be appropriate. Also, CEDA stresses debate adaptation to the audience, even if that audience is a single judge. They may use wit and humor to PERSUADE you, as well as all of the traditional techniques of sound argumentation covered by the 8 categories above. Remember, the debaters are **learners,** help them to become better advocates by rewarding them when they skillfully use tools of argumentation and persuasion to communicate their ideas to you in a clear, complete, logical, analytical, organized, evidenced, and pleasant manner. The debaters and their teachers depend on your comments for feedback in these areas in order to learn. Please assist them in learning by providing as specific and extensive commentary as appropriate. Thank you for your time in this effort.

Reproduced by permission of Raymond Bud Zeuschner. Copies of this ballot are available from the Executive Secretary of the Cross Examination Debate Association.

FIGURE 15–1

Division ________ Round ________ Room ________ Date ________ Judge ____________

Affirmative # _____ School ______________ Negative # _____ School ______________

Rate all speakers and both teams on a scale from 30 (Superior) to 1 (Poor)
Rank each debater in order of excellence (1st for best, 2nd for next best, etc.)

Rankings must be consistent with ratings; ties in rank are not permitted.

		rating	rank			rating	rank
1st Aff.	______________ (Name)	_____	_____	1st Neg.	______________ (Name)	_____	_____
2nd Aff.	______________ (Name)	_____	_____	2nd Neg.	______________ (Name)	_____	_____

Aff. TEAM rating . . . . ________ Neg. TEAM rating . . . . ________
(Teams should be rated on a 30-point scale; do NOT total individual speaker points.)

COMMENTS AND BASIS FOR DECISION:

In my opinion, this debate was won by ____________ (Aff. or Neg.) representing ______________ (School and/or #)

______________________ (Judge's name) ______________ (School)

Reprinted by permission of the American Forensic Association.

FIGURE 15–2

Full advantage should be made of one's own evidence strength and the deficiencies of the evidence used by the opponents. Debaters should utilize any of the tests for evidence discussed in Chapter Six. Analysis should also be a key skills area, so any conceptual errors that debaters can identify in their opponent's arguments will be crucial.

Finally, refutation will be an important skills area, so debaters should be comprehensive in the refutation of their opponent's case. Shortcuts in refutation, such as cross-application, and perhaps even the grouping of arguments, might be considered by a skills assessment judge as a reflection of poor refutational skills.

Stock Issues

The stock issues paradigm identifies several issues that are crucial to the strength of the affirmative case. In this paradigm, the affirmative always has the burden of proof, and the burdens are clear and specific. Since this paradigm is applicable only to policy advocacy propositions, the stock issues pertain to the affirmative plan. The stock issues that are almost always considered are:

1. significance of harm
2. solvency
3. inherency
4. cost–benefits

Strengths and weaknesses. Stock issues assessment is not difficult for most debaters to comprehend or for most judges to explain and follow. The paradigm utilizes issues that are well defined. As a result of this clarity, most decisions are clear. Issues might be decided closely, but once the issues are decided, the final decision should be easy. If the affirmative fails to satisfy any of the issues, they lose.

The major weakness of this paradigm is that it has a rather narrow application. As we said, it applies only to policy advocacy propositions. Judges who utilize the stock issues paradigm for policy controversies therefore have no consistent model to apply to debates on other types of propositions.

Another apparent weakness is that the burdens are heavily heaped upon the affirmative. This might lead to an unequal opportunity for a side to prevail. The negative has to win but one of the stock issues, the affirmative, by contrast, must win all of them.

Debater adaptation. Debaters adapting to this paradigm have little difficulty determining which issues to focus on. Using Case Outline I as a reference, the case areas that would be important to a stock issues judge are:

1. The extent of unemployment (I.A.).
2. The relationship between unemployment and stress (I.B.1).

3. Extent of Solvency (relationship between I.A. & B. and the Plan).
4. The question of whether fundamental change is needed to solve the problem.
5. Can the Affirmative proposal be adopted with creating disadvantages?
6. Is the Affirmative proposal topical?
   a. Does it provide "guarantees?"
   b. Do they provide employment opportunities for *all* unemployed U.S. citizens?

For the affirmative, the task is formidable. The negative may focus on any one or more of the issues that they feel is stronger for them.

The affirmative has little room to adapt in this paradigm—they must meet all of the issues requirements, presumably with equal priority. The negative, on the other hand, might be able to discard arguments utilized for judges of other paradigms and strengthen their arguments on any of the stock issues.

Policy Choice

The policy choice paradigm is patterned after the decision-making process of the policy maker, and this is the way our civic deliberative bodies conduct business. Two policy systems are compared and the judge chooses between them. Obviously, this paradigm applies only to policy advocacy propositions.

Strengths and weaknesses. The strength of this paradigm can be seen when contrasted with the stock issues approach. The latter focuses on only a few stock issues. The policy maker, however, considers a wider range of issues, which makes the comparison of the two policy systems more comprehensive.

With the policy choice paradigm, the affirmative still has the burden, and the negative retains presumption. But an advantage of the policy choice paradigm is that the burdens are somewhat more evenly distributed in the debate. As discussed above, stock issues assessment focuses the assessment on the affirmative policy system; the negative needs defend nothing—they need only defeat the affirmative proposal. In policy choice, however, the negative must defend a policy system; this system may be the status quo, or the status quo which has been repaired, or a counterplan.

Debater adaptation. The major task for the debater will, of course, rest on questions of solvency. Unlike the stock issues approach, however, the solvency questions will be applied to *both* policy systems, and not just the one proposed by the affirmative. While presumption lies with the negative in most cases, the negative must do more within this paradigm than with stock issues, as indicated above.

Utilizing Case Outline I, we can see the difference in what debaters should do for a policy choice judge. Stock issues will in all likelihood still be considered, but will be applied to both systems. So the question of solvency, assuming that the problem has been adequately established, will be applied to both the affirmative plan and the present system or an alternative system offered by the negative.

Because policy choice judges require the comparison of the policy systems, minor repairs and counterplans make more sense for a policy choice judge than for a stock issues judge. Presumably, the more specific the choices the better. Using the example, if the negative concedes that unemployment is a problem, they might offer a nonresolutional alternative to the affirmative proposal. This would certainly be appropriate for a policy choice judge.

Hypothesis Testing

This paradigm is very different from the previous ones. Hypothesis testing is patterned after the decision-making process of the scientist. The proposition is analogous to the hypothesis, and the debate is analogous to the experiment that tests the hypothesis. Presumption is against the hypothesis, as in science, and the burdens for proof on the affirmative.

Strengths and weaknesses. This model can be applied to any controversy, and to any proposition. Another strength is seen when this model is compared to the policy choice paradigm: in the latter, two policy systems are compared and one is chosen, no matter what. If both policy systems are bad, or morally repugnant, the judge guided by the policy choice approach must nevertheless choose one of them. The hypothesis testing paradigm allows a judge to reject the affirmative proposal (the hypothesis) without making an endorsement of any alternative.

A possible weakness of this paradigm is that the standards for judging the hypothesis are unclear. On what basis will the hypothesis be tested? What is the experiment designed to test? What issues are relevant to the judgment made by the judge? The answers to these questions might not be answered adequately before the debate, which will make the adaptation by the debaters to the judge a difficult task.

Debater adaptation. The hypothesis testing paradigm is similar to the stock issues approach: The important issues are tested against the affirmative case; as a result, the negative task is more narrow. If the negative defeats any significant portion of the affirmative case, the hypothesis or proposition will not be adopted.

When adapting to policy propositions, issues of solvency become paramount. The extent of the problem, while still considered, is not as important as the ability of the affirmative to solve the problem. Therefore, both the affirmative and negative teams should concentrate their time and effort on those issues.

When adapting to nonpolicy propositions, the criteria will not be the paramount concern—the *application* of the criteria will be the key voting issue. While the negative should dispute the criteria if it does not suit them, their main concern should be the application of the criteria to the observations. In Case Outline II, the focus of the debate should be on whether pornography is harmful to third parties (III.A. & B.).

The observation on presumption would be absolutely useless if argued before a hypothesis testing judge, because for them the affirmative always has the burden and the negative always has presumption. This is so regardless of the type of proposition, or its wording.

Judicial

This paradigm is patterned after the decision-making process of the jurist. Chiam Perelman, who favors this approach to the evaluation of argument, writes:

> This effort to resolve incompatabilities is carried on at every level of legal activity. It is pursued by the legislator, the legal theorist, and the judge. When the judge encounters a juridical antinomy in a case he is hearing, he cannot entirely neglect one of the two rules at the expense of the other. He must justify his course of action by delimiting the sphere of application of each rule through interpretations which restore coherence to the juridical system. He will introduce distinctions for the purpose of reconciling what, without them, would be irreconcilable.[5]

This paradigm considers the positions of the two sides, which we assume are irreconcilable. In other words, both the affirmative and negative positions cannot be accepted at the same time—they are mutually exclusive. This paradigm follows the process by which a jurist resolves such irreconcilable differences in a court of law.

To reconcile incompatabilities of law, a jurist weighs the positions offered to him by some standard of law, or often by some non-legal standard. Regardless of the specific nature of the standard, it is almost always value-ladened. The various positions are placed in a hierarchy of non-coherent arguments.

The model as it is applied to debate has similar characteristics. The following proposition is illustrative: *Resolved, that liberty is more precious than law.* The affirmative might present examples of situations in which liberty appears to be paramount to law. The negative, on the other hand, will cite examples in which law surpasses liberty in importance. As Perelman suggests, the judicial paradigm does not require the judge to reject either set of observations. The judge will search for a standard to measure the two sets of observations and, having determined that standard, will prioritize the sets accordingly.

In other words, the judge can agree that in some situations law is paramount, and in others liberty is more important. The fundamental question that the judge must then answer concerns which of the circumstances are more significant. Depending upon the standard used by the judge, the hierarchy may differ.

In this paradigm, standards or criteria for evaluation are crucial. Because of this focus, the paradigm is especially well adapted to nonpolicy propositions, although it can be applied to any brand of controversy.

Strengths and weaknesses. Perelman suggests the strength of this paradigm above. Juridical decision-making is carried on in a number of arenas and gaining competence in understanding that process is a valuable educational benefit. We will not all be jurists, but most of us will certainly be affected by their decisions. Understanding how those decisions are made is an important lesson; this lesson can be learned by adapting to the model in a debate.

A strength mentioned above is that this paradigm is applicable to all kinds of propositions. It is particularly suitable for propositions other than policy advocacy.

There is a major disadvantage to the paradigm: presumption is unclear. Both positions are considered equally. The observations are considered in isolation, then a common standard is applied to all of them, and they are prioritized.

When it is applied to policy propositions, the question of presumption is not vague. Since the writings of Archbishop Whately, there has been presumption in favor of existing policies or institutions. Therefore, the burden lies with the team suggesting change, and this holds true for the judicial paradigm. But in propositions other than policy advocacy, neither team is suggesting change, and the paradigm is unclear as to where the presumption lies in those cases.

In hypothesis testing, presumption is always in favor of the negative, but in the judicial model it is not so clear. A judge working from this perspective might impose other standards to determine presumption. One standard, taken from the legal arena, is in terms of "plaintiffs" and "defendants." In the following proposition, the defendant seems to be the negative: *Resolved, that the United Nations is obsolete.* The affirmative would be making the charge (the plaintiff), the negative would be defending the existing institution (the defendant).

The judicial model is not without complexities, and these complexities might make it difficult for the inexperienced debater to adjust to a judge utilizing the judicial model.

Debater adaptation. Debaters adapting to this view of decision-making must be careful to focus their arguments on those issues that underly criteria for evaluation. For policy debates, the criteria for evaluation will include the issues that justify action; for nonpolicy debates it will focus on the standards by which observations are evaluated.

Utilizing Case Outline I, the issues that justify action are those found in the contentions that establish the extent and nature of the problem (I & II). Whereas for the hypothesis testing judge issues of solvency would be paramount, for the judicial judge solvency will be a secondary issue. It will still be necessary for the affirmative team to establish solvency, but the judicial paradigm will lead the judge to be more concerned with the issues of need.

When adapting to the judicial paradigm in propositions other than policy, the issues are certain: issues of criteria are fundamental. In Case Outline II, the definition of legitimate is perhaps the most important issue in the debate (I. B.). The affirmative ought to be able to defend it well and the negative ought to have reasons to undermine it.

The only circumstance in which the negative could ignore this issue is if they were certain that the criteria offered by the affirmative could be applied to other examples to "warrant" a rejection of the proposition (alternatives to III. A. & B.).

Finally, the affirmative team would be perfectly safe in claiming presumption. The placement of burden and presumption depends on the justification argued and on the wording of the proposition. The reasons argued in Case Outline II seem legitimate. The negative also appears to have several legitimate arguments on their side. In other words, in adapting to the judicial paradigm, the affirmative presumption argument is legitimate. If the case was aimed at the hypothesis testing judge, however, the presumption argument would be useless.

Tabula Rasa

This paradigm is a view that the judge should have no set model in mind when entering the debate round. A *tabula rasa* judge prefers that the paradigm of evaluation be determined during the debate, based upon the arguments of the debaters. The *tabula rasa* judge has no notion of which paradigm is best.

Strengths and weaknesses. The strength of this paradigm is educational value. For debaters to be able to argue for one paradigm over the other necessitates an understanding of the paradigms. If the debaters learn them, this is indeed a benefit.

This paradigm encourages debaters to think about what they are doing, and might lead them to be more creative than they otherwise might be. Another benefit of the paradigm is that it can, of course, be applied to any proposition.

The weaknesses are obvious. The standards are vague. Inexperienced debaters would have difficulty participating in a debate within this paradigm. Morever, the debate might degenerate into a controversy over paradigms rather than focusing on the proposition.

The paradigm is also risky for the judge. If neither team argues for any standards for evaluation, the judge must then choose some criteria. Obviously the paradigm does not offer a good opportunity for adaptation in that event.

Debater adaptation. For this paradigm, adaptation is easy: anything is legitimate. The debaters should determine which paradigm or which standards for evaluation are most advantageous to their position and then argue that the judge ought to apply those standards to the issues.

Summary

The goal of debate is education. It is to teach students how to argue more effectively and how to persuade their audiences with more facility.

Goals of debate evaluation also include education or pedagogy. In a real sense a debate judge is a teacher. A debate judge is also a mediator in that the evaluator carefully weighs issues with only a personal paradigm to restrict his options. A judge is also an arbitrator, in that only a finding for either of the two competing positions is possible. The judge cannot endorse any other position.

There are six currently utilized paradigms of evaluation: (1) skills assessment, (2) stock issues, (3) policy choice, (4) hypothesis testing, (5) judicial, and (6) *tabula rasa*. Skills assessment focuses on the hierarchy of communication and refutational skills as the basis for evaluation. Stock issues approach to evaluation identifies several issues that are fundamental to the success of the affirmative case; the negative must win at least one of these to prevail.

The policy choice paradigm compares two policy systems, one presented by the affirmative, and one, usually the present system, defended by the negative. Hypothesis testing is patterned after the decision-making process of the scientist. It places the burden for proof completely on the affirmative, and the decision is made on the acceptability or unacceptability of the affirmative case. Within the paradigm there is no necessary comparison between policy systems.

The judicial paradigm looks at a controversy as jurists would. It allows for a resolution of controversies by applying standards that will account for the observations of both sides. A rejection of either set of observations is unnecessary. The criteria, once applied, will lead to a determination of which set of observations is more reliable.

Finally, the *tabula rasa* paradigm is one that forsakes preconceived notions of evaluation standards. It encourages debaters to offer arguments regarding which standards should be used, which in turn encourages the debaters to learn the standards.

Notes

1. Robert Rowland, "Standards for Paradigm Evaluation," *Journal of the American Forensic Association,* 18(Winter 1982), 133–140.
2. Evaluation criteria has been offered by several studies. See Kim Giffin, "A Study of the Criteria Employed by Tournament Debate Judges," *Speech Monographs,* 26(1959), 69–71; Frederick Williams, Ruth Ann Clark, and Barbara Sundene Wood, "Studies in the Dimensionality of Debate Evaluation," *Journal of the American Forensic Association,* 3(1966), 95–103; Frederick Williams, Sally Ann Webb, and Ruth Ann Clark, "Dimensions of Evaluation in High School Debate," *Central States Speech Journal,* 17(1966), 15–21; Judee K. Burgoon, "Evaluation Criteria as Predictors of Debate Success," *Journal of the American Forensic Association,* 12(Winter 1975), 1–4.
3. Rowland, pp. 134–140.
4. Burgoon, p. 4.
5. Chiam Perelman and L. Olbrechts Tyteca, *The New Rhetoric,* trans. John Wilkinson and Purcell Weaver (South Bend: University of Notre Dame Press, 1969), pp. 414–415.

Questions and Exercises

1. What are the three goals of debate evaluation?
2. How are debate judges both arbitrators and mediators?
3. What are the six paradigms of evaluation discussed in the chapter?
4. What are the strengths and weaknesses of each paradigm?
5. What are the distinctive features of each paradigm?
6. Compare and contrast the burdens of the affirmative team within the context of each paradigm.
7. Compare and contrast the burdens of the negative team within the context of each paradigm.

Suggested Readings

Allen, Mike and Dowdy, Lisa. "An Analysis of CEDA and NDT Judging Philosophies." *CEDA Yearbook, 1984.* California State University, Northridge: Don Brownlee, 1984, pp. 74–79.

Brydon, Steven. "Judging CEDA Debate: A Systems Perspective." *CEDA Yearbook, 1984*. California State University, Northridge: Don Brownlee, 1984, pp. 85–88.

Gaske, Paul, Kugler, Drew and Theobald, John. "Judging Attitudes and Paradigmatic Preferences, CEDA Debate: A Cumulative and Construct Validity Investigation." *CEDA Yearbook, 1985*. California State University, Northridge: Don Brownlee, 1985, pp. 57–66.

Miller, Thomas and McVay, Kenneth. "An Audience Analysis Curriculum: Its Theory, Practice and Implications." *CEDA Yearbook, 1984*. California State University, Northridge: Don Brownlee, 1984, pp. 65–73.

"Special Forum: Debate Paradigms." *Journal of the American Forensic Association*, XVII (Winter 1982), 133–160.

Weiss, Robert. "The Audience Standard." *CEDA Yearbook, 1985*. California State University, Northridge: Don Brownlee, 1985, pp. 43–49.

APPENDIX A

A Transcript of a Debate on a Policy Proposition

Edited by John K. Boaz

The Thirty-Eighth National Debate Tournament, sponsored by the American Forensic Association and the Ford Motor Company Fund, was held at the University of Tennessee in Knoxville, Tennessee, on March 30–April 2, 1984.[1] The sixty-two participating teams debated the 1983–84 intercollegiate debate proposition: "Resolved: That Any and All Injury Resulting from the Disposal of Hazardous Waste in the United States Should Be the Legal Responsibility of the Producer of that Waste."

Eight preliminary and four elimination rounds, all using cross-examination debate format, resulted in this final debate between Dartmouth College and the University of Louisville.[2] Representing Louisville on the affirmative were Mark Whitehead and Cindy Leiferman, and representing Dartmouth on the negative were Mark Koulogeorge and Leonard Gail. Judges awarded the decision to the negative team from Dartmouth College.[3] Critiques of the debate by the final round judges follow the transcript. The text of the debate follows:[4]

First Affirmative Constructive:
Mark Whitehead, Louisville

Good day. We are very pleased to be here in the final round, really pleased, and we would like to thank the following people: Dr. Russell Church, tournament host of the University of Tennessee; Dr. David Zarefsky who's done a very fine year as Director of this, or whatever his role is, you know, that type of thing; the University of Louisville debate squad, Lynn and all the guys, including Steve, Tim, Rich, Julie, Mr. Liptak, of course, Mr. Bill, Denny and the boys, especially Dan and Dave who have sung this song before, assistant coach of the year Gary Padgett, Joe Franko, especially Tim Hynes who's helped us a lot, and I'd like to thank Cindy for giving me a great year this year, and she would like to bring a special thanks to a person who's been a great contribution to her career, Professor Pfau, and of course all the debate community, because there are a lot of other people who deserve to be here, you

Dr. Boaz is Associate Professor of Communication at Illinois State University and a former President of the American Forensic Association.

[1] The tournament director was Professor David Zarefsky of Northwestern University, and the tournament host was Professor Russell Church of the University of Tennessee.

[2] The debate was held in the Ballroom of the Hyatt Regency Knoxville on April 2, 1984. Coaches of the two teams were Professor Tim Hynes of the University of Louisville and Professors Herb James, Ken Strange, and Tom Ryan of Dartmouth College. The sixteen teams qualifying for the elimination rounds were from the University of Arizona, Bates College, Baylor University, Claremont-McKenna College, Dartmouth College (two teams), Emory University (two teams), Harvard University, University of Kentucky, University of Louisville, Loyola Marymount University (two teams), Northwestern University, Southern Utah State College, and Suffolk University.

[3] Judges for the debate were Professors Tony Derosby (Bates College), John Katsulas (University of Iowa), Roger Solt (University of Kentucky), William Southworth (University of Redlands), and Robert Rowland (Baylor University). The decision was 4-1 for the negative team.

[4] The debate was edited from a tape recording. Except for the correction of obviously unintended errors and, where necessary, the insertion of case outline references (I, A, 1, etc.) this is as close to a verbatim transcript as was possible to obtain from the recording. An outline of arguments developed in the debate is provided in the Editorial Analysis section at the end of the transcript, which the reader may wish to consult occasionally for clarity. Evidence cards and other materials used in the debate were supplied to the editor immediately following the debate by the participants. Sources of the evidence have been verified as indicated in the footnotes, which also supply the exact quotation and other information when necessary. When the source was not located after a reasonable search or was not available to the editor, the term "source indicated" is used in the footnote together with any additional information provided by the debaters. For help in locating sources in this debate, the editor gratefully acknowledges the assistance of the library staff of Illinois State University and of William Putman, editorial assistant for JAFA.

know, especially like Lewis and Bill and both Johns from Harvard.[5]

We offer the following proposal, you know, of the resolution. Historically the United States has generated vast amounts of hazardous waste. Professors Walker, Gould, and Woodhouse provide documentation in 1983 when they state: "Wastes from weapons production include approximately eighty million gallons of highly radioactive solutions and sludges stored in steel tanks and a large quantity of less radioactive wastes in shallow-earth disposals."[6] In 1983, the *New York Times:* The DoD [Department of Defense] was the primary culprit when it said: "The military operates about 83 percent of Federal hazardous waste sites (or about 3 percent of all such facilities), generating 500,000 tons of waste—such as solvents, hydraulic fluids, fuels, munitions—yearly."[7] Furthermore, the Armed Forces insured the disposal of tons of waste yearly as the *Wall Street Journal* says in 1983: "According to some estimates, the armed forces alone must dispose of more than 400,000 tons of liquid wastes annually."[8]

The mere existence of hazardous wastes itself poses a serious risk for those involved with its disposal as Professors Willrich and Lester of MIT stated in 1977: "In the past, the U.S. government's record of management has been marred in a sufficient number of instances to be a cause of concern. An inevitable legacy of our nuclear age, radioactive waste constitutes a potential Nth century hazard."[9] It is just as apparent that as long as the government produces hazardous waste and it is being disposed of by the military there is a constant risk of injuries. Cindy and I support the resolution that "any and all injury resulting from the disposal of hazardous waste should be the responsibility of the producer of that waste."

Regrettably the current judicial system failed to provide legal responsibility as we note in contention (I): Duty-to-warn denied. Because the government is responsible for tortious injuries enjoined by military personnel, it seems only just that the government fulfill that responsibility by providing adequate information to those about to be subjected to a hazard or those who were subjected. Litigation should not be a prerequisite to redress as Professor Tredway advocated in '82: "The successful legal recourse for a hazard-exposed veteran is a separate consideration from what the government should do to provide relief. When implementation of a military program places soldiers at risk of harm through explosion of hazardous substances, the responsible agency or military department should initiate a program of systematically identifying and warning all affected servicemembers. The veteran should not have to litigate in order to be appraised of that hazard."[10]

Indeed the courts recognize the legitimacy of this as Professor Packard notes in 1979: " '[T]he Army . . . has been aware for some time that those servicemen who were obliged to witness the 1953 nuclear detonation were likely to suffer physically from the exposure.' *Id.* The court's decision granting the appellant the requested warning, may imply that knowledge of this danger created a duty on the part of the Army to act affirmatively in order to mitigate the injuries which it caused."[11] Unfortunately the lower court's decision became the exception rather than the rule. Instead the courts continued to bar servicemen's suits by applying the Feres doctrine, a judicially created exemption of the FTCA [Federal Tort Claims Act] waiver of sovereign immunity. Morina documents in 1983: "Because the failure to warn was a continuation of the in-service injury covered by the *Feres* doctrine, the failure to warn claims likewise were barred by *Feres*."[12] Hislop-Brumfield further explained that the Feres doctrine resulted in denial of tortious action for hazardous exposure this year: "The court nevertheless determined that Brook's injuries were only remotely related to his military duty and therefore allowed

[5] Lynn Bearden and Steve Gibson were the other Louisville team at the 1984 NDT. Tim Allison, Rich Puzsczwicz and Julie Graves are current Louisville debaters. John Liptak and Bill Campbell were 1982 NDT participants from Louisville. Denny Crumb is the Louisville basketball coach. Dan and Dave Southerland of Louisville won the 1982 NDT. Mike Pfau coached Cindy Leiferman while she was at Augusta College of South Dakota. Lewis Lamb is a debater at West Georgia College, and Bill Brewster is a debater at Emory University. Jonathan Weiner and Jonathan Massey debate at Harvard University.

[6] Charles A. Walker, LeRoy C. Gould, and Edward J. Woodhouse, eds., *Too Hot to Handle? Social and Policy Issues in the Management of Radioactive Wastes* (New Haven, Conn.: Yale University Press, 1983), p. x.

[7] Wayne Biddle and Margot Slade, "The Pentagon As Polluter," *New York Times,* 21 August 1983, p. 8E.

[8] Andy Pasztor, "Pentagon's Waste Sites Represent Huge, Neglected Crisis, Critics Say," *Wall Street Journal,* 22 July 1983, p. 19.

[9] Mason Willrich and Richard K. Lester, *Radioactive Waste: Management and Regulation* (New York: The Free Press, 1977), pp. 19–20.

[10] Lora Tredway, "When a Veteran 'Wants' Uncle Sam; Theories of Recovery for Servicemembers Exposed to Hazardous Substances," *American University Law Review,* (Summer 1982), p. 1110.

[11] "Comments," *New York Law School Law Review,* 25 (1979), 392.

[12] J. Thomas Morina, "Denial of Atomic Veterans' Tort Claims: The Enduring Fallout from *Feres v. United States,*" *William and Mary Law Review,* 24 (1983), 289.

recovery. It must be noted that the *Brooks* cause of action only allows recovery in rare situations when the government is somehow at fault but the negligence is not related to military duty."[13] Therefore, veterans exposed to toxic substances have no recovery under this rule. Hence, as long as the courts continue to recognize the existence of the continuous tort theory, recovery will be denied. Szykowny confirmed in 1982 when he says, "Since the *Feres* test for intramilitary immunity is 'whether plaintiffs' injuries have as their genesis injuries alledgedly sustained incident to the performance of military service,' courts have rejected the view that an injury does not occur until its manifestations become apparent. Under a continuous tort analysis, injuries which can be traced to the service are not compensable, even though the injuries do not manifest themselves until after the person has attained civilian status."[14]

Recent history confirms that subsequent decisions hold a contradictory rationale with respect to the duty-to-warn or in this case failure to warn. Although the Thornwell case was successful in obtaining a court recognized the duty to warn suit, other lower courts have rejected the Thornwell rationale as Hislop-Brumfield explained in '83: "Several cases have departed from the holding of *Thornwell* on facts so similar to *Thornwell* that their holdings impliedly or expressly reject the post service tort. In the Laswell v. Brown case, the Eighth Circuit Court of Appeals expressly rejected the post service tort."[15]

The result is a denial of recourse as she continues: These veterans are not receiving any redress for their injuries. Unless the court accepts the post service tort these veterans will remain non-compensated.[16] Additionally, the withholding of veteran information by the government infringes upon the soldier's right to know what he is being exposed to since the exposure could prove life threatening. Hislop [Brumfield] says in 1983: "The frequency of new medical discoveries make the cure for cancer and other diseases more likely. Surely a veteran should have the right to know the possibility of contracting cancer so that he may take advantage of these medical break-throughs. In any case, the veteran should be made aware of the increased potential for these diseases so early medical treatment can be sought."[17]

Such denial of information eliminates any hope of compensation as the *Pacific Law Journal* concluded in '83: "The military has exposed servicemen to toxic substances and used them as human 'guinea pigs' and then discharged them ignorant of their fate. Veterans have had little success with their attempts to penetrate this immunity."[18]

Independent of whether causation can be proven, the only hope the serviceman has of successful redress lies with the government obligation to warn of the potential hazards. Tredway explained the rationale last year: "Even if the veteran does prevail, however, going forward with the claim will entail substantial problems of proof. Notwithstanding, the difficulties involved in litigating a claim of post-discharge tortious conduct, such litigation is presently the veteran's most realistic possibility for recovery for any of the judges associated with in-service exposure to hazardous substances."[19]

Thus, regardless of the compensation, efficacy of government responsibility should be established as she concludes: "Regardless of the propriety of the court's holding in *Jaffee II,* the individual liability is impractical for those plaintiffs under discussion in this Comment. When the effects of tortious conduct are not manifest until long after an initiating event, the responsible individuals may be unavailable. Moreover, the limited resources of the individual will restrict the amount of monetary damages. Public policy dictates a different course of action."[20]

In addition, Sable concludes and says: "The court then made it abundantly clear . . . an individual's injury cannot be subject to the scrutiny of the court," because of sovereign immunity "no justice can exist. . . . 'If such be the law in this country, it sanctions tyranny.' "[21]

Therefore, we offer the following proposal:

Section I, the mandates. Congress shall express its intent of allowing U.S. military servicemen recovery from any and all injuries resulting from the disposal of hazardous waste by amending the MCA [Military Claims Act], Section 2733 of Title 10 such that military servicemen shall not be exempt from the waiver of sovereign immunity through application of incident to service bar in suits for failure to warn as parallel with other provisions of the MCA statutes. The amendment will supersede relevant portions of

[13] Lorna Hislop-Brumfield, "Judicial Recovery for the Post-Service Tort: A Veteran's Last Battle," *Pacific Law Journal,* (January 1983), 338.

[14] T. E. Szykowny, "Duty to Warn as an Inroad to the *Feres* Doctrine: A Theory of Tort Recovery for the Veteran," *Ohio State Law Journal,* 43 (1982), 272.

[15] Hislop-Brumfield, pp. 343–4.

[16] "So, in spite of the V.A.'s statutory scheme, veterans exposed to toxic substances during or after service are receiving no compensation for their injuries." Hislop-Brumfield, p. 353.

[17] Hislop-Brumfield, p. 353.

[18] Hislop-Brumfield, p. 354.

[19] Tredway, p. 1139.

[20] Tredway, p. 1126.

[21] James Samuel Sable, "Sovereign Immunity: A Battleground of Competing Considerations," *Southwestern University Law Review,* (1980–81), 461.

conflicting legislation, U.S. codes and/or equivalents. Settlements under other statutory benefits will be set off any award under the MCA. Failure to warn will be recognized as the post-discharge tort compensable with the MCA statute, and the United States government shall accept indemnification for payment of claims leveled against the military officials.

Section II, implementation. Funding through general federal revenue. Enforcement through appropriate judicial proceedings including the availability of judicial review to ensure that any and all injuries resulting from the disposal of hazardous waste should be the legal responsibility of producer of that waste. Any non-topical or unconstitutional plan provisions will be severed with the remaining provisions remaining in full force and effect. Debate speeches will serve as history with affirmative speeches indicating what we mean.

The next contention, contention (II), I guess this is, duty-to-warn solves. (A) By ensuring that all servicemen have the opportunity to sue for failure to warn upon governmental neglect of its duty to warn, individual rights will be protected as well as governmental interests. Szykowny explains in 1982: "Failure to warn theory still preserves military autonomy; yet, it also restores veterans' right to sue under the FTCA for some injuries, affirms the government's responsibilities to those who have faithfully served in the military and better allocated to government the risks of those losses from military service."[22]

(B) Additionally such a duty imposed upon the government would prevent needless death and suffering as Hislop-Brumfield explained last year: "The post-service tort would impose a duty on the government to inform veterans of their exposure to harmful substances and would require follow up care after discharge. The imposition of this duty could prevent the birth of defective children to chromosome-damaged servicemen and prevent the early deaths of servicemen who, once informed of their exposure could seek early medical care."[23]

(C) Duty-to-warn ensures an even balance between the rights of government versus servicemen as is historically validated by the Schwartz decision. Szykowny again elucidates in 1982: "The *Schwartz* decision does not conflict on policy grounds with the reasons typically employed by the courts to support the *Feres* decision. For example, military discipline will not be endangered if a plaintiff has, like Schwartz, attained civilian status. Second, Veterans Administration benefits would serve only to mitigate the damage recovery that the failure to warn tort will provide. It should be noted that the *Schwartz* decision does no more than restore to a plaintiff the right to trial by jury at the expense to government of weakening a blanket immunity and obviating some administrative decisions of the Veterans Administration."[24] Furthermore, any hindrance to federal activities is more than outweighed by the moral and just implications incumbent upon providing the relevant information to military personnel. Szykowny again concludes: "The interrelationship of the military to the soldier still in the service is characterized by the latter's dependency and lack of free choice. It would be a rather harsh doctrine that disavowed any obligation to a veteran. When the military has knowledge of the potentially lingering effects of a dangerous exposure of a serviceman, the moral and just result of warning the serviceman outweighs any inconvenience to government that may accompany such a duty."[25]

We offer the following underview. (III) Feres is justified. Although Feres is the barrier to the area the extension of government legal responsibility, that structural obstacle is warranted. The rationale must be upheld. Since the alternative compensation mechanism exists which ensures a course of redress for psychological or physical injury to servicemen, there exists no basis for rejecting the premise of the Feres decision which balanced the needs of the governmental immunity against the rights of the military to court access. The VA (Veteran's Administration) system ensures such a forum for damage redress as Major Donaldson says in '83: "In the *Feres* decision, the Supreme Court referred to these statutory provisions as 'systems of simple, certain, and uniform compensation for the injuries or death of those in the Armed Forces.' "[26]

The equity of system suffices as he continues and says: The VBA [Veterans Benefits Administration]" . . . serves a dual purpose: it not only provides a swift, efficient remedy for the injured serviceman, but it also clothes the Government in the 'protective mantle . . . of limitation-of-liability provisions.' "[27]

In addition in the Jaffee case, the Jaffee case went on to state: "The court noted that soldiers injured incident to service were guaranteeed compensation under the Veterans' Benefits Act. . . . The court later pointed out that '[i]t is important to remember that what we are called upon to decide is simply whether

[22] Szykowny, pp. 280–1.
[23] Hislop-Brumfield, p. 353.

[24] Szykowny, p. 275.
[25] Szykowny, p. 274.
[26] Howard L. Donaldson, "Constitutional Torts and Military Effectiveness: A Proposed Alternative to the *Feres* Doctrine," *The Airforce Law Review,* 23, (1982–1983), 197.
[27] The Supreme Court is quoted here in Donaldson, p. 197.

the plaintiffs are entitled to money damages, in addition to the compensation provided by Veteran's Benefits. . . .' "[28]

The alternative is a comprehensive program enacted by Congress of governmental redress. As the same thing continues: "Congress has enacted a rather comprehensive system of benefits for military personnel and definite and uniform compensation for injuries or death of those in armed services, in addition to medical and hospital treatment."[29]

Donaldson discusses with the legitimate basis of Feres in 1983 when he said: "[T]here are sound legal reasons for continuing the *Feres* defense to the *Bivens* actions. One reason is that some personal injuries resulting from constitutional violations are compensated under the Veterans Benefits Act."[30]

Furthermore, such a system is superior for it ensures a balance of competing interests. Lehmann says in 1982 when he said: "It further opined that the claimants were in fact better off under the VBA because no litigation is required. *Id.* Other courts that have denied wrongful death actions have recognized that because the VBA provides death benefits to wives and children of servicemen, denial of their claims under the FTCA would not leave them uncompensated."[31]

Hence, there is no justification to dismissing these types of cases as Donaldson says in '83: "[E]ven if the lower federal courts have held 'in mistaken reliance on what in *Feres* is not even dicta, that there is absolute intra-military immunity for willful torts,' this mistaken reliance is the rule today, and there are very sound reasons for continuing this rule."[32]

Finally, the rationale of Feres being legitimate does not imply that the Government should not be responsible for all injuries. Cyze explains in 1980 when he says: "The *Feres* rulings regarding its plaintiff are incorrect in view of the considerations in *Brown.* Furthermore, it is significant that the *Feres* opinion does not discuss the application of the Feres Doctrine to the underlying facts. Rather, it seems designed only to support the existence of the Doctrine. However, this does not necessarily negate the use of *Feres* to aid in the development of a workable and clear guide which would yield consistent determinations of governmental liability to its servicemen."[33]

Tredway further elaborated upon the unique justification for duty to warn as he [she] says in 1982: "More important, the rationale for sovereign immunity is especially inappropriate when the consequences of such exposure are latent and the government failed to appraise those involved of the potential harm, either before *or* after such persons were discharged from the military."[34]

Hislop concurred in 1983 when she said: "[T]he military has a duty after the veterans are discharged to rescue them from the harm caused during service. The post-service tort theory allows governmental immunity for injuries inflicted on servicemen during military duty but demands recovery for injuries the veterans incur after discharge."[35]

In addition Tredway outlines in 1982 when she said: "When service members regain civilian status and the government breaches a duty owed to them, the United States should be held accountable under the FTCA. That the government's omission is associated with a prior military activity or that the omission presently involves a military-related program or policy should not preclude injured veterans from litigating the merits of the failure-to-warn claim."[36]

Finally, such a policy is consistent with current compensation programs. As Hislop-Brumfield explains in 1983: "Modernly, V. A. benefits have not been interpreted as placing an upper limit on liability. As a practical matter the benefits are not compensating these veterans as the courts have expected. Therefore, the post-service tort remedy is consistent with *Feres* and *Stencel* and should be accepted by the courts."[37]

Hence, a consistent rational policy emerges as she finally concludes in 1983: "When analyzed in light of *Feres,* the post-service tort does not conflict with any of the reasons expressed by the Court for upholding military immunity."[38]

Cross-Examination:
Leonard Gail questioning Whitehead

Gail: Can counterplans be topical? Whitehead: I don't think that they can. Gail: OK.

Gail: What type of hazardous waste does the government produce? Well, first of all, explain any injuries produced by government agencies. White-

[28] Wei-Wei Chiu "TORTS—Military Service Immunity—There's No Cause of Action Implied Under the Constitution Against Government Officials for Intentional Constitutional Torts Occurring Incident to Military Service," *Villanova Law Review,* (1981–1982), 875.
[29] Chiu, p. 866.
[30] Donaldson, p. 195.
[31] Richard S. Lehmann, "The Effect of the *Feres* Doctrine on Tort Actions Against the United States by Family Members of Servicemen," *Fordham Law Reiew,* (May 1982), 1257.
[32] Donaldson, p. 180.

[33] D.A. Cyze, "The Federal Tort Claims Act: A Cause of Action for Servicemen," *Valporaiso University Law Review,* (1980), 572.
[34] Tredway, p. 1097.
[35] Hislop-Brumfield, p. 335.
[36] Tredway, p. 1138.
[37] Hislop-Brumfield, p. 353.
[38] Hislop-Brumfield, p. 347.

head: Well, I mean there's a lot of disposal, and I believe the first couple of cards even under the first contention—ah no, that'd be . . . Gail: Anyone has been harmed? Whitehead: Pardon me? Gail: They indicate anyone has been harmed? Whitehead: Well, there's a number of cases that are brought forth to the courts. Gail: To the courts. Tell me about the . . . Whitehead: You know, they think they're harmed.

Gail: Tell me about the MCA. What type of system is this? Whitehead: It's a review board. Gail: What's the difference between the MCA and the VA? Whitehead: Well, we went through this last time. I believe what happens is . . . I'm not real sure what the difference is, but there is some type of difference in the review systems between the two.

Gail: Would a counter plan that had the VA use the duty-to-warn be topical? Whitehead: I don't know. Gail: Why would it be different from the affirmative? Whitehead: Why would it be different from the affirmative? Let's see, the counterplan that does the VA, that had VRA do the duty-to-warn. I mean, we're saying that these servicemen . . . . I mean we're talking about like past injuries where the government has failed to warn—right? OK, so that'd be different. Gail: But future injuries cannot be compensated for? Whitehead: Oh, I mean, you know, if that's the case then we would have a residual advantage. Gail: All of these injuries that happened as a result of hazardous waste disposal tomorrow—people who did not—who were warned would not be given benefits? Whitehead: If it lived up to the standards, right. I mean, if the government fulfills its obligation to warn these people, yeh, we're just saying that they have failed in the past, and right now those claims are barred, and we let them get access to pursue those claims.

Gail: In the MCA how does one prove that they—how does the government prove it was given a duty-to-warn—that they gave a duty-to-warn? Whitehead: I don't know what the standards are? Gail: You don't know how your duty-to-warn is proven? Whitehead: I mean, this is all done in the MCA Act, you know, I mean, that's like saying to me recite the rules of civil procedure, I mean, I can't do that. Gail: Well, tell me what the MCA Act says. It's in your plan. Whitehead: What? Gail: The MCA says. What the Act is. Whitehead: About what? Gail: About the burdens of duty-to-warn. Whitehead: OK, Give me the plan. I mean. Gail: I saw the words MCA on the plan. I want to know what the MCA does on duty-to-warn, what standard it utilizes. Whitehead: I don't know. Gail: You've no idea. When the government claims that it gave the duty-to-warn. Whitehead: I mean, I think there's a reasonable presumption here that if a serviceman is exposed without his knowledge, I mean, you know, you say you go out on maneuvers . . . Gail: I'm asking, how does the government prove it gave a duty-to-warn? Whitehead: Well, I mean, if a guy goes out on maneuvers and they're using CBW [Chemical and Biological Warfare] or something. Gail: Doesn't the President of the DoD say we warned him? Does his father say he was warned? Does his commanding officer say he was warned? Whitehead: Yeh, I would assume it's something like a commanding officer, something within the military structure. I'm not sure, OK? I don't know. Gail: That's all.

First Negative Constructive:
Mark Koulogeorge, Dartmouth

On behalf of Dartmouth College, Lennie and I would like to thank the NDT, the Board of Trustees, Dr. Zarefsky and the tournament staff for a well-run tournament. We would also like to thank Professor Church and all the Tennessee Volunteers for their warm hospitality. Finally, I would like to thank my friends at Dartmouth, Herb, Mark Weinhart, Meredy, Karen, Craig, and everyone at home. A special thanks to Mr. Gail and my mom and dad who came 500 miles to see us. But, most of all I'd like to thank the people who have made my term at Dartmouth College the last three years in debate, certainly worthwhile, that's Kenny, Lefty, and Tommy. And I'd like to dedicate this round to my partner, Lennie, whom I not only admire but truly love as a friend.[39]

First, a counterplan is that causes of action for military servicemen shall be removed. The VA will be the exclusive forum for the military benefits.

Discipline. (I) First disadvantage. (A) subpoint, discipline hurts. (1) litigation hurts. Dunas, 1982: "[G]eneral discipline in the military would be threatened if soldiers were permitted to challenge every military decision made. . . ."[40] Jaffee, 1981: "The *Feres* decision discussed immunity for injuries arising 'incident to service,' and no compelling distinction can be made under that rationale for the type of injuries that occur during that service. Litigation over intentional torts would appear to disrupt military discipline and undermine military decisionmaking as much as tort suits for negligence."[41]

(2) subpoint, chill. Donaldson in 1983: "The *Wallace* court did not adequately address the potential for disrupting military effectiveness because it ignored the 'chilling effect' on decisionmaking of the

[39] Herb James, Tom Isaacson, Mark Weinhart, Meredith McClintock, Karen McGaffey, and Craig Bridner. Ken Strange, headcoach; Steve Mancuson, assistant coach, 1983; Tom Lyon, assistant coach, 1984.

[40] Source indicated: Dunas v. U.S., 1982, 544 F Supp. 10 (1).

[41] Jaffee v. United States, 663 F. 2d 1226 (1981), p. 1235.

litigation itself, notwithstanding the actual merits of the case."[42] Jaffee, 1981: "While the Tort Claims Act would not make them personally liable in these circumstances, the prospect of adversarial civilian scrutiny might inhibit the exercise of military discretion."[43]

(B) subpoint, impact. Lieutenant Colonel Kunnell, 1980: "The services simply cannot function without [discipline], and the country that fails to require its military forces to preserve discipline, that is, responsiveness and obedience to its lawful authority, will soon find itself defenseless, its forces turned into uncoordinated gangs and individuals. Apart from failure in its mission, the members will become a threat to the peace of the Republic. . . . "[44] McKinney in '77: "Militarily speaking, the mission of the unit must be the primary goal of every officer and noncommissioned officer. Secondly, they must provide for the welfare and morale of their subordinate troops. To reverse these traditional roles will cause defense capabilities to collapse beyond a state of preparedness and readiness."[45] Freedman in '82: If the alliance can hold together and project a serious military capability, it probably can keep the Soviet Union in check.[46] Dyer, 1977: Therefore, it would appear that despite the passage of time America's commitment to Europe is still more clearly demonstrated by troops (via tripwire) than by an ambiguous weapons system.[47]

Morina, 1983: "The military discipline rationale has survived extensive criticism and remains a strong justification for the bar against servicemen's F.T.C.A. suits."[48]

(II) Second disad, spending. (A) Brink evidence. We're going to have a big interest rate push absent the budget compromise. *Fortune,* April 1984: "An uneasy truce may be about to end on the interest rate front. Short term rates remain in the narrow range they have occupied since last August. . . . Private credit demands have been unexpectedly strong, the dollar has weakened, and the Fed still seems determined to cap credit growth. *Interest rates could well break into new territory by midyear.*"[49] Sullivan, March '84: " 'Unless there's some abatement in credit market pressures in the next few weeks' the prime could reach 12 percent. . . . "[50]

(B) subpoint, budget downpayment decreases interest rates. It prevents any increase. McCracken, February '84: "And a good 1984 'downpayment' (to use the current buzzword) would do a lot for interest-rate levels and the readjustment of exchange rates so essential for redressing our severe trade imbalance."[51] *Fortune,* '84: "If Congress and the Administration agreed on a package for substantial cuts in the federal deficit, interest rates wouldn't have to go up. Volcker has testified that a $50-billion-a-year reduction would lower rates by one percentage point—a more precise calculation than seems possible in this murky area."[52] Weidenbaum, 1984: "The 'first installment' of deficit reductions agreed upon by the White House and Republican Congressional leadership is a useful first step."[53]

(C) subpoint, any new spending destroys the budget compromise that's going on right now. *Union Leader,* March 1984: "Reagan told House Republicans, . . . [and] [h]e delivered the same message to GOP senators, 'if anyone sends me this tax package and at the same time does not include the spending cuts, I will veto the tax package.' "[54]

Reagan in '84: " 'But I do think that we should try to concentrate on the less contentious issues,' he quickly added. 'If we all focus on what's doable, we can get something done for the American people.' "[55] Weakening on the spending side empirically has impeded past compromise measures as [Donald T.] Regan explains in 1983: "I was on the contingency tax earlier, but as it stands now, Congress is not coming through with the remainder of the deal. . . . Therefore the deal is off."[56] *New York TImes,* April 17, '84: "What must be avoided in the weeks ahead is a political stalemate"[57] which is exactly what the plan would be.

(D) subpoint, snowball. Snowball, Titus, 1983: "Funding a special project to benefit a relatively small number of people conflicted with the 'Reaga-

[42] Donaldson, pp. 191–192.

[43] Jaffee v. United States, p. 1232.

[44] Ludolf R. Kunell, III, "The Functions of the UCMJ in Maintaining Air Force Readiness," *The Reporter,* (April 1980), 50.

[45] Source indicated: McKinney (NCOA), 1977, p. 250.

[46] Source indicated: Freedman, AWPR, Nov. 1982, p. 23.

[47] Source indicated: Dyer, 1977, p. 235.

[48] Morina, pp. 265–6.

[49] Dodd May, Jr., et. al., "Fortune Forcast: Mounting Pressure on Interest Rates," *Fortune,* 2 April 1984, p. 38.

[50] Source indicated: Sullivan, 20 March 1984, W.P. Dean Witter.

[51] Paul W. McCracken, "Gobbling Up the Economic Pie," *Wall Street Journal,* 28 February 1984, p. 32.

[52] May, p. 39.

[53] Source indicated: Wiedenbaum, 19 March 1984, p. A 18 or 19.

[54] "Reagan Firm on Deficit Package," *The Union Leader,* 22 March 1984, p. 1.

[55] Ronald Reagan quoted in Storer Rowley, "Reagan Insists He'll Work to Cut Deficit," *Chicago Tribune,* 28 January 1984, p. 1.

[56] Donald T. Regan quoted in Stephen H. Wildstrom, "Why Regan Can't Jawbone the Deficit Away," *BusinessWeek,* 24 October 1983, p. 45.

[57] Dan Rostenkowski quoted in Jonathan Fuerbringer, "Pact on Deficit: Near and Yet So Far," *New York Times,* 17 March 1984, p. 11.

nomics' approach to fighting inflation through the reduction of federal expenditures."[58] *Congressional Quarterly,* '82: "Those groups see the possibility of a national workers' compensation program or a national product liability law lurking behind the asbestos problem."[59] It is generally high as Titus explains in 1983: "A second problem is cost: compensating an unknown number of victims could run into the billions of dollars. . . ."[60]

Make this, I guess, (D2), compensation will spread to other groups, especially in an election year. *Environmental Reporter* explains in 1983: " 'The history of the last several decades teaches us one very troubling lesson, McGrath said. 'Congress is generally incapable of leaving income distribution schemes alone, much less of pruning them back.' "[61] McGrath in 1983: "[I]f we were to adopt a governmental solution as to one of these problems but not to others, that would raise an issue as to why we would favor one group of claimants over others."[62] *Environmental Reporter,* '83: "Disjointed consideration of what are economically, socially, and politically related topics makes no sense, McGrath said in citing various proposals to amend the superfund law to cover toxic waste site injuries and to provide compensation for asbestos-related illnesses, cancers caused by radiation, Agent Orange contamination, and uranium mining-related diseases,"[63] indicating once you do one compensation, it politically spreads out and you get the big snowball. *Environmental Reporter,* '83: "McGrath said that however new legislation is fashioned, 'there is a dire risk that the original brilliant scheme will be turned into an economic monster.' He added that 'in an era of limited resources, it also threatens to reduce our future flexibility to deal with the other problems of our society.' "[64]

(E) subpoint, equals stock market. *Business Week,* 1984: "The stock market responding positively to every hint out of Washington that the deficits will be reduced, and negatively to every indication that they will not."[65]

Business Week, 1984: "Another drop in the stock market and a rise in interest rates would surely push the economy back into recession."[66]

Hollings, '84: "In short, we are dealing with our survival as a productive, harmonious community. We cannot wait 1 year to attack the deficits. In 1 year we might be back in recession, and then no one will want to take the necessary steps. The time to act is now. . . ."[67] The impact is war and LDC [less developed country] growth. Erlich, '81: "To put the brakes on material economic growth now would be to condemn the majority of the world's population to lives of misery."[68] *South* magazine, February, '83: "The UN Committee for Development Planning has warned that if the present situation persists, it will result in 'extensive human suffering in many of the poorest developing countries, as well as risks of widespread political instability."[69]—without growth. *Futurist,* 1980: "The possibility of a second Great Depression in the 1980s is not something to be taken lightly. Even if the likelihood of such a development is low—as most professional economists think—the consequences would be extremely grave. The collapse of living standards would be calamitous for many millions of poeple, and the political and social consequences would threaten the stability of democratic institutions. Even worse, an economic crisis could lead to a world war, as the bitter experience of the 1930s demonstrated so powerfully."[70]

Case. (I) First contention. (A) national security outweighs *Feres.* Brennan in 1981: "military (or national) security is a weighty interest, not least of all because national survival is an indispensible condition of national liberties."[71] This is Jaffee, 1981: "This is a difficult and troubling decision. The Supreme Court has stated, however, that the interests of the society as a whole are advanced by holding certain individuals acting in special capacities free from legal action. Military service appears to be a situation where the Court would not independently

[58] Source indicated: Titus (UNLV), JHPPL, Summer 1983, p. 288.

[59] Elizabeth Wehr, "Manville Bankruptcy Adds to Pressure: Action Expected Next Year on System for Compensating Victims of Asbestos Disease," *Congressional Quarterly Weekly Report,* 23 October 1982, p. 2731.

[60] Source indicated: Titus, p. 278.

[61] "Hazardous Waste: Victim Compensation Seen as Dire Risk by Administration Task Force Chairman," *Environment Reporter,* 28 October 1983, p. 1151.

[62] Source indicated: McGrath, DOJ, 1983, 10-28, *Chem. Reg. Reporter.*

[63] "Hazardous Waste: Victim Compensation Seen As Dire Risk by Administration Task Force Chairman," p. 1151.

[64] "Hazardous Waste: Victim Compensation Seen As Dire Risk by Administration Task Force Chairman," p. 1151.

[65] "Defuse the Deficit Crisis Now," *Business-Week,* 26 March 1984, p. 146.

[66] "Defuse the Deficit Crisis Now," p. 146.

[67] Sen. Hollings, "A Budget Plan to Cut Our Deficits Before They Stall Our Recovery," *Congressional Record,* 25 January 1984, p. S155.

[68] Paul and Anne Ehrlich, "Extinction or a Strategy of Conservation," *Bulletin of the Atomic Scientists,* (June/July, 1981), p. 27.

[69] Editorial, "Say Goodbye to Backseat Drivers," *South,* February 1983, p. 6.

[70] Edward Cornish, "The Great Depression of the 1980's," *Futurist,* (June 1980), 29.

[71] Justice William Brennan quoted in Jon P. Bruinooge, "Mobilization for a European War: The Impact of Habeas Corpus," *Air Force Law Review,* (1980–1981), 274.

grant a new cause of action under the Constitution."[72] Now even if the present system does not—even if the present system is wrong and there is no military justification, the fact that society has postulated that fact means it can be a competing consideration and outweighs.

(B) assumes unjust military system. This is from Levine in 1980: "[A different Supreme Court under] Chief Justice Burger no longer felt compelled to distrust the military justice system and firmly recognized that the military necessity for order and discipline may outweigh the need for constitutional safeguards for servicemembers."[73]

(C) military objectives are different. Parker v. Levy in 19[74] I don't know, whatever it is: "This Court has long recognized that the military is, by necessity, a specialized society separate from civilian society. We have also recognized that the military has, again by necessity, developed laws and traditions of its own during its long history. The differences between the military and civilian communities result from the fact that 'it is the primary business of armies and navies to fight or to be ready to fight wars should the occasion arise.' "[74] This is from Neutze, 1973: "[U]nfettered free expression is inconsistent with military efficiency. What may be innocuous in civilian life may well be disastrous in the military."[75]

(D) argument, military system suffices. (1) Generally. Kuhnell, 1980: "The Supreme Court has recently reiterated its recognition of the need for a separate system of military justice and further recognized that the military constitutes a separate society which requires a separate body of law to fulfill its mission."[76] *Michigan Law Review* in '79: "Military law, like state law, is a jurisprudence which exists separate and apart from the law which governs in our federal judicial establishment. This Court has played no role in its development."[77]

(2) Subpoint, superior knowledge. Seaman, 1971: "The extent to which the exercise of military expertise or discretion is involved. Courts should defer to the superior knowledge and experience of professionals in matters such as promotions or orders directly related to specific military functions."[78]

(E) subpoint, promoters prove. Captain Ellis, 1982: "The reluctance of the judiciary to review the promotion actions of selection boards is rooted not only in the court's incurable lack of knowledge of the total grist which the boards sift, but also in a preference not to meddle with the internal workings of the military."[79]

(F) subpoint, speech rights prove. Neutze in 1973: "[I]mportant considerations such as discipline, morale, and obedience to orders demand that the right of free expression be more circumscribed among military personnel."[80]

(G) no equal protection violation. Rhodes, '76: "Refusing military members access to the courts for full redress of incident-to-service injuries is not inappropriate per se, but a decision to single out the service members as a class should be based on sound policy considerations."[81]

Now, they argue below, right to know. Well, here it is, Cye.

(H) subpoint, right to know, not recognized at present because of risks in application. O'Brien in 1981: "The Supreme Court's failure to denominate a First Amendment right to know . . . does not reflect insensitivity to the political ideal of freedom of information and an informed public. Rather, it reflects a refusal to engage in extra-constitutional decision-making."[82]

(I) subpoint, potential impact of recognition is disastrous. (1) subpoint, escalates press restrictions. O'Brian in '81: "[T]he right to know inevitably leads to judicial determinations of what the public does and does not have a right to know, and thus invites restrictions on freedom of speech and press in the form of prior restraints."[83] (2) subpoint, this is judicial tyranny. O'Brien in 1981: "The proprietary of governmental openness with respect to documents and other materials, or public access to facilities such

[72] Jaffee v. United States, pp. 1239–40.

[73] Stanley Levine, "The Doctrine of Military Necessity in the Federal Courts," *Military Law Review*, (Summer 1980), 6.

[74] Levine, p. 9.

[75] Dennis R. Neutze, "Yardsticks of Expression in the Military Environment," *The JAG Journal*, (Spring 1973), 183.

[76] Kuhnell, p. 50.

[77] The Supreme Court in Burns v. Wilson, 346 U.S. 137, 140 (1953) is quoted in "Notes: From *Feres* to *Stencel:* Should Military Personnel Have Acces to FTCA Recovery?" *Michigan Law Review*, (April 1979), 1112.

[78] Mindes v. Seaman, 453 F. 2d 197 (1971), *Federal Reporter*, Second Series, Volume 453 F. 2 d (St. Paul, Minnesota: West Publishing Company, 1972), pp. 201–2.

[79] The court in *Brenner v. United States* [202 Ct. Cl. 678 (1973)] is quoted in L. Neal Ellis, Jr., "Judicial Review of Promotions in the Military," *Military Law Review*, (Fall 1982), 138.

[80] Neutze, p. 203.

[81] Robert L. Rhodes, "The *Feres* Doctrine after Twenty-five years," *Air Force Law Review*, (Spring 1976), 41.

[82] David M. O'Brien, "Reassessing the First Amendment and the Public's Right to Know in Constitutional Adjudication," *Villanova Law Review*, (November 1980), 61.

[83] O'Brien, p. 7.

as prisons and other governmental institutions, pose issues of public policy reserved for the legislative and executive branches. The First Amendment neither requires nor permits judicial formulation of information policies via the denomination of novel and unenumerated rights."[84] It is irrelevant if the plan—the administrative form. It is the same type of justification that will be used in the future.

(J) subpoint, uniqueness. O'Brien in '81: "A majority of the Supreme Court has not recognized affirmative first amendment rights for the public and the press to receive or obtain access to governmental information."[85] O'Brien in '81: Quoting Justice Rhenquist, concurring in Gannett: "[I]t is clear that this Court repeatedly has held that there is no First Amendment right of access to in the public or the press to judicial or other governmental proceedings."[86] "The Court has never recognized any right of access to governmental facilities, whether in the public generally or in the press."[87]

(K) subpoint, pre-empts or applies to judicial, constitutionally-based action only. I'll get to that later. (IV) Mass noun, please, topicality. (A) subpoint, definition of mass nouns. Number modifiers are inappropriate, and do not use an indefinite article with the word "a." Ware, Calgary, 1975: "[T]he distinction between count nouns and mass nouns is determined by the quantifiers and determiners that are appropriate to the nouns. Count nouns are distinguished by their taking the indefinite article, 'many,' 'few,' 'one,' and other number words. I shall call these enumeratives. Mass nouns are distinguished by the appropriateness of what I shall call amassives, words like 'much,' 'little,' and 'less,' "[88] Waste is clearly a mass noun. You would say "much hazardous waste" instead of "many hazardous waste," and topic does not say "a hazardous waste."

(B) subpoint, mass nouns mean the group is covered. Cartwright in 1975: Some of the characteristics of Strawson's feature noted that do not introduce particulars into our discourse but only general features and that their unmodified subjects as Quine stated. They do not divide their reference, not because of their function as singular terms, but because they go along with singular terms,[89] indicating they all have the same characteritic, and that's why you use the singular, not the plural. It is a mass, to look at as one.

(C) subpoint, grammar rules determine. We will defend examples which are in a prepositional analogous to the topic: A mass noun (waste) modified by another mass noun (disposal) in the prepositional phrase (disposal of hazardous waste). Cartright in '75: "The crucial difference in all these cases is not lexical but 'structural'; the *relevant* ambiguity is not to be gleaned from the sense of such words as 'apple', 'beer', 'metal', or 'experience' but from the grammatical structure of those contexts in which they occur."[90]

(V) Underview. Illegal dumping. The (A) subpoint will be, most circumvent contracts. Choi and Daly in 1983: "[The DoD] relies primarily on civilian contract firms to treat or ultimately dispose of hazardous waste. In 1981, for instance, the department disposed of 51,000 tons on its own sites. . . . "[91] Now, this argument really climbs it, in the present system they can sue right now for some of it, the part that's contracted out.

The (B) subpoint will be the uniqueness. Presently the use of mechanisms to get away from the high costs, etc., as they go abroad and dump on Honduras, on these poor people overseas, and they die. The plan gives them an added incentive, because you can sue for this now, and that not happen in Honduras.

Environmental Reporter, 1983 noted: "Synar asserted that the subcommittee's review of DoD contractors' handling of wastes showed that . . . Manifests listing the final disposal locations of the PCB wastes were falsified; An attempt was allegedly made by American Electric Corp. to ship ten of thousands of gallons of the toxic material to Honduras with falsified papers; and, Dozens of contaminated transformers and capacitors and tens of housands of gallons of PCB-contaminated oils obtained from Defense facilities remain 'unaccounted for.' "[92]

[84] O'Brien, p. 60.
[85] O'Brien, p. 47.
[86] O'Brien, pp. 37–8.
[87] O'Brien, p. 32.
[88] Robert X. Ware, "Some Bits and Pieces," *Synthese,* (September/October 1975), 379.
[89] "Indeed it is at least tempting to say that the unmodified mass nouns and plurals of (1) and (2) are not to be salvaged as full-fledged singular terms at all, that these sentences share some of the characteristics of Strawson's feature-placing statements and 'do not introduce particulars into our discourse' but only 'general features,' and that their unmodified subjects function in the way Quine describes the use of mass nouns as a lexical class. They do not divide their reference, not because of their function as singluar terms, but because they do not in (1) and (2) 'go along with singular terms . . . in purporting to name a unique object each.' " Helen M. Cartwright, "Some Remarks about Mass Nouns and Plurality," *Synthese,* (November/December 1975), 405.
[90] Cartwright, p. 400.
[91] Source indicated: Choi and Daly, DMJ, 4th Quarter 1983, p. 36.
[92] "Hazardous Waste: Defense Does Not Assess Qualifications, Monitor Contractors, House Panel Reports," *Environment Reporter,* 19 August 1983, p. 653.

The next underview is (VI) no harm presently. (A) subpoint, the right is ill defined. How do you weigh this percentage bodies like of your own case? If I win one life, they are certainly greater than the other rights. (B) subpoint, no harm presently. They have not given you any evidence saying that there is any harm to these people. *Environmental Reporter,* August 1983: "The majority of significant problems have been identified, and cleanup programs are under way, Daley said, adding that the department does not know of any cases where immediate health or environmental threats exist."[93] He continues: "To date, only three installations—Rocky Mountain Arsenal, Redstone Arsenal, and Pine Bluff Arsenal—have shown evidence of contaminant migration . . . indicates the limited scope of the problem within the Army."[94] HEW claims in 1981 that monitoring solves. "Colonel John Spence, Commander of the U.S. Army Toxic and Hazardous Materials Agency, told the senators . . . 'You haven't cleaned up,' Spence acknowledged, 'but at least you know where it's going.' "[95] OK, so they've cleaned up now.

(VII) Topicality disadvantage. I'll argue, reasonability is stupid. (A) argument would be that it de facto delimits the topic. What is reasonable? The affirmative simply states they are reasonable and there is no way truly to debate it out. (B) subpoint, it's the rule; it's the best definition. (1) subpoint. Rules run both ways. When they have their choice to decide affirmative or negative, they knew the rules, and this should be binding on them. (2) subpoint is if you are against the rule you should still accept it. It is the rule that's there to prevent people from abusing these things. If, for example, you say, I don't like the rule: I think topicality should be reasonability. If you continue to do this, especially in the final round of the NDT, people will backlash, and they'll do things such as making a case list or no new arguments.

(C) subpoint, can't clearly define. *CJS* [*Corpus Juris Secundum*], 1980: "The term 'reasonable' is a factual expression not ascertainable by reference to rule, law or formula. . . ."[96] So, I think we're going to do good things on topicality. Our "splaining" evidence is excellent, as Lisa would say.

Cross-examination:
Mark Whitehead questioning Mark Koulogeorge

Whitehead: I would like to discuss the evidence on discipline, if I could please. Koulogeorge: OK. Whitehead: Now, I would like to know how much of this assumes like general litigation against the government versus a duty-to-warn scenario, or a failure-to-warn scenario. Koulogeorge: I can't really quantify. . . . Whitehead: OK. Koulogeorge: . . . and breakdown the evidence. Lennie gave it to me. I assume it applies. I trust him. Whitehead: So you don't really know, right? So, if we can show somehow that this stuff is talking about like our old case where you just go ahead and compensate versus the—'cause I think that . . . Koulogeorge: Right, right. What's going to happen is you're going to have testimony in the tribunal, and that's going to cause the lack and the breakdown of discipline. Whitehead: . . . affirmative evidence, make some type of distinction between—like straight compensation schemes versus failure-to-warn scheme. I mean, I thought that was for . . . Koulogeorge: Well, if you want to make that argument, make it. Whitehead: OK. Koulogeorge: I mean, do you want to split a question? Whitehead: All right, so you don't really know that it would or distinction it makes? Koulogeorge: You're embarrassing me in front of my parents. That's not nice. [Laughter]

Whitehead: Now let's see. The impact of the discipline disad means that checks the Soviet Union and then what's the impact of that? I mean, what—does the Soviet Union expand somewhere, or what's the deal? Koulogeorge: Oh, the evidence is pretty good in terms of war and discipline. Whitehead: I see—there's a card that says war? Koulogeorge: Yeh, as a matter of fact. Whitehead: What's the scenario. Koulogeorge: I guess the lack of discipline causes the Soviets to encroach on Europe. Whitehead: Uh, huh, OK.

Whitehead: "The" is the modifier. It means an entire group of, right? Like "the" crowd means all "the" crowd. Koulogeorge: It depends on the structure, and that's our standard on topicality. Whitehead: So like, for example, in the grammatical sense grammatical use, like in the use of a prepositional phrase? Koulogeorge: Yes. Whitehead: Like—um—let's see, "of the group." Koulogeorge: Well. Whitehead: That would be a prepositional phrase. Then if I say, I am of the group, that would be one of an entire group. Koulogeorge: That's because "I" isn't a mass noun. The structure is mass noun modifying mass noun. Whitehead: OK. I see. Good.

Whitehead: Now these people are cleaning up right now in the DoD, right? Koulogeorge: Uh, some of it gets cleaned up. Some of it gets thrown into Honduras. Whitehead: Pardon me? Koulogeorge: Yeh, some of it gets cleaned up, yes. Whitehead: OK. I would like to see the evidence on Honduras, if I could please. Koulogeorge: C'est bien.

[93] "Hazardous Waste," *Environment Reporter,* 12 August 1983, p. 618.

[94] Source indicated: Marienthal, 1980, p. 67.

[95] Source indicated: *HW Report,* July 1981, p. 2.

[96] "Reasonable," *Corpus Juris Secundum,* 75, (1983), Cumulative Annual Pocket Part (Brooklyn, New York: The American Law Book Company, 1983), p. 109.

Whitehead: Now, who's cleaning up? Is the federal government cleaning up? Koulogeorge: Actually in some cases the EPA cleans it up and then gives back to the federal government, and in some cases the DoD. Whitehead: OK. So, in other words, when soldiers are cleaning this up, they do have the potential to be exposed to it. Koulogeorge: I don't know if it's soldiers. OK. The first argument is, a lot of it is civilian contracted. OK. So that takes you out of everything. Whitehead: OK. Koulogeorge: You would sue the contractor. Whitehead: Is the counterplan conditional? Koulogeorge: No. Whitehead: Are topical counterplans OK? Koulogeorge: Yeh, sure, why not? Whitehead: Why is topicality a voting issue? Koulogeorge: It's one of the rules of the game. Whitehead: OK. That's the only reason, right? Koulogeorge: As of now, yeh. Whitehead: How about jurisdiction? Jurisdictionally? Is that a reason? Koulogeorge: Well, as long as there's clash. I don't know what jurisdiction is. Whitehead: OK. Jurisdiction is. . . . Koulogeorge: Fairness is always an issue. Whitehead: OK. Some way to divide ground, right? Koulogeorge: Well, that's neat initially to decide which case you are. Whitehead: or which side you are? Koulogeorge: You know, for example, you could be . . . Whitehead: So there's some type of jurisdiction there. Koulogeorge: I disagree. Whitehead: Very well.

Second Affirmative Constructive:
Cindy Lieferman, Louisville

(I) This case only establishes a failure to warn, not a duty to warn. That will become clear. [unintelligible] he talks about in national security. First of all, that's [unintelligible] for courts, not administrative. Second, it's not true. There's no rationale for this. Cyze in '80: "[T]he effect of maintenance of discipline . . ."[97] is not an effect which would result and has never been explained. Second or third argument, beats justification. Zillman in '82: "[I]t is unfortunate to justify all incident-to-service cases on disciplinary grounds. It is unfair to the military plaintiff to offer specious reasons to deny his suit."[98] Fourth argument, no risk is discipline. Zillman '82: "[N]o citizen-control objectives counsel against the elimination of intramilitary FTCA remedies."[99] Fifth argument is irrational. Should reassess. *Michigan Law Review* says: "[C]ourts . . . simply redefined the limits of military discretion. In light of those developments, the reliance on Feres in deference to 'military autonomy' must be reconsidered."[100] Sixth argument does not justify defeat. That's Antin in 1980: "Although the military's emphasis on discipline and respect for authority is certainly understandable under wartime conditions, there is no justification for an inordinate emphasis upon protecting military discipline when events transpire which are not unique to military service."[101]

Seventh argument, he says, vote for the resolution today, and we need you to have to justify it today. On two, he says that . . . he says, assumes that it is unjustified. First of all, that's irrelevant. Second of all, courts, not administration. Second, doesn't justify it in peace. Third argument, does not warrant immunity. *Michigan Law Review* in '79: "There is a need for protecting military discipline. . . . Yet we have seen that these issues no longer completely bar judicial review."[102] Fourth argument, it's overextended. Too broad. Dawson in '82: ". . . *Feres'* protection of military discipline may be too broad, thus necessitating legislative examination."[103] This argument does not justify denial. Reed in '80: "Military discipline . . . has not evolved into a firm prerequisite for the application of intramilitary immunity and the resulting denial of recovery to military plaintiffs."[104]

He says, three, discipline is unique with us. Discipline is not key, right there. Second of all, doesn't justify denial up above. He says, military have now. Please group. First of all, [unintelligible]. First argument on courts say it's OK, is disproven with three case IAC on duty-to-warn. Second argument, we don't use courts; we use administration. He says, superior knowledge, but you do it with affirmative. One—he says, five and six—please group. We maintain this acting through military, and second of all, it ignores that you can cross-indemnify in the plan. Third, I argued up above. He says, seven, no equal protection violation, but we don't claim that. We claim day in court, and should hold the person responsible.

He says, right to know. First of all, we don't claim right to know is absolute. Second of all, it is not

[97] "Whether or not the 'effect of the maintenance of discipline' can somehow be attributed to *Feres, Brown* does not explain what are the effects which will result. Furthermore, the Court does not articulate how suits by a serviceman for torts committed by a civilian government employee, by a military member of a different branch of the service, or by a serviceman of a lower rank, will affect discipline." Cyze, p. 555.

[98] Donald Zillman, "Intramilitary Tort Law: Incidence to Service Meets Constitutional Tort," *North Carolina Law Review,* 60 (1982), 513.

[99] Zillman, p. 517.

[100] "Notes: From *Feres* to *Stencel,*" *Michigan Law Review,* (April 1979), 1117.

[101] Norman B. Antin, "Constitutional Tort Remedies: A Proposed Amendment to the Federal Tort Claims Act," *Connecticut Law Review,* (Spring 1980), 523.

[102] "Notes: From *Feres* to *Stencel,*" p. 1118.

[103] Dawson, "In Support of the *Feres* Doctrine and a Better Definition of 'Incident to Service'," *St. John's Law Review,* 56 (1982), 502.

[104] Michael Reed, "Jaffee v. United States: Feres Doctrine at the Cliff's Edge," *University of Pittsburgh Law Review,* 42 (1980), 121.

unique. The courts have already established that there's a right to know. Worthy of three court cases. Third, this is talking about courts, not administrative. Fourth, this is talking about compensation. Now, we claim compensation, not right to know. Fifth argument, we establish a failure to warn here, not a duty-to-warn. Seventh argument, it's not a constitutional right, and we don't establish it as a constitutional right in the plan.

Eighth and last argument is that we establish legislative right to know, which we do not, but rather a failure to warn which means you could sue.

Please go to (IV) collective noun. First of all, (1) no distinction. Bergen [Evans] says in '57: "Strictly speaking, a collective is a singular noun with a plural meaning," but it "is not clearly singular or clearly plural."[105] (2) doesn't alter meaning. Evans and Evans in '75: "A few mass nouns, such as *ash* and *ashes* . . . have both a singular and a plural form. . . . But it should be noticed that there is not the usual difference in meaning between the singular and plural form."[106]

(3) resolution usage does not mean collective. Epstein says, "Identifying which hazardous wastes . . . ,"[107] and he pluralizes, indicating you should do it.

(4) argument is verbage supports. (a) subpoint, "the" denotes singular. Evans in '57: "When not used in speaking of a unique thing, *the* means 'that particular one out of the lot of them.' "[108] (b) subpoint, "that" specifies. Evans '57: "When *that* qualifies a following noun . . . it is a demonstrative adjective."[109] (c) subpoint, parameters support. Define as *a* by-product. (5) argument, we meet. The government as the producer is legally responsible for all the hazardous waste of that producer.

(6) argument, best interpretation. Alternative wording. If they would want all producers to be legally hazardous that they would have read "injuries resulting from the disposal of hazardous waste be the legal responsibility of producers of those wastes.

He says, (VII) reasonability standard, but (1) why should we do this, and (2) why would it not be bad if we're reasonably in jurisdiction. He says, second, it is best if we use reasonability to determine best. He says, three, the rules of chess, but that's a backlash. Would not be from a final round transcript. Second argument here is that that's irrelevant. What you need to do is use the word 'jurisdiction' in this round. Third argument is you should use it as an instructional test, and we only need to be reasonable.

Export death. First of all, it talks about government to, but is not government. Second, it's irrelevant. It is not talking about hazardous waste injury here. We're talking about failure to warn. Third, there's no uniqueness here. Three court cases would have indicated. Would trigger. Also, clean-up evidence on case would have triggered. Fourth, no threshold, no indication we cause the net increase if they're doing it now. Fifth argument is—specific link, gives us the right to turn this thing in IAR if they ever do it.

Sixth and last argument, it's empirically not true. We've got three cases now indicating that if there was a motive they were shifted to you. That's to beat this empiricism burden to win.

On harm. First of all, it's the injured one that is injured now. The first card in IAC indicates that. Second, evidence is not specific to the affirmative. It's talking abut CBWs. Third, there's no disadvantage here, no indication why you should reject. Fourth argument, process is paramount. *University of Pennsylvania Law Review*—I'm sorry, Easterbrook in '82: "Several have argued that process is valuable in itself because it treats each person as an equal. . . . Such dignitary considerations are exceptionally important. . . ."[110]

Second argument, it is the essence of life. March '82: Outcomes are generally less significant . . . than process. Process is the meaning of life.[111]

Third, you vote for most freedom. Evans in '65: Fundamental . . . to judge all processes is that of freedom of individual choice.[112] Last argument is that it preserves life. That evidence comes from the *University of Pennsylvania Law Review:* "[F]reedom from absolute, arbitrary power is so necessary to, and closely joined with a man's preservation, that

[105] "Collective Nouns. Strictly speaking, a collective is a singular noun with a plural meaning. But the term is used loosely by many grammarians and may be applied to almost any noun that is not clearly singular or clearly plural." Bergen Evans and Cornelia Evans, *A Dictionary of Contemporary American Usage* (New York: Random House, 1957), p. 99.

[106] "Mass Nouns," in Evans and Evans, p. 99.

[107] "Identifying Hazardous Wastes. Identifying which hazardous wastes are being released or threatened to be released into the environment will require access to technical data." Samuel S. Epstein, Lester O. Brown, and Carl Pope, *Hazardous Waste in America* (San Francisco, Calif.: Sierra Club Books, 1982), p. 283.

[108] "The," in Evans and Evans, p. 506.

[109] "That," in Evans and Evans, p. 504.

[110] Frank H. Easterbrook, "Substance and Due Process," *1982 Supreme Court Review* (Chicago, Ill.: The University of Chicago Press, 1982), p. 115.

[111] "Outcomes are generally less significant—both behaviorally and ethically—than process. It is the process that gives meaning to life, and meaning is the core of life." James G. March, "Theories of Choice and Making Decisions," *Society,* November/December, p. 38.

[112] Source indicated: Evans, 1965, p. 22.

he cannot part with it but by what forfeits his preservation and life together."[113]

(DA II) Spending, please. First argument, (1) there's no increase in liability. Antin in 1980: "[P]artial elimination of sovereign immunity will facilitate nonstatutory judicial review of Federal administrative action without exposing the Government to new liability. . . ."[114]

Second, we certainly have long term—(2) this would be a long term increase. No increase in the problem is short term causing disad.

In terms of (3) there's enough money now, mounts said in '78: If the bill were passed today, it would be approximately $400,000. It would be enough to go through fiscal year 1984.[115]

Fourth argument, (4) it justifies the resolution now. That's all we have to do. We have enough money.

Fifth argument, is that (5) insignificant money sought. Senator Hatch in '82: These veterans say "that the money is needed for their victims is not large. They are trying not so much to get money, but to get justice."[116]

Sixth argument, is (6) this isn't the problem. Congress rejected when they consider of the passage of the FTCA.

Seventh argument is (7) no threshold. The increase would have to be in the future, indicating it would not happen.

Eighth argument is (8) no precedent established here. That evidence comes from Jordon in '79: "We would not be setting precedent in permitting an open-ended service connection for those disabilities that we know to be the result of radiation exposure."[117]

Ninth argument is (9) his evidence—next argument, I'm sorry, is that their evidence does not apply. That's talking about open ended compensation processes. We do not have open ended compensation. Tenth argument, (10) perception is they're going to pass a bill. *Congressional Quarterly* in '84: "The House by voice vote Jan. 30 passed a bill (HR 1961) authorizing disability compensation benefits for Vietnam-era veterans who suffer from three diseases. . . ."[118]

Eleventh argument is (11) there's no political pressure with increase. Pfau in '81: "[A] more limited approach, and the claims for its efficacy, can produce quiescence, which would underpin the support for other seemingly non-competitive alternatives."[119] The twelfth argument is historically invalidated—validated with Bikini, etc.

On the impact, first of all, (1) there's no increase in interest rates. That is what the *U.S. News & World Report* says in '84: " 'Big deficits create high interest rates.' As it turns out, that isn't true."[120]

Second argument here is that (2) there's no down payment as Kirschter says in '84: "In essence, the President's deficit reduction plan consists of nothing more than rhetorical exhortation."[121] Third argument is (3) there's no bipartisan agreement. *Boston Globe* in '84: "As things stand now, the President's language in the budget message would appear to rule out a bipartisan approach to the deficit problem. Instead, the stage appears set for . . . warfare."[122]

Fourth argument, (4) a Democratic coalition would break. *Wall Street Journal* says in '84: "[T]he Democrats are in no mood for bipartisanship. The next question is whether they are in the mood for anything that would bring the budget under control."[123] In the sad spirit of things, the prospect seems to be for no money down.

[113] John Locke quoted in Richard B. Saphire, "Specifying Due Process Values: Toward a More Responsive Approach to Procedural Protection," *University of Pennsylvania Law Review,* (November 1978), 118.

[114] Antin, p. 509.

[115] "Let's say if the bill were passed today, it would be approximately half of the fiscal year. We would look at an increase of perhaps $300,000 to $400,000 during this fiscal year, as the worst case. And even if that occurred, we have sufficient funds in our current appropriation to take care of that, and we also have good enough lead time now to be able to go to fiscal year 1984 and make appropriate adjustment for it." James A. Mounts, "Military Claims Amendment," Hearing before the subcommittee on Administrative Law and Governmental Relations of the Committee on the Judiciary, House of Representatives, Ninety-eighth Congress First Session, on H.R. 597, Military Claims Amendment, March 23, 1983, Serial No. 5 (Washington, D.C.: U.S. Government Printing Office, 1983), p. 74.

[116] Orrin G. Hatch, "Radiation Exposure Compensation Act of 1981—Part 2," Hearing before the Committee on Labor and Human Resources, United States Senate, Ninety-Seventh Congress, Second Session, on S. 1483, April 8, 1982 (Washington, D.C.: U.S. Government Printing Office, 1982), p. 160.

[117] Robert Jordon, "Veterans' Claims for Disabilities from Nuclear Weapons Testing," Hearing before the Committee on Veterans' Affairs, United States Senate, Ninety-Sixth Congress, First Session, June 20, 1979 (Washington, D.C.: United States Government Printing Office, 1979), p. 223.

[118] "House Approves Agent Orange Disability Pay," *Congressional Quarterly Weekly Report,* 4 February 1984, p. 229.

[119] Michael Pfau, "The Present System Revisited Part Two: Policy Interrelationships," *Journal of the American Forensic Association,* 17 (Winter 1981), 153.

[120] Walter Wriston, " 'A 50-50 Chance' Business Will Sputter in '84," *U.S. News & World Report,* 20 February 1984, p. 53.

[121] Dick Kirschten, "Blueprint for a Campaign," *National Journal,* 4 February 1984, p. 215.

[122] Thomas Oliphant, "Reagan Plans $925b Budget," *The Boston Globe,* 1 February 1984, p. 13.

[123] "Review and Outlook; No Money Down," *Wall Street Journal,* 9 February 1984, p. 26.

Fifth argument is that (5) agreements are irrelevant. *U.S. News* says in '84: "Even if . . . Reagan's call . . . for a bipartisan 'down payment' on deficit reduction is successful, that won't change the picture much. The 100 billion dollars the President wants to shave from the deficit over the next three years . . . is merely a ripple in the sea of red ink that now is engulfing the nation."[124]

Sixth argument is that—(6) turn, and you need to stop. Holmes says in 1984: Congress needs to get it going before it can muster the political will necessary to get serious about spending cuts.[125]

Seventh argument is that (7) it will overheat. A subpoint, it will occur. *U.S. News and World Report:* " 'What you're getting now is the stimulative effects of all of the elements of the budget—the defense buildup, the tax cuts—that propel an economy forward.' "[126] B, subpoint, will increase interest rates. Herman in '84: "[I]f the economy continues to expand at a rapid clip, the risk of a rise in interest rates 'obviously exists.' "[127]

Eighth argument is (8) not decrease in the economy. Brownstein in '84: "Deficits should be reduced, George Ball said, 'but they are not insupportable. As a practical matter, they are not going to capsize the economy.' "[128]

Please go to discipline. Overview on the counterplan. First of all, it's not competitive, you could ban courts and still go through the MCA. Second of all it is unreasonable. You could ban all turnarounds to disads. Third, it's a disad. There'd be tyranny without access to a forum. Fourth, it's illogical. Democracy presupposes three branches. Hence, you shouldn't uphold. Fifth argument, presumption against. Judicial system has historically existed. Sixth argument, it's irrelevant. Courts still prove the disad is not unique—use now thereby—taking out the reasons that we would cause. Seventh, is repugnant. Means you ban rights in order to get esoteric advantages. Eighth, case is a priori. We argue process is paramount. Ninth argument, it is short term advantage. You should have access and enough to check tyranny. Tenth argument is a turn—it denies due process. Evidence comes from Haynes [Shea] in 1975: " 'The right to a prior hearing' before governmental deprivation of life, liberty, property is recognized as the 'fundamental requisite' of due process."[129] The twelfth argument is that it would be unconstitutional, would mean you'd deny people their property without due process, and hence would be void. Thirteenth argument is to reverse benefits for affirmative, so we could ban turns to our positions. Fourteenth, no defense of constitutionality—1NC position presupposes policy-making. Fifteenth argument is the widespread discretion for affirmative; we can amend our plan, and allow it to going. Sixteenth argument is the turn argument, and that is the VA denies due process. Poteet in '79: "Instructions from the VA . . . are vague and incomplete. . . . [T]his constitutes a clear and unmistakable error denying the veteran due process."[130] Last argument is the turn, it denies constitutional remedies. Donaldson says in '82: These conclusions . . . the VBA provided swift, efficient remedy . . . leave these unconstitutional torts . . . infringement for [unintelligible].[131]

(DAI) Turn to discipline please. First of all (1) talks about litigation, not MCA. Second of all, (2) proves the disad is not unique. Third, (3) talking

[124] Monroe W. Karmin and Robert J. Morse, "Drowning in Debt," *U.S. News and World Report,* 13 February 1984, p. 18.

[125] "Senate Finance Committee Chairman Robert Dole (R-Kans) notes that a deadline facing the deficit cutters will occur in May, when legislation extending the temporary debt ceiling comes up for renewal. Dole warns that unless progress on the deficit is apparent, there may not be enough votes in the Senate to pass the extension. If so, the government would not be able to pay its bills. That could turn out to be the crisis Congress needs before it can muster the political will to get serious about spending cuts." Peter A. Holmes, "Two Step Path to Budget Control," *Nations Business,* March 1984, p. 27.

[126] Milton Hudson quoted in Karmin and Morse, p. 19.

[127] Paul Volcker quoted in Tom Herman and Edward P. Foldesay, "Bond Prices, in Sluggish Trading, End Little Changed on Fears of Higher Rates," *Wall Street Journal,* 1 March 1984, p. 44.

[128] George Ball quoted in Ronald Brownstein, "Republicans and Democrats Troop to Wall Street for Money and Support," *National Journal,* 4 February 1984, p. 214.

[129] Richard J. Shea, "Constitutional Law—The Anti-Injunction Act—Due Process Considerations where IRS Actions Threaten First Amendment Liberties—Bob Jones University v. Simon; Alexander v. "Americans United, Inc.," *Boston College Industrial and Commercial Law Review,* (January 1975), 282.

[130] Al Poteet, "Veterans' Claims for Disabilities from Nuclear Weapons Testing," p. 226.

[131] "The Veterans Benefits Act provides a comprehensive disability retirement system for servicemen injured in the line of duty and a related system of benefits for veterans and their dependents. In the *Feres* decision, the Supreme Court referred to these statutory provisions as 'systems of simple, certain and uniform compensation for the injuries or death of those in the Armed Forces.' And in the *Stencel* case, the court emphasized that this type of compensation scheme 'serves a dual purpose, it not only provides a swift, efficient remedy for injured servicemen, but also clothes the Government in the "protective mantle . . . of limitation-of-liability provisions." ' However, these conclusions leave a void of uncompensated torts stemming from infringements of military members' constitutional rights because this no fault statutory scheme does not address violations of constitutional rights unaccompanied by any personal injury defined as 'disabling' under the applicable Veteran's Administration regulations." Donaldson, pp. 197–8.

about criminal, does not compare to our case. Fourth, (4) it does not affect [unintelligible]. We talked about failure to warn here, not increase. Fifth argument is (5) indemnification in the plan takes out. Sixth argument, (6) they cite courts which conclude affirmative. Seventh argument, (7) case outweighs. Evidence is from Milford in 1982: "In a democracy we have far more to fear from the lack of military accountability than from the lack of military discipline. . . ."[132] Next argument is (8) no decrease in discipline. Lehmann says in '82: "Subjecting the military to diverse standards of care and liability would not interfere with the performance of its vital function because the relationship between the claimant and the United States. . . ."[133] Next argument is the (9) turn, courts decrease discipline. Milford in '82: "A second argument, and the one that has been at the core of all later decisions in the area, is the belief that review by civilian courts would undermine discipline."[134] Next argument is (10) irrational. Lehmann in '82: "Actions brought by civilians or off-duty servicemen . . . may involve second-guessing military orders. . . . Yet, these actions have never been thought to sufficiently threaten military discipline so as to warrant their dismissal."[135] Next argument, (11) turn—increase discipline. *Michigan Law Review* in '81: "The exercise of authority in a manner consistent with both military interests and personal rights promotes discipline more effectively than irrational authoritarianism."[136] Next argument, (12) does not justify immunity. Whalen in '82: " '[M]ilitary discipline' does not offer a cogent reason to bar servicemen's actions except in a limited number of cases."[137]

Next argument is, (13) turn. We deter torts. *Michigan Law Review* in '81: "Civil damages are intended . . . to deter tort feasors from engaging repeatedly in such conduct. Official immunity may undermine these fundamental goals."[138] Next argument, (14) is turn—we get increased AVF efficiency. Broudy in '82: "If the veterans were treated with the proper respect and entitlements . . . it would encourage more young men to join the military services, which would of course strengthen our military."[139] Next argument is (15) turn, the VA has greater risk. Stewart and Lieberman in 1982: "The inadequacy of the health-care system . . . [of the VA] has a negative impact on morale. . . . [I]ts gross shortage of capability makes it largely incapable of responding to a sudden mobilization requirement."[140] Next argument, (16) it's not unique. (a) subpoint, officers liable now. Burgess says in 1980: "If a military official is unable to sustain the burden of proving he acted reasonably and in good faith, he will be held liable for damages."[141] (b) subpoint, the courts are reviewing now. Hislop-Brumfield in '83: "[T]he courts have infringed on military autonomy when the rights of servicemen were receiving less protection than a court would provide and the judicial infringement on military discipline and autonomy was not great."[142] Next argument in here is that—(c) subpoint, FTCA encourages such suits. Chiu in '82: "[S]tatutory military policy encourage complaints about and redress of intramilitary wrongs."[143] Next argument is (17) there's no link. Extending coverage would not decrease. Reed said in 1980: "[C]ourts have consistently highlighted the fact that to allow recovery could have no detrimental effect on military discipline."[144] Next argument, (18) proves case legitimacy. Dawson in '82: "[O]ne district court" stated "that the incident to service inquiry should be limited to whether the particular suit would undermine discipline. . . . [T]his approach has not gained general acceptance. Indeed, if disruption of military discipline were the only criterion, it is submitted that the *Feres* plaintiffs may very well have recovered."[145] Next argument, (18) no value absent the resolution. Claudine Schneider says in 1982: I certainly appreciate . . . threat to order and discipline. Neither of these are preserved or strengthened by turning a blind eye to negligence and errors.[146]

[132] Lewis M. Milford and Ronald Simon, "Is Uncle Sam Toying with Veterans?" *Clearinghouse Review,* August/September 1982, p. 318.

[133] Richard Lehman, "The Effect of the *Feres* Doctrine on Tort Actions against the United States by Family Members of Servicemen," *Fordam Law Review,* (May 1982), 1266.

[134] Milford and Simon, p. 317.

[135] Lehman, p. 1265.

[136] "Intramilitary Immunity and Constitutional Torts," *Michigan Law Review,* (December 1981), 328.

[137] Thomas J. Whalen, "*Feres* and *Stencel* Revisited: Liability of the United States for Contribution and Indemnity in Cases Involving Servicemen," *The Forum* (Fall 1982), 113.

[138] "Intramilitary Immunity and Constitutional Torts," pp. 314–5.

[139] Alice P. Broudy quoted in "Radiation Exposure Compensation act of 1981—Part 2," Hearing before the Committee on Labor and Human Resources, United States Senate, Ninety-seventh Congress, Second Session, on S. 1483, Salt Lake City, Utah, April 8, 1982 (Washington, D.C.: U.S. Government Printing Office, 1982), p. 45.

[140] Jim Stewart and Paul Lieberman quoted in "The Feres Doctrine as It Relates to Private Claims," Hearing before the Subcommittee on Agency Administration of the Committee on the Judiciary, United States Senate Ninety-Seventh Congress. Second Congress, on the Feres Doctrine as it Relates to Private Claims, April 14, 1982, Serial No. J-97-110 (Washington, D.C.: U.S. Government Printing Office, 1982), p. 41.

[141] Gail M. Burgess, "Official Immunity and Civil Liability for Constitutional Torts Committed by Military Commanders after *Butz v.* Economou," *Military Law Review,* (Summer 1980), 54.

[142] Hislop-Brumfield, p. 350.

[143] Chiu, pp. 278–9.

[144] Reed, p. 121.

[145] Dawson, p. 508.

[146] "I certainly appreciate that allowing for law suits within the military can present a threat to order

Please go to (IV) topicality. That is, standards. A.subpoint. Only need to be reasonable. Epstein says in 1982: "The legal system regulates many formal relationships . . . between the public and those who . . . dispose of hazardous wastes. One of the most important concepts governing these . . . is 'reasonableness'."[147] B.subpoint, he says, no best definition. Alexander in '69: "It is a mistake to think of definitions as being either right or wrong, provable or disprovable."[148] C.subpoint, discretion is necessary. *Roberts Rules of Order:* The wise presiding officer will never rule an amendment out of order as not germane unless he is absolutely sure he is right.[149] Two, judicial model. *Golden v. City of Oakland* says, Interpretation of statutes . . . the courts . . . to interpret . . . reasonable.[150] D.subpoint, agencies should get deference. Smith and Guenther in 1981: "The United States Supreme Court has ruled that an agency's interpretation of the statutes it administers deserves great respect and should be followed unless there are compelling indications it is wrong, especially when this interpretation is contemporaneous with the statute it administers."[151] English scholars concur. Ullah in 1981: "One way of expanding our knowledge of words is by taking a word one step beyond its generally recognized meaning."[152] Meaning that it would be better if you distorted these. Hall in 1981—sorry.

and discipline. Neither of these, however, are preserved or strengthened by turning a blind eye to negligence and errors. It would be a mistake to allow ourselves to hide behind an abstract concept and not deal with a problem that is apparently very real." Claudine Schneider quoted in "The Feres Doctrine As It Relates to Private Claims," p. 7.

[147] Epstein, p. 258.

[148] Hubert G. Alexander, *Meaning in Language* (Glenview, Ill.: Scott, Foresman and Company, 1969), p. 113.

[149] "There are borderline cases where a presiding officer will find it difficult to judge the germaneness of an amendment. Whenever in doubt he should admit the amendment or, in important cases, refer the decision to the assembly." Henry M. Robert, *Robert's Rules of Order Newly Revised* (Glenview, Ill.: Scott, Foresman and Company, 1970), p. 115.

[150] "Interpretation of Statutes is an exercise of judicial power, and it is the duty of courts, within framework of statutes, to interpret them so as to make them workable and reasonable," Golden v. City of Oakland 49 Cal. App. 3d 284, *West's California Reporter,* Vol. 122 (St. Paul, Minn.: West Publishing Company, 1975), p. 400.

[151] Patrick Smith and Jerry D. Guenther, "Notes: Environmental Law: Protecting Clean Air; The Authority of Indian Governments to Regulate Reservation Airsheds," *American Indian Law Review,* 9 (1981), 94.

[152] Rena Ullah, "Letters to the Editor," *New York Times Magazine,* 1 March 1981, p. 94.

Cross-Examination:
Mark Koulogeorge questioning Cindy Leiferman

Koulogeorge: To describe a characteristic about the ocean, would you agree that they would use a singular term, the singular, as the verb? Leiferman: No. Koulogeorge: Could you say, the ocean are "waterfull"? Leiferman: You could say oceans are . . . Koulogeorge: Oceans, right. So when you add an "s" it becomes a different, it requires a different verb than when you had . . . Leiferman: Well, it depends on what the preceding . . . Koulogeorge: Why? Wait, let's look at "ocean are waterfull." Leiferman: There's a difference here. Koulogeorge: What is the difference? Leiferman: "Ocean" does talk about one collective body. Hazardous waste refers to one collective body. Hazardous wastes, you know, that means that there is plural. If they wanted you to have hazardous waste, they mean include it all like you'd include nuclear waste. Koulogeorge: Where do we . . . but the topic does not have an "s," correct? Leiferman: Exactly, which means that only have to do all of the waste you specify, not all waste. Koulogeorge: Why? Where do you read into the topic that it is all of the waste that the affirmative specifies. Leiferman: Because if it was different it would have said those hazardous wastes . . . Koulogeorge: Wait, wait a second, those hazardous wastes would require plural. It wouldn't require that you specify one, correct? Leiferman: That's exactly the argument. Koulogeorge: How can you specify one waste? Leiferman: Because like if I say this is a hazardous waste, I'm saying this pile of it. Koulogeorge: This. OK.

Koulogeorge: Let's talk about your spending answers. Can you explain your turnaround on the bottom, please. Leiferman: I'm sorry, where are you at? Koulogeorge: Spending. Leiferman: Yeh, talk about overheating now, and the only way to stop it is for acts to spend now. Koulogeorge: Wait. When you . . . Leiferman: No, right now. Koulogeorge: The Government is overheating, so it increases its spending. Doesn't that raise aggregate demand? Leiferman: No, you have increase in spending to check the overheating. Otherwise . . . Koulogeorge: How can increased spending check—overheating means the economy is being strained, correct? Leiferman: No, overheating means it's growing way too fast. Koulogeorge: Right, its being strained. There are inflationary pressures. Is that correct, or not? Leiferman: Man, I don't know. I'm really bad. I don't know that much about—Mark says, yeh. Koulogeorge: OK, so if prices are getting real high, you spend more, you bid up prices more correct? Leiferman: Now, if the government. . . Koulogeorge: All right. Now tell me this? We have five apples and five . . . Leiferman: No, that's the . . . Koulogeorge: You spend more, demand goes up, price goes up, right, Ms. Freedman? [Laughter] Let me see all the evidence.

Second Negative Constructive:
Leonard Gail, Dartmouth

We're at then the twelfth response, the counterplan is unconstitutional. [Unintelligible] is all you make. The [unintelligible] response over [unintelligible] is the important thing. It argued that [unintelligible] still can be assigned in administrative tribunals, and that is their term which gives us the right-to-know on the case. Their argument here is that the administrative tribunal, the MCA would be guaranteed—RVA would be nonconstitutional right which proves that their MCA can grant it, the same exact thing which an administrative tribunal will [unintelligible]. Group this point together. First of all, extend her response on the disad is rational. They should be suing now. That empirically denies the disad. Take these arguments at their face value. That is empirically denied.

Two subpoint, the disad is not true. Terrible. There's no harm. There's no invasion of Western Europe. They never argue any type of [unintelligible]. I think that's fundamental. The third response is it's empirically denied again. Bring up the argument that officers are suing now. This is the [unintelligible] doctrine and that is not hurting discipline. There is no effect on discipline at all.

OK. Now, [unintelligible] (IV) standards. All these are irrelevant to the grammar standards we set up. All these reasonable, best definition, assume some level of grammar which I will beat. A. subpoint, they [unintelligible] be reasonable. First of all, drop the [unintelligible], argument, [unintelligible], etc.

Second subpoint, it's the role of the [unintelligible]. We deal with that on the other side. B. subpoint, no best definition. First of all, there can be a better definition, and the way you should determine that is by comparing the two. The two subpoint issues determine what is better by grammar, and I'll explain after a while that grammar is how you determine. A. subpoint—or I'll explain it here. Important to interpretation. *Corpus Juris Secundum* explains: "The ordinary rules of grammar will be applied for the purpose of ascertaining the meaning of a statute. . . ."[153] McNeece versus Wood: Courts take judicial notice of the following facts: The true signification of all English words and phrases, and of all legal expressions.[154]

B. subpoint, when you're in doubt about things, viz., reasonability, best definition, you vote on grammar. *Corpus Juris Secundum* explains in '53: "Such rules of grammar may, however, influence a doubtful case and are controlling when there is nothing in the statute not in accord with them."[155]

C. subpoint, we should assume that framers understood grammar rules. They continue: The legislative power, in enacting a law, is presumed to have understood the ordinary and elementary rules of construction of the English language, and the court must therefore construe the law according to the context and approved usage. . . .[156]

D. subpoint, grammar is Key to determination of intent. *Corpus Juris* continues: "The legislature is presumed to know the meaning of words and rules of grammar. . . "[157] *Iowa-Illinois Gas* in 1950: Quoting another case, "It is also a well-recognized rule of construction that legislative intention is to be deduced from the language used, and the language is to be construed according to its plain and ordinary meaning."[158]

E. subpoint, reading in ambiguity is unreasonable. *Corpus Juris* explains in '53: "Where context of words in act did not make it apparent that a different meaning was intended from that clearly conveyed by the words when construed according to the ordinary rules of grammar, and in order of grammatical arrangement in which they were placed in the act, there was neither justification nor excuse for reading into the act an ambiguity in order to make the act mean otherwise than what any layman acquainted with the ordinary rules of grammar must naturally understand it to mean."[159] The point is, there's no ambiguity if you look at grammar rules. Those are a priori, and we win those on the other side.

Please group three to E. together on those things. First of all, they assume some type of legislative paradigm. Well, lives are at stake. There should be no absorption. Two subpoint, you don't look at debate implications. We explained that above. Third subpoint is, you must look at grammar a priori which we explained above. The fourth is [unintelligible] topicality is not a voting issue. There's a rule in the NDT. You need—arguing topicality is educational, and you know, to be limited to the resolution, and take a priori jurisdiction, and all those various reasons.

F. subpoint, went beyond the distinction is OK.

[153] "Rules of Grammar," *Corpus Juris Secundum,* Vol. 82 (Brooklyn, N.Y.: The American Law Book Co., 1953), p. 682.
[154] Source indicated: McNeece v. Wood, Cal 260 P, p. 818.

[155] "Rules of Grammar," p. 683.
[156] "Rules of Grammar," p. 682.
[157] "Rules of Grammar," p. 682.
[158] Quote is from the case of Jefferson County Farm Bureau v. Sherman, 208 Iowa 614, 226 N.W. 182 and referred to in the case of Meredith Publishing Company v. Iowa Security Commission, 232 Iowa 666, 6 N.W. 2d 614, speaking of the well-defined canons of statutory construction. Both are cited in Iowa-Illinois Gas and Electric Company et al. v. City of Bettendorf et al., 41 N.W. 2d 1, *North Western Reporter,* Second Series, Vol. 41 (St. Paul, Minn.: West Publishing Company, 1950), p. 4.
[159] "Rules of Grammar," p. 682.

That is explained above. That is not the rule of the NDT, and should not be for its debate implications.

Mark's argument, reasonability standard A. subpoint, defacto delimits. Group her arguments together. First of all, [unintelligible] do not want her to. Each [unintelligible] in isolation doesn't [unintelligible]. B subpoint, the rule is best. We argue the bold rule. Group her arguments together. She clearly misses the argument that when they chose affirmative, they knew about the rule, and we would have done the same.

B. subpoint, backlash. She says, it's not [unintelligible]. She asserts the argument would be the same; in fact it would be magnified. Because it would be in the transcript, change would be in print. Ignore. The next response is irrelevant to act. This is not true. He should look at the implications, and that's why you have to look then. She says it's a threshold issue which proves our point. You have to meet minimum grammar standards before you can ever cross the threshold.

Mass noun. We will run intellectual circles around them here. The first response is no distinction. This evidence is awful. First of all, it refers to collective nouns, and all of our arguments in the first negative draw a distinction between mass and collective. Collective nouns are "army" and "committee," whereas mass nouns are "food" and "hazardous waste," things that are indistinguishable, and that's all that's in the first negative's cards.

[Unintelligible]. The evidence says "may." I'm not making the Stanford-type argument that evidence says "may." My point here is merely that "may" means it depends on the construction in the sentence, and that's why all of our arguments apply. It assumes the grammar. It assumes the form of the verb. All that is clear, and all of our rules apply.

Third, [unintelligible] is that you have to look at the construction to determine the meaning. This evidence is in the vernacular. What does this mean? I argue you have to look at context.

Two subpoint, doesn't alter meaning. Get a look at this evidence. A few mass nouns such as [unintelligible] and [unintelligible] have both singular and plural meanings. What in the world does that mean? First of all, it merely says, you know, "may" once again which depends on construction which we explain above.

·Two subpoint is that it doesn't give you the construction. I would say those arguments you have not [unintelligible] where it's used as the subject, not where it's using a mass noun as a direct object modifying a mass noun.

The third response is it's [unintelligible] in the construction of the resolution, and the fourth response is it assumes the plurality—would have said hazardous waste which I explain above.

They say three, resolution didn't mean collective. This argument is basically if they want the responsibility for all waste they would have said waste. First of all, that would have allowed cases that would have just gone to hazardous waste, and you should have been doing more than one hazardous waste. You'd have made legal responsibility for waste. That would have been plural. So you know, that doesn't cut it.

Two subpoint is in text is irrelevant. You have to look at the resolution on its face, and the way you do that is by looking at the grammatical construction.

Third subpoint once again it is a collective noun which is completely irrelevant.

The fourth response here is [unintelligible] are not animals. Epstein talks about hazardous waste are being responsed which is hazardous waste as the subject, but hazardous waste with a direct object and an indefinite article as the grammar as rules state in first negative means each and every which I will explain below.

Four. Verbal usage. A. "The" denotes [unintelligible]. First of all, "the" is not in front of hazardous waste. Seems clear to me. Two, evidence doesn't apply. The evidence merely says when [unintelligible] speaking of a unique thing, "the" means that particular one out of a lot of them. That's merely saying the ocean is red when you point and you're not using it in speaking and you say the ocean is red, but if you say the oceans are wet, you mean each and every ocean. Furthermore, that's not using the word "the" in grammatical construction as it is in the topic where the disposal, "the" is in front of a mass noun, and when "the" is in front of a mass noun it means each and every disposal. OK. OK. And that's the third—I narrow his construction. All our standards apply.

B. subpoint. Would have said; well, that specifies. That waste equals all [unintelligible]. First of all, "that" does not make waste a count noun. Ware explains in '75: "What needs to be clear is that by referring to this water and that water we have not thereby referred to countables. We cannot say how many waters we have referred to."[160]

Two subpoint, "that" is synonymous with hazardous, and we only argue the plan must cover all hazardous waste.

Third response, could not say "those" waste; mass nouns take the singular which is the essence of our argument. Jespersen in '33: The singular is used with most mass words.[161] So, all their arguments are [unintelligible].

[160] Ware, p. 388.

[161] "The singular without any article is used with mass words—material and immaterial." Otto Jespersen, *Essentials of English Grammar* (University: University of Alabama Press, 1933), p. 213.

C. Parameter. This is irrelevant. First of all, mass nouns are in the singular form and use no article; thus the parameter proves our argument that hazardous waste is a count noun. Jespersen explains: "The singular without any article is used with mass words. . ."[162] A hazardous waste would mean one, but since they say, without anything in front of it, hazardous waste is, you mean each and every hazardous waste. You didn't say a hazardous waste was, you know, that would be different, but they say hazardous waste is. That proves our point.

Two subpoint is parameters often define words in the singular. The public utility topics say all public utilities are topic and defines public utility in the parameter.

Third response is grammar is secondary to the topic which is rather ambiguous. And the fourth response is you're defining a word. You always do that in the singular.

The fifth response is all they can hope for, that they are legal responsibility. The government is the producer of the—They can pick the producer and make them responsible for all waste produced by that producer. This is wrong. First of all is, they have to do each and every. It is quality argument as well as quantity. That have to do each and every type of hazardous waste, and the government does not produce each and every type of hazardous waste. Hence, they don't meet each and every.

The two subpoint is look at the debate cases. This delimits. Pick the producer in Georgia, and make him legally responsible.

The third response is this is a justification argument. It merely means that the government should be responsible on other things.

The fourth response is government must be responsible for all waste then. You can pick the producer, but that would mean the producer would have to be responsible for each and every waste. It doesn't say its disposal, so the government according to that standard would have to be responsible for each and every waste ever produced anywhere in the United States, and clearly this plan doesn't meet it, and that's why that's a bad word.

Sixth response, alternative wording. First of all, they didn't need to use alternative wording. Mass noun means all. Two subpoint would have said "a" hazardous waste if they didn't mean all. Third subpoint, would have said some hazardous waste if they didn't mean all. Jespersen explains in '33: "*Some* as used with a mass-word indicates an unknown or unspecified quantity. . ."[163]

(DAI) Disad—If I can find it—judicial activist. A. subpoint, plan increases confidence. First of all by guaranteeing, by increasing [unintelligible]. Jaffee explains in '81: "That any judicial tribunal in the world, in the last fifth of this dismal century, would choose to place a class of persons outside the protection against human rights violations provided by the admonitory law of intentional torts is surprising. That it should be an American court will dismay persons the world over concerned with human rights and will embarrass our Government."[164] This ripples as explained on the discipline argument. More evidence comes from Schuck in '83: "The court's institutional power—its capacity to further the goals of the legal system by influencing the behavior and value of other participants—depends not only upon the acceptance of its rights declarations but upon the credibility of its sanctions."[165]

Two subpoint, it needs to ripple. I explain that above. You need a change as Burger explains in '82: "The public opinion polls indicate that people still have confidence in the judicial function, both federal and state. But unless we change things, we're not going to be able to maintain the public's confidence."[166]

The B. subpoint is, this leads to activism. All the above evidence indicates. *National Review* explains in '82: "Every time a court creates a new constitutional right against government or expands, without warrant, an old one, the constitutional freedom of citizens to control their lives is diminished."[167] Nonet and Selznick explain in 1978: "[E]very legal order [of courts] has a repressive potential because it is always at some point bound to the status quo and, in offering a mantle of authority, makes power more effective."[168] The argument is, is that currently people are going uncompensated in courts. When you take those out of court even if you don't guarantee them money, you don't make the courts look bad, increasing confidence in the courts, causing them to be activist which is bad.

Cross Examination:
Cindy Lieferman questioning Leonard Gail

Lieferman: Are the parameters binding? Gail: No. Lieferman: No. So, why should you look for the framers' intent then? Gail: You shouldn't. Lieferman-

[162] Jespersen, p. 213.
[163] Jespersen, p. 180.

[164] Jaffee v. United States, p. 1250.
[165] Peter H. Schuck, *Suing Government: Citizens Remedies for Official Wrongs* (New Haven and London: Yale University Press, 1983), p. 26.
[166] Warren E. Burger, "Unclogging the Courts—Chief Justice Speaks Out," *U. S. News & World Report,* 22 February 1982, p. 36.
[167] Robert Bork, "The Struggle Over the Role of the Court," *National Review,* 17 September 1982, p. 1139.
[168] Phillipe Nonet and Phillip Selznick, *Law and Society in Transition: Toward Responsive Law* (New York: Octagon Books, 1978), p. 29.

man: You shouldn't ever look at the intent? Gail: No. Lieferman: OK.

So, how do you resolve whether or not. . . Gail: Grammar rules. Lieferman: Just grammar rules? What if deferring to an interpretation would give you precision in that grammar rule? Gail: It wouldn't. It would give you what they supposedly meant. It would tell you nothing about the grammatical construction. Lieferman: Now, when someone defines a clause, like when we're reading from these people that define what. . . Gail: They may be defining it incorrectly grammatically. Lieferman: Well, then we can't presuppose that they're grammatically correct when they give definitions either, right? Gail: That's not true. Well, I guess that is fairly true, but that doesn't answer the argument that you should be debating the resolution as it is. Gail: Well, then why should the analysis of this guy in the book that you're quoting be now this grammarian is even grammatically correct? Gail: What? Lieferman: Well, if you can't look at the intent and you're not sure if they used grammar correctly. . . Gail: You look at the examples he uses. Lieferman: But how do we know that the examples you used or the evidence you cite. . . Gail: Because they're parallel construction which your evidence isn't. Lieferman: Then why aren't the parameters binding, if it is parallel construction? Gail: How in the world is that relevant? Parallel construction is. . . Lieferman: That doesn't matter, Lenny, I want you to explain why the parameters wouldn't be binding on parallel construction. Gail: Parallel construction is a parallel example of a similar sentence grammatically. I go home. He goes home. Is parallel construction. Lieferman: That means that if the two are the same, you change one word. That's all that parallel functions means. Gail: No, it means the same grammatical construct. We want parallel construction when you come up with an example of a mass noun modifying a mass noun. Lieferman: Why should this card—Ware—I think his name is Ware. I don't know, Ward, somebody. I don't know. Gail: Which card? Lieferman: This card I'm going to read to you right now. This guy is not a grammarian. How do we know that he is using that in the right context. Gail: What makes you think he's not a grammarian? Lieferman: Well, it says he's from the University of Calgary. Gail: That's because he's a professor of English there. Lieferman: Now, why would that give more credence than our professor of English at different. . . Gail: I think for starters your evidence was talking about collective nouns, not mass nouns. Second of all, you don't know why your evidence says that, and third of all you've got a class. Lieferman: All it says is "what needs to be clear is that by referring to this water and that water we have not thereby referred to countables." I mean that doesn't talk about collective versus mass. Gail: It is saying "water" is a mass noun. When you say "that water," you can mean the plural, all water, each and every water by using the singular. You gotta get down the grammar rules here in order to truly comprehend the argument.

First Negative Rebuttal:
Mark Koulogeorge, Dartmouth

(DAII) Spending. They have dropped all the evidence saying political snowball and other people make the claim, so the fact that they increase the compensation, it gets me the big kick getting to the disad.

She argues, One, no increase in liability. First of all, no they must spend. Their evidence on the third argument of all proves that. That's the way they get their advantage, because it's compensation. Two subpoint, you spur other groups. All my evidence takes out all their arguments. His evidence [unintelligible] specific is from late 1983. It is this the reason you should not do it right now, especially once the new pressures give it to you. She argues, too long term. No, you must be a spending program now. They must still appropriate which breaks the budget talks. Two, subpoint, Reagan and congressional perception are still there. Reagan does not want to increase the dole amount, and this is exactly what the plan is, a dole out to these people, the servicemen, which they do not be compensated. Three subpoint, it still gets you the other group which we'll win below.

He argues 400,000. First of all, that's not true in fiscal year '85. That might have been true in fiscal year '84, and that assumes that there's a lot of time left in the fiscal balance. Two subpoint, the main link is of the groups, and once we get the perception of the snowball—I read six cards in the first negative constructive all saying it gets to the big, and the big economic clubs. She's not responsive.

She argues, four, justifies reasons. First of all, no, this is a policy DA [disadvantage]. She's not arguing how she can [unintelligible] test this out. It is irrelevant.

She argues, five, can still get the money. First of all, irrelevant. The new programs will kick in all the other people which we argue below gets us the disad. Two subpoint, spending programs come in layers. *Wall Street Journal* says in 1979 that these spending programs tend to bring out, layer other spending programs. And again, once one passes, others will tag along.[169]

She argues, sixth, DoD irrelevant. First of all, no,

[169] "Spending programs often result in a layer of spending programs which become permanent." G. William Miller, "Blumenthal Says 'Downturn' May Become Deeper, Longer If Inflation Isn't Curbed," *Wall Street Journal*, 16 July 1979, p. 3.

that's wrong. This evidence just says that they wanted them to spend money, but I'll argue in this present context, it is not justified [unintelligible].

On seven, she says, recession. First of all, any spending will cause the disad. Reagan evidence, 1984, from one week ago. Now number two, you must avoid. That is the argument from Rostenkowski from March 17, 1984. It still meets the present budget talks. All her '84 evidence is from February, before Reagan introduced the now $150 billion deficit [unintelligible], and that's why they're out to lunch.

She argues, eight no press into the service. First of all, the evidence is old. It is a 1982 blurb from [unintelligible] saying my bill wouldn't set a precedent. I mean that's no reason you can accept it. Ours gives a specific rationale, an election year precedent.

She says, nine, our evidence does not apply. She does not explain this argument whatsoever. I still get the [unintelligible] of the disadvantage which kicks us into bigger spending.

She says, ten, not deliver the benefits. [unintelligible] continued on the above arguments which I went on one, two, and three.

She says [unintelligible] political pressure right now. Yes, it is. I will argue the uniqueness of the C. subpoint originally, that the [unintelligible] will pass without the plan.

She argues, twelve, Bikini. First of all, that's in the past. Not a new spending program. D. subpoint, we argue on the brink right now. Any additional spending programs kicks in the disad.

Now, the quasi substantive arguments. She argues, one, no increase in interest rates. First of all, this evidence is a complete blurb. Should not accept it. Two subpoint, X in all the evidence saying the decrease in the impact. Three, empirically. *Wall Street Journal,* March 2, 1984, indicates perception. That Dow hears when Governor Thompson indicated a tax hike. The stock market went up 14.86 points and noted that Mr. Reagan might consider raising taxes.[170] They want that because it decreases deficits, and that's empirical. Three subpoint, how? Supply and demand. You increase the amount of demand in the capital markets [unintelligible] and it takes it out. Fourth subpoint, all the preponderance of the evidence shows this is true. *Time* magazine, March 5, '84: "All things holding constant, if all things are held constant, the higher deficits build, the higher interest rates will ultimately be."[171] And there's no reason not to accept that.

She argues, downpayment rhetorical. First of all, this evidence is ridiculous. It just—that's all it is, is a blip, it says rhetorical. Two subpoint, it is not, the nineteen is not the concrete offer. It was when Reagan said in the State of the Union Address; it is not the new offer which we argue in the [unintelligible]. Three subpoint—ok.

She argues below, bipartisan approach necessary. First of all, Democrats work a bipartisan approach *Wall Street Journal,* 1984: "In contrast Jones has noted that 'putting all my eggs in the basket of a bipartisan budget agreement,' "[172] and he's the Oklahoma Democrat who chairs this thing. Two subpoint, his evidence is not talking about the President's program which we argue independently will pass, and [unintelligible] specific there. This is from the *Wall Street Journal* 1984: If we're going to—oh, no, make the third argument. Democrats want to do this; it helps them. *Wall Street Journal* in '84: "If we're going to elect a Democratic president this year, we ought to be trying to take care of the deficit right now. On the other hand, if Ronald Reagan is to be re-elected we still ought to reduce the deficit, because that's how we can save the social programs."[173] So, the Democrats have the absolute motive which argues for the cuts.

She goes, four, Democrats not need bipartisan. This is the February bill, not the March which we argue will pass. And now all that evidence is dropped.

She argues, five, agreement in [unintelligible] because of ripple effect. First of all, does not explain

[170] "On Tuesday, USA Today's front page flashed one of its typically pithy summaries: 'Hint of Tax Hike Refuels Dow's Rally.' The idea here—apparently offered seriously by some market analysts—was that the stock market rose 14.86 points Monday becaues Gov. Jim Thompson of Illinois came out of a meeting with the president and said Mr. Reagan might consider raising taxes after Congress gives him the spending cuts he wants." Source indicated.

[171] "But most would argue that if all other factors are held constant, the higher deficits go, the higher interest rates will ultimately be. The proposition is as simple as the law of supply and demand: if Government sharply increases its demands for credit because it is running larger deficits, then the price of credit tends to rise." Charles P. Alexander, et. al., "Economy and Business," *Time,* 5 March 1984, p. 65.

[172] "In contrast to the speaker, House Budget Chairman Jones says he's 'putting all my eggs in the basket of a bipartisan budget agreement.' The Oklahoma Democrat argues deficit reductions won't occur without bipartisan cooperation, and that it makes sense for congressional Democrats to try to work out a good-faith compromise with the president." Dennis Farney, "Democrats Are Divided on Budget Stance As Bipartisan Blame for Deficit is Feared," *Wall Street Journal,* 1 February 1984, p. 3.

[173] "If we're trying to elect a Democrat president this year, we ought to be trying to take care of some of that deficit now, so it won't be such an awful problem for him in 1985,' he says. 'On the other hand, if Ronald Reagan is reelected, we still ought to try to reduce the deficit this year. Because if we don't, the social programs we care about will be all the more vulnerable next year." James Jones quoted in Farney, p. 3.

how any type of ripple. How does this increase? Two subpoint, ours is long term which gives you growth and depression. Three argument, on the brink right now. That's the evidence from 1984. *Business Week,* 1984: "Even a one-percentage-point rise would trigger another wave of small-business failures. . ."[174] They continue: "[A]ccelerating credit demand could push rates even higher and eventually put the brakes on economic expansion."[175] *New York Times,* March 1984: "Interest rates are already too high. If forced higher . . . another recession is likely."[176]

She argues, six, turnaround, political will. First of all, no. You cannot delay. If you delay you have to do it after the election. The toughest stuff gets too high. *U. S. News,* February '84: " 'The longer the deficits are expected to persist,' Feldstein warns, 'the greater are the risks to our economic future.' "[177] *Business Week,* '84: The momentum of spending programs and interest costs are clearly mounting rapidly. Some spending, particularly for indexed entitlements . . . will skyrocket in coming years. Limited revenue. The time to act is indeed now.[178] Weidenbaum in 1984: "[T]he longer they wait, the worse the problem will get. Payments on the debt will continue to rise. Federal projects, civilian and military. . . ."[179] They must stop.

She has a turnaround on the bottom on [unintelligible]. First of all, no. We argue they increase aggregate demand which takes in greater spending, causes disad. Two subpoint, overconsumption. Bacon in '84: We're overconsuming right now. We're going to have to under consume in the future. We're really lowering the living standard.[180] And three subpoint, this evidence is simply not true. We've given that argument below.

Now, go to their case extensions. Right, all the other arguments are taken above. Now, due process. First of all, always must consider the practical implications. Without there is no [unintelligible]. Lempert in 1981: One might think practical considerations like these which have little to do with due process. . . . Yet Justices who are charged with overseeing the federal courts as well as with upholding constitutional rights. . . .[181] Two subpoint, assumes balancing interest which the present system does. Three subpoint, not an end by itself. Bundy in '68: We can see the law of itself is not good, but an instrument which derives a value from that which it prevents.[182] Four subpoint, pure procedural view is incomplete. Tribe in '84: The constitutional theme of perfecting the processes of governmental decisions is radically indeterminate and fundamentally incomplete.[183] Next subpoint, constitution—no, that's enough.

Right to know. Look, the way they get their advantage on duty-to-warn, telling people, giving the right to know, that's only [unintelligible]. She says, not [unintelligible]. Yes, the evidence of the first contention says that. It do so. That's the way they get the solvency. She says, courts apply and the courts in compensation right now. These are all assertions which are not responsive.

X number a, b subpoint on setting [unintelligible] failure to know, but the failure to know is because the government didn't tell them which gives them the right to know and de facto justifies the extent of the judicial tyranny.

She says, six, [unintelligible] constitution. That's a turn.

Now, I think I'm winning a decent risk. All she does is put seven responses here.

I don't know what to say. I've had a great time the

[174] "Interest Rates Begin to Bite," *BusinessWeek,* 26 March 1984, p. 31.

[175] "Interest Rates Begin to Bite," p. 30.

[176] Editorial, "Poverty and Mr. Meese," *New York Times,* 6 March 1984, p. 22.

[177] Martin Feldstein quoted in Monroe W. Karmin and Robert J. Morse, "Drowning in Debt," *U. S. News and World Report,* 13 February 1984, p. 21.

[178] "The momentum of spending programs and interest costs are clearly mounting rapidly. Some spending, particularly for indexed entitlements and defense, will skyrocket in coming years. At the same time, programmed tax cuts will limit revenue growth. The time to act is now." "How to cut the Deficit," *BusinessWeek,* 26 March 1984, p. 52.

[179] Quotation concludes: ". . . move inexorably forward. Even the most marginal program is difficult to stop." Murray L. Weidenbaum, "Fully Tackle the Deficits," *New York Times,* 19 March 1984, p. 17.

[180] "We're overconsuming now but we're going to have to underconsume in the future. We're really talking about burdening the next generation and lowering their standard of living." James Fralick quoted in Kenneth H. Bacon, "The Outlook: Reagan's Rising Burden of Debt Service," *Wall Street Journal,* 19 March 1984, p. 1.

[181] "One might think that practical considerations like these, which have little to do with due process, should be given no weight when a clash of constitutional values must be resolved. Yet justices who are charged with overseeing the federal courts as well as with upholding constitutional rights may be more influenced by perceived practicalities than by doctrinal analysis." Richard O. Lempert, "Civil Juries and Complex Cases: Let's Not Rush to Judgment," *Michigan Law Review,* (November 1981), 90.

[182] "Or perhaps we can think of the law not as something good in itself, but as an instrument which derives its value less from what it does than from what it prevents." McGeorge Bundy, "A Lay View of Due Process," in Arthur E. Sutherland, ed., *Government Under Law* (Cambridge, Mass.: Harvard University Press, 1956), p. 365.

[183] Laurence H. Tribe, "The Puzzling Persistence of Process-Based Constitutional Theories," *Yale Law Journal,* (May 1980), 1064.

last two years, and I love a lot of you, in fact all of you.

First Affirmative Rebuttal:
Mark Whitehead, Louisville

He said they can do business through the VA. First of all, we're just talking about the VA denies, not that there is any way that we increase although there is no disad there.

(DAI) In terms of the new disad, first of all, there's three cases on the first card that will take that out. Second of all, the turnaround is discipline. If this is the case and we win, and he grants that that means that there's no discipline here. Third subpoint, I mean it has been empirically denied on Bikini and other rights that they did. Fourth subpoint, this talks about new constitutional rights we offer them now; it is not talking about rights that are consistent with rights that have already been done. Fifth subpoint, you know we don't increase the courts. There's no impact to the disad anyway.

Now, we'll turn to the right to know on the case. Now all this is talking about is the courts already have this type of thing. This is all asserted plus the fact here that we only do a failure to warn. This is the last answer, and the courts will not necessarily to do it, and there's no right to look at it which is all dropped in INR.

The process stuff now. Just group his arguments together. First subpoint, we maximize both pragmatic and procedure, you know. It is the essence of that. That's what it is talking about. Second of all, the rules, the decision rule that we give is vote for the most freedoms. That's argument number five. Third subpoint here is there is no reason to assume—does not assume good rights like we do. And fourth subpoint if this is the case then it beats the new disad that he runs.

(DAII) Spending now, I believe. First argument, he says that they must spend dollars. First of all, this alters the concept which you do not do this. If we do go to court they will not necessarily get their claim. If they say too no long term increase, you know, that it's going to talk about breakup in the perception, we say perception should be gone now. On third, monies now. He said that was in '84, but all we need to do is justify [unintelligible] in '84, and they have already appropriated that money.

In terms of drop down to number five now, he said new programs can cause snowball. No, first of all the status quo would have already done it. The compensation bill that we passed is already for this specific type of thing. These things would have already broken down the perception.

On seven, threshold. He says, any new dollars, but, first of all, we don't spend, and even if we do, it's all talking about long term after the election anyway, or after the continuous spending resolution.

On eight no precedent, he says, old. He says it's the Hatch evidence. It is not call for the card. It's the A-vets bill. But that is not what we do. On that evidence not apply, he says, don't explain, but, yes, we're talking about it. We don't compensate.

On ten, best policy. He says, above. But all we say is the perception is already broken, and this will produce snowball.

On eleven, [unintelligible] policy is not unique. We say there is no increase in political pressure. I want to just—to do a couple of things. On no increase interest rates, he gives three evidence. First of all, actually no link between deficit and interest rates. According to Gross in 1984: "Nor can a close relationship be found between deficits and high real interest rates."[184] On number two, he says, no down payment. First of all, he says, bad card, but no, this is actually a deficit doing this type of thing as *Washington Post* says on March 18, 1984: "The suggestion that this small decrease somehow opens the way to a larger resolution of the deficit is simply wrong."[185] In terms of three subpoint, nobody has to follow an agreement. He says, we were. First of all, no, that is not the case. They have the choice to stay high according to Koretz in '84: Stratszheim also predicted that "Most foreign capital came to the U.S. for sound economic reasons and will stay."[186] In other words, foreign capital will come in and solve these types of interest rate arguments.

(IV) Topicality. Our standards. Now, I will say that any type of blowing up, this is a new type of quantitative study, new arguments which I don't think that they are going to do anyway, are justified. He says, one [unintelligible] delimits. First of all, no. We say that actually reasonability is OK. More evidence comes from *West's General Digest* which says, "[S]trict meaning and arrangement of individual words are not as persuasive . . . as are reasonable meaning of the words in accordance with legislative objective."[187] Second subpoint here, contextually, within the hazardous waste context. Epstein continues and says, "The legal system regulates many formal relationships within society, including . . . disposal of hazardous wastes. One of the most

[184] George Gross, "Budget Deficits: Do They Matter," *Nation's Cities Weekly,* 16 January 1984, p. 4.

[185] "The Rose Garden Budget," *Washington Post,* 18 March 1984, p. C6.

[186] Donald H. Straszheim quoted in Gene Koretz, "Two Who Pooh-Pooh: A Deficit Disaster Scenario," *Business Week,* 19 March 1984, p. 16.

[187] "Statutes, Meaning, In General," *West's General Digest,* Sixth Series, Vol. 12 (St. Paul, Minn.: West Publishing Company, 1983), p. 1114.

important concepts governing these relationships is 'reasonableness.' "[188]

In terms of the D. subpoint, he said, no better definition. First of all, yes, you need the better definition you just simply can't compare the best. [That is] what this evidence talked about.

He says grammar. First subpoint, no. Grammar is decrease is better according to Johnson in 1983. If you stop worrying about the fine points of grammar the language will get better not worse.[189] Second subpoint, decrease grammar is actually better. According to Barnett in '77: "The real barrier to universal understanding is grammar."[190] Third subpoint, actually should get rid of on balance. *Commonweal* says in '81: [Unintelligible]. At the end of the day I felt the strain of a whole day of trying to use the correct subject and verb.[191] And so as you know it's just talking about better communication.

He says if A. subpoint, decrease in interpretation, that's about actually better. He said, decrease in controls, but no. You actually increase the communication and understanding. He says, should assume no grammar. First of all, this assumes some type of—this is talking about the parameters, but he said, parameters are not that binding, but even if that's the case, it defines the hazardous waste as a byproduct.

He says, context is irrelevant. First of all, no. The affirmative has the right to define it according to Anderson in '76: "Statutory language is often ambiguous and its meaning unclear. In trying to determine what the legislature intends . . . , they may refer to . . . floor debates on the law in question."[192] Second subpoint, ambiguity is essential for some things. According to Levi in 1949: "The categories used in the legal process must be left ambiguous in order to permit the infusion of new ideas."[193] Third subpoint here, is precision here is unrealistic. Levi says in 1979: "[R]easoning by example has moved so far ahead as to make it clear that the suggestive influence of the word is no longer desired."[194]

Now, in terms of C. subpoint, discretion. He says, you must weigh it. No, it assumes the same type of process, just like debate. He says, talking about life, but life's value is made by the process that it must go through. They say, it's different, but no, that's dealt with above as to whether or not it applies. He says, grammar's OK. That's above. He says, equals not a voting issue, but, yes, it is. Because it's talking about the same subpoint. He drops D. on agencies which means you defer to us to see what we mean, and E. subpoint on scholars. He says, not so. We say, the way to do it is to take the words one step beyond their generally recognized meaning which means we can distort.

In terms of reasonability and in terms of the best definition, he says, it's OK and in effect to change the rules. That's up above plus the fact that we can clarify anyway.

On the best definition, he says, the search for words is magnified, and first of all, this assumes perception, but it also does not assume our right to at least have ambiguity in those types of statutes. He says, within the jurisdiction the implications are OK, but that's all explained. He says, threshold not talking about standards, but those are all dealt with above as to whether or not we could do these.

Our arguments, first, one on illegals. He says [unintelligible], but first of all, the hazardous waste can be, types of things like radiation exposure etcetera which means that can hurt the individual. Third subpoint, this all explained when, you know, once you look at the context of that. That means the context will actually be explained by us which means you could interpret them later on.

On second, equals changed meaning. First of all, the "s," when he pluralizes the waste tends to show that. Second of all, modifiers like types of things—modifiers like, you know, like modifies prepositional phrases will be our correct uses.

He says, five, resolution equals and allows two cases. First of all, so what if there's two cases. No reason for that. He says, grammar. Well, that's up above. He says, collective noun. We'll deal with that in just a second. He says, usage is analytical. First of all, they're all modified by injuries of disposal. That modifies disposal, and if that's the case, it's the subject of that.

Four a, he says, equals case. He says, not hazardous waste, but that we equal the one producer of all waste. He says, two, evidence does not apply, but the only reason is because the government's the only one that does that.

[188] Epstein, p. 258.

[189] "Stop worrying so much about finer points of grammar, the linguists say. Relax. Talk in a way that comes naturally. Don't pay attention to whether that poor Joe said *me* or *I*. Get used to the idea that there's nothing wrong with vernacular English. The language will get better, not worse." Flora Johnson, "Us against Them," *Ambassador,* April 1983, p. 83.

[190] Richard S. Barnett, "The Grammar Barrier," *National Review,* 18 February 1977, p. 210.

[191] "At the end of the day I felt the strain of a whole day of trying to be sure my verbs and subjects agreed as to number." "Talk English Good: How Newspeak Impacts Us," *Commonweal,* 13 March 1981, p. 146.

[192] James E. Anderson, *Public Policy-Making* (New York: Praeger Publishers, 1975), p. 82.

[193] Edward H. Levi, *An Introduction to Legal Reasoning* (Chicago, Ill.: University of Chicago Press, 1949), p. 3.

[194] Levi, p. 6.

I'm going to drop down to the fifth argument on hazardous waste, one producer. He says, pick a producer, but no, it's talking about everyone else is already liable. Second of all, this is the only person that makes all of one particular waste. And third subpoint, all alternative producers are all liable right now. On six, alternative wording, he says, judiciary in waste. First of all, no. This is justified in IAC, you know, so it was justified. Second of all, each and every one is done with these types of things. For all injuries, you know, companies already cover right now. So, all we do is simply fill the gap. Plus the fact that if we win these standards, you know, it's OK to vote for us.

Second Negative Rebuttal:
Leonard Gail, Dartmouth

(DAI) Once we win these arguments, any risk of [unintelligible] nuclear war outweighs. Dropped Mark's risk analysis in the INR. You get any worse, we win. They say, we're proceeding to [unintelligible], and it's an end in itself. It is good. Dropping the arguments it must be substantive. [Unintelligible]. The alternative to [unintelligible] to all [unintelligible] in INR is dropped. He says, two, most—and three, group together. First of all, process is not an end by itself. Secondly, you must consider the implications. You have to, that's the way you have your process. Third response, destruction of demand, and admits it's rhetorical. In [unintelligible] view, it's inevitable. [unintelligible]. His fourth response, extend the impact. It is empirically denied. We have it now, all this arguments [unintelligible]. This disad does come out with a minute left. They have missed it, dropped the argument that the plan uniquely increases confidence in the courts. That's A.I., because people are going on confidence.

He says, three, case in the first affirmative. First of all, the disad was clearly linear. Mark argued that on the B. subpoint. Two, cards [unintelligible]. Second of all, drops [unintelligible]. 1982 indicating that even though this plan's administrative, he won't go to other places. He argues this on two, turnaround, on ripple, on discipline. No, at best this turns back on them, because the courts will be more interventionist. [unintelligible] the ripple, and that gives me all the turns on the other side, and my argument, unlike [unintelligible] said couldn't be turned, was the reason why conventional knowledge could which all my takeouts don't take out.

The third response here, the [unintelligible] empirically denied. Our argument is that this—you know, that—no, I don't see how that's important. This plan is military servicemen now, and this increases here, and it's linear. All those responses apply. That say, no new rights. Irrelevant. Increase confidence. Then the courts go to new rights. They say courts don't increase, but we stopped the bad perception on them. More evidence comes from Wasby in '78: "Public opinion is an important part of the Court's environment affecting the judges' strategies discussed in the previous chapter."[195] Bates [Spaeth] explained in '79: "[T]he Court's policy-making capacity—based on the respect and reverence accorded Justices."[196] Beth in 1982: "Judicial review is democratic in the sense that it is accepted by most people, if in no other way. Such an institution can only survive so long as the general public and officialdom as well accepted it, both in principle and in practice."[197] And my subsumes that the legislatures would have acted if real rights would have been denied. No impact. [unintelligible] linear risk. And I believe we're flipped out discipline on the other side.

(DAII) Spending. Overview. All evidence is not take out. Spreads to other issues. Political issues. Our evidence says, if you set up a new class of injury which doesn't even mean you compensate people, you gain the harm. They say, political snowballing. He says, he doesn't claim. Yes, you know, it is one that you set up a new class. I'll explain more about [unintelligible] they do compensate. You have to look at the plan. It argues that in the past people who were not given duty-to-warn will be compensated, and that's made clear in the cross examination.

Second response, long term. They say, can do it [unintelligible]. No, perception here. March seventeenth, no new program. Even the plan itself would be a new program which would destroy the budget compromise. Second response, want to increase. They say, just in 1984. One clearly new. Never given anywhere else. Second of all, that's not an

[195] Stephen L. Wasby, *The Supreme Court in the Federal Judicial System,* (New York: Holt, Rinehart and Winston, 1978), p. 34.

[196] "The sole weapon the Court has at its disposal is its moral authority, and though moral authority may appear to be a fragile weapon when compared with dollars, nightsticks, nuclear weapons, and other weapons of *Realpolitik,* the Court's policy-making capacity—based on the respect and reverence accorded Justices, the perceived legitimacy of the court's decisions even when they are disapproved of by substantial segments of society, and the factors described in Chapter 1—compares favorably with these tangible forms of persuasion, whether they are gently or roughly applied." Harold J. Spaeth, *Supreme Court Policy Making: Explanation and Prediction* (San Francisco, Calif: W. H. Freeman and Company, 1979), p. 196.

[197] Loren P. Beth quoted in Charles M. Lamb, "Judicial Restraint on the Supreme Court," in Stephen C. Halpern and Charles M. Lamb, eds., *Supreme Court Activism and Restraint* (Lexington, Mass.: Lexington Books, D.C. Health and Company, 1982), p. 11.

option. It has to be topical. Now, you have to [unintelligible] the resolution now. Third response is, this is clearly illegitimate. You could just [unintelligible]. Do the, you know, do the plan ten years back, and then, you know, you don't have the harm of the present system. It's ridiculous. You know this is a new argument [unintelligible].

Fourth response, justifies. They say, [unintelligible] do the bill already. No, this is only talking about the House approving some spending measure. It's not since March seventeenth compromise which is important, and the snowball kicks in. And it just wasn't passed.

Drops all the arguments. Any new program. Rozinsky, February '80: Democrats hope for it. No, precedent. We argue the evidence is old and only a blurb. He says it's not, and they don't do it. They create a new class. Hance was talking about [unintelligible] which is irrelevant, and it was a blurb in 1982.

Any new program, and they do compensate people, because of the past. Duty-to-warn may not in the future, but the past, they're compensating, because there was no duty-to-warn. Ninth response, evidence to comply. They say, doesn't talk about it. We say, they don't deny the thesis, that's clear. We say, ten, in the past. They said, perception is broken. Now, all the above response take out. It never occurred in absence of March seventeenth. Eleven, political pressure. They say, no increased pressure, but drops all the uniqueness evidence on the C. subpoint. We're winning that cold.

On the argument, substantively. Perception, new programs come in layers, and they dropped the INR extension remark. Even though this program may not cost money, it will lead to other programs which will cost money. New programs come in layers.

On the arguments itself. [unintelligible] no link. They need a card here. First of all, that merely indicates they're not related. You know, that they're not causative. Our argument is that they're clearly correlated. We've argued, empirical. [unintelligible] subpoint, they're important. They say, it does it too. First of all, drop to Mark's from the argument, then it's logical, the fourth response, it's logical, supply and demand. More people wanting money equals increased bidding—drives up interest rates. They argue the third response, foreign countries. First of all, that's irrelevant. It has taken on new [unintelligible] in our evidence. The United States increases its, and that drives up U.S. interest rates. The impact does not come from comparison to foreign interest rates. And pull through all of our arguments that it will pass.

First of all, underviews. Pull through one hundred and fifty billion over three years. Second, it's efficient to stop any increase in interest rates now. We don't claim to eliminate the deficit, only to prevent future increases.

Third response is presumption is the key. An interim measure is for, first, they're prevent an increase in interest rates. Fourth response, can't delay. Failure to pass a small program prevents acts in the future.

Now, look at Koulogeorge in the INR. All the impacts plus the number six, delay, cannot delay.

Now, first of all, I'll give my conclusion for the round. I think we've won on all my issues, and on Mark, he's done a tremendous job. Second, I just don't know what to say at a time like this, I've thought about it late at night, you know, when you're lying asleep, and, you know, what am I going to say at the end of my last rebuttal after debating as hard as I can for seven years, and it's taken up so much, and I just dont know what to say. I would like to say that it's really important that you work hard in debate and that you do well, but I would trade it in for personal happiness any day, because I think that that is more important. You can be great in debate, but if you're not happy, nothing matters.

Second Affirmative Rebuttal:
Cindy Leiferman, Louisville

(DAI) He grants IAC—the last card that we read is that we maintain *Feres,* and *Feres* is bad and destroys court system which means that we do not increase credibility of the court. His first argument, he says plan increases the confidence in the courts. MCA is not a court, hence there is no increase in court confidence. Second of all, if anything, we turned this. We say, courts are bad, and we take them out of the courts indicating a net turn.

On ripples, we win discipline turns indicating the courts are bad on discipline. Turn his ripples argument there, because we've increased discipline to courts to turn the ripples back at him.

Three, he says that our argument on three is not important, but it says we've had three cases now indicating that they should be able to show empirically that the disad happened. All we really argue is on four. He says that we increase confidence, the increase rights. No, we argued MCA should have access, and we decrease confidence in courts saying that the courts are bad. He says, we stop with destruction of courts. But no, it's a turn. We say the courts are bad.

Fourth argument in IAR was dropped indicating there's no evidence indicating the MCA would increase the confidence in courts which means that there is no link to this disad.

Now what you have here is no increase or decrease on courts. Second, we turn this thing, because we think courts are bad, and third, there's no causality, because you could still go to the court under the affirmative indicating there is no change in the court perception.

Please, go to where we argued no harm. He says, any risk equals negative. First of all, no, he grants our evidence on process is life, and there's been no answer for that. Second, he grants my decision rule in 2AC that says you vote for most freedom indicating that even if they win spending, this a priori consideration. There has been no answer.

On his processes, he says, substantive. We are. We give you the process of the day in court plus compensation meeting his criterion, meaning that the decision rule kicks in. He says, not an end in itself, but we combine due process and a day in court indicating we meet the end in itself and again it's substantive which meets the decision rule. He says, empirically denied. That doesn't justify further infringements and also drops his decision rule, the answer to substantive and procedural, and again the decision rule means you vote for most freedom.

(DAII) Please go to spending. At the top. He says, snowball. New class. First of all, this evidence talks about open-ended compensation, and we do not do open-ended compensation. We go through the MCA which means you go and you get your claim if you are injured. It is not blanket compensation. Second argument, none of this evidence was related specifically to the MCA which cuts this link. Third, we don't cause this link. He drops my first argument, my number one in 2AC that says there's no increase to the liability with the passage of the plan. Also dropping number three that there's enough money to cover through the '84 season. He drops number five that says they don't want lots of money so even if they compensate there wouldn't be an increase in the amount of money that they would have to pay out for those claims.

On specific answers, number one, he says they do compensate, but that is future only. The plan is not retroactive, and he never argues that it should have been until then, and that's too late, in rebuttals. Second, it's irrelevant. If we indicate we have enough money now. That was the number three response. He says, off our third argument. We say the plan would give it, but that's—I argued above plan would not trigger it. He says, new argument on why you should vote for the resolution. First of all, I think it's not. My fourth argument in 2AC is that it justifies the resolution now which means you can vote on that. Second argument, we have enough for 1984, and that's the time is now, and that is what you vote on. You vote today for whether the resolution should be voted for, not next week which indicates that if we show it's justified in 1983–84 resolution, it'd be OK. He says, it's illegitimate, but now the resolution only exists in the 1983–84 topic. That's all we need to do—is justify the existence of the resolution is in that time frame, and we have enough money in that time frame.

Second argument, it beats snowball. No evidence indicates that we would snowball before the 1984 season is out, indicating that even if it gets snowballed doesn't mean that you would vote against the disad, and he grants that. This is all new on illegitimacy, also which cuts against it.

On snowball. First argument is that is an open-ended compensation, but we don't do. You must prove that failure to warn before you get the money. Therefore, it is not related to compensation. Second, it's empirically not true. He drops my evidence that read on number nine, or number ten, I'm sorry, in 2AC that says we've passed the compensation bill through the House. Now, if it's true that every time you pass a bill these pressures inevitably cause it to snowball. That means the snowball process is already started which means the disad will prove itself not true in the future independent of affirmative action which means you don't vote against us on that.

Third, he drops my eleventh argument I mean he misses the turn, and he didn't catch it. It's the Pfau evidence and it says that political pressure would be gone if you passed short-term programs which means you pass our programs, and there will not be increased pressure. There will not be increased snowball, and he does not answer number eleven.

His next argument. He says, won't pass. First, he says, this is brand new. He never argues that before. Second, it's irrelevant. If the pressures are inevitable, they'll act on a bill as well. Third, there is no link to the affirmative indicating that this is an open-ended process.

Now, on where he talks about the Hatch bill. He says, we created a new class. First argument is [unintelligible] argument. We never created a new class, because the MCA already covers it anyway. Scholl in '81: The military claims act provides an administrative remedy for property damage, personal injury or death. . . . The MCA is expressly excluded military or civilian personnel whose injuries or death. . . . This remedy, therefore, is available only to civilians,[198] indicating that everybody else is already covered, but the military. Not a new class.

Second argument, it beats the disad. The bill has already created a new class for A-vets etcetera which we do not do. He says, failure to warn equals compensation. You pay out enough money for that, so no increase in spending. Second, there is no precedent to affirmative. Number eight, we would

[198] Debra Sholl, "The Nevada Proving Grounds: An Asylum for Sovereign Immunity," *Southwestern University Law Review,* 12 (1981), 661.

argue, implicitly we disapprove the disad, because it is open ended.

He says, one. He says, they're broken. He's beaten above, and does not explain the bill does not beat the perceptions. He says D. subpoint equals the uniqueness, but it never pacifies and internally you get the perception.

On the impact, he says, perceptions other than cost. First of all, they have passed the budget by then, so it's irrelevant. Even if it's true, the snowball would be years and years from the budget appropriations process. Second, the turn to the disad is not unique. Compensation bill would have caused internal pressure, and contribute to the snowball. Third, affirmative is the best interpretation, if any only open-ended program inevitably causes, bills and the compensation of vets, etcetera which causes a new class would certainly cause it. All I want here—the fourth argument is that the decision rule does not kick in now. Does not assume the compensation bill does not assume the political pressures turn and is not specific to the MCA. For the snowball, all these new programs would be post-budget negotiations, so there would be no impact.

Now, we've got four big things going here. First, there is no link to the MCA. Increases. Second, there's no snowball link to us, and we turn it implicitly with the passage of the compensation bill. The third that we've got the status quo beats it, and we've got the decision rule that rights outweigh process.

Uhm, it's a good round but a... I don't know what I can say.[199] This activity means a lot to me. I feel sorry for you guys that couldn't be up here. [Applause].

[199] Leiferman's emotions prevented her from expressing appreciation in a way she wished to at the end of the actual round. She later wrote: "As this round comes to an end, I realize that four years of friendship and fun also end. This activity is a very valuable part of my life and thus I'd like to thank all of those people who have helped me through the years: John Williams, Lorel Peterson-Deatherage, Mark, the Augie and Louisville debaters along with the two most talented, intelligent, and loving coaches one could ever hope to work with—Mike Pfau and Tim Hynes. In addition, I'd like to extend a deep sense of gratitude to a wonderful group of friends who've always been around to share both the joys and sorrows of this activity: Erik Walker, Melonie Gardner, Robin Jacobsohn, Bill Brewster, Ricki Robbins, the Toms from Harvard, Lewis Lamb, Scott Forester, and the rest. Finally, and especially warm thanks to Alex Pritchard. Again, thanks everyone, for four fantastic years."

APPENDIX B

A Transcript of a Non-Policy Debate

The following is a transcript of a debate that was held as an exhibition at the annual Fall Workshop of the Southeast Cross-examination Debate Association. The debate was held in September of 1985. The affirmative team, from the University of Tennessee, was Mr. Phil McGill and Mr. Scott Greer. The negative team, from the University of South Carolina, was Mr. Tad Stephenson and Mr. Kevin Sargent. They were debating the proposition: *Resolved, that significant government restrictions on coverage by the U.S. media of terrorist activities are justified.* For instructional purposes and to facilitate readability, there has been slight editing of the transcript. Footnote references follow directly after the sentence to which they apply, and the footnotes themselves follow the text of the debate.

First Affirmative Constructive:
Mr. Phil McGill, University of Tennessee

The University of Tennessee stands firmly resolved that significant government restrictions on coverage by the U.S. media of terrorist activities are justified. We begin our analysis with observation one: definitions. Subpoint (A), from *Webster's New World Dictionary*, "significant: Having or expressing a meaning; important; momentous."[1] Subpoint (B) "restrictions", according to *Webster's:* "Having certain limitations put on or being confined."[2] Subpoint (C) "coverage", from the *American Heritage Dictionary:* "The extent to which something is observed, analyzed or reported."[3] Now this brings us to subpoint (D) "media", from *Webster's:* "any means, agency or instrumentality; specifically a means of communication."[4] This brings us to subpoint (E) which is "terrorism." We refer to *Webster's* again: "the use of force or threats to demoralize, intimidate, and subjugate; especially such use as a political weapon or policy."[5] This brings us to our last subpoint which is (F), "activity." *Webster's* defines it as: "any specific action or pursuit."[6]

As a measurement for justification, we offer observation two: decision rule. The University of Tennessee feels that the lives of the victims and of potential victims must hold the paramount value in this debate. As Robert Rabe put it in 1979: "As declared, the First Amendment is not absolute and specifically 'the right to speak and publish does not carry with it the unrestrained right to gather information.' Just as this government has both the right and the duty to prohibit certain forms of speech as in libel and slander, the government, too, must expend every effort to protect the safety and lives of the hostages, even if the latter dictates limiting the rights of the press. The right to life is, of course, the most basic and paramount."[7] It is our objective as the affirmative to prove that the lives of such victims warrant restriction. Although at times, some specific policy ramifications of the resolution may or may not require observation, it is our objective to defend the resolution as one of "quasi-policy." David Zarefsky referred to such a resolution in the 1980 *C.E.D.A. Handbook:* "First is what I would label the quasi-policy proposition. It does not advocate a specific plan of action, yet one is implicit within the statement of the proposition."[8] We will argue that the concept of coverage restrictions is justified in terms of the value of human life. We feel this to be a sufficient warrant for an affirmative ballot.

The University of Tennessee offers one compelling justification: media restrictions on coverage of terrorist activities are warranted. Delineate to subpoint (A): Terrorist activity is significant. From *U.S. News and World Report* in '85: "A decade ago, the world experienced an average of ten incidents of terrorism per week: assassinations, bombings, air hijackings, kidnappings, maimings, or attacks on facilities. The average now, nearly ten a day."[9] Clearly, if the past is in any way indicative of the future, the threat will continue to grow.

Now, judging the threat of life, liberty and the pursuit of happiness is greatly significant, we now contend subpoint (B). Terrorism is vitally dependent upon the media. Alex P. Schmid and Janny de Graaf reported in 1982: "yet terrorism and mass communication are linked to each other. Without communication there can be no terrorism."[10] Walter Laquer echoed this conclusion in *Harper's* magazine in March of '76: "The media are the terrorist's best friends. The terrorist act by itself is nothing. Publicity is all."[11] Schmid and de Graaf sum up: "Violence, to become terroristic, requires witnesses."[12] We now subdivide into subpoint one, Proximity promotes terrorism. With the recent growth of the electronic media, newsgatherers can now obtain information from the far corners of the earth, transfer it back to a central location and distribute it to those far corners with relative ease and speed. According to Schmid and de Graaf in '82: "The shrinking of time needed to relay events made possible by the communication revolution is a major element which has increased the usefulness of the media for terrorists."[13] The same source continues to point out: "The location of the foreign press correspondents has made one of the determinants of the location of the struggle. While wars attract journalists, journalists attract terrorists."[14] We now move to subpoint two, Proximity exists for continued terrorism. Specifically, the University of Tennessee argues that the frequency and the severity of attacks will increase. Yonah Alexander points this out in the *Journal of International Affairs* in '78: "As Richard Clutterbuck asserted, 'ideas travel through the normal news media. People watching and listening to the reports get ideas about doing the same things themselves.' That is, the more news reports about bomb scares the more bomb scares there are likely to be. The reports about plane hijackings lead to more plane hijackings."[15]

Now, the link between the media and terrorism is undeniable, so we move to subpoint (C). Restrictions are justified. We will contend that the breach in this link will offer a solid means of reducing terrorism and its impact on innocent citizens. Turn again to Schmid and de Graaf: "Terrorism cannot be understood only in terms of violence."[16] Terrorism does not exist to kill somebody but to affect those other than the victim. For empirical proof we once again turn to Schmid and de Graaf: "Violence aims at behavior modification by coercion. Propaganda aims at the same by persuasion. Terrorism is a combination of the two."[17]

We conclude with a strong reaffirmation of our initial stance and ask for your concurrence.

Cross-Examination:
Mr. Stephenson questions Mr. McGill

Stephenson: O.K. now significance. Are there any kinds of standards there? Any kinds of numbers we can measure in this round? McGill: Well, we give you that down where we talk about how terrorism has increased. Stephenson: So how are we to compare? The number of lives, is that it? McGill: No, I would argue that it's the weight of values. Stephenson: Why is the definition then equal to "meaning, important, momentous." I mean lives are important, they're momentous aren't they? McGill: To give you some scale of measure. Stephenson: Let's go to your terrorism definition. Action the primary intent of which is to instill fear through violence, right? It's not talking about non-violence, right? McGill: No, I would argue that it's talking about violence and intimidation -- causing fear and alarm. Stephenson: So violence or potential violence then, right? McGill: Yes. Stephenson: O.K. Let's go to your justification observation. (A) subpoint -- terrorist activity is significant. Now, the CIA study predicts an increase. What is the motive for an increase in terror? McGill: Well, as Rabe points out in 1AC that terrorists believe they need to one-up themselves. To be able to get as much coverage as last time they need to blow up something a little bigger, a little better. Stephenson: O.K. While you are on that -- that's little 2 subpoint -- the propensity for continued terror. Now the Alexander in 78 card says publicity leads to more hijacking, right? McGill: Right. Stephenson: Does he ever talk about the level of hijacking increasing? Doesn't he just say that the level stays the same? That it leads to more and more hijackings, but not an increase? Doesn't he say that it is a stable level if you give them what they want? McGill: I just know what the card says -- that media is producing more terrorist hijackings. Stephenson: Does it actually say that it increases the absolute number of terrorist acts or does it say that this month you're going to have two acts, the next month you're going to have two acts, and the next month you're going to have two acts? McGill: Alexander didn't tell us that. Stephenson: He didn't tell us that? McGill: No. Stephenson: O.K. Let's see -- terrorism for effects not murder. So that means that the motive is just to gain publicity not just to go out and commit mass murder? McGill: Right. They don't care about the victims themselves, its just how they intimidate the people besides the victims. Stephenson: O.K. If we can establish the motive then, its just symbolic -- not for the murder. It's that they want to get their message across? McGill: Right. For propaganda. Stephenson: Thank you very much.

First Negative Constructive:
Mr. Kevin Sargent, University of South Carolina

On the second observation on decision rule I will have five responses: Number one, the affirmative does not advocate a single decision rule. What is crucial to understand in this round is that the affirmative actually is advocating a set of values -- the protection of life contingent upon censorship and order. Their values are life, order and censorship, they are a set. Number two, even if you grant affirmative sole possession of life protection decision rule, they must demonstrate that this is the best criterion by which to judge the round. I will suggest that other decision rules could be at least as important and equally good. For example, general freedom and democracy distinct from the First Amendment. Of what value, after all, is life without freedom. Number three, long-term tradeoff. There exists a possibility that emphasis on short-term life savings may come at the expense of long-term death and suffering and this will become clear in the 2NC counter values. Number four, affirmative fails to meet their own decision rule. We will argue that unrestricted media coverage best meets life protection decision rule as we will make apparent. Number five, negative value grouping is the best. We will also include protection of life as part of our non-resolutional value matrix, but in addition, Tad and I will include freedom and expression as being part of a superior value grouping.

Large observation number one, self-regulation is a non resolutional and superior value option. Little one subpoint, The media is improving itself. Bassiouni, 1981: "...the media are becoming more responsible and self-critical than in their often sensational past ..."[18] Two, empirical examples demonstrate self regulation. Yonah Alexander in 1978: "The *Chicago Sun-Times* and the *Chicago Daily News*, already mentioned, the *Courier Journal* and the *Louisville Times*, *United Press International* and *CBS News* have unilaterally determined internal guidelines for coverage."[19] Three, they balance responsibilities. Bassiouni in 1982: "The media have demonstrated increasing awareness that

during terrorist incidents they must balance their responsibility to provide full and fair coverage with their responsibility not to exacerbate the threat to life and impede effective law enforcement management."[20] In four we will argue, self regulation is the only option in an open society. Bell, in 1978: "Beware of those offering solutions to terrorism. There are no solutions in open societies. There are advisable attitudes, incremental protection from the violent, and the assurance as yet without takers, that the greatest danger from the enemy is that the enemy is us. The terrorists cannot bomb down an open society, but an act of parliament can close one."[21] Now number five, ambiguity is crucial -- you must vote against regulation. Number six, self-regulation provides the basis for cooperation. The media and the police can cooperate. Bassiouni in 1981: "... self-restraint voluntarily adopted by the media ... would furnish a basis for cooperation in media law enforcement regulations."[22] Number seven, Cooperation is the only way to limit terrorism. Bassiouni again: "Democratic institutions work best, however, where there is provision for flexibility and forebearance on each side. Any direct collision over first amendment freedoms would merely shift the problem to a higher conflict of values and postpone steps toward the prevention and control of terror violence.
Consequently, the public interest can only suffer and the terrorists objective be aided should active enmity characterize media-government regulations."[23] Finally, in eight, the impact. The affirmative must now justify resolutionally inherent government restrictions in light of the evidence above that indicates self-regulation is the best, in fact, the only strategy to deal with terrorism.

Large observation number two, unrestricted media coverage is essential to incident resolution. Specifically in little one subpoint, media reduces pressure. Alexander in 1978: " ... the roles of the media are not always detrimental. There are situations where the media, by publicizing an incident, have, in the words of Special Agent of the FBI Conrad Hassel, 'relaxed the pressure of the terrorist finger.'"[24] Second, it provides crucial information. Bassiouni in 1981: " ... media coverage can provide law enforcement with otherwise unavailable tactical and intelligence information."[25] Third, media is an essential bargaining chip. Bassiouni again: " ... media coverage is frequently the most effective bargaining tool that a negotiator has in dealing with terrorists."[26] Number four, media integrates terrorists into the system. Cofman in 1977: " ... coverage of such events is helpful. It allows these people to have some method of ventilating their anger and frustration, in making known their grievances. The more coverage given, the more they are likely to see themselves part of, rather than outside the system."[27] Number five, media prevents police overreaction. Schmid and de Graaf in 1982: " ... police forces might be deterred from ending the situation at the expense of the hostages through the presence of the media ..."[28] Number six, media limits public anxiety. Bassiouni in 1981: "The media perform several important functions, among which is controlling rumors by disseminating accurate information to the public of dangers present at the site."[29] Number seven, lack of information produces the worst risk. Now, the following evidence is the only one in the round which evaluates risk and it tells you to vote against regulation. Paper on Terrorism, in 1977: " ... the greatest possible risks (are) involved in wild and reckless rumors and exaggerated, provocative word-of-mouth reports."[30] Finally, in eight, value-benefit analysis rests clearly with unrestricted media coverage. Bassiouni in 1981: " ... the problems created by media coverage can be offset by the directly related benefits it provides, in addition to other benefits of society which derive from the media's informational and watchdog roles."[31]

Please go to the justification. On the (A) subpoint -- they want to say that terrorist activity is significant. I will have three responses. Number one, no, terrorism is not quantitatively significant. That is from Bassiouni in 1981: "...the actual harm resulting from international terrorism in its present manifestations is not quantitatively significant."[32] Number two, you should avoid exaggeration of the terrorist threat. This is from Laquer in 1978: "Similar caution is required if one is to avoid exaggerating the importance of terrorism today. It is true that no modern state can guarantee the life and safety of all its citizens all of the time, but it is not true that terrorists somehow acquire 'enormous power' (to quote our editorialists) if they kidnap a few dozen citizens as in Holland, or even a dozen oil ministers, as in Vienna."[33] Now, number three, the affirmative must quantify the harm from terrorism that is directly linked to the media coverage. I suggest that they cannot do that.

On the (B) subpoint where they tell you that terrorism is caused by the media. I will have four responses. Number one, no conclusive evidence. That is from Bassiouni in 1981: "It is essential to recognize, however, that conclusive evidence of the terrorist-media relationship has not...been presented."[34] Two, no empirical research. Schmid and de Graaf in 1982: "...there is no empirical research that could unequivically provide a direct statistical correlation between media coverage and terrorism."[35] Number three, lack of study precludes policy decisions. That is from Bassiouni in 1981: "The inconclusiveness of research on the various psychological effects on the public of terror violence at this point appears to preclude any state regulation of subsequent coverage. In this context, it will be suggested that media self-regulation in the form of general guidelines or licensing procedure is most appropriate."[36] Number four, above evidence justifies non-resolutional studies value decision. The evidence above makes it clear that more study is necessary for resolutional assessment. I will suggest that such a course is superior and non-resolutional to media and government.

Now, specifically on the (C) subpoint where they tell you that restrictions solve. Number one, they must quantify the degree of solvency in order to weigh against possible counter value harms, and Tad will make that clear in 2NC. Number two, they must prove solvency from the media terrorists. They must solve for specifically that harm. If they don't have that link, then no justification is present. Number three, international agreements are better than government restrictions. That is from Bassiouni in 1981: "...the most promising means of deterring terrorism is effective enforcement and implementation of...existing conventions and, particularly, greater cooperation between states in the areas of extradition and penal matter."[37]

Go back to studies. Schmid and de Graaf, which they use, is not a good study. They admit in 1982: "Given the paucity of previous research in the field, our study cannot be anything more than exploratory."[38] The affirmative evidence admits that even their own study is exploratory. Vote for self regulation and non-resolutional studies.

Cross Examination:
Mr. McGill questions Mr. Sargent

McGill: On your second observation. What was your fifth subpoint? Sargent: Eliminates cooperation. McGill: Now, on this observation two, what is the main thesis of it? Sargent: That you need unrestricted media coverage for incident resolution. McGill: O.K. Sargent: In hostage situations. McGill: O.K., so you are saying that media is good because they relieve pressure? Sargent: That's right. McGill: Do they always do this? Sargent: The evidence says that on balance that in most situations they do. Well, in some cases they do harm. McGill: But on balance they are good, right? Sargent: Well, yes and they are getting better all the time because they are self regulating. Where they have had bad effects in the past they are acting to correct that. McGill: O.K. Let's talk about self regulation. Sargent: Sure. McGill: Are you saying that the media wants self regulation? Sargent: Well, we are saying that the media understands the responsibility that they have to balance their informational capacity with the needs of the hostages or whatever the terrorist situation is. McGill: So you claim that self regulation will work? Sargent: Not only will it work, it is the only possible solution. McGill: Now again, is this on balance it will work? Sargent: Not only does the evidence say on balance, it says that if you restrict them with media regulations that they get really angry at the police and they can't work together and in the long run you won't have any solution to terrorism. McGill: On justification subpoint (C). Your last point. What was your last point? Sargent: That international agreements on extradition and penal matters are the real solution if you want to solve terrorism, and that is clearly non resolutional. McGill: How are we going to do this? Sargent: It doesn't matter. It is just a non resolutional option. We are not going to defend it as what we should do, just as another possibility. In fact, it's the best way. McGill: Can I see your card on that please? Sargent: Sure. McGill: Also, I need your card above that. On your subpoint three about studies. Sargent: Yes, on studies. McGill: I also need a card on your second subpoint. Sargent: O.K. McGill: Let's see if I got this straight on justification. You're saying that terrorism is not quantitatively significant? Sargent: It is not now. McGill: Not now? Sargent: But it is going to get worse if you restrict it I think. McGill: If you restrict what? Sargent: If you restrict the media. McGill: Thanks.

Second Affirmative Constructive:
Mr. Scott Greer, University of Tennessee

In his first observation he argues self regulation. He says the media themselves can do the restricting -- that we don't need government restrictions. Group responses one through four together. I would say number one, the evidence he gives you doesn't say solvency. The right to life is the only right you have in this round as far as values are concerned. Now, if the negative team is going to argue self regulation, they have to meet the criteria of the round and they are unable to do so at this point. Number two, the decision rule is absolute at this point. That will be given to you in observation two. I would argue number three, self regulation will never occur. J.B. Bell in 1978 explains: "We of the Western Press have yet to come to terms with international terror. If we thought about it more and understood its essence we would probably stop writing about it or we would write about it with a great deal more restraint."[39] Clearly, the man is admitting to himself that he is not doing it. I would argue number four, they will not take the responsibility. Same source continues: "A.M. Rosenthal of the New York Times speaks for many when he insists that it is not the responsibility of the media to accept such self-restraint."[40] Number five, they do not desire it in the first place. Same source: "The news industry does not want to limit coverage. Even if continued coverage might invite governmental intervention, that is, censorship."[41]

Of course, what we are arguing is that you nip it in the bud. You go ahead and stop it right now because they are not going to do it themselves. The negative doesn't tell you that they could solve even if the media self regulates. Please go to argument number five. He says that ambiguity is crucial. I'm going to argue that on the next one. On six, seven, and eight, he argues that it allows police cooperation and so on. Number one, he never gives you an on balance measurement between the first amendment and the right to life, which Rabe says you have to do. He just says that police are going to cooperate. But people are dying. If they are going to argue that self restraint is working right now, I have a simple question. Why are people still dying from terrorist acts? Obviously it doesn't solve. Please go to number two on this, that you have to stick with the Rabe evidence. It is the best in the round.

Now go to the second overview. First five arguments together. I would argue number one, it's a ludicrous assertion. What he is suggesting that you do is to accept that terrorism occurs and then deal with it. What we the affirmative suggest is to stop it completely from ever happening in the first place, instead of trying to deal with it when people die or are taken hostage. We are simply saying we should never have people taken hostage in the first place. I think it makes much more sense. I would argue number two, the affirmative is given solvency on this argument alone and that is enough to win the round. Please go to six, seven, and eight. He says that public anxiety goes down and that the lack of information is crucial. I would argue number one, media distorts. *Los Angeles Times* in '85: "Even when the crisis itself was in full swing, the hostage taking didn't seem to inflame the American people, in part because we could see the hostages and their captors practically arm-in-arm on the air as the crisis grew old, in part too, because persistent exposure to televised calamities may have given us all asbestos sensibilities. We get annoyed, we don't seem to get inflamed."[42] Number two, media distortion is harmful. Same source: "'We've decriminalized terrorism' moaned one Capitol Hill observer of television after watching all the coverage. 'Of course, they do encyclicals on the evils of what they're doing as they go along' he said of the networks, 'but they'll never change.' Bernard Goldberg, looking back at the whole bizarre spectacle for a CBS News report, called it 'theatre of the absurd.' It was, and the networks had been selling the tickets for the full run of the show."[43] Three, Schenck is analogous. Now this 1919 case says that you can't yell fire in a crowded theatre. That is what the media is doing by distorting terrorist activity. They are overblowing America's image of this. They are clearly causing bad policy. *Legal and Other Aspects of Terrorism* in 1978: "Obviously, there are First Amendment rights involved which may be affected. But the Court, in an early case, *Schenck* v *U.S.*, 249 U.S. 47 (1919), compellingly acknowledged that 'the most stringent protection of free speech would not protect a man in falsely shouting fire in a theatre and causing panic.' More than two decades later, the Court reaffirmed that 'when particular conduct is regulated in the interest of public order'and the regulation results in an indirect, conditional, partial abridgement of speech, the duty of the courts is to determine which of these two conflicting interests demand the greater protection under the particular circumstances presented."[44] We have clearly shown that in the particular circumstance presented that the right to life outweighs.

Please go to case now. Observation two criteria. He argues that we are not advocating one rule, that it is a set of rules. I'll give him that. Now on number two he says that we have to demonstrate that it is the best. Number one, no, all we have to do is show that we are reasonable -- that's the affirmative right to give a 1AC. I think that is pretty clear. Now, he never denies reasonability and to that extent I suggest that you accept it. Number two, he gives you no counter decision rule, only that the first amendment is most important. Rabe tells you that that is not true. He does not document anything in 1NC. I suggest that you stay with Rabe. On his argument on long-term tradeoff, we have to wait for 2NC on that. He says we do not meet the decision rule. Of course, I think we do. His last argument is that freedom of expression is most important. Rabe says that you can balance those. That is my first argument. My second argument is that he merely asserts that you have to do this -- I would suggest that you stick with Rabe. Now, on number three, I will extend little (a). The First Amendment must be violated at times. In a majority opinion Chief Justice Vinson explains in 1951: "An analysis of the leading cases in this Court which have involved direct limitations on speech, however, will demonstrate that both the majority of the Court and the dissenters in particular, cases have recognized that this is not an unlimited, unqualified right, but that the societal value of speech must, on occasion, be subordinated to other values and considerations."[45] Of course small (b) is the Schenck case. That was given to you above. I think criteria is very clear.

Please go to justification. On the (A) subpoint he says that we don't have quantitative significance. I would argue number one, that his evidence from Alexander is from 1981. Number two, he gives you no figures and I think that is what quantitative significance is all about. Number three, 1AC gives you a very strong quantitative significance in that it tells you that it has gone from one a week to ten a day. That is about quantitative enough for me. Please go to his next argument -- avoid exaggerations. That is talking about terrorists taking power. We aren't talking about that. We are simply saying that they shouldn't kill. That's good enough for us. Now (B) subpoint. He says no conclusive evidence and goes all the way down with this. Number one, that is extremely unfair. To that extent you should not debate affirmative on this topic. Number two, he never argues any presumption in the round. I would argue that is a moot issue. Number three, by the same token negative evidence must be thrown out. It is not conclusive either. To that extent you have no evidence in the round and you might as well go home now. Now on the third argument -- you can't affirm the resolution. The evidence doesn't say that -- just that it is difficult. It is not impossible. It is possible and we are showing you how. Now on the fourth argument he says that Schmid and de Graaf is exploratory. That's no problem because that is the only study we have -- they use it too. Now on (C) subpoint. He demands quantified solvency. Please group. Number one, he never denies 1AC evidence which is crucial. He has granted you the cards on solvency. He's merely pressing us on quantification. I would suggest to you that if you feel like, at the end of this round, that one life can be saved because of the adoption of the resolution that's good enough because criteria has been granted. Now later he argues that international agreements can solve. Number one, that is unfair because the negative assumes that these things will come into effect. I would suggest that it is an unfair standard because they are relying on fiat. To that extent we can fiat as far as our case is concerned because they are running fiat. To that extent you have to vote affirmative. I would argue overall that if you feel like we can save one single life in this round you have to advocate the resolution. Self regulation doesn't work. Otherwise, there would not be terrorism. Negative team is saying that you let terrorism exist and deal with it then. Affirmative says as Barney Fife would -- nip it in the bud.

Cross Examination:
Mr. Sargent questions Mr. Greer

Sargent: 100% of terrorism is media linked? Greer: Any terrorism is media linked which you have not denied that we have solved. And that gives you the resolution. Sargent: Wait a minute. Specifically on my second observation on incident resolution. Your response is that it assumes that it will occur anyway and that affirmative will solve? You are saying it doesn't matter right? Greer: The whole thrust of your argument is that let everything that is happening now continue to happen and then deal with it after they take them hostage. Sargent: And you are saying that you will solve 100% of terrorism? Greer: Any lives we save, in light of the decision rule is good enough. Sargent: You're evading the question. Greer: No, I'm not. Sargent: You admit at least, that if we affirm the resolution there will still be some terrorism taking place? Greer: That's fair enough. Sargent: In terms of self regulation -- I need all the cards on that. Greer: O.K. Sargent: Why is it that the press is unwilling to regulate themselves? Greer: It sells. Sargent: What sells? Greer: Coverage of these kinds of things. It sells advertising. Sargent: In terms of quantified significance, what is the percentage of terrorism? That ten a day is media caused terrorism? Greer: The evidence doesn't indicate that. Sargent: Then how do we evaluate the level of significance versus counter values? Greer: We haven't heard the counter values. So, I don't know. Sargent: How much terrorism is caused by the media? Greer: Evidence in "B" Subpoint and "C" Subpoint says a lot. Sargent: Wait a minute. Greer: A lot is enough. If we save one life, by granting the decision rule, that is enough. Sargent: O.K. Media distorts information. That card is in '78? Greer: No in 1985. Sargent: Let me see that card. O.K. What about Schmid and de Graaf? What are you saying? That all the evidence in the round needs to be thrown out? Greer: If there is no conclusive evidence, then why debate it? Sargent: Are we arguing that it shouldn't be debated or that we should not justify future policy? Greer: I don't know. What are you arguing? Sargent: O.K. Thanks.

Second Negative Constructive:
Mr. Tad Stephenson, University of South Carolina

At the end of this round one thing will be clear. Counter terrorism is still a form of terrorism.

Position one, that is value hierarchy. Subpoint (A), Democracy is more important than order. Martha Crenshaw in 1983: "...protecting democracy is more essential than maintaining order. The threat of terrorism is not grave enough to justify the establishment of garrison states in a neofuedal system."[46] Subpoint (B), Freedom overrides even effective prevention of terror. Center for Constitutional Rights in 1984: "...it cannot be sufficiently stressed that this aim overrides in importance even the objective of eliminating terrorism and political violence as such. Any bloody tyrant can solve the problem of political violence if he is prepared to sacrifice all considerations of humanity and to trample down all constitutional and political rights."[47] Subpoint (C), That is that you must eliminate less restrictive means. That is what makes Kevin's argument in 1NC so crucial. Restriction of freedom must be the last alternative. You must have least restrictive means.

I would argue in position two that the inverse of the resolution is actually true. (A) subpoint. More open media is the way to solve terror. From Harold Coffman in 1978: "[Media] coverage of such events is helpful. It allows these people to have some method of ventilating their anger and frustration in making known their grievances. The more coverage given, the more likely they are to see themselves as part rather than outside the system."[48] (B) subpoint indicates that there is no affirmative solvency. Even if you buy the argument that media might somehow increase the incidence of terrorism, restrictions won't solve. C, none of affirmative evidence indicates an increase in terrorism caused by the media. All the affirmative cards say is that it causes a maintenance of terrorism. They don't say an increase actually caused by media. Kevin in 1NC says to quantify the link. It is dropped cold in 2AC. The position is clear. The inverse of the resolution is true.

I will now go to my third position and that is terrorist catharsis. Restrictions equal an increase in terror. Subpoint (A), current motives produce low level violence. The actions are symbolic, they are not meant to kill. That goes very well with what they said in 1AC. So, they have to grant the motives for current terrorism. Little one, possible support limits terror. Brian Jenkins in 1975: "...terrorist violence may be self limiting in the sense that terrorists depend to a degree on the support of some constituency or the toleration of at least some governments. Too much violence could provoke harsh reactions and greater international cooperation against the terrorists."[49] Little two, current motive is against mass murder. Scott Fenn in '81: "Terrorists generally have made limited efforts to seek support... [T]hey have concluded that their objectives would not be advanced if they used these potent weapons to create incidents of mass destruction."[50] In little three I would argue that, it is empirically true. Alexander in '83: "No mass casualties and widespread disruptions to vital systems of industrialized nations have yet resulted from a single terrorist attack. [T]errorists have found it politically and morally expedient to restrain the level of violence. Had it been otherwise, they could have used conventional weapons to cause major disasters in our extremely vulnerable society by attacking, for example, hazardous chemical plants."[51] (B) subpoint, and that is that restrictions provoke increased terror. Little one, consensus of evidence. So, now you have empirical evidence and you have consensus of evidence. Subdivide to small (a), we refer for support on Alexander in '83: "Should effective governmental and intergovernmental responses deny terrorists their sought-after publicity, they are likely to change tactics, increase their audacity and escalate their symbolically oriented acts through high technology weapons."[52] Small (b), Schmid and de Graaf in '82: "To introduce additional laws and guidelines to keep these terrorists from presenting their grievances and frustrations with violence may even increase the level of violence."[53] Small (c), Crenshaw in '83: "Terrorism serves as a safety vent for letting off dangerous pressures. Better to let this vent continue to function and even from time to time let terrorism succeed than to allow worse substitutes to develop should the forces presently causing terrorism be frustrated. Frustration and failure would also encourage the expansion of terrorism."[54] Now my cards are specific to increase. All they can show you is a maintenance because no cards show an actual increase in the level of terror. No cards can link it to the media. All of my cards are specific to that. Now my cards are specific and they have dropped Kevin's responses. 2AC was cold on that. Little two, empirically this is true. Alexander in '78: "The media also played a helpful role in establishing a vital link between authorities and the public at large in connection with the May-June 1977 South Moluccan incident in Holland. During that episode daily news releases containing bits of information on details not crucial to developing strategy and tactics satisfied the public's appetite for information, as well as conveyed an image of official responsibility and effective crisis management."[55] That card is specific to escalation not maintenance which is the status quo. (C) subpoint, is escalation equals voting issue priority one. Little one, terrorism is relatively low at present. Little two, there is a huge potential for escalation. Little three, no restriction can overcome escalation. No matter what kind of restriction it is, if you restrict that equals escalation. Now I will go to subpoint (D) and that is impacts. Little one, restrictions will lead to chemical and biological terrorism. Go to Bell in '78: "The scenario builders have constructed even more dread possibilities, involving the whole spectrum of chemical weapons, nerve gas, hallucinogens, and various lethal and dangerous agents, some legally available, others that can be created by the knowledgeable. Such scenarios are not all that impossible."[56] Little two, and that is in terms of nuclear terrorism. Wolf in '81: "The prospect of terrorists becoming capable of nuclear blackmail...is surely not a happy one, but the warning signs are out, including the possibility of individuals, as distinct from governments, using and exploiting atomic weapons."[57]

Position number four, freedom values are paramount. Subpoint (A), restrictions violate the values of freedom. Little one, restrictions equal the ultimate loss of values. Danforth in '81: "In an era when terrorism is on the increase, a democratic society must resolve that it will continue to stand firmly for its set of values. To abandon those values in the face of a threat, or to accommodate ourselves to the strident demands of those who resort to violence is to give the terrorist the victory they seek, and to encourage similar outbreaks in the future."[58] I will argue in little two, terrorism is the price of values. That is the card that Kevin read in 1NC. Subpoint (B), I will argue that Reagan will use counter-terrorism to repress all dissent. Stephanie Ferrior in '84: "The Reagan administration had adopted policies which affect adversely a broad range of human rights. The rhetoric of anti-terrorism has become the administration's weapon in its campaign against political dissent, especially in matters of foreign policy and international human rights."[59] Reagan will use it to repress dissent and then you will have impacts such as these. (C) subpoint, impacts. Little one, democracy, free speech, association. Ferrior supports us again in 1984: "Anti-terrorism is already being used as a scare tactic to chill free speech and association among groups where there is no evidence of violence or criminal activity. As the example below illustrates, there is already a serious problem of FBI overreacting in the name of combatting terrorism."[60] Little two, other impact is loss of value base. Affirmative says let's destroy some values in order to save other values. That simply makes no sense at all. Especially when you have chemical and biological weapons in terms of increase which they can never show.

Cross Examination:
Mr. Greer questions Mr. Stephenson

Greer: By giving people the right to life we are taking away something else? Stephenson: Right. Greer: O.K. Now, if we give free press and people are dying, what is the negative advocating? Stephenson: We are not advocating a policy system. Greer: I know. But if you are advocating a free press then you have to be advocating lives being lost, right? Stephenson: What we advocate is open press equals fewer deaths. Greer: Where was that given? Stephenson: It's the second position. Greer: It's the entire second position? Stephenson: Yes. Greer: O.K. Consensus of evidence tells us that the inverse of the resolution is true, right? That a lot of people die? Stephenson: Well, you're going to have some deaths no matter what. Greer: Oh. So, the inverse of the resolution is not true all the time? Stephenson: No. You don't understand. You are going to have some terrorists that are going to do it whether they get publicity or not. That's why we wanted you to quantify the causal link. You won't do that so we are talking about the consensus of evidence to the contrary. Greer: And what does that say? Stephenson: It's a whole lot closer to quantification than yours. Greer: Does it exclude any deaths from media terrorism? Stephenson: No, that's what I'm talking about. Greer: What? Stephenson: What I'm saying is that inevitably you're going to have terrorism. It's not realistic to say you can totally eliminate it. You're going to have it. The question is at what level are you going to have it. Is it going to be symbolic or is it going to be on the level of mass destruction. Greer: Right. Stephenson: If you restrict you get mass destruction. Greer: O.K. Do we have any restrictions whatsoever now? Stephenson: Not that I know of. Greer: O.K. Let's go to the first position. You say we are going to garrison states. Doesn't Zarefsky say in 1AC that we are not advocating a policy? Stephenson: You are concentrating on one part of one card and saying that that is a policy system the negative defends. That's not the case at all. What the card says is that democracy is more important than order. And then it gives a little bit of analysis as to why. Greer: O.K. Don't you have people existing in that democracy in order for it to function? Stephenson: It's a whole set of values. If you destroy one, it can have impact on all the rest. Greer: Doesn't Rabe say in 1AC that you can conflict the two? Stephenson: Sure. But the critical issue here is how do you balance those within different sets of values. And we will contend that you do it with no restriction and that is a better set of values because you get more life and still have freedom. Greer: The last thing is, you are talking about the level increasing right? That we are not showing the level of violence actually increasing? Stephenson: Right. Greer: Doesn't the mere existence of a threat pose a risk though? Stephenson: No. Greer: If I have a loaded gun pointed at you with only one bullet in it for a long time, isn't that a threat? Stephenson: No, the reason that is a bad example is because it distorts causality in that relationship. What we are talking about here are the motives to commit terror. Greer: What? Stephenson: If you restrict you increase the motives for mass destruction. That's the only causal evidence in the round. Greer: All right.

First Negative Rebuttal:
Mr. Kevin Sargent, University of South Carolina

Starting on the second observation on decision rule, I will focus on my second argument -- show that the affirmative standard is best. In first negative I simply argued that the affirmative decision rule must be demonstrated to be the best decision rule with which to evaluate the round. Number one, that is never done. He only says they have to be reasonable. Reasonability only has to do with topicality and has nothing to do with defending decision rules. I tell you there are other equally important decision rules independent of First Amendment, like general freedom and expression. Now, I will argue number three, apply the Bell evidence in the self regulation brief that tells you that the only way you can have an open society is when you have self regulation of the media. You must avoid government regulations and that is the only way to evaluate the round. I will suggest number four, this decision rule can now be evaluated as a reason for a negative ballot in the round.

Please go to my first overview on self regulation. He got up here and has five responses. But all of them basically say that the press is unwilling to regulate themselves and haven't done a very good job of it. Of course, I will argue number one, every single card is from 1978. Number two, the evidence that I read from 1981 says that they are improving and the evidence from 1982 says they they are getting even better. Number three, in the latest incident in Beirut we have an instance where the press showed more than willingness to restrict and to balance their responsibility. Number four, I want the specific card that tells you that they are willing to balance responsibility. That's a really good card, it tells you that the policy that is most likely to balance is self regulation. Number five, I also want that it is the only option in an open society. At the end of this round, if you want an open society and the elimination of terrorism, you're going to have to vote negative.

Specifically go to the sixth and seventh subpoints -- the basis for cooperation with the police and that cooperation is the only way to decrease terrorism. He makes a very drastic mistake. He says only that there is no problem with restricting the First Amendment. Number one, the First Amendment restriction is not the harm. That is not what I am claiming here. Number two, the evidence I read tells you that the restriction leads to a confrontation between the media and the police. Number three, the next card tells you that if you have that kind of confrontation, that kind of enmity between the police and the media, you can never solve terrorism. If lives are important to you and the elimination of terrorism, again, the only way to vote in the round is for self regulation and against governmental restrictions on the media.

Please go to the second observation on incident resolution. His only argument here is that we accept that it's going to happen and that is some sort of fatalism on our part. Number one, unless affirmative evidence on solvency is 100%, which clearly it isn't, it will continue to occur. Number two, please pull the specific reasons that if you restrict the media, you're going to have lots of people dying. For instance, police overreaction is dropped. You need it for a bargaining chip, dropped. It provides information, it reduces pressure, all dropped. Go to anxiety and the public. All he can say here is that the media distorts information. I will argue number one, the evidence I read above says that the media is improving. Number two, the best evidence in the round from 1977 says that the elimination of media coverage equals rumors and word of mouth and that is the worst risk. This is the only evidence in the round which evaluates risk and it suggests you vote against government regulation. Number three, I want the last card that I read from Bassiouni which says that value benefits analysis rests clearly against the resolution. It is dropped.

In terms of significance,there is never any quantified link. It is irrelevant. In terms of studies. We are not advocating that any policy be adopted, we are simply saying that you should not vote for the resolution without adequate study. Number two, that is all we have to do in this round.

First Affirmative Rebuttal:
Mr. Phil McGill, University of Tennessee

Let's deal with the first VO. I will deal with that on case when we talk about distortion. On two where he talks about open media, I will also deal with that on case about media distorts. But let's go to three, his big one. What I want here is that the inverse is wrong because people are still dying today. That is very important. If the inverse were true, people would not be dying because we would have no terrorism.

Let's talk about the so-called consensus evidence. That is empirically false because we are still having terrorism now. Let's go down to the impact -- high tech weapons and the rest. Number one, it is a contradiction. Look at where he talks about the motive is not mass murder. But what is chemical and nuclear warfare? It is nothing but mass murder. I would suggest that is contradictory and should be thrown out of the round. But let's go down to his last one -- violates freedom. I would argue that it is a very circular argument. If you lose life, you lose speech; if you lose speech, you lose life. To the extent that the negative is arguing in a circular motion there is no logic.

Now let's go on case side. All the definitions pull through. Let's go to where they talk about the decision rule. Where they say that we are unreasonable, I would say it is not true. But number two, Scott establishes that it's the best criteria because there is no counter criteria. All the negative tells us is that speech is good. They never give us any other type of counter criteria. So, you must vote affirmative. Also I want that the First Amendment is not absolute, and Scott's extensions on Rabe. That is very important. It tells us that the Supreme Court says that it is O.K. to abridge some rights. That is important because the Supreme Court gives us power to abridge some rights. It takes out Tad's arguments about decreases democracy.

Go down to justification where restrictions are warranted. Where he talks about reasonability. Group all those together and apply Rabe's card that the right to life is the paramount issue. I would argue that the Supreme Court has given the power to override the First Amendment in order to protect life. Rabe tells us that life is paramount.

Go down to subpoint (B). What I want here is that it is difficult to affirm the resolution but not impossible. That is very important. That still gives us the opportunity to justify restrictions. What I want is subpoint (C). He drops it and that gives us solvency. So we have solvency in this round.

Go to observation one, on self regulation. Group them all together. What I want here is all the evidence that says that self restraint does not work -- it beats all his responses here. Down to six and seven where he talks about police cooperation. I say that Scott takes that out in 2AC and that life outweighs. On two, he drops solvency in 1NR. To that extent we have solvency already. To that extent any arguments against it drops out of the round.

Down to where he talks about media distorts. Number one, the cards are from '85. Number two, we have shown that the Supreme Court has allowed it. You can't falsely yell fire in a crowded theatre.

Second Negative Rebuttal:
Mr. Tad Stephenson, University of South Carolina

Off-case position number one leaves me with an empty feeling. I have democracy is more important than order and it is dropped. I will go to (B) subpoint because that is most critical in the round. Freedom overrides prevention of terrorism. Now even if you don't buy any solvency arguments in the round, neither team is going to have solvency. Even if you think that, you have to look at the base level of values and that should be clear in this round that even if you could eliminate terrorism, freedom is still going to be more important. Now there are no responses to that in this round. All he says is life, but he can't get to the point of complete protection of life. That is irrelevant at this point. (C) subpoint -- less restrictive means -- is also punted. I would argue that anything that is less restricted and will solve is justified. Because that is the criteria that they set up. They say if you save one life, it is justified. Less restrictive means also do the same.

Position number two, inverse of the resolution. Now all that they argue is that media distorts. Of course, I will pull (B) subpoint. Even if there is a causal relationship, it doesn't mean restrictions will solve. Catharsis can still be true, and they don't have any evidence to deny that.

That is what I will go to next and that is terrorist catharsis. First response is that people are dying today. Number one, perfection is impossible -- some people are going to die anyway. Number two, one life is enough and that is their criteria. If you get one net increase that is enough to vote for. Number three, the best criteria is net harm and I suggest that restrictions are worse. That is undenied. He says empirically that is false. That is an assertion. There is no evidence for that. Number four, affirmative drops all evidence in 1AR. They drop the consensus evidence. Even their own source grants us that catharis will occur. Number five, motives are clear and the current motives are those of symbolic violence, not for increase. That means the round.

Next, they say it's a contradiction because current motives contradict mass murder. Number one, restrictions change the motive. If you restrict, they will go to mass technology which will kill lots of people. Number two, current motive is symbolic and that's the one that produces low levels of violence. You have the absolute links. I want to pull all the impacts across. (C) subpoint, restrictions equal escalation and a voting issue.

Position four, he says that we are circular. What I suggest is that that is why you have a set of values. It is not circular. What we say is that you get life through freedom. They want life through censorship. We say our set is better.

Now in terms of case decision rule. He says in second response that we have no counter criteria. Of course, he drops that in 1AR. I suggest that the counter criteria is the set of values and democracy is more important than order. Even freedom outweighs absolute prevention of terror. He says First Amendment is not absolute. But note that the Supreme Court does not restrict the press and I suggest that a free press is O.K. He says that Rabe's right to life is paramount. And I suggest that the set of values is what is going to be paramount and in that we still have a free press.

Now in terms of self regulation. Go down to where he says it does not equal solvency. First response, all affirmative analysis is on limits. Self regulation is in terms of balance. Number two, there is no affirmative solvency either and that is what they had to show you at that point. They had to quantify some solvency and they didn't do it. All they say is that we show no counter solvency. Number three, only in an open society can you do anything about it. You have to preserve freedom. It is the prerequisite to any kind of solution. I would go to third response in 1NR. You can never solve terror if you have the police and media confrontation. That is what restrictions produce.

All I want in observation two, incident resolution, is that a lot of people die from police overreaction. That is punted. All I want is seventh and eighth responses that lack of information is the worst risk. And the net value benefit is in terms of unrestricted media. Now those are completely dropped. I would argue any argument in terms of First Amendment -- the Supreme Court does not restrict.

Second Affirmative Rebuttal:
Mr. Scott Greer, University of Tennessee

On his first position off-case. I'm going to argue that Phil's distortion turnaround, which was initially offered in 2AC, is good enough to beat all of this. Now you have no freedoms because as a result of distorted information you have bad public policy. That is clearly what evidence is indicative of in 2AC and that was completely dropped. Number two, freedoms are no longer important because you no longer know what you're doing with them. You have distorted information and that, my friends, is a bad value. All of that was dropped. He wants to extend least restrictive means. But if they are beaten on case side, which I suggest they are, then you don't have least restrictive means and you are left, by default, to voting for the resolution.

Please go to second position. The first argument is that we have the inverse of the resolution now. Tad grants in cross-ex that we do not have restrictions now. To that extent, terrorism should stop. I don't see it stopping. Two, you don't have a net saving of lives because he grants you sustenance of terrorism. To that extent, people are dying, whether it's increasing or not does not matter, it does not beat the only decision rule in this round. And that means you vote affirmative by default. All of his consensus evidence is clearly empirically false because you have to save lives, but he grants you sustenance of death. He is saying he can't be 100% solvent. To that extent, why run least restrictive means?

Please go to bottom. He talks about CBW and nuclear war. What I'm going to argue is that his partner runs self regulation. To that extent he is accruing the disadvantage himself. They are restricting themselves. The position flips right back in their face and it's all over now. If that is true and we are having self regulation right now, we shouldn't be sitting in this room in the first place because we would be blown away.

Last position. He says freedom is most important. I argue that distortion takes that out and that's good enough. Please go to self regulation. My first response in 2AC is good enough. If you're going to run a minor repair or whatever you want to call it, you've got to show that it solves. They want to argue you can't. That is unfair. Two, if they run this then they will accrue his partner's disadvantage. To that extent, I would say its a contradiction. Now, at the bottom, he wants to argue that this is the only way to keep the police from shooting the media or something like that. Arguably, I would say the disadvantage would come before that. I say throw them both out. That's the fair thing to do because they contradict.

On the second overview, I would argue that he grants (C) subpoint on solvency. They haven't touched it in rebuttals. To that extent, I would say that we have solvency. On the bottom I argue media distortion. That is harmful and Schenck is analogous. I have no responses on my flow. To that extent it turns right back in their face and turns all counter criteria arguments off case.

Please go to our criteria. First argument is clear. No counter criteria in the round. Reasonability is no longer even an issue, because it's the criteria for the round by default. Rabe says that's what you have to do. That you have to balance life and freedom. I would argue that life is more important because you cannot have or express any freedom if you are not alive. That is clearly what the Supreme Court and Rabe say. He drops First Amendment on bottom, Phil extends, 2NR drops. That beats all 2NC off case criteria. Please go to (A) and (B) subpoints. He's granting you sustenance of death. That is significant enough for us. We argue that inverse of the resolution is false. Go with the resolution. All I want on (B) subpoint is that they have no presumption arguments. Negative cannot win on that and just because it is difficult does not mean that it is impossible.

Last thing on here is solvency. Least restrictive means require that their minor repairs have to work. Affirmative is given solvency. You don't know about negative because they are accruing disadvantages and they are contradicting each other. I think you should vote affirmative.

Notes

1. *Webster's New World Dictionary*, 2nd ed. (New York: Simon and Schuster, 1980), p. 1325.
2. *Webster's*, p. 1213.
3. *The American Heritage Dictionary*, 2nd ed. (Boston: Houghton Mifflin, 1982), p. 334.
4. *Webster's*, p. 882.
5. *Webster's*, p. 1469.
6. *Webster's*, p. 14.
7. Robert L. Rabe quoted in *Legal and other Aspects of Terrorism* (New York: Practicing Law Institute, 1979), p. 185.
8. David Zarefsky, "The Criteria for Evaluating Non-policy Argument," *C.E.D.A. Handbook*, 1980, p. 10.
9. *U.S. News and World Report*, 99 (July 22, 1985), 39.
10. Alex P. Schmid and Janny de Graaf, *Violence as Communication: Insurgent Terrorism and the Western Media* (London: Sage, 1982), p. 9.
11. Walter Laquer, "The Futility of Terrorism," *Harper's*, 252 (March 1976), 104.
12. Schmid and de Graaf, p. 14.
13. Schmid and de Graaf, p. 14.
14. Schmid and de Graaf, p. 15.
15. Yonah Alexander, "Terrorism, the Media and the Police," *Journal of International Affairs*, 32 (1978), 104.
16. Schmid and de Graaf, p. 14.
17. Schmid and de Graaf, p. 14.
18. M. Cherif Bassiouni, "Terrorism, Law Enforcement and the Mass Media: Perspectives, Problems, Proposals," *The Journal of Criminal Law and Criminology*, 72 (1981), 23.
19. Alexander, p. 111.
20. Bassiouni, 139.
21. J. Bower Bell, *A Time For Terror: How Democratic Societies Respond to Revolutionary Violence* (New York: Basic Books, 1978), p. 278.
22. Bassiouni, 30.
23. Bassiouni, 31.
24. Alexander, 1978, p. 107.
25. Bassiouni, 31.
26. Bassiouni, 31.
27. Quoted in Alexander, 1978, p. 107.
28. Schmid and de Graaf, p. 139.
29. Bassiouni, 31.
30. Bassiouni, 31.
31. Bassiouni, 31.

32. Bassiouni, 7.
33. Walter Laquer, *The Terrorism Reader: A Historical Anthology* (Philadelphia: Temple University Press, 1978), p. 252.
34. Bassiouni, 14.
35. Schmid and de Graaf, p. 108.
36. Bassiouni, 33.
37. Bassiouni, 11.
38. Schmid and de Graaf, p. 1.
39. Bell, p. 50.
40. Bell, p. 50.
41. Bell, p. 48.
42. *Los Angeles Times*, 5 July 1985, Section I, p. 23.
43. *Los Angeles Times*, 5 July 1985, Section I, p. 23.
44. Rabe, p. 184.
45. *Dennis* v *U.S.*, 341 U.S. 494, 1951.
46. Martha Crenshaw, *Terrorism, Legitimacy, and Power: The Consequences of Political Violence* (Middletown, CT: Wesleyan University Press, 1982), p. 146.
47. Stephanie Ferrior, *House Hearing on Terrorism, Subcommittee on Civil and Constitutional Rights,* HR 5613, August 2, 1984, p. 37.
48. Harold Coffman in Alexander, 1978, 106.
49. Brian Jenkins, *International Terrorism: A New Mode of Conflict* (Los Angeles: Crescent Publications, 1975), p. 20.
50. Scott Fenn, *The Nuclear Power Debate: Issues and Choices* (New York: Praeger, 1981), p. 160.
51. Yonah Alexander and Lawrence Freedman, eds., *Perspectives on Terrorism* (Wilmington, DE: Scholarly Resources, 1983), pp. 226-227.
52. Alexander, 1983, p. 227.
53. Schmid and de Graaf, p. 171.
54. Crenshaw, p. 80.
55. Alexander, 1978, p. 107.
56. Bell, 1978, p. 108.
57. John B. Wolf, *Fear of Fear: A Survey of Terrorist Operations and Controls in Open Societies* (New York: Plenum Press, 1981), p. 107.
58. John Danforth in Benjamin Netayahu, *International Terrorists: Challenge and Response* (New Brunswick, NJ: Transaction Books, 1982), p. 121.
59. Ferrior, p. 54.
60. Ferrior, p. 37.

APPENDIX C

Recent Intercollegiate Debate Propositions

National Debate Tournament Topics

1971–72 RESOLVED, that greater controls should be imposed on the gathering and utilizing of information about United States citizens by government agencies.

1972–73 RESOLVED, that the federal government should provide a program of comprehensive medical care for all United States citizens.

1973–74 RESOLVED, that the federal government should control the supply and utilization of energy in the United States.

1974–75 RESOLVED, that the power of the presidency should be significantly curtailed.

1975–76 RESOLVED, that the federal government should adopt a comprehensive program to control land use in the United States.

1976–77 RESOLVED, that the federal government should significantly strengthen the guarantee of consumer product safety required of manufacturers.

1977–78 RESOLVED, that United States law enforcement agencies should have significantly greater freedom in the investigation and/or prosecution of felony crime.

1978–79 RESOLVED, that the federal government should implement a program which guarantees employment opportunities for all United States citizens in the labor force.

1979–80 RESOLVED, that the federal government should significantly strengthen the regulation of mass media communication in the United States.

1980–81 RESOLVED, that the United States should significantly increase its foreign military commitments.

1981–82 RESOLVED, that the federal government should significantly curtail the power of labor unions in the United States.

1982–83 RESOLVED, that all United States military intervention into the internal affairs of any foreign nation or nations in the Western hemisphere should be prohibited.

1983–84 RESOLVED, that any and all injury resulting from the disposal of hazardous waste in the United States should be the legal responsibility of the producer of the waste.

1984–85 RESOLVED, that the United States federal government should significantly increase exploration and/or development of space beyond the mesosphere.

1985–86 RESOLVED, that more rigorous academic standards should be established for all public and elementary and/or secondary schools in the United States in one or more of the following areas: language arts, mathematics, natural sciences.

Cross Examination Debate Association Topics

1971–72 RESOLVED, that the United States should withdraw all its combat forces from bases located outside the Western hemisphere.

1972–73 RESOLVED, that the penal system of the United States should be significantly improved.

1973–74 *First Semester:* RESOLVED, that victimless crime should be legalized. *Second Semester:* RESOLVED, that the United States should reduce its commitments to Israel.

1974–75 *First Semester:* RESOLVED, that the federal government should grant amnesty to all those who evaded the draft during the Vietnam War. *Second Semester:* RESOLVED, that American television has sacrificed quality for entertainment.

1975–76 RESOLVED, that education has failed at its mission in the United States.

1976–77 RESOLVED, that legal protection of accused persons in the United States unnecessarily hinders law enforcement agencies.

1977–78 RESOLVED, that Affirmative Action promotes deleterious hiring practices.

1978–79 RESOLVED, that a United States foreign policy significantly directed toward the furtherance of human rights is desirable.

1979–80 RESOLVED, that compulsory national service for all qualified United States citizens is desirable.

1980–81 *First Semester:* RESOLVED, that protection of the national environment is a more important goal than the satisfaction of American energy demands. *Second Semester:* RESOLVED, that activism in politics by religious groups harms the American political process.

1981–82 *First Semester:* RESOLVED, that unauthorized immigration into the United States is detrimental to the United States. *Second Semester:* RESOLVED, that the American judicial system has overemphasized the rights of the accused.

1982–83 *First Semester:* RESOLVED, that a unilateral freeze by the United States on nuclear weapons production and development would be desirable. *Second Semester:* RESOLVED, that individual rights of privacy are more important than any other Constitutional right.

1983–84 *First Semester:* RESOLVED, that United States higher education has sacrificed quality for institutional survival. *Second Semester:* RESOLVED, that federal government censorship is justified to defend the national security of the United States.

1984–85 *First Semester:* RESOLVED, that the method of conducting presidential elections in the United States is detrimental to democracy. *Second Semester:* RESOLVED, that the United States is justified in providing military support to nondemocratic governments.

1985–86 *First Semester:* RESOLVED, that significant government restrictions on coverage by the United States media of terrorist activity are justified. *Second Semester:* RESOLVED, that membership in the United Nations is no longer beneficial to the United States.

APPENDIX D

Flowing a Debate

Flowing a debate or *taking a flow* is a method of keeping notes in an educational debate. The name "flow" might seem like an odd name for taking notes, but actually the word describes the process accurately. Taking notes on a debate requires that the advocates follow the argument by the opposition and indicate their responses to those arguments. As the debate progresses, the notes follow the arguments across the page—the pages flow with the arguments.

The principles of effective flowing are relatively simple to understand and relatively few in number. They are as follows:

1. Prepare in advance for the task
2. Outline all arguments in the order presented
3. Use key words, abbreviations, and symbols
4. Connect arguments to their responses
5. Flow throughout the debate

We will consider each principle individually.

Prepare for the Task

The beginning debater needs to maintain certain attitudes and acquire certain skills before attempting to flow a debate. To be effective as a debater the student needs to make a commitment to careful listening. This means that he or she must devote significant energies not only to "hearing" the arguments of the opposition, but to sincerely trying to *understand* those arguments. Moreover, the debater must learn to listen in an objective and detached manner. Often debaters will listen with aggressive and hostile attitudes without any real desire to understand the argument being offered. Such attitudes can be counterproductive since they encourage selective listening and premature argument selection. The debater with such an attitude will often stop listening and begin preparing his or her own arguments before understanding the meaning of the message.

After debaters have determined the proper attitude, then they should also make certain that their behaviors and preparation allow them to follow through with objective note taking. Materials for the debate ought to be "ready" to use before the debate begins. This means that the evidence files, the brief outlines, the blocks, and other materials should be well organized and conveniently located. The debater should eliminate unnecessary clutter. Disorganized materials will inevitably lead to a disorganized performance in the debate.

The debater should also have the proper materials to flow the debate: two long legal pads (8½ × 14 inches), a multi-color pen, or two pens in different colors (flowing each side in a different color will ease delivery of responses), and any necessary preflows. Pre-flows are the outlines of arguments that the debater uses frequently in a debate. These will speed the process of flowing and will ease the barriers to effective listening. Pre-flows are prepared before the debate round and are designed to fit in the space on the flowsheet available for those arguments. For example, most debaters will pre-flow the affirmative case they are using. The case can be pre-flowed because it is absolutely certain that it will be presented. It is best to do as much work as possible before the debate begins. In most debates, second negative speakers can flow most of their arguments as well. All speakers will likely have a few and perhaps many frequently-used arguments that can be pre-flowed. The debater may wish to pre-flow on adhesive labels that can be lifted off the page and replaced a number of times. These kinds of labels are available in most office supply stores.

Finally, debaters should not engage in behaviors that are counterproductive to effective listening and flowing. Examples of such behaviors include discussing arguments with colleagues and searching for evidence cards or lost briefs or blocks while the opposing debater is speaking, which will result in poor listening and ineffective flowing. Ineffective flowing will ultimately lead to poor refutation, unnecessary arguments, misunderstanding, and loss of credibility.

Outline Arguments as Presented

Effective outlining skills should be acquired and polished before attempting to flow debate. If a debate fails to outline effectively, the debate will be hard to flow and arguments will become confused and disorganized. If the opposing team is well organized they will indicate outline signposts. They will speak with such phrases as "contention one" or "subpoint a." If a debater records the signposts as they are presented, then s/he will have an outline of the arguments at the end of the speech.

When a debater outlines the arguments of a speech s/he should outline the speeches in the order presented. Debaters should turn one of their two legal pads so that the bound edge is at the left-hand side. This flow will be for the case issues and arguments—those arguments that deal with the justifications for the proposition and for the refutation of those arguments.

The legal pad should be divided into seven columns. The first affirmative speech should be flowed in the column next to the bound edge. The plan, however, should not be flowed on this pad, since the arguments in response to the plan do not directly respond to the case arguments. The arguments should be flowed in order, as they are presented in the debate. If additional pages are necessary, it is better to use them rather than to crowd everything onto a single page.

The first negative speech will usually be direct refutation of the first affirmative and should be outlined side-by-side in the second column. The second affirmative should be flowed in the third column in like manner. Figure A–1 is illustrative.

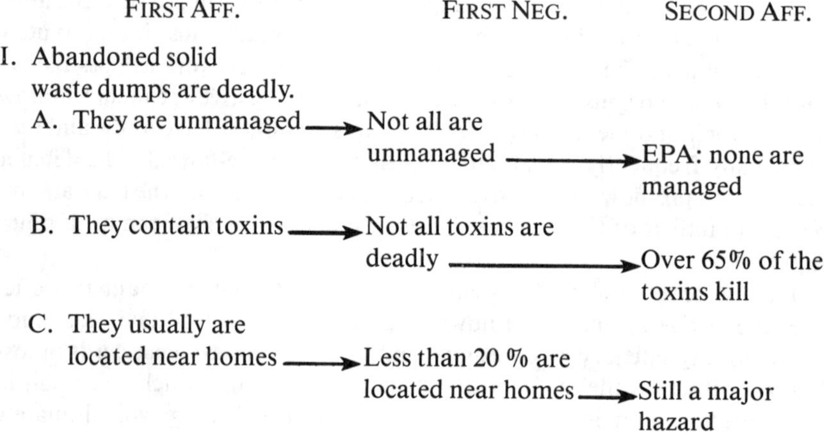

FIGURE A–1

During the rest of the debate, the case issues should be outlined in the remaining columns of the first pad.

The second negative constructive speech will usually consist of plan attacks (if the proposition is policy advocacy) or counterwarrants (for any other proposition). We suggested that the plan not be flowed on the first pad so that the second pad can be used to flow the plan arguments, or the counterwarrant arguments. If they remain separated, the debate will remain more organized than it might otherwise.

The column on the right of the plan attack, or the counterwarrants, is for first affirmative rebuttal and responses to the plan attacks or counterwarrants. The next two columns to the right are for the last two rebuttals of the debate.

In many debates the outline of the arguments will be relatively straightforward because each speech will follow the original outline of the affirmative case with the exception of the plan or counterwarrants. In any given speech, however, a debater may decide to organize his or her speech in a different manner. For example, s/he may choose to talk about the "most important argument," which may be in the middle of the outline of the previous speech. If this happens, then the opposing debaters should locate that argument and flow the response next to the relevant part of the outline. A well organized debater will make this easy to do by indicating the outline signposts both before and as s/he speaks, which will aid the opposing debaters and judge in keeping an organized flow.

Abbreviate When Possible

When a debater outlines an argument delivered at a conversational rate, flowing complete sentences are impossible. Even complete phrases are often too ambitious. Since some debaters speak more rapidly than a conversational rate, it is necessary to flow only key words, using abbreviations and symbols whenever possible.

Debaters should develop a set of abbreviations and symbols that will create a kind of "debate shorthand" to assist their note taking. Some abbreviations and symbols will be usable on all debate topics. For example, "SQ" for status quo, or "DA" for disadvantage will always be useful abbreviations for the policy debater. Mathematical symbols are also useful abbreviations. For example, an equals sign (=) could represent a number of verbs including: "is," "results," "creates," "does," and "causes." Figure A–2 provides a list of commonly used abbreviations and symbols.

How much should a debater write down? This is a question asked frequently by the beginning debater. Generally, the more information the debater has noted, the more effectively s/he can argue. As a debater becomes more proficient, s/he learns to record an increasing amount of information. Again, more information is better retained through the use of key terms, abbreviations, and symbols than when trying to capture complete sentences. A debater will be unsuccessful attempting the latter, and will miss information in the attempt.

Connect Arguments and Responses

In a good debate with a lot of clash, there will be a response for every argument presented in the first affirmative and in turn like responses presented in the first negative, and so on throughout the debate. It is very important that in any debate each debater keeps a record of the clash or lack of clash between arguments. After the first affirmative, the arguments can be connected to arguments in the first negative, and so on throughout the debate. Figure

A–3 illustrates the procedure. When an argument is not answered, the debater may wish to connect the argument to an "NR" or "X," symbolizing that there were no responses refuting the point. Or the debater may choose to simply leave the space blank; either the blank spaces or the appropriate symbols will remind the debater that an argument has been dropped from the debate.

av advantage
aff affirmative
atyp atypical
a+ add-on
bd board
CH CEDA Handbook
cp counterplan
ccp conditional counterplan
cv countervalue
cx cross-exam
da disadvantage
dec decision
def definition
doc document
dths deaths
ev evidence
ex example
fd funding
hcp hypothetical counterplan
hg hasty generalization
imp impact
inh inherency
insig insignificant
JAFA *Journal of the American Forensics Association*
lip legislative intent plank
meth methodology
mr minor repair
n/a does not apply
neg negative
np non-policy
NYT *New York Times*
o/b on balance
ov overview
o/w outweigh
pf *prima facie*
pma plan meet advantage
pmn plan meet need
ps present system
reas reasonable
res resolution
rr resolution refutation
sig significance
sgl single
solv solvency
stand standard
sq status quo
ta turnaround
tp topicality
tx taxes
w/o without
WSJ *Wall Street Journal*
USNWR *U.S. News & World Report*
uv underview
xt extratopicality
∅ no response
= is, does, create
≠ is not, does not
$ money, funding
↗ increase, enhance
↘ decrease, diminish
=? maybe
? challenge, conditionality
statistics, numbers
1AC, 1NC, 2AC, 2NC, 1NR, 1AR, 2NR, 2AR the speeches in the debate

FIGURE A–2 Commonly used flow sheet abbreviations and symbols.

OBS II. Porn = VC
A. Only criminals → 1. others too
2. voting issue

OBS III. Crit.
A. Risk to others → 1. good crit.
2. porn = risk
B. ↑ harm = ↑ rest.
C. ↓ harm = ↓ rest.

Cont. I. Porn ≠ bad
A. No society harms → 1. sex crimes ↑
2. ♀ ↓ respect
3. fear ↑
B. Benefit – ↓ agg. → 1. studies are flawed
C. ≠ harm crit.

Symbols/Abbreviations

agg-aggression
amt-amount
app-apply
censor-censorship
crit-criteria
ev-evidence
FS-free speech
govt-government
imp-important
leg-legitimate
meth-methodology
neg-negative
porn-pornography
resp-response
rest-restrictions
VC-victimless crimes
↓-decrease
↑-increase
= -is, are
≠ -is not
♀ -women

RESOLVED, that victimless crime laws are outside the legitimate function of government.

FIGURE A-3

Flow All Speeches

Especially when debaters are just beginning, they should flow all the speeches of the debate, including their own responses as they are preparing. All debaters should also flow their partner's arguments, even if they do not expect to use them or to defend them. Flowing those arguments will enlarge the debater's understanding of their case and their opponent's case and will assist in developing other arguments in the debate. There is even value in flowing the second affirmative rebuttal; even though no one will respond to this speech, debaters are benefited in future debates by keeping a complete record of past debates. Successes and failures can be better assessed, and strategies for improving debating skills can be designed with more certainty.

APPENDIX E

The AFA Code of Ethics

Preface

The American Forensics Association, as a professional organization for forensics educators, believes that forensics programs and tournaments ought to provide environments where students can become intelligent, effective and responsible advocates and communicators. We believe in equality and fair play in all forensics competition, and we therefore promulgate the following Code of Forensics Program and Forensics Tournament Standards for Colleges and Universities in the hopes that the guidelines outlined here will serve to govern and regulate effectively the conduct of forensics competition in the United States.

Article I: Competitor Standards

1. A tournament contestant is to be an officially enrolled undergraduate in good standing at the college or university he/she is to represent in forensics competition.

- **A.** A contestant is considered "officially enrolled" when he/she is duly registered in accordance with institutional regulations as an undergraduate student at the college or university he/she is representing in competition.
- **B.** A contestant is considered an "undergraduate" if he/she is registered as a bachelor or associate degree seeking student at the institution he/she is to represent in competition and is not in possession of a BA degree.
- **C.** "Good standing" shall be determined by rules and policies set by the institution the forensics competitor is representing in competition.

2. A tournament contestant is eligible for competition in a maximum of eight time blocks.

- **A.** The forensics tournament season shall be considered divided into two time blocks: (1) July-December, (2) January-June.
- **B.** A student shall have used his/her eligibility in a given time block if he/she participates in three or more forensics tournaments:
  - **1.** A student shall be considered to have participated in a tournament if he/she competes in at least half of the scheduled preliminary rounds of the tournament.
  - **2.** A tournament is defined as a forensics contest involving at least four schools in which at least four rounds of debate or two rounds of individual events are held, decisions are rendered by judges and awards given. This definition does not include summer workshop tournaments.
  - **3.** A student's participation in individual events shall not count against his/her eligibility to compete in debate, and vice-versa.

3. Students are free to transfer from one college to another so long as the transfer is not the result of an unscrupulous effort by one school to cause the student to transfer to it in order to receive financial compensation and/or other rewards for forensics competition.

- **A.** "Unscrupulous" is used here to refer to cases where the college that the student transfers to initiates contact with the student and makes an offer of financial compensation if the student transfers.

B. The PRC will determine if a student's transfer is the result of unscrupulous recruiting efforts based on the facts of the individual case. It is the burden of the school alleging unscrupulous recruiting to provide proof to the PRC that the school that the student transfers to initiated the contact with the student and the decision to transfer was motivated by the promise of financial compensation and/or other rewards for forensic competition.

4. Under unusual circumstances, involving valid educational or professional justifications, students who have received bachelor degrees may participate if:

A. The student has never competed in forensics as an undergraduate.

B. The coach who desires to let the student compete informs the chair of the PRC of this decision and the reasons for it, and a majority of the PRC agrees that the student has valid reasons for participating.

C. Such students may participate for a maximum of two time blocks.

D. The above eligibility rules shall not restrict additional eligibility requirements established by either the NDT or NIET Committees or by the individual tournament directors.

Article II: Competitor Practices

1. Forensics competitors shall not use fabricated or distorted evidence.

A. Evidence is defined as factual material (statistics and examples) and/or opinion testimony offered as proof of a debater's or a speaker's contention, claim, position, argument, point or case.

B. Fabrication of evidence refers to falsely representing a cited fact or statement of opinion as evidence when the material in question is not authentic. Fabricated evidence is so defined without reference to whether or not the debater or speaker using it was the person responsible for fabricating it.

C. Distorted evidence refers to misrepresenting the actual or implied content of factual or opinion evidence. Distorted evidence is so defined without reference to whether or not the debater or speaker using it was the person responsible for distorting it. Distortions shall be judged by comparing the challenged evidence against the material as it appears in the original source. Distortions include, but are not limited to:

1. quoting out of context.

2. misinterpreting the evidence so as to alter its meaning.

3. omitting salient information from quotations or paraphrases. MLA standards will be considered advisory with respect to this standard.

4. adding words to a quotation which were not present in the original source of the evidence without identifying such an addition.

5. failure to provide complete documentation of the evidence (name of author(s), source of publication, full date, page numbers and author(s) credentials where available in the original) when challenged. Debaters and speakers are expected to be in possession of the forms of documentation listed here at the time they used any evidence which was challenged.

2. In individual events which involve original student speech compositions (oratory/persuasion, informative/expository, after dinner/epideictic, rhetorical criticism, impromptu, extemporaneous or other similar speaking contests), the speaker shall not commit plagiarism.

A. Plagiarism is defined as claiming another's written or spoken words as one's own, or claiming as one's own a significant portion of the creative work of another.

B. A speech in individual events competition is considered plagiarized when the student presenting it was not the principal person responsible for researching, drafting, organizing, composing, refining and generally constructing the speech in question.

3. Forensics competitors are expected to do their own research.

A. Persons other than the forensic competitor (undergraduate students, graduate student or instructor/coaches) are not to be charged with the responsibility for doing a forensics competitor's research.

B. This provision shall not be construed to prevent coaches or assistants from engaging in limited research designed to:

1. teach research techniques
2. provided limited examples of high quality research
3. identify areas of research which students should pursue, and
4. provide the coach with the working knowledge necessary to function as effective critic with respect to the debate or speech topics being investigated by his/her students.

4. All forensics participants are expected to compete honestly and fairly. Students are not to intentionally lose debates or perform badly in individual events rounds for the purpose of allowing other competitors to benefit as a result. Directors of forensics, judges and coaches are not to encourage dishonesty in competition by asking students to purposely lose or do poorly in rounds of forensics competition.

Article III: Tournament Practices

1. Tournament directors must ensure that all participants compete on a more or less equal basis.

A. A debate team should not meet the same team during preliminary rounds of a tournament unless:

1. There are so few teams entered that it would be impossible for the tournament to proceed, in which case the two teams should switch sides the second time they meet, or
2. The schools entering the tournament have agreed to suspend the provision that teams not debate each other twice in preliminary rounds.

B. So far as possible, debate teams should debate an equal number of preliminary rounds on each side of the debate proposition.

C. Speakers in individual events shall not be repeatedly matched against the same opponents in a given event, unless:

1. the tournament cannot proceed otherwise, or
2. the schools attending the tournament agree to suspend the provision that speakers should not repeatedly meet the same opponents in a given round of individual events.

D. So far as possible, speakers in individual events contests should rotate speaking positions.

E. Judges for forensics contests shall be assigned in accordance with these stipulations:

1. A judge shall not be assigned to judge his/her own team.
2. A judge shall not judge the same debate team or student speaker in one particular individual event twice during a tournament's preliminary rounds unless there is no way to avoid this conflict. In such cases:

a. the judge will hear the debate team on the opposite side, unless it is impossible to do this or the schools competing agree to suspend this provision, and

b. the judge will hear the student speaker compete against as many different opponents than those involved in the judge's first hearing of the speech, unless it is impossible to do this or the schools competing agree to suspend this provision.

3. A judge shall not judge debaters or speakers where there is a conflict of interest possible, such as:

a. the judge has previously coached in college a debater or speaker he/she is to hear,

b. the judge was, within the last two years, the coach of the school whose team or speaker he/she is to hear

c. the judge was, within the last two years an undergraduate student forensics competitor at the school whose team or speaker he/she is to hear.

4. Prior to the start of the tournament, all judges shall have an opportunity to declare themselves ineligible to hear specific debate teams, speakers, or events.

5. The practice of allowing debate

teams or individual events speakers to prevent a specific judge from hearing a particular team or speaker is permitted only when:

a. all teams or speakers are given an equal chance to declare judge strikes prior to the start of the tournament,

b. all teams and speakers are granted the same number of strikes -- the number to be determined by the tournament director(s), and

c. The procedures for removing strikes (if any) are stated openly to all competitors.

2. Tournaments should be completely and fairly advertised.

A. The levels of competition expected should be specified.

B. If the tournament has more than one division of competition, eligibility requirements for the divisions shall be clearly defined in the tournament invitation.

C. The basis for advancing competitors to the elimination rounds, and/or for awarding trophies or prizes, shall be specified either in the tournament invitation or in written or oral statements presented to all tournament participants prior to the start of the first round of the tournament.

D. The rules governing all competitive events (event description, procedures, time limits, etc.), shall be clearly specified in the tournament invitation.

3. All tournament rounds are open on a space available basis to any and all interested observers, who may take notes. Participants, coaches of the teams involved, judges or authorized researchers (with the tournament director's approval) may tape record any tournament round of competition.

4. Tournament judges are obliged to provide detailed and constructive criticism of any and all rounds of competition they evaluate. Judges are expected to provide written comments on the ballots provided by the tournament. These written comments should be made available to all the competitors a judge has heard by the conclusion of the tournament. All provisions of this article shall apply to high school and college competitors.

5. Tournament directors should ensure that:

A. Results are made available to all contestants as soon after competition ends as is humanly possible.

B. Their tournament is not run to benefit financially the host school. An anticipated profit in excess of 10% of total entry fees is considered excessive.

C. Their tournament runs smoothly and efficiently, with breaks in between rounds for power-matching minimized whenever possible.

D. All results are kept secret if that is specified by the tournament rules.

Article IV: Adjudication Procedures

1. Anyone wishing to initiate a formal complaint may do so by sending six copies of the charges, in writing, to the Chair of the PRC. The complaint must:

A. Indicate the specific section(s) of the Code allegedly violated.

B. Name the person(s) charged with the alleged violation(s).

C. Indicate the factual circumstances and events associated with the alleged violation(s).

D. Include all necessary supporting documents which would constitute, at least, a prima facie case that there is reason to believe that a violation of the Code may have occurred.

E. Include the addresses and phone numbers of the person making the complaint.

2. The PRC, upon receipt of six copies of the charges, will inform, in writing, the person charged with an alleged code violation. The person charged will be informed of the nature and extent of the charges against him/her. The person charged may supply any relevant information in his/her defense in regard to the charges. Six copies of any material supplied should be sent to the Chair of the PRC.

3. Once all materials are gathered, the PRC members will independently review the case and determine if there is reason to believe that a code violation has occurred.

A. If the PRC agrees, by majority vote, that there is insufficient proof of a violation, the charges will be declared dropped and all parties to the dispute informed.

B. If the PRC agrees, by majority vote, that there is sufficient evidence to support the charges made, the Chair of the PRC will inform all parties of this fact and will schedule a formal hearing as soon as possible involving the members of the PRC, the accused and the person bringing the complaint. The location of this hearing will be determined by the Chair of the PRC with the location being as convenient as possible to all parties. The hearing shall occur as soon as it can be feasibly scheduled. The accused will have the right to make an oral defense at the hearing, and can be represented by legal counsel if desired. The complainant will have the same rights. At the conclusion of the hearing, the PRC will vote on the charges. At least a 4-1 vote is required to convict the accused of a Code violation. Following the verdict of guilty, the PRC will determine the penalties to be imposed in accordance with Article V of the Code. A majority vote will be required to impose penalties.

4. The accused may appeal both the verdict and the penalties determined by the PRC.

A. The appeal will be made to the President of the AFA, who will appoint a special three-person appeal board composed of impartial members of AFA.

B. The appeal board will review all documents gathered by the PRC, and will also listen to tape-recordings of the formal hearings.

C. The appeal board may gather any additional information it deems necessary to judge the case from any of the parties (the accused, the complainant, or the PRC).

D. The accused and the complainant have the right to present an oral argument to the appeal board. If so desired, the appeal board will set up a convenient method for allowing either the accused or the complainant to address it. The accused and the complainant have the right to counsel in these instances.

E. A majority vote of the appeal board is necessary to overturn the PRC's actions.

Article V: Penalties

1. Directors of forensics, assistants or coaches found guilty of entering ineligible students in forensics competition will:

A. Have their names published in the AFA Newsletter with a note of censure.

B. Have the notice of censure conveyed in writing by the AFA President to appropriate officials at the offending institution.

2. A student declared ineligible will be barred from national competitions or awards sponsored in whole or in part by the AFA. Notice of this action will be published in the AFA Newsletter, with a letter sent by the AFA President to appropriate officials at the offending student's school informing them of the student's ineligibility for competition in forensics.

3. In instances of evidence distortion and/or fabrication, the judge(s) shall automatically award the decision in the debate to the opposing team and give the offending speaker zero speaker points, noting the violation of the rules of evidence on the ballot as the reason for the judge's decision and points. In individual events, the judge(s) will treat evidence distortion and/or fabrication by giving the offending speaker zero points and by dropping that speaker from the speaker rankings to be assigned at the end of the round. The judge(s) will note the violation of the rules of evidence on the ballot as the reason for the points and no-rank given.

4. Speakers found guilty of plagiarism will be disqualified from the round in which the plagiarism occurred, with zero speaker points and no rank assigned and plagiarism noted on the ballot as the reason for the judge's action.

5. A judge who makes a decision on the basis of evidence distortion, evidence fabrication or plagiarism will immediately report his/her action to the tournament director. The tournament director will, as soon as possible, investigate the incident and determine if the offending speaker should be declared ineligible for further competition, elimination rounds or award at the tournament. Directors should base such decisions on the severity of the case involved.

6. Tournament directors must report, to the Chair of the PRC, any and all instances of judge decisions granted for reasons of evidence distortion, evidence fabrication or plagiarism. If the Chair receives, in any given academic year, two such complaints involving the same student, the student will be declared ineligible for national competitions or awards sponsored in whole or in part by the AFA for a period of 12 calendar months from the date of the second offense. The student will be informed when notification of the second offense is received. The student has the right to appeal that the penalty should not be imposed, under the appeal procedure outlined in Article IV, Section 4 of the code. Notice of the student's ineligibility for national competitions sponsored by the AFA will appear in the AFA Newsletter, with a letter by the AFA President sent to appropriate officials at the offending student's school.

7. Forensics squads found guilty of using non-competitors for primarily research purposes will have a note of censure published in the AFA Newsletter, with written notice of the censure communicated by the AFA President to appropriate officials at the offending school. The squad will be barred from national competitions sponsored in whole or in part by the AFA for a period of 12 calendar months from the date when the PRC ruled the school to be in violation of this part of the Code.

8. Tournament directors found guilty of violating any section of Article III of this code will be subject to any or all of the sanctions listed below, as deemed justified by the PRC.

A. Censure of the offending tournament.

1. The PRC finding that the tournament had violated the Code will be published in the AFA Newsletter.

2. Appropriate officials at the offending school will be notified in writing by the AFA President of the decision to censure the tournament.

3. In cases where the PRC determines the Code violation to be severe, the tournament will not be allowed to publish its dates in the next AFA tournament calendar following the PRC's decision that the tournament was in violation of the Code.

B. Tournament probation.

1. When a tournament is found guilty of a Code violation on a second separate occasion, the tournament may be put on probation; viz. the results of the next occurrence of the tournament, following the PRC's decision to place it on probation, cannot be used for the purpose of qualifying forensic participants for national tournaments sponsored in whole or in part by the AFA.

2. If a tournament is placed on probation, this decision will be printed in the AFA Newsletter Tournament Calendar edition covering the tournament season in which the probation will be served, with notification that this tournament's results cannot be used for the purpose of qualifying forensic students for national competitions sponsored in whole or in part by the AFA.

3. Probation will be for one year. When the probation ends that fact will be reported in the AFA Newsletter Tournament Calendar issue.

9. Tournament directors should forward names of all judges who fail to turn in written ballots for all the preliminary rounds they judge at a tournament to the Chair of the PRC. Any school which leaves a tournament with all of the preliminary round ballots it should have, and assuming there is no valid explanation for missing ballots, may notify the Chair of the PRC of the judge(s) who failed to provide ballots. If a judge is guilty of failing to provide written preliminary round ballots for all rounds judged by the end of the tournament on two occasions, the judge shall:

A. Be subject to censure by notification in the AFA Newsletter, and
B. Be declared ineligible to be hired as a judge at any national competition sponsored in whole or in part by the AFA.
C. Be informed when notification of the second failure to turn in ballots is received. The judge to appeal that the penalty should not be imposed, under the appeal procedures outlined in Article IV, Section 4 of the Code.

10. Forensics directors, coaches, assistants of judges found guilty of asking students to throw rounds of forensics competition will be subject to the penalties listed under section 1 of this Article.

11. A student transferring from one school to another as a consequence of unscrupulous recruiting will be ineligible to participate in the next national tournament sponsored in whole or in part by the AFA occurring after the PRC's decision that the transfer resulted from unscrupulous contact initiated by the school to which the student transferred.

Reprinted by permission of the American Forensic Association from *AFA Newsletter*, 4 (No. 3, June, 1982), 12-14.

Index